Windows XP

POWER HOUND

OTHER MICROSOFT WINDOWS RESOURCES FROM O'REILLY

Windows XP

POWER HOUND

Preston Gralla

POGUE PRESS™
O'REILLY®

Beijing · Cambridge · Farnham · Köln · Paris · Sebastopol · Taipei · Tokyo

Windows XP Power Hound
by Preston Gralla

Copyright © 2005 O'Reilly Media, Inc. All rights reserved.
Printed in the United States of America.

Published by O'Reilly Media, Inc., 1005 Gravenstein Highway North, Sebastopol, CA 95472.

O'Reilly books may be purchased for educational, business, or sales promotional use. Online editions are also available for most titles (*safari.oreilly.com*). For more information, contact our corporate/institutional sales department: (800) 998-9938 or *corporate@oreilly.com*.

Editor:	Sarah Milstein
Production Editor:	Genevieve d'Entremont
Cover Designer:	Ellie Volckhausen
Interior Designer:	David Futato

Printing History:

October 2004:	First Edition.

 This book uses RepKover™, a durable and flexible lay-flat binding.

ISBN: 0-596-00619-5
[M]

Table of Contents

The Missing Credits

About the Author

 Preston Gralla is the author of more than 30 books about computers and the Internet, which have been translated into 15 languages, including *Windows XP Hacks* and *Internet Annoyances*. He has been writing about technology since the dawn of the PC age, and has been an editor and columnist for many national newspapers, magazines and Web sites. He was the founding editor of *PC Week*; a founding editor, then editor, then editorial director of *PC/Computing*; and executive editor for ZDNet/CNet.

Preston has written about technology for numerous magazines and newspapers, including *PC Magazine, Computerworld, CIO Magazine, Computer Shopper*, the *Los Angeles Times, USA Today*, the *Dallas Morning News* (where he was a technology columnist), and many others. He has been a columnist for ZDNet/CNet, and is currently a columnist for TechTarget.com and PriceGrabber.com, and editor-in-chief of the Case Study Forum. His commentaries about technology have been featured on National Public Radio's *All Things Considered*, and he has won the award for the Best Feature in a Computer Publication from the Computer Press Association. Under his editorship, *PC/Computing* was a finalist for General Excellence from the National Magazine Awards. Email: *preston@gralla.com*.

About the Creative Team

Peter Meyers (editor) had been using and disliking Windows operating systems for more than a decade—until the arrival of Windows XP. At O'Reilly Media he works as an editor on the Missing Manual series. Peter lives with his wife and cat in New York City. Email: *peter.meyers@gmail.com*.

Sarah Milstein (editor) is O'Reilly's senior editor for Missing Manuals and the author of *Google: The Missing Manual*. She lives with her dog in New York City. Email: *milstein@oreilly.com*.

Susan Stellin (editor) is a freelancer writer and editor. She writes the Practical Traveler column twice a month for the *New York Times* travel section, and her articles about travel and technology have appeared in *Travel + Leisure*, *The New York Observer*, *The International Herald Tribune*, *The New York Post*, *Business 2.0*, *Industry Standard*, and *Interactive Week*.

Nan Barber (copy editor) co-authored *Office X for the Macintosh: The Missing Manual* and *Office 2001 for Macintosh: The Missing Manual*. As the principal copy editor for this series, she has edited the titles on iPhoto, Mac OS X, AppleWorks 6, iPod and iTunes, and Windows XP. Email: *nanbarber@mac.com*.

John Cacciatore (copy editor) has worked as an event specialist and freelance writer for many a moon. Among his passions: Asian cuisine, Cheers reruns (starring Coach or Woody), and his 23-year-old Rawlings baseball glove that still picks 'em clean at short. Email: *j_cacciatore@yahoo.com*.

Dave Carrano (technical editor) is a systems administrator and generally helpful Windows guy for O'Reilly in Cambridge, MA.

Acknowledgments

This book had a longer birth than many, and I'd like to thank its many editorial midwives, among them Sarah Milstein, Susan Stellin, and Peter Meyers, for helping bring it to term. In addition, the O'Reilly production staff worked hard to bring this book to life. And, as always, thanks to my family, who put up with too many late-night deadlines.

The Missing Manual Series

Missing Manuals are witty, superbly written guides to computer products that don't come with printed manuals (which is just about all of them). Each book features a handcrafted index; cross-references to specific page numbers (not just "see Chapter 14"); and RepKover, a detached-spine binding that lets the book lie perfectly flat without the assistance of weights or cinder blocks.

Recent and upcoming titles include:

Mac OS X: The Missing Manual (Panther and Tiger editions) by David Pogue

FileMaker Pro 7: The Missing Manual by Geoff Coffey

iPhoto 4: The Missing Manual by David Pogue

Introduction

Windows XP is the most powerful, stable, useful, and all-around fun operating system Microsoft has released yet. From networks that work to desktop icons you can customize—and everything in between—this operating system *rocks*. Yet millions of people around the globe use it every day and have *no idea* what it can do for them. You don't have to be one of them.

This book takes you under the hood, helping you find easier, faster, and better ways of using virtually every aspect of Windows XP, from the Start menu to the software that lets you watch movies on your PC.

Almost all of the hints in this book work whether you're using the XP Home Edition or XP Professional. If a hint covers the Home Edition, it also applies to XP Professional, which has all the features of the Home version, plus a bunch of extras. If a hint covers XP Professional only, it's noted.

Note: If you're not sure which version you have, head to the Start menu or desktop and right-click My Computer, then choose Properties, and in the dialog box that opens, click the General tab. The System area of the tab tells you whether you have XP Home or Pro.

How This Book Works

Most computer books are set up to teach you a whole program, from start to finish. Not this book. Instead, it gives you the cream of the crop, and each hint can stand on its own. While many of the hints are, in fact, inter-related (who would want to know about wireless Internet tricks without also finding out about security?), a lot of the hints here involve a single trick or solution that isn't related to any other hint in the book.

The cool thing about this arrangement is that you can just open the book anywhere, read a hint, marvel at how cool it is, and then jump back 63 pages to read about another amazing trick. Think of it as the "Choose Your Own Adventure" of computer books.

A Special Note: The Registry

Some of the hints in this book require you to work with the *Registry*, a vast database inside Windows XP that contains *all* your system settings and vital stats. Because you can edit the settings, the Registry is a very powerful tool for customizing XP. (In fact, you actually change the Registry all the time without knowing it. For example, whenever you change a setting using the Control Panel, behind the scenes XP changes the Registry to put that new setting into effect.)

If you've never used the Registry before, fear not—you can easily master it. Chapter 15, "The Registry," is devoted to teaching you exactly what you need to know to run the Registry tricks throughout this book. Despite the geeky nature of the Registry (and the weird language in the Registry hints), Chapter 15 is surprisingly digestible, and it walks you through the process for running the Registry tricks. Your grandmother could catch on in about 15 minutes. Seriously.

Some Experience Required

This book assumes that you already know the basics of Windows XP. It doesn't explain how to log in, create an account, use menus, or other basics. (You might think of this book as a sort of intermediate sequel to *Windows XP Home Edition: The Missing Manual* and *Windows XP Pro: The Missing Manual*.)

Once you have some experience with the operating system, this book can help you progress from anybody-can-do-this to power hound.

About → These → Arrows

Throughout this book, you'll find sentences like this one: "Open the My Computer → C: → Windows folder." That's shorthand for a much longer instruction that directs you to open three nested folders in sequence, like this: "On your hard drive, there's an icon called My Computer. Open that. Inside My Computer, there's a folder for your C: drive. Open that. Inside your C: drive is your Windows folder. Open that."

Similarly, this kind of arrow shorthand helps to simplify the business of choosing commands in menus, such as File → New → Window, as shown in Figure 1. You'll also see this arrow notation used to indicate which tab or pane of a dialog box you're supposed to click: "Choose Tools → Options → General," for example.

Note: Since its initial release, Microsoft has released a number of upgrades to the system (page 291 tells you all about these upgrades—they're called *Windows Updates*). The upgrades don't alter the basic functioning of the operating system, but there's a chance one of them has changed slightly some of the menus and screens you see in this book. So don't fret if what you see onscreen is a little different than what's in the book—the same hints still apply.

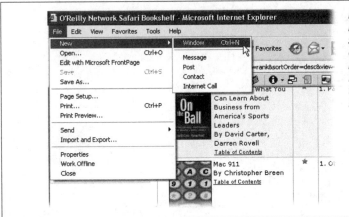

Figure P-1:
In this book, arrow notations help to simplify folder and menu instructions. For example, "Choose File → New → Window" is a more compact way of saying "From the File menu, choose New; from the submenu that appears, choose Window," as shown here.

About MissingManuals.com

At *www.missingmanuals.com,* you'll find news, articles, and updates to the books in the Missing Manual and Power Hound series.

But the Web site also offers corrections and updates to this book (to see them, click the book's title, then click Errata). In fact, you're invited and encouraged to submit such corrections and updates yourself. In an effort to keep the book as up to date and accurate as possible, each time we print more copies of this book, we'll make any confirmed corrections you've suggested. We'll also note such changes on the Web site, so that you can mark important corrections into your own copy of the book, if you like.

In the meantime, we'd love to hear your own suggestions for new books in the Missing Manual and Power Hound lines. There's a place for that on the Web site, too, as well as a place to sign up for free email notification of new titles in the series.

Getting Started

There's more to getting started with Windows XP than just turning on your computer. With XP, the most stable and customizable version of Windows developed so far, you can tweak pretty much every aspect of how your computer looks, starts up, and shuts down—plus a whole lot in between.

The hints in this chapter help you get more out of Windows XP's most basic functions.

Startup and Shutdown

Start up and shut down faster, get yourself a new startup splash screen, and get rid of useless error messages. After you read the hints in this section, you'll never again settle for sitting down at your PC and fumbling for the On button.

1-1   Instant Startup

Windows XP seems to take a few light years to start up. Happily, you can change that. The secret? Don't shut down your computer. Instead, put it on Stand By, a kind of deep freeze your PC can recover from almost instantly. A nice bonus of Stand By is that you can leave your programs running—meaning they're standing at attention when you pull your computer out of hypnosis.

To invoke this handy trance, choose Start → Turn Off Computer → Stand By (instead of Start → Turn Off Computer → Turn Off). In Stand By mode, your computer appears to be turned off, but in fact uses a trickle of power to stay just barely on (the system stores everything in its short-term memory, or *RAM*). Then, when you use your mouse or keyboard, it springs to life almost instantly rather than going through the normally lengthy startup procedure.

Note: Don't use the Stand By method all the time. When Windows XP shuts down and starts up again, it does various bits of housekeeping that keep it running smoothly—like cleaning out its memory. But it can't perform those chores when your PC is just Standing By, so over time your machine can slow down dramatically. The solution? Every few times, shut your computer down completely.

1-2   Instant Startup for Laptops

The downside to Stand By mode is that even though it uses just a smidgen of power, it does continue to suck power. If you use a laptop, leaving it in Stand By for more than 20 minutes or so can dribble you into oblivion. In these cases, set your computer to Hibernate. It'll take your computer a little longer to wake up from Hibernate, but this mode draws considerably less power.

To put your computer in this hibernation state, choose Start → Turn Off Computer as you normally would. Then, when the shut down dialog box opens, press Shift to change the Stand By button to a Hibernate button (Figure 1-1). Click it, and your computer appears to go to sleep.

To wake your computer up, press the power button—merely jiggling the mouse or pressing a key doesn't do the trick.

Tip: If you have a laptop, you can set Windows XP to *automatically* slip into Stand By or Hibernate mode when you shut the lid—a nice way to bypass the Start menu altogether when you want to grab your computer and run to a meeting or class on another floor. Choose Start → Control Panel → Power Options, and then click the Advanced tab. Under "Power buttons," the first choice is "When I close the lid of my portable computer"; use the menu to choose Stand By or Hibernate. If your laptop resists slipping into Stand By, see hint 10-5.

Figure 1-1:
Left: The Stand By button changes to a Hibernate button (right) when you press Shift.

Right: To use hibernation, you need a little room on your hard disk because that's where Windows XP stores everything you want to leave open. To find out whether you've got the room, choose Start → Control Panel → Power Options, then click the Hibernate tab—which has a "Disk space for hibernation" section that does the math for you.

Note: Like Stand By, Hibernate does not run your computer through its normal regime of startup/shut-down exercises. If your machine doesn't go through its paces every few days, it can accumulate gunk in the memory that slows it down. Avoid this irritating sluggishness by doing a full-blown shutdown a couple of times a week.

1-3 Nixing the Startup Screen

Every time you start up your PC, Windows XP puts a screen in front of your face that serves no purpose other than giving Microsoft extra advertising. You can easily make this splash screen history by using a little-known Windows XP feature called the System Configuration Utility.

Although hiding this screen won't hasten your PC's start up time, killing the ad can make your morning routine a tad less heraldic. Here's how.

Click the Start button, and then choose Run. In the blank box that appears, type *msconfig* and then press Enter. When the System Configuration Utility opens, choose the BOOT.INI tab, and then select NOGUIBOOT, as shown in Figure 1-2. Click OK or Apply. A little box pops up asking if you want to restart your computer now, for the changes to take effect immediately, or later. Click "Exit without Restart" if you want to wait. The next time you turn on your PC, the startup routine is pleasingly splash-free.

Note: You can also make this change from the *command line,* a separate window that lets you type commands directly to the operating system, without using menus or the normal interface. For more about using the command line, see page 103.

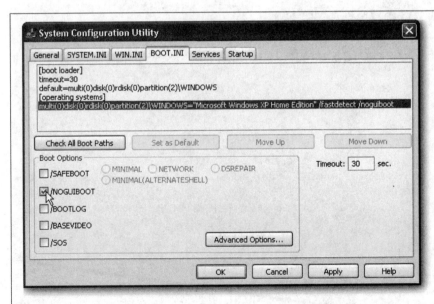

Figure 1-2:
Stopping the Windows XP splash screen from loading on startup is only one of the many ways the System Configuration Utility can help you take control of Windows XP. The box on page 4 explains more about making changes in BOOT.INI, and page 280 gives the lowdown on using the Services and Startup tabs to take charge of your operating system.

1-4   Changing the Startup Screen

The previous hint told you how to nix the startup screen. But if a blank screen is too minimalist for your taste, you can add a picture instead. BootXP, available from *www.bootxp.net*, lets you choose from hundreds of pics available online, or it can help create your own. Here's how to use it to change your startup screen.

Note: BootXP is *shareware,* which means you can try it out for free. If you keep using it, there's a $7.95 fee.

---

1. **Download, install, and run the program.**

   When you run BootXP, it starts by asking where you want to store your boot screens. The program comes set to create My Computer → C: → WINDOWS → Resources → Bootscreens. Unless you can think of a better place to keep them, click OK to confirm this folder and let BootXP finish launching. Don't be put off if the interface looks confusing at first—it's not that tough to use.

POWER USERS' CLINIC

Troubleshooting with Boot.ini

The System Configuration Utility lets you make changes to a startup file called boot.ini. By altering the file, you can control which processes run when you fire up the computer. This little program is good to know about, because turning off your startup processes individually is a good way to narrow down certain problems. Figure 1-2 shows you the boot.ini options. Here's what happens when you turn each of them on:

/BASEVIDEO. This option starts Windows XP using the standard VGA driver instead of your normal video driver. Use it if you're having trouble starting Windows XP due to a problem with a video driver (for example, if your screen doesn't display properly, or you get an error message about a problem with your monitor or video).

/BOOTLOG. This option logs information about the boot process to the file ntbtlogl.txt, which lives in your My Computer → C: → Windows folder. Turn on /BOOTLOG if you're troubleshooting startup problems, and then after you've booted, examine the ntbtlogl.txt file for error messages.

/SAFEBOOT. This option forces Windows XP to start in *Safe Mode,* which means the system loads the fewest *drivers* possible (drivers are little programs that help various pieces of hardware attached to your computer work with the operating system). /SAFEBOOT is another handy option

when Windows XP isn't starting up properly because it can help you figure out whether a driver is causing the problem.

When you turn on /SAFEBOOT, you can also choose which version of Safe Mode to use (click one of the buttons next to /SAFEBOOT). In MINIMAL mode, Windows XP loads only the minimum set of drivers necessary to start your computer. If you need to access the Internet or your network when you're in Safe Mode, choose NETWORK mode instead, so that Windows XP loads the minimum set of drivers plus networking drivers. In MINIMUM (ALTERNATE SHELL), Windows XP loads the minimum set of drivers and boots into the command prompt, making this strategy the ideal alternative if Windows XP is causing you so many problems you can't even view the interface. You can ignore the DSREPAIR option, since it's useful primarily to network administrators.

/SOS. This option displays the name of each driver as it loads and provides a description of what's going on during the boot process. It also offers other information, including the Windows XP build number, the service pack number, the number of processors on the system, and the amount of installed memory. When you're on the phone with tech support, the agent may ask you to start up this way and read off some information about your PC.

---

2. **Select the Your Boot Screens tab.**

   If you have any graphics or boot screens in My Computer → C: → WINDOWS → Resources → Bootscreens, the program displays a list of them.

   If you don't have any boot screens stored, click the Get Boot Screens button to have BootXP search several Web sites that have downloadable boot screens. (If you find any you like, make sure to download them to My Computer → C: → Windows → Resources → Bootscreens.)

Note: You can also create screens from scratch using a graphics program. Put them in Windows → Resources → Bootscreens, and then, when you open them in BootXP and click Convert To Boot Screen, BootXP converts them to the format Windows XP requires: 640×480 pixels and 16 colors.

---

3. **To choose a new boot screen, click the file in the list, and then from the selection screen that appears, click OK.**

   As in Figure 1-3, the program shows the graphic you've chosen on the left side of the screen, and how it looks as a boot screen on the right.

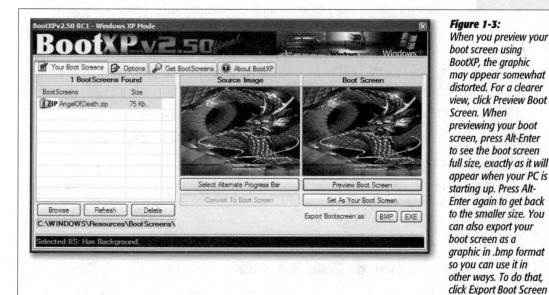

Figure 1-3:
When you preview your boot screen using BootXP, the graphic may appear somewhat distorted. For a clearer view, click Preview Boot Screen. When previewing your boot screen, press Alt-Enter to see the boot screen full size, exactly as it will appear when your PC is starting up. Press Alt-Enter again to get back to the smaller size. You can also export your boot screen as a graphic in .bmp format so you can use it in other ways. To do that, click Export Boot Screen as BMP in the bottom right corner of the screen.

4. **To confirm this is the boot screen you want, click the Set As Your Boot Screen button.**

   That's it. You've now got yourself a shiny new startup picture.

1-5   Good Housekeeping for Speedier Startups

If you're tired of waiting…and waiting…and waiting while Windows XP starts up, you're in good company. But you can leave the unwashed masses behind by running *boot defragment,* a process that puts all the startup files next to each other on your hard drive, thereby helping the operating system start up more quickly. Defragmenting may speed the startup process by five seconds or more depending upon how badly your boot files are scattered all over your hard drive.

On most computers, boot defrag—as geeks call it—comes turned on, so every time you defragment your hard disk by choosing Start → All Programs → Accessories → System Tools → Disk Defragmenter, your boot files get defragmented along with all the other files. Defragment your drive once a month for best performance.

But what if you're flossing regularly and you're *still* molding over waiting for your computer to boot up? If you've inadvertently turned off boot defrag, you can run the Disk Defragmenter until the cows come home and see no startup benefit. To make sure boot defrag runs every time you defragment your system:

1. **Run the Registry Editor.**

    For information about how to run and use the Registry Editor, see page 328.

2. **Go to My Computer → HKEY_LOCAL_MACHINE → SOFTWARE → Microsoft → Dfrg → BootOptimizeFunction.**

    This is the Registry key that controls how the Windows XP defragmentation process works.

3. **Change the Enable string value to *Y* if it is not already set to *Y.***

    If for some reason the Enable value isn't present, create it as a new string value.

4. **Exit the Registry and reboot.**

    From now on, whenever you run the Disk Defragmenter, it makes sure your boot files are all in one place.

Tip: For more powerful defragmentating options, see the box on page 7.

1-6   Killing the Error Messenger

Windows XP likes to keep you apprised of problems on your system by popping up messages when if finds something wrong—a nice service. But nothing's more annoying than getting the same error message every time you start the computer, especially if you have no way to fix the problem (say you improperly installed some software or inadvertently disabled a driver nine months ago). Luckily, you can quash these error messages before they appear.

Note: When you turn off error messages that display on startup, you're disabling *all* startup error messages, not only those you'd prefer not to see. So if you turn them off, you risk missing important Windows XP error messages.

To kill error messages: Launch the Registry Editor (page 328), and go to My Computer → HKEY LOCAL MACHINE → SYSTEM → CurrentControlSet → Control → Windows. Create a new DWORD called NoPopupsOnBoot and give it a value of *1*. Exit the Registry and reboot. Error messages will bedevil you no longer.

1-7 Customizing Your Startup Process

Hidden on your PC are *startup folders* that tell your computer to launch certain programs every time you turn it on. Every account has its own startup folder, and the system has a common folder, too. The cool thing about these folders is that you can use them to customize how your PC greets you.

For example, if you want your email program to open automatically when you turn on your computer, startup folders are the place to turn.

You can find the common startup folder by opening Windows Explorer and choosing My Computer → C: → Documents and Settings → All Users → Start Menu → Programs → Startup. Individual startup folders live at Documents and Settings → [Your Account Name] → Start Menu → Programs → Startup; [Your Account Name] is whoever is currently logged in.

To *prevent* programs in either folder from running automatically, simply delete their shortcuts. (In Windows Explorer, you can spot shortcut icons by the label "shortcut" next to them.)

ADD-IN ALERT

A Better Disk Defragmenter

For most purposes, Windows XP's Disk Defragmenter (page 6) works just fine. But sometimes you need a more powerful utility. If you want to schedule the defragmentation process, for example, or you're a system administrator who needs to perform this task on multiple PCs, consider an alternative to XP's Disk Defragmenter. Two of the best are available as try-before-you-buy software: Diskeeper and Perfect Disk.

- **Diskeeper.** This defragmenter is ideal for anyone who takes care of multiple computers on a network. Diskeeper automatically defragments a disk when it starts up, lets you schedule defragmentation on several computers, and is easy to install on multiple PCs. Available at *www.execsoft.com,* Diskeeper costs $29.95 for personal use and $44.95 for corporate users..

A free version, called Diskeeper Lite Freeware, is available too, but it defragments only one disk at a time and doesn't allow scheduling.

- **Perfect Disk.** Like Diskeeper, Perfect Disk is best for network administrators who want to schedule defragmentation on multiple machines on a network. Perfect Disk defragments hard drives even if they only have a little bit of free space available (normally a road block), and it also works on files that Windows XP's built-in defragmenter won't touch, such as the Windows page file. The program is available at *www.raxco.com.* It's free to download and try, but costs $44 per PC if you decide to keep it.

To *force* a program to run automatically when you start up the computer, you can add a shortcut to one of these startup folders. In Windows Explorer, find the executable file for the program you want to add to your startup process. (An executable is the file that launches a program, identified with the extension *.exe*; for example, *word.exe* for Microsoft Word.) To locate the executable file you want, right-click the program icon on the Windows desktop and choose Properties from the shortcut menu. The name and location of the executable file appear in the Target box. Now that you've got your executable file at the ready, drag it to the startup folder you want to customize. Once you've put the executable file in the startup folder, Windows automatically creates a shortcut and launches the program when you boot up.

POWER USERS' CLINIC

Change the Location of Your Startup Folders

If you'd like, you can change the location of your startup folders. In fact, you can make any folder become the common startup folder or your individual startup folder. That way, you can choose any name and location that's easy for you to remember. For example, you may want to create and use a folder called My Computer → C: → All Startup for the common startup folder, and My Computer → C: → [Your Name] Startup for your individual startup folder.

To change the location of the current account's Startup folder, first run the Registry Editor (page 328), and then go to My Computer → HKEY_CURRENT_USER → Software → Microsoft → Windows → CurrentVersion → Explorer → User Shell Folders → Startup. The file has a string value for

the location of the folder, like *C:\Documents and Settings\ Joe Schmoe\Start Menu\Programs\Startup,* for example. To change the location of the startup folder, edit this string to refer to any folder on your hard drive; for example, *C:\ YourStartup.* Exit the Registry and reboot for the change to take effect.

To change the location of the common Startup folder, go to My Computer → HKEY_LOCAL_MACHINE → SOFTWARE → Microsoft → Windows → CurrentVersion → Explorer → User Shell Folders → Common Startup. The string value should be *C:\Documents and Settings\All Users\Start Menu\Programs\Startup.* Again, this string can lead to any folder on your hard drive; for example, *C:\AllStartups.* Exit the Registry and reboot to make the change take effect.

Tip: If you're having startup problems and you want to determine whether any of your startup programs are to blame, you can have Windows ignore those programs when you boot—without deleting their shortcuts from the startup folder. That way, you don't have to waste your time deleting and then recreating the shortcuts.

Here's how: When you log in, type your account name and password in the logon box, and then press Shift as you click OK—and continue to hold down Shift until the desktop appears. When you follow this procedure, Windows XP doesn't run any programs in your startup folders, but it doesn't delete them either. They'll run as usual the next time you boot up. For more on this Safe Mode, see page 308.

1-8   Automating Reboots and Shutdowns

Rebooting or shutting down your PC should be quick and painless. But in Windows XP, you have to go through several clicks and menu choices and manually shut down programs that are running. Rome was built in less time than it takes to turn off your computer.

But relief is at hand: You can create reboot or shutdown shortcuts to perform the routine for you. Once you've got the shortcut icons on your desktop, all you have to do is double-click one to have the computer shut itself down. For maximum efficiency, create a shortcut that reboots your computer (to restart it if your system crashes, for example) and another that shuts it down.

Here's how to create a shutdown icon:

1. **Right-click your desktop, and in the menu that appears, choose New → Shortcut.**

    A wizard appears asking you to fill in the location of the item.

2. **Type the command *shutdown*, but don't press Enter. Instead, follow the command with a space and one of several *switches*.**

    A switch is a letter that follows a command and customizes how the command works. Here's a list of the switches you can use with the *shutdown* command. Note that you can use more than one, in any combination.

    - -s. Shuts down the PC. Use when you want to do a basic system shutdown.

    - -l. Logs off the current account. Use when you don't want to turn off your computer, but you want to log out of the current account quickly.

    - -t *nn.* Indicates the amount of delay, in seconds, before the shutdown begins. So if you want to delay it for 10 seconds, you would use -t 10. Use when you don't want an immediate shutdown, but instead want the shutdown process to start after a few seconds. That way, you have a chance to close any open programs before the system shuts down.

    - -c *"messagetext".* Displays a message in the System Shutdown window. You can use a maximum of 127 characters, but you have to enclose the message in quotation marks. Use if you want to issue a warning to anyone using the computer that the system is about to shut down, like "Hasta la vista, baby!"

    - -f. Forces any running applications to shut down (safely). That way, you won't have to close them yourself.

    For example, *shutdown –r –t 01 –c "Rebooting your PC"* reboots your PC after a one-second delay and displays the message, "Rebooting your PC."

    Type in your command and switches, and then click Next.

3. **Type a name for the shortcut, and then click Finish.**

    A good name might be Shutdown, or Log Off and Reboot.

That's it. Your shortcut is ready to roll.

1-9   Speedier Shutdown Times

If your computer takes its sweet time turning off, you can easily goose the shut-down process.

One reason it takes so long for Windows XP to shut down is that it waits for any open programs and *services* (see the box on page 10) to call it a day before turning itself off. If you think you don't have any programs running, think again—they're just invisible, or what geeks call running in the background.

Things get sluggish when Windows tells a task to shut down but the task doesn't respond, leading Windows to wait politely for 20 seconds before forcing the task to end. You can speed things up by shortening the amount of time Windows XP waits. To do so, run the Registry Editor (page 328) and then:

1. **Go to My Computer → HKEY_CURRENT_USER → Control Panel → Desktop.**

2. **Edit the WaitToKillAppTime value.**

   This value controls the amount of time that Windows waits, in milliseconds, before closing a program that isn't responding. The value comes set at 20000, which is 20 seconds. Put in a smaller value, such as 10000 or 5000.

3. **Edit the HungAppTimeout value, which does essentially the same thing as WaitToKillAppTime.**

   Again, the preset value is 20000. Enter the same number here that you entered for WaitToKillAppTime.

4. **Go to My Computer → HKEY_LOCAL_MACHINE → SYSTEM → Current-ControlSet → Control.**

   Edit the WaitToKillServiceTimeout value, which controls the amount of time that Windows waits, in milliseconds, before closing a *service* that isn't respond-ing. It should be set to 20000. Put in the same value that you entered for HungAppTimeout.

5. **When you're done editing, exit the Registry.**

   You have to reboot in order for the new settings to take effect.

UP TO SPEED

Windows Services

Every time you start your PC, Windows runs a series of *ser-vices,* which are background tasks that your PC needs for one reason or another. For example, one service automati-cally checks to see whether Microsoft has any Windows XP updates you should download. Another service automati-cally configures laptops to let them connect to wireless net-works. Yet another service puts files in a print queue for printing.

You don't necessarily need the services that automatically load on startup, however, and some can slow down your system or even cause conflicts. To find out how to delete unnecessary ones, see page 280.

1-10 Other Software that Can Control Startups and Shutdowns

Windows XP gives you some control over how your system starts up and shuts down. But if you want to do detailed things, like scheduling shutdowns, third-party software is the way to go. Here are a few programs you can download:

• For full startup management, you can't do better than **Advanced StartUp Manager.** This program is best for creating different *startup profiles*, which optimize your PC for certain tasks when you turn it on. You can, for example, customize a startup profile for the times you're mostly using the Internet, and another for when you're working in a graphics program. For Internet sessions, you can have programs like instant messengers and audio and video players launch automatically, ready when you are. On the other hand, if you need to run a graphics program, you might want to have very few programs running, so your system can devote resources to your graphics program. Advanced StartUp Manager is shareware and free to try; it's $19.95 if you decide to continue using it. Get it from *www.rayslab.com.*

• For a less powerful (but free) program, try **Startup Control Panel.** This small program, which runs via the Control Panel, lets you decide which programs Windows XP runs on startup the next time you boot your PC. (It controls which programs start only the next time, not every time after that.) You can download it from *www.mlin.net.*

• To better handle shutdowns, try **Switch Off.** This free utility runs in your system tray where it's easily accessible and lets you schedule things like shutdowns, restarts, disconnecting your dialup connection, and locking your workstation. It's free and available from *http://yasoft.km.ru/eng/switchoff.*

ADD-IN ALERT

Startup and Shutdown Controls

As you've learned in this chapter, startup and shutdown are two of the most tedious processes in computing; they always seem to take longer than they should. While starting a PC is never going to be as quick or easy as turning on a light, you can shave precious seconds off your daily workload by trying the options described below. (For more hints and downloads for startup and shutdown, see page 11.)

• **Shutdown Now!** This piece of software gives you just about every option you can imagine for shutdown. You can specify that Windows XP launch or load applications automatically before shutdown (to perform housekeeping tasks like defragmenting your hard disk, for example), schedule shutdowns, delete all the files in a particular directory before shutdown...the list goes on and on. ($19.50 shareware; *www.dworld.de.*)

• **OSL 2000.** If you boot more than one operating system on your PC, check out this program. It lets you boot from up to 100 separate operating systems (such as multiple copies of Windows XP or other versions of Windows) or boot from a second hard disk. Other features include an automatic boot timer, and the ability to uninstall operating systems if they cause problems. If you need 100 operating systems on one computer, you should probably keep that information to yourself. ($25 shareware; *www.osloader.com.*)

Controlling Your Monitor and Sounds

You spend half your life looking at and listening to your computer. Why settle for lame displays and cacophonous sounds? This section reveals stunning monitor and sound tricks that most people don't even know about. Some are just for fun (like building a customized startup sound), while others are powerful work tools (like attaching additional monitors).

1-11   Insta-Mute

Here's a quiz: You're blasting the latest Yeah Yeah Yeahs CD or your favorite Internet radio station when your phone rings. (You can't hear the phone, but you can see it flashing.) What do you do?

Answer: In the system tray (also known as the notification area), which is in the far right corner of the taskbar at the bottom your screen, click the volume icon—the small, round icon that looks like a speaker. A dialog box, shown in Figure 1-4, appears. When you choose Mute, the sound stops immediately.

Figure 1-4:
To mute sounds and music, choose Mute. You can also increase or decrease the volume by dragging the slider up or down.

1-12   The Silence of the Modem

If you're not a big fan of the squeaks, beeps, and static you hear whenever your phone modem dials, you can nix the screeching. Choose Start → Control Panel → Printers and Other Hardware → Phone and Modem (alternatively, at the command prompt or in the Run box, type *telephon.cpl* and then press Enter). In the dialog box that appears, choose Modems → Properties → Modem, and then drag the slider in the "Speaker volume" area to Off, as shown in Figure 1-5. Click OK until you're out of the dialog box. The next time you use your modem, you're greeted by blessed silence.

1-13   Personalizing Your PC's Sounds

Windows XP plays washy, electronic noises when it wants to alert you to things like the arrival of email or the intrusion of an error message. Who needs more tinny beeps in life? Instead, you can swap in, say, your dog's woof for new email or your mother's voice for errors.

You can easily add any sound you like, as long as your PC has a built-in microphone. Most PCs made in the last several years have them, and if yours doesn't, you can buy a cheap plug-in mic at any electronics store.

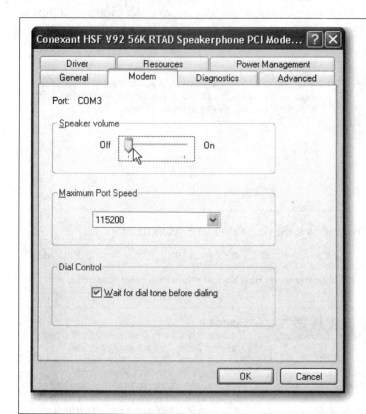

Figure 1-5:
When it comes to modem volume, you have two choices: On or Off. If you want to make the modem sounds quieter or louder, you can use the slider that controls the overall sound in Windows XP, explained on pages 12 and 106.

Here's how to record and add a new sound. If you already have a sound you want to use, and it's saved as a .wav file, skip down to step 4.

Tip: You can download sounds from the Internet—just make sure they're .wav files. *www.wavcentral.com* is a great place to find them.

---

1. **Open the Sound Recorder by choosing Start → All Programs → Accessories → Sound Recorder.**

   Figure 1-6 shows the Sound Recorder.

Tip: For a quicker way to get to the Sounds and Audio Devices Properties dialog box, at the command prompt or in the Run box, type *mmsys.cpl* and then press Enter.

---

2. **Click the Record button, record your sound clip, and when you're done, click the Stop button.**

Speak (or bark) in a normal tone of voice, about six inches from the microphone. Remember to keep the clip short, because you don't want to endure a long clip every time you get new email, for example. A few seconds is plenty.

Figure 1-6:
When you're recording, Windows tells you how many seconds the sound will last. This clip will be a looong startup sound, as Sound Recorder shows that it's already at 60 seconds.

3. **Choose File → Save and save the file to a folder or your desktop.**

Note the location and the file name (it ends in .wav). Exit the Sound Recorder.

4. **Now tell Windows XP to use your new sound when you start your PC.**

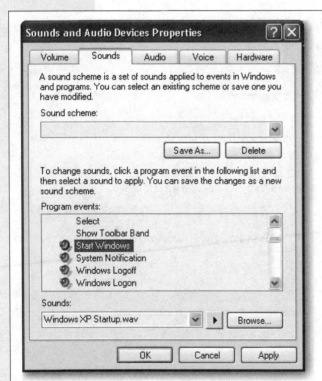

Figure 1-7:
The Sounds and Audio Devices Properties dialog box doesn't limit you to changing the Start Windows sound. While only those events with a small speaker next to them already have associated sounds, you can make Windows XP play sounds for any event, and you can change the existing sounds. Highlight an event, then browse for and select a sound the same way you customized the Start Windows sound.

To do so, choose Start → Control Panel → Sounds, Speech, and Audio Devices → Sounds and Audio Devices. On the Sounds and Audio Devices Properties dialog box that appears, click the Sounds tab. In the "Program events" list, shown in Figure 1-7, select Start Windows—or whatever event you want to associate with your sound.

Click Browse and locate the .wav file you just recorded (or the existing file you want to use). Select it and click OK. When the Sounds and Audio Devices Properties dialog box appears again, click OK.

5. Restart Windows.

When it starts up again, it greets you with the sound you recorded.

1-14 Building Sound Themes

In the previous hint you learned how to customize an individual sound. But you can build entire sound *themes* (groups of related system sounds), and you can even switch among themes as the mood strikes you. This trick's just for fun—don't expect it to boost your productivity.

To build a sound theme:

1. **Record as many sounds as you want to include in your theme.**

   Follow the steps in the previous hint or download new sounds (in the .wav format) from the Internet. An excellent place to find them is *www.wavcentral.com*.

2. **Once you've assembled the sounds you want to use, choose Start → Control Panel → Sounds, Speech, and Audio Devices → Sounds and Audio Devices.**

   Under "Program events," assign different sounds to each event. Once you've customized all the events, click the Save As button near the top of the dialog box, give your theme a name, and then click OK. You can close the dialog box now or create more themes before exiting. Your changes take effect immediately.

3. **To switch among themes, open the Sounds and Audio Devices dialog box, and choose from among the themes in the "Sound scheme" menu.**

That's it. You're styling—soundly.

1-15 Visual Reminders

Setting your system to chime when it's accomplished something—like successfully downloading a file—is a great way to stay on top of what your PC is up to. But if you've got Led Zeppelin blasting out of your speakers, you're not going to hear those useful sounds. And if you fail to notice that your all-important quarterly report has finished downloading, and you go fishing instead of reading it, you're gonna get fired. Better to have some handy *visual* reminders to supplement your alert sounds.

To help, Windows XP has a little-known feature called SoundSentry. It's designed to assist people with hearing difficulties, but it's also ideal for times when your PC's sound system is otherwise occupied.

To use SoundSentry, choose Start → Control Panel → Accessibility Options → Accessibility Options (if you're at the command prompt or in the Run box, type *access.cpl* and press Enter). In the dialog box that opens, click the Sound tab and turn on the box next to Use SoundSentry, as shown in Figure 1-8. Now select the visual warning you want to display when the system makes a sound. For example, you can have it flash the active window as a visual cue. Click OK. Voila! Your machine is giving you every possible clue that it's done something noteworthy.

Figure 1-8:
SoundSentry was designed for people with hearing difficulties, but it's useful for others as well. If you don't like your music interrupted by system sounds, use it to flash visual alerts at you, rather than play sounds, when Windows wants to get your attention.

1-16   Adding Sounds to Microsoft Office

Microsoft Office, unlike Windows XP, doesn't include system sounds. But if you're a fan of audio feedback from your PC and have Office XP or Office 2000 installed, you can make Word, Excel, and your other Office programs sound off, too.

Note: Unfortunately, if you have an older version of Office, Microsoft doesn't provide any way to add sound.

Go to *http://office.microsoft.com/downloads/2002/Sounds.aspx,* and download and install the Office Sounds add-in. Now open any Office application, choose Tools → Options → General, turn on "Provide feedback with sound," and then click OK. You've just made Office chatty.

If you want to turn off specific sounds or use different ones than those provided, choose Start → Control Panel → Sounds, Speech, and Audio Devices → Sounds and Audio Devices, and click the Sounds tab. In the Sound Events list, scroll down to Microsoft Office, and select the sound you wish to turn on, turn off, or change. Then follow the instructions for "Personalizing Your PC's Sounds" on page 12.

1-17 More Screen Real Estate with Virtual Desktops

No matter how big your monitor is, it's not big enough. And if you're running multiple programs in Windows XP, the problem can get out of hand, with windows on top on windows on top of windows. In less time than it takes to say, "ten-program pileup," you've lost an important document.

The best way to manage the problem is with multiple *virtual desktops,* which are separate versions of the Windows XP desktop, each complete with its own look and feel, and each of which can be running its own separate programs. You can have up to four such desktop environments running at once. For instance, you can have one desktop for sending and receiving email and browsing the Web, another for downloading and playing music, another for using your word processor and spreadsheet, and so on. You can quickly switch among the desktops, or take a global view of your work and see them all at a glance, as in Figure 1-9. It's like adding Pentaflex folders to a crammed file drawer—suddenly, you can find things.

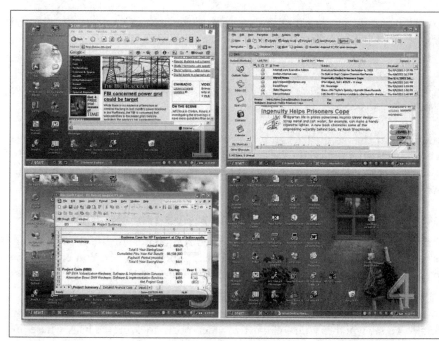

Figure 1-9:
The Virtual Desktop manager can display all four of your desktops simultaneously. To switch among them, you just click the screen you want to go to.

You can create virtual desktops with a free Microsoft PowerToy called Virtual Desktop Manager, available for download from *www.microsoft.com/windowsxp/ downloads/powertoys/xppowertoys.mspx.* It's one of several free utilities from

Microsoft, including the exceedingly useful TweakUI (page 28), and the Alt-Tab Replacement (page 20).

After you've downloaded the program, follow its installation wizard (which doesn't require you to restart Windows), then turn it on by right-clicking the taskbar and choosing Toolbars → Desktop Manager. A new toolbar appears on the taskbar, to the left of the system tray, as shown in Figure 1-10. You now have four virtual desktops at your disposal, numbered 1 through 4.

Figure 1-10:
Controls for the Virtual Desktop Manager appear in the taskbar, just to the left of the system tray.

At first, the desktops are identical, since you haven't customized any of them. To switch to any of them, click the desktop's number. When you do, that desktop takes up your full screen. Treat it as you do your normal Windows XP desktop: You can change its background the way you normally would or run whichever programs suit the task at hand. For example, you can run your email program and an instant messenger in an Internet-themed desktop but keep a word processor and spreadsheet open in a desktop focused on productivity (switch to the latter when your boss is looking).

To see all desktops at a glance, click the leftmost icon. A screen appears like the one in Figure 1-9, where you can click the desktop you want to visit.

Tip: If you're not a fan of the mouse, you can switch desktops using a keystroke shortcut like Ctrl+Alt+1, Ctrl+Alt+2 and so on. Simply right-click the taskbar, choose Configure Shortcut Keys, and choose a key combination for each desktop.

If you want to change the background of each desktop—a great way to help keep track of them—right-click the taskbar and choose Configure Desktop Images. In the dialog box that appears, pick from the backgrounds listed or browse your hard drive for a picture you want to use.

1-18   Expand Your Screen Real Estate with Two Monitors

If virtual desktops don't get you enough screen real estate, go with the real thing: Use two monitors and spread Windows XP across both of them. You can use the two monitors as one large, continuous desktop. The extended desktop stretches across the two displays, treating them as one monitor.

You can achieve this feat only if your computer has two video ports or if you have a laptop. To see whether your PC has two video ports, look on the back where the monitor is plugged in. The monitor is plugged into a video port, so if you have another port just like it, you're in business. Many computers have only one video port, and if that's the case with yours, you're out of luck—unless you buy a new graphics card with two ports. In the case of the laptop, you can use the built-in monitor and the second monitor in concert with each other.

Here's how to create your amazing two-monitor setup:

1. **Attach the second monitor to your computer.**

   If you have a desktop machine, plug the monitor into the free video port. If you have a laptop, it will have a free video port in the back, so plug it in there.

2. **Right-click your desktop and choose Properties → Settings. Icons for two monitors appear, as you can see in Figure 1-11.**

   The monitor labeled 2 should be the monitor you just installed. Turn on "Extend my Windows desktop onto this monitor."

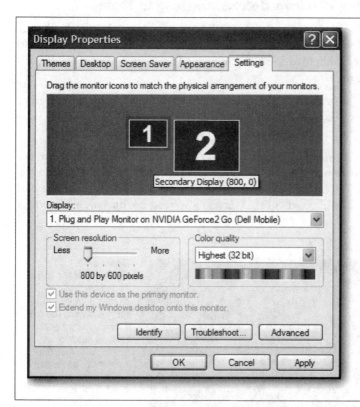

Figure 1-11:
When extending your desktop to two monitors, drag the icons for monitors in this dialog box until they match the way you want your desktop to span the two monitors—above, below, or side-by-side.

3. **With monitor 2 selected, move the Screen resolution slider to your preferred resolution.**

   If the monitor flickers, you may need to change the monitor's refresh rate. To do so, click the Advanced button, choose the Monitor tab, and try increasingly higher rates until you find the best one.

4. Click OK. The Display Properties settings dialog box reappears.

The arrangement of the two monitors determines how the desktop extends from one to the other. Initially, they are side-by-side, so that the second monitor extends the desktop to the right, but you can rearrange the icons so that the second monitor extends the desktop in any direction. When you're done rearranging the icons, click OK. Your Windows desktop now spans both monitors.

Individual Windows Tricks

A window is a window is a window…or is it? As you'll see in this section, there's a surprising number of ways you can tinker with how individual windows work.

1-19   Previewing Windows Before Switching to Them

When you press Alt-Tab at the same time, Windows displays a box with all your open programs and windows. To switch among them, just hold down Alt and keep tabbing until you've highlighted the one you want. This tactic is one of the biggest click-savers in Microsoft history.

But when you use Alt-Tab, you're flying blind: you can't preview a window before switching to it. This behavior becomes problematic when you have several windows open in a program and don't know which you'll be switching to.

Here's a simple solution: the Microsoft PowerToy called Alt-Tab Replacement, which you can download from *www.microsoft.com/windowsxp/pro/downloads/powertoys.asp*. After you install it, whenever you use Alt-Tab, you get a preview of the window to which you're switching. You can also read its title bar, as shown in Figure 1-12.

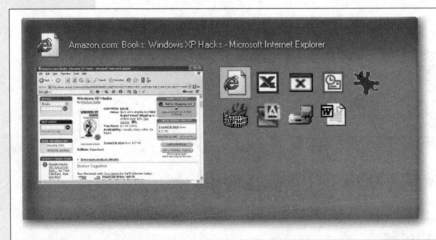

Figure 1-12:
The Microsoft PowerToy Alt-Tab Replacement displays a preview of each window as you tab through. This program takes up much more screen space than the normal Alt-Tab feature, but the preview makes it well worth it.

1-20   Manage Groups of Open Windows

As you've probably figured out by now, when you have several windows open in a program at once, they group together into a single button on the taskbar when minimized, with a small arrow at the right-hand side. Right-click the button, and a listing of all its open windows pops up, as shown in Figure 1-13 on the top. To switch to any of the windows, click it.

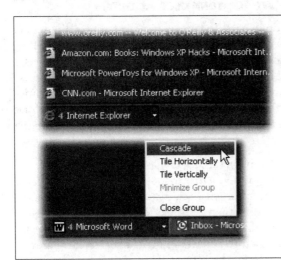

Figure 1-13:
Top: When you have several open windows in an application, they group together in a single entry on the taskbar, which you can expand by clicking.

Bottom: Save yourself time and keystrokes by managing open windows using this right-click menu.

Don't settle for the single-window switcheroo, though. The taskbar lets you manage the entire program group and view them all at once, close them all simultaneously, or minimize them if they're open. Right-click the entry, and the menu shown in Figure 1-13 (bottom) appears. You can choose to display them in a cascade, arrange them like tiles horizontally or vertically, close them all at once, or minimize them if they're maximized.

When you cascade them, the windows appear one behind the other, offset slightly, so that you can see the front one fully while the ones behind it are partially obscured (you can still see their title bars). Cascading is best when you don't need to see the contents of individual screens, but you do want to see the title bars clearly.

When you tile windows, they spread out like tiles on a floor. No window obscures another, but each window is tiny, so you often can't see the entire name in the title bar. Use tiling when it's important to distinguish the contents of the screens, albeit in a shrunken size.

User Accounts and Logons

Windows XP gives you a quite a bit of control over the way you log on and what you can do with user accounts. Here's where you'll find out how to use your own customized picture for your user account, how to make sure you use a password no one can crack, and other insider secrets.

1-21   Using Your Own Picture for Your User Account

One of the best things about Windows XP is the way you can customize it to reflect your personality, not the collective wisdom of a Microsoft marketing committee. And one of the best ways to customize it is to use your own picture on your user account rather than one provided by Microsoft. Rubber duckies, soccer balls, plastic frogs, and Kung Fu masters are all well and good, but you might want something more personal (and attractive) next to your name. After all, you see that picture not only when you log on to your PC, but also every time you bring up the Start menu.

For your user account, you can use any picture as long as it's in .gif, .jpg, .png, or .bmp format. Once you've decided on the picture, choose Start → Control Panel → User Accounts, then select the account with the picture you want to change. Next, choose "Change my picture" and then "Browse for more pictures." Now navigate to the folder that contains the picture you've selected. Choose the picture, and then click OK. Your new picture appears in the Current Picture area of the User Accounts screen, as shown in Figure 1-14. It also turns up on your logon screen and on the Start menu.

Note: If you have a digital camera or scanner attached to your PC, a button appears on the User Accounts screen that lets you snap or scan a picture and then immediately use that picture for your user account.

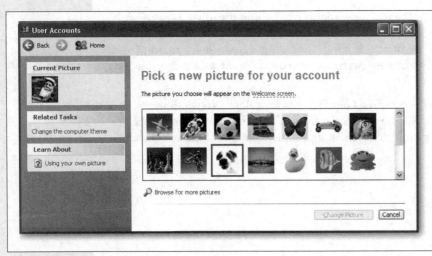

Figure 1-14:
Windows XP has a set of pictures you can use for your user account. The currently active picture appears in the upper-left part of the screen.

Tip: You can quickly get to the screen pictured in Figure 1-14 by going to the Start menu, then simply clicking the picture at the top. (On some systems, there may be no picture available.)

1-22   Fast User Switching

If several people use your PC and each person has a separate account, you can make it easy to snap from one account to another by turning on Windows XP's Fast User Switching feature. It lets several people log on simultaneously and then quickly switch between accounts without logging off the current account.

The cool thing is that whatever you're doing in the first account keeps running when you switch to another account. So for example, your account could be retrieving an email with a very large attachment. If someone else logs on to her account and uses the computer for word processing, your email download continues in the meantime.

Note: You may encounter performance trade-offs when you use Fast User Switching. Every active program uses up CPU cycles and RAM. Even idle accounts running in the background can suck up resources, too. As a result, you may notice a slowdown on your PC when more than one account at a time is logged in.

To turn on and use Fast User Switching:

1. **Log on as an administrator and choose Control Panel → User Accounts → "Change the way users log on or off."**

   The screen pictured in Figure 1-15 appears.

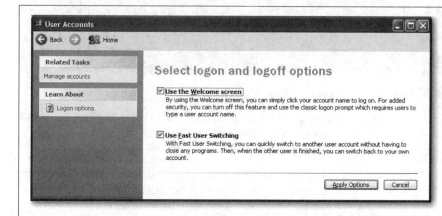

Figure 1-15:
When you turn on Fast User Switching, one person can keep his tasks running in the background, while another person logs on and uses the computer.

2. **Turn on "Use Fast User Switching," and then click Apply Options.**

   Fast User Switching is now ready to roll. To switch to another account, press the Windows logo key+L. When the Welcome screen appears, you can log onto another account as you would normally.

1-23 Create a Random Password

Anyone who guesses your password can break into your account and have the run of your computer. Frequently, the passwords that people use for their PCs are very easy to guess. You'd be surprised at how many people, for example, use the word "password" for their user account. You don't have to be The Amazing Kreskin to guess that one.

The best way to keep yourself safe is to have Windows XP automatically create a random password for you that will be very hard for others to guess. Here's how to do it:

1. Choose Start → Run, type *command* in the Run box, and press Enter.

   A command prompt appears, with a blinking cursor to the right.

2. Type the command *net user username /random,* but change *username* to the name of the account you're giving a new password.

   A prompt appears, telling you the random password to use to log on to the account. Be sure to write it down somewhere safe in case you forget, ideally not on a Post-it stuck to your monitor.

UP TO SPEED

Password Safety Rules

Using a randomly generated password will help keep your password safe. But if you'd rather choose one of your own, follow this advice to create a password that's hard to guess:

- Use at least seven characters in your password, and make sure they're a mix of numbers, uppercase letters, and lowercase letters.

- Don't use the names of your spouse or children or anything else obviously associated with you.

- Make the letter and number sequences random, rather than spelling out words.

- Change your password once a month.

1-24 Create a Password Reset Disk

It can be easy to forget your password, especially if you create one no one could guess—not even you. That leads to a major dilemma: What to do if you've forgotten your password and can't get into your account?

The best way to avoid this predicament is to create a Password Reset Disk. This disk allows you to change your password even if you can't remember your old password to log on to your PC. Just pop the disk into your computer when you forget your old password, and you can then log into your account.

Make sure to create the Password Reset Disk *before* you forget your old password, because you need to know your current password to create the disk.

To create the disk:

1. **Make sure you're using the account for which you want to create the disk.**

   To be extra sure, you might want to log out and log back in to the right account.

2. **Choose Control Panel → User Accounts.**

   A dialog box opens, offering a sort of command central for managing user accounts.

3. **Click your account and choose "Prevent a forgotten password" from the Related Tasks pane.**

   The Forgotten Password Wizard launches. Follow its instructions for creating the disk.

From now on, if you enter the wrong password when you log on, Windows XP prompts you for the disk so you can get into your account. Keep in mind that you can only have one Password Reset Disk for each account, so if you create a new one, the old one won't work. Also make sure to keep the disk in a safe place…and remember where you put it.

1-25 Set Disk Quotas for Users

When several people use the same PC, it's easy for the hard disk to become overrun with files. If a family member downloads digital music, videos, and movies, for example, that one space hog can quickly fill up a hard disk. However, you can solve the problem by setting limits on how much disk space any one person is allowed to occupy. You can also establish quotas on an individual basis.

Note: You can only set disk quotas on disks that use *NTFS*, a special Windows file system. To see if yours does, open Windows Explorer, then right-click your C: drive and choose Properties. On the General tab, look next to File System. It tells you whether your disk is NTFS.

Setting quotas that apply to everyone

To set disk quotas, log on as an administrator, and right-click your C: drive (or whatever drive you're setting quotas on) and choose Properties → Quota. The screen pictured in Figure 1-16 appears.

Turn on Enable Quota Management to allow disk quotas. As shown in Figure 1-16, you can set a quota for each account, and you can also set a specific warning level so a person gets alerted when he's nearing his limit. If you select the checkbox next to "Deny disk space to users exceeding quota limit," folks will get an "insufficient disk space" error message when they try to save a file but have reached their limit.

When you click OK, you get a warning message that Windows is about to rescan your disk, which may take several minutes. Click OK, and after scanning, the quotas go into effect.

Setting quotas individually

The quota limit above applies to every person who uses the PC, except for the administrator, who has no limits. However, you can set different quotas for each person who uses the PC as well. To do that, right-click the C: drive and choose Properties → Quota → Quota Entries. You get a list of all user accounts and details about their disk usage, including the amount of disk space used, the quota limit, the warning level, and the percent of their quota currently used.

To change the quota limit and warning level for a particular employee, student, or family member, double-click that account name. When the Quota Settings dialog box appears, set the quota limits here just as you did on the Quota tab of the disk's Properties panel, and then click OK. Repeat for each potential space-hogger you want to reign in.

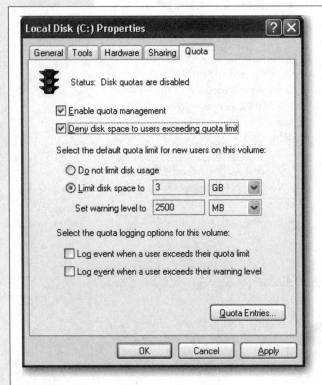

Figure 1-16:
You can limit the amount of storage each person who uses the computer gets, and even set warning levels so Windows will warn folks ahead of time when they approach their limit. Go a step further and have Windows create a log that tracks when anyone's account reaches its warning level or quota.

The Desktop and Interface

Like most operating systems, Windows XP comprises the things you experience as the computer itself—stuff like the desktop, the Start menu, the icons and cursors—in short, what people call the *interface* (and what geeks call the *user interface* or *UI*).

One of the most effective ways to get more out of Windows XP is to make the interface look and work the way you want it to. This chapter includes more than two dozen hints on how to customize your desktop, Start menu, taskbar, Control Panel, icons, cursors, and themes. Basically, you can give your computer a makeover: Think of it as a reality TV show for your PC.

Desktop Makeover

The desktop is the screen you see after your computer boots up. Most people think of it as the place where all those program icons live. But like your actual desk, there's no reason your Windows desktop should be cluttered up. Figure 2-1 shows you how to jump to the desktop, and the rest of this section gives you tips for taking control of it.

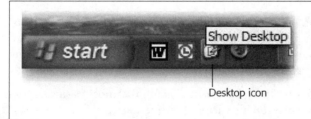

Desktop icon

Figure 2-1:
Most people don't realize that the Quick Launch bar (to the right of the Start button) contains an icon that brings up the desktop and automatically minimizes everything else to the taskbar. If you mouse over this light blue icon, you see the label "Show Desktop." It's indispensable when you want to get to your desktop with just a quick click. (If you don't see the icon, turn it on in the Taskbar and Start Menu control panel.)

2-1   The Easiest Way to Customize Your Desktop

It's a no-brainer: If you want to customize your Windows XP settings—including the desktop—download TweakUI, a free utility from Microsoft. TweakUI is part of a suite of utilities from Microsoft called XP PowerToys, and it's far and away the best one. In fact, TweakUI appears throughout this book because of the astonishing number of things you can do with it.

Microsoft supplies XP PowerToys but it doesn't *support* them, meaning if something goes wrong, the company's tech support agents won't help you out. Fortunately, TweakUI almost always works as it should.

Note: TweakUI works only if you have Windows XP Service Pack 1 or higher installed. To check your version of Windows XP, open My Computer, and then choose Help → About Windows. The window that opens gives you the version of Windows XP you have, including the service pack number.

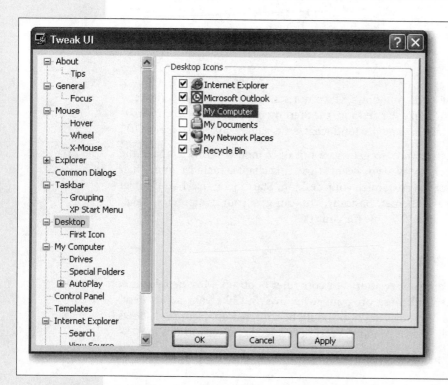

Figure 2-2:
You can also use TweakUI to have Windows XP display either My Documents or My Computer as the first icon on the desktop, in the upper-left corner—the position easiest to hit with the mouse. Choose Desktop → First Icon, and then click the icon you'd like first.

Download TweakUI from *http://www.microsoft.com/windowsxp/pro/downloads/ powertoys.asp* (it takes just a few seconds). Save it to your hard drive and then run the installer (which takes another few seconds). Open the program by clicking Start and choosing All Programs → PowerToys for Windows XP → TweakUI.

Once you've got TweakUI running, you can use it for the most basic desktop maintenance: whether to display or hide icons for Internet Explorer, Microsoft

Outlook, My Computer, My Documents, My Network Places, and the Recycle Bin. If you don't use any of these icons (either because you never use these items or because you reach them through the Start menu or other places), get rid of 'em. Conversely, if you're constantly searching in vain for, say, My Documents or My Network Places, then add those icons to your desktop. Simply open TweakUI, and in the panel at the left, click Desktop, and then turn on or off the icons of your choice, as show in Figure 2-2.

Note: TweakUI does a whole lot more. Hints throughout this book help you get the most out of it.

2-2 Changing the Standard Desktop Icons

If you don't like the way a desktop icon looks, or if you want to change one because it's confusingly similar to another icon, you can swap in a new picture. Right-click the one you want to change, choose Properties → Shortcut → Change Icon, and then browse to the icon you want to use. (You can find a large collection of icons in the file C: → Windows → System32 → SHELL32.dll.)

Unfortunately, if you try this procedure on the icons for My Computer, My Documents, My Network Places, and the Recycle Bin, you'll be out of luck: they have no Change Icon option. But don't fret—you *can* change their pictures. For reasons known only to Microsoft's brilliant engineers, these four icons store that option in a completely different place.

POWER USERS' CLINIC

Changing Really, Really Recalcitrant Icons

A number of icons—including those for Microsoft Outlook, Internet Explorer, Network Neighborhood, and others—don't officially let you change them at all. You can't alter them by the normal method of changing a desktop icon, and you can't alter them using the technique outlined in hint 2-2. You can, however, use a Registry hack to apply any icon you want to them.

To use the Registry hack, you need to know the CLSID (Class ID) for the icon you want to change. Here's a listing of the CLSIDs for icons you can change this way:

- **My Computer.** {20D04FE0-3AEA-1069-A2D8-08002B30309D}

- **Recycle Bin.** {645FF040-5081-101B-9F08-00AA002F954E}

- **Microsoft Outlook.** {00020D75-0000-0000-C000-000000000046}

- **Internet Explorer.** {FBF23B42-E3F0-101B-8488-00AA003E56F8}

- **The Internet.** {3DC7A020-0ACD-11CF-A9BB-00AA004AE837}

- **My Network Places.** {208D2C60-3AEA-1069-A2D7-08002B30309D}

Once you've got the right CLSID, run the Registry Editor (page 328), go to HKEY_CLASSES_ROOT → CLSID, and look for the CLSID subkey for the icon you want to change. Open the subkey and then the DefaultIcon subkey under that. For example, to change the icon for My Computer, open the subkey My Computer → HKEY_CLASSES_ROOT → CLSID → {20D04FE0-3AEA-1069-A2D8-08002B30309D} → DefaultIcon. Change the Default value by typing in the path of the icon you want to use—for example, *C:\MyIcons\ New.ico*. Exit the Registry. You may have to reboot in order for the new settings to take effect.

Here's the secret: Right-click the desktop and choose Properties → Desktop → Customize Desktop, which brings up the Desktop Items dialog box, shown in Figure 2-3. Select the icon you'd like to change, then click Change Icon and choose one of the icons that appear. Once you've chosen the picture you want to use, click OK until you're out of the dialog boxes. Admire your new icon.

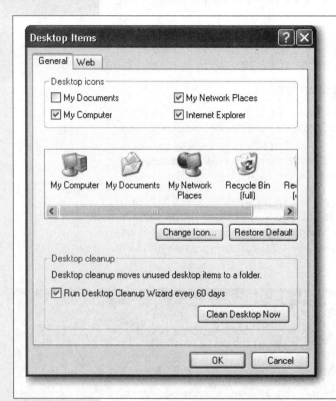

Figure 2-3:
If you want to change an icon to a picture you have stored on your hard drive, simply select the icon that you'd like to alter, click Browse, and then navigate to and highlight the file. Click OK until you've closed all the dialog boxes.

2-3   Cleaning Your Desktop Automatically

Over time, as you install programs and futz with your system, your desktop can become clogged with icons that you rarely (if ever) use, making it harder to hit your heavy-rotation icons. The good news is that you can have Windows clean up the mess for you, automatically deleting the deadbeats (that is, icons you haven't used for the past 60 days).

Right-click the desktop and choose Properties → Desktop → Customize Desktop to bring up the Desktop Items dialog box, shown in Figure 2-3. To have Windows sweep away icons you no longer use, click Clean Desktop Now.

Tip: If you want Windows to perform this service every two months (which is a good idea), simply turn on "Run Desktop Cleanup Wizard every 60 days." Each time it's about to start cleaning, Windows asks if you want the wizard to run, so you can always opt out.

2-4   Adding a Run Icon to Your Desktop

If you frequently use the Run box, then you know it's a time-saving way to launch a program—you simply type a few letters of its name. So why waste time going to the Start menu to open the Run box? Instead, put its icon on your desktop or in your Quick Launch bar. Once you've got the icon in place, you can launch the box with a swift double click.

To do so, click Start, and then drag the Run icon to the desktop or the Quick Launch bar. You'll know you're clear to drop it on the bar when the Stop circle turns into a vertical line, though you may have to wiggle around a little to get the line.

Tip: If you create a desktop icon and you'd like to give it a name other than the standard *&Run*, right-click it, choose Rename, and then type, say, *Percy.*

2-5   Rearranging Your Desktop Icons

Little-known fact: You can orchestrate the way icons appear on your desktop. You can arrange them by name, by icon type, by the last time someone worked on (modified) them, or by their size (assuming they're different sizes, of course). You can also force them to align in a grid or float freely—an aesthetic choice. And you can even hide all your desktop icons, so you see only your wallpaper, as shown in Figure 2-4. This is the desktop for neatness freaks: no muss, no fuss, no distractions. (Even if you hide your icons like this, by the way, you can still run the programs from the Start menu.)

Figure 2-4:
You can hide all of your desktop icons by right-clicking the desktop and, from the shortcut menu, choosing Arrange Icons By, then turning off Show Desktop Icons. If you set up your desktop with no icons, you get to enjoy an unsullied scenic view like this one, but you rely more heavily on the Start → All Programs menu to launch applications. See hint 2-11 for advice on customizing this menu.

To rearrange your desktop icons, right-click the desktop, choose Arrange Icons By (Figure 2-5), and then choose one of these options:

- **Name.** Arranges the icons in alphabetical order.

- **Size.** Arranges the icons in size order, measured in pixels.

- **Type.** Arranges icons by type of program, although there seems to be no rhyme or reason as to how Windows decides which program is which type. More than anything, it seems to arrange the icons randomly.

- **Modified.** Arranges icons by the order in which you last made changes to them or added them to the desktop. For example, icons for the most recently added program appear furthest to the right and at the bottom.

- **Auto Arrange.** Arranges icons in rows starting with the left-hand side of your screen. When you delete an icon, XP automatically re-arranges the remaining icons in rows, filling in the space taken up by the one you deleted. When you add an icon, XP automatically adds it to the right row. Auto Arrange uses whatever sort order you've chosen—for example, if you've chosen to arrange the icons by name, it places them in rows alphabetically.

Note: If Auto Arrange is turned on, you can't drag your icons around freely; they automatically slide back into place according to the arrangement you've chosen (for example, alphabetical). If you want to move individual icons, turn off Auto Arrange. Otherwise, keep it turned on to maintain your spiffy desktop scheme.

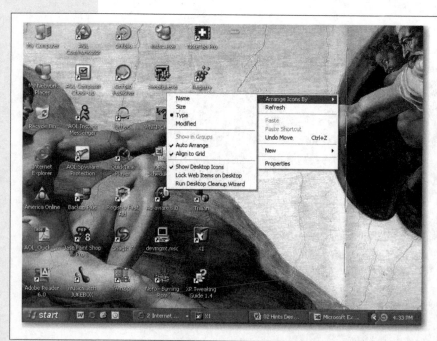

Figure 2-5:
This menu, in addition to letting you wrest control of your icons, also lets you run the Desktop Cleanup Wizard, which removes icons whose programs you haven't recently run. Hint 2-5 explains how it works.

- **Align to Grid.** Places icons along an imaginary grid on your desktop so they're all aligned neatly.

- **Lock Web Items on Desktop.** If you've used a Web page as your background, turning on this option locks the page in place, so no one can move or resize it.

POWER USERS' CLINIC

Removing the Recycle Bin and AOL Icons

If you're a desktop minimalist, you might be tempted to trash the Recycle Bin. But, if you try to delete it by highlighting it and pressing Delete…nothing happens. Once again, the Registry can come to your rescue, letting you can the bin. (When you use this method, the Recycle Bin still works as it does normally; you're only removing the icon, not its function.)

To delete the Recycle Bin icon from the desktop, run the Registry Editor (page 328) and go to My Computer → HKEY_LOCAL_MACHINE → SOFTWARE → Microsoft → Windows → CurrentVersion → Explorer → Desktop → NameSpace. Delete the key {645FF040-5081-101B-9F08-00AA002F954E}, then exit the Registry and restart your machine.

Once you've removed the icon, however, there's no longer an obvious way to see what you've got *in* the bin. You can view files in the Recycle Bin by going to the folder in My Computer → C: → RECYCLER that starts with S-1-5. Deleting files from this folder (by highlighting them and pressing Delete, for example) *empties* the Recycle Bin.

On some systems, you also can't delete the America Online icon using conventional methods. But you can remove it using the same technique you used for removing the Recycle Bin. Instead of deleting the Recycle Bin key, delete the key {955B7B84-5308-419c-8ED8-0B9CA3C56985}. Doing so won't delete America Online, just its desktop icon, so you can still run AOL from the Start menu or directly from Windows Explorer.

2-6   Slapping Your Favorite Web Page on Your Desktop

Windows wallpaper makes a fine desktop background, but you can use your favorite Web site instead—complete with live links and regular updates whenever you're online. You can even split the screen and have a Web page occupy any desktop space that's not taken up by icons. The cool thing about this trick is that you can see your favorite Web page without launching a browser. And if you're a news junkie, you can set a news site as your desktop background and have the latest news piped directly to you all day long.

Note: If you're online and click a link from your Web-page-as-desktop, your regular browser snaps to attention and takes you to the linked page.

ADD-IN ALERT

Giving Windows XP a Makeover

You can give Windows XP a digital makeover by changing its icons, wallpaper, buttons, and overall look (page 51). For help with *skinning* (i.e., altering the look), Window-Blinds is the best software for XP. Once you install it, you can use the program's canned skins to change the style of

title bars, buttons, toolbars, and so on. For example, you can give your PC a metallic appearance, or go for a retro look. If that's not enough, you can download other skins from the WindowBlinds Web site, or even build your own ($19.95 shareware; *www.windowblinds.net*).

To put a Web page on your desktop, right-click the desktop and choose Properties → Desktop → Customize Desktop → Web. To have Windows use your browser's homepage, turn on My Current Home Page, as shown in Figure 2-6. To choose a different home page for your desktop, choose New, and in the dialog box that appears, type in the Web site's URL.

Once you've chosen your Web page, click OK twice to have Windows display it on your desktop. If you want Windows to update the page more frequently than once a day, here's what to do. Right-click the desktop, choose Properties → Desktop, click Customize Desktop, and then click the Web tab. Highlight the event you want synchronize, then click Properties, and then choose the Schedule tab. Select the schedule you want to tweak, and then click Edit. In the dialog box that appears, choose the Schedule tab and then click Advanced. Turn on "Repeat task," and set a new schedule (if you want the update to occur around the clock, set the duration for 24 hours). Click OK until you've closed all the dialog boxes, and you're done.

Figure 2-6:
If you're online, you can click Synchronize to have Windows grab the latest version of your desktop Web page. You can also set a schedule to automatically synchronize the page. Right-click Properties, then choose the Schedule tab. Select "Using the following schedule(s)" and then click Add. Set a daily schedule, and finally, click OK.

Note: When you set a Web page as your wallpaper, it acts like a window of its own—and it comes with a bar at the top that lets you resize the window and drag it around just like any garden-variety desktop window. If you want the window to stay put, turn on "Lock desktop items."

Normally, when you right-click the desktop, Windows shows you a menu for desktop options. But if you have a Web page set as your wallpaper, when you right-click, Windows instead shows you the same menu you'd see if you right-clicked a Web page in Internet Explorer. This feature is great if you want to view the source code for that page. But if you need to change your desktop options, you need the standard desktop shortcut menu.

There are two ways to get that menu: (a) Right-click any part of your desktop that doesn't display the Web page and that isn't an icon, or (b) if the Web page takes up the whole screen, resize the window as described above and then right-click the desktop.

2-7   Special Effects for the Windows Desktop

Like a high-octane action movie, Windows XP features a bunch of special effects that make things look snazzier. For example, the system lets you add or remove shadows under the menus that appear on the desktop and other system windows. These effects may not make you George Lucas, but they can help you customize the system's appearance.

To control which effects appear, right-click the desktop and choose Properties → Appearance → Effects to get the dialog box shown in Figure 2-7.

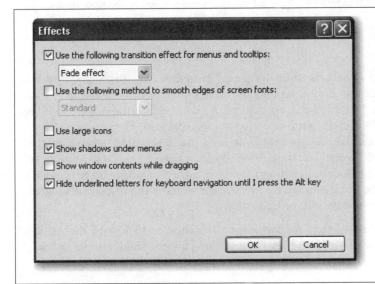

Figure 2-7:
The Effects dialog box lets you turn on or off Windows XP's special effects. Keep in mind that the more effects you use, the more stress you put on your computer. If you have a newer machine, the effects shouldn't have an impact on speed. But if you have an older computer, going hog-wild with the effects may slow things down.

Here's what the effects do:

- **"Use the following transition effect for menus and tooltips."** This option lets you control how menus and tooltips slide into place. If you turn it on, Windows gives you a choice between a fade effect, in which the menu or tooltip quickly fades in, and a scroll effect, in which the item drops down quickly, like a scroll unfurling.

- **"Use the following method to smooth edges of screen fonts."** If you're sitting in front of a CRT monitor, don't bother with this option. But if you're using a laptop or an LCD screen on which fonts can appear somewhat ragged, turning on this feature helps smooth them out. The system gives you a choice between Windows XP's standard method of smoothing fonts or a Microsoft technology called ClearType. ClearType is superior to Windows XP's normal font-smoothing technology, so always use this choice.

• **"Use large icons."** If you find the regular-sized icons too small to see clearly, turn on this feature to have Windows supersize the pictures.

• **"Show shadows under menus."** Turn on this feature to have Windows display handsome, three-dimensional shadows behind menus, as shown in Figure 2-8.

Figure 2-8:
Left: Placing shadows behind menus gives Windows XP a handsome, rich look.

Right: But you can turn the shadows off if you prefer a more staid decor. Shadows are a good example of an effect that eats up computing power, so if your machine is running with all the enthusiasm of a snail on Thorazine, nix the shadows.

• **"Show window contents while dragging."** Normally, when you grab a window by its title bar and drag it around the screen, the contents inside the window move with it. But this behavior requires a lot of computing power, so if your machine is a few cycles short of a Happy Meal, dragging the contents of a window around can take longer than ordering a Big Mac with a personally monogrammed beef patty. Better to have Windows move only the outline of a window when you drag it, letting the contents snap in when you're done dragging. Leave the feature turned on to move the window and its contents together; turn it off to move the outline separately.

• **"Hide underlined letters for keyboard navigation until I press the Alt key."** This mystery sentence is the key to controlling a surprisingly simple option. As

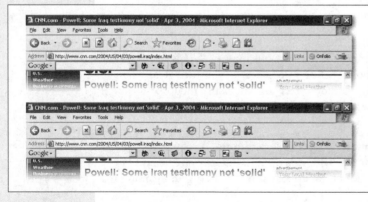

Figure 2-9:
Top: If you want to use the keyboard instead of the mouse to reach menus, underlined letters tell you which key to press along with Alt. This setting doesn't use up many system resources, so using it on older machines won't stall out your PC.

Bottom: If you find the underlines aesthetically unpleasing, you can turn them off.

you know, nearly all Windows programs let you reach the menus via keyboard shortcuts instead of the mouse. For example, in Internet Explorer, you can get to the File menu by pressing Alt+F. On a program's menu bar, Windows XP clues you in to the shortcut by underlining the letter to press with Alt in order to bring up that menu (Figure 2-9).

Normally, the letters appear underlined all the time. But if you find the underlining ugly or distracting, you can turn it off and have Windows underline the letters only when you press Alt.

Note: Not all programs respond when you change this setting. Word, for example, leaves the underlined letters turned on all the time, even if you turn them off here.

The Start Menu

The Start button (in the lower left-hand corner of your screen) is your gateway to just about everything in the operating system. You use it to open programs, customize your computer via the Control Panel, and shut down your computer. In fact, you probably use the Start menu more than any other part of Windows. This section shows you how to reorganize the menu, make it work more quickly, and generally train it to behave the way you want it to.

2-8   Making the Start Menu Jump to Attention

When you click around the Start menu, you may notice a delay between the moment you select a menu item and the time Windows gets around to displaying it. Since you're not getting any younger, it should come as good news that you can eliminate the delay. Or, if you have slower reflexes (or if you like moldering away in front of your monitor), you can lengthen the delay.

To do it, run the Registry Editor (page 328) and then:

1. **Go to HKEY_CURRENT_USER\Control Panel\Desktop.**

   This Registry setting controls many aspects of how the desktop works.

2. **Find the string value MenuShowDelay.**

   This value tells Windows how long it should pause when you highlight an item on the Start menu. It comes set to 400 milliseconds.

3. **Change the value to 100 or 200.**

   A setting of 100 or 200 speeds up the menu noticeably; anything less is imperceptible. If you want a longer delay, change the value to something greater than 400.

4. **Exit the Registry.**

   You many need to reboot in order for your new settings to take effect. If the new settings are too fast or too slow, re-edit the Registry.

2-9   Switching to the Classic Start Menu

Windows XP has a lot of bold, new features—including an outsized Start menu that takes up a ton of room. If you're a back-to-basics kind of person and prefer the way the Start menu worked in previous versions of Windows, you can easily switch back to the classic look. Figure 2-10 compares the two.

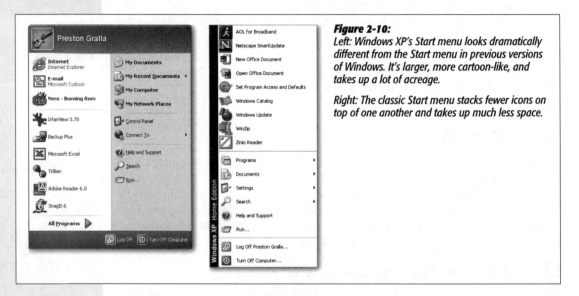

Figure 2-10:
Left: Windows XP's Start menu looks dramatically different from the Start menu in previous versions of Windows. It's larger, more cartoon-like, and takes up a lot of acreage.

Right: The classic Start menu stacks fewer icons on top of one another and takes up much less space.

To switch to the classic Start menu, right-click the Start menu, choose Properties → Classic Start menu, and then click OK.

2-10   Tweaking the Start Menu

Windows XP lets you decide how many programs appear on the Start menu, and to some degree, which ones appear and how they're arranged.

Get started with the customization process by right-clicking the Start menu and choosing Properties → Start Menu → Customize. The Customize Start Menu dialog box opens, displaying the options on the General tab. Figure 2-11 explains the three choices Microsoft's engineers saw fit to give you.

2-11   Customizing the Most Frequently Used
Programs List

One of the Start menu's more useful features is the list of programs that appears right above the All Programs button (Figure 2-12). For your menu-ing pleasure, you can set the number of programs Windows includes on the list.

To do so, right-click the Start button and choose Properties → Customize → General. The Customize Start Menu dialog box appears. Change the number next to "Number of programs on Start menu" (you can choose any number between 0 and 30).

To clear all of the current programs from the list—say you've been using several programs recently that you're not going to run anymore—click Clear List. Now you can start fresh.

Figure 2-11:
Change the size of the icons on the Start menu by choosing either Large icons or Small icons. To change which Internet browser and email programs appear at the top of the Start menu, select them from the drop-down lists in the "Show on Start menu" area. If you turn off the Internet and E-mail boxes, these programs disappear from the menu.

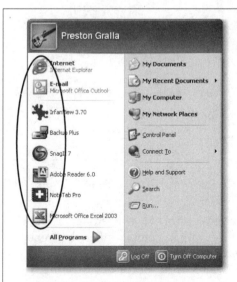

Figure 2-12:
Windows XP keeps track of the programs you use most frequently and automatically puts their icons on the Start menu.

Suppose there's a program you want to access quickly that's not on the list, or, conversely, there's a pesky program on the list you no longer want there. In these circumstances, you have to make those changes from within the Start menu itself.

- **To delete a program**, right-click it and select "Remove from This List."

- **To rename a program** on the list, right-click it and choose Rename.

- **To add a program**, click the Start button and then the All Programs menu. From All Programs, right-click any program you want to add, and then drag it to the list.

2-12 More Advanced Start Menu Tricks

You can do some deep-tissue customization of the Start menu. Use the Advanced dialog box shown in Figure 2-13.

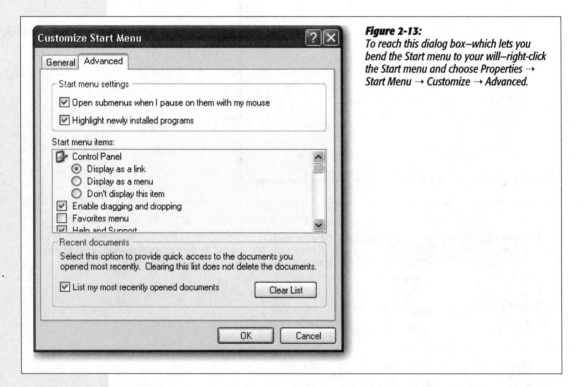

Figure 2-13:
To reach this dialog box—which lets you bend the Start menu to your will—right-click the Start menu and choose Properties → Start Menu → Customize → Advanced.

The Advanced dialog box has three sections that let you change how the Start menu looks and behaves. Here's what each does:

- **Start menu settings.** This panel gives you control over two settings. If you select "Open submenus when I pause on them with my mouse," the submenu opens automatically after a short delay when you hold your mouse over any of the small arrows next to a Start menu item, such as the one next to My Recent

Documents. You can change the amount of delay, as described in hint 2-8. (If you don't turn on this option, you have to click an arrow to open a submenu instead of just holding down the mouse.)

When you turn on "Highlight newly installed programs," any new program you've just installed appears highlighted the next time you choose the All Programs menu. This option makes it easier to find that brand-spanking new file-compression program you're just dying to use.

- **Start menu items.** This section lets you determine the items that show up on the Start menu and also tweak some Start menu behavior. You can decide whether to display My Computer, My Documents, My Music, My Network Places, and several other items on the Start menu (by selecting "Display as a link" or "Display as a menu"), or hide them instead (by selecting "Don't display this item").

You can also control features such as whether you can reorganize the Start menu by dragging and dropping items to another part of the menu (to use that feature, select "Enable dragging and dropping"). Finally, you can choose whether to display the "Help and Support" link, a link to your computer manufacturer's Web site, or a link to the Printer and Faxes folder.

- **Recent documents.** If you want the documents you've opened recently to appear on the Start menu, turn on this option. Should you want them *not* to appear—say you share a computer and you don't want others to see what you're working on—turn it off.

2-13   Organizing the All Programs Menu

When you click All Programs on the Start menu, it displays a cascading menu that lets you run any program you have on your PC. When you take your computer out of the box, the list is alphabetized, but as you download new programs, XP usually adds the latest additions to the bottom of the list—essentially throwing alphabetical order out the window. This nonsense makes it difficult to find the program you want quickly (and defeats the purpose of your elementary school training).

WORKAROUND WORKSHOP

Handcrafting the All Programs Menu

Windows Explorer can help you organize the All Programs menu more quickly. After all, the All Programs menu is nothing more than a collection of shortcuts found in two folders, My Computer → C: → Documents and Settings → [Your Account Name] → Start Menu, and My Computer → C: → Documents and Settings → All Users → Start Menu.

For programs that you want to appear at the top of the All Programs menu, place their shortcut icons in one of the Start Menu folders (depending upon whether you want the item to appear only on your All Programs menu, or on everyone's All Programs menus). Put the shortcuts for programs that you want to appear on the *lower* part of the All Programs menu in the Start Menu → Programs subfolder, again depending on whether you want the item to appear only on your All Programs menu, or on everyone's.

Fortunately, there's a way to restore order to the All Programs menu. In fact, you can create any order you want, like alphabetizing the list or organizing it by frequency of use. What could be more efficient than placing programs you frequently run at the top of the menu, and programs you rarely use at the end?

- **To move any item** on the menu, simply drag it where you want it to appear.

- **To delete an item,** right-click it and then choose Delete.

- **To sort the entire menu** in alphabetical order, right-click an item and choose Sort by Name.

- **To sort a submenu** in alphabetical order, right-click the item in the submenu and choose Sort by Name.

The Taskbar

You probably don't pay much attention to the *taskbar*, the bar across the bottom of your screen that shows what programs are currently running, along with the time, the Start button, and a bunch of other icons you may never have noticed. But ignore the taskbar at your peril—this little powerhouse offers many ways to make your computer time more efficient. This section has all the details.

2-14   Launching Web Pages from the Taskbar

Memo to speed demons: you can jump directly to Web pages without opening a browser first. Here's the trick: add an address box to the taskbar. Then, whenever you type in the address of a Web site (such as *www.oreilly.com*), your browser opens and heads straight to that site.

To add the address box, right-click the taskbar; in the menu that appears, choose Toolbars → Address. (You may have to select "Lock the Taskbar" to remove the checkmark first.) The word *Address* appears toward the left end of the taskbar. To the left of the word Address there's a handle—a small dotted line you can grab and drag. Drag the handle to the left to reveal a white box, shown in Figure 2-14. When you type an Internet address in the box, your browser launches and goes directly to that site.

Note: If you want to lock the address box in position, right-click the taskbar and select "Lock the Taskbar."

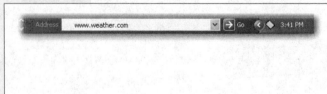

Figure 2-14:
Adding an address box to the taskbar is a big time-saver, since it lets you visit Web sites without opening your browser first. You don't need to click the Go button after entering a Web address; simply press Enter after you type the URL (and you don't have to type http:// either—just start with www).

2-15   Adding Files, Folders, and Disks to the Taskbar

The Internet address bar you added to the taskbar in the previous hint is a kind of *toolbar*—in essence, a shortcut that lives on the taskbar. You can create other kinds of toolbars as well, containing things like shortcuts to a specific folder, document, or drive. If you constantly head to Windows Explorer for a particular item, add that item to the taskbar for faster access.

Here's how. Right-click the taskbar and in the menu that appears, make sure "Lock the Taskbar" is turned off (if it's checked, select it to remove the checkmark). Then choose Toolbars → New Toolbar. The New Toolbar dialog box, shown in Figure 2-15, appears. In the New Toolbar dialog box, browse to the folder, disk, or document you want to add to the taskbar. Click OK.

Figure 2-15:
If you don't like a toolbar you've created, you can get it out of your face. Right-click the taskbar, choose Toolbars, and turn off the one you want to delete. (If you change your mind, you have to recreate that toolbar from scratch.)

Once you're done, the title of the item you added appears on the taskbar next to a double arrow. Click the double arrow to open your new item, as shown in Figure 2-16.

2-16   Hiding Icons on the Bottom of Your Screen

Many utilities and programs that run in the background on your computer, such as antivirus software, add their icons to the *notification area*, the area on the far right end of the taskbar (also known as the *system tray*). Some of the icons in this area are useful (like the volume button, described on page 12). But the tray can get cluttered with useless icons, so you may want to hide the flotsam.

To stash away the icons you don't regularly use, right-click the taskbar and choose Properties. The "Taskbar and Start Menu Properties" dialog box appears. In the notification area, select "Hide inactive icons." Figure 2-17 shows you how to *unhide* them.

To handpick which icons you hide, reopen the "Taskbar and Start Menu Properties" dialog box (right-click the taskbar and choose Properties), and then click the Customize button. The Customize Notifications dialog box appears, as shown in

Figure 2-16:
When you click the double-arrow next to a folder you've added to the toolbar, the contents of the folder appear in a pop-up menu (here the folder is Cloning). If you create a toolbar for a folder that contains a lot of files, the pop-up menu can get unwieldy. Consider doing a little housekeeping to make things tidier, by creating subfolders for some of your files, which makes it easier to use the toolbar to get to the file you need.

Figure 2-17:
Top: Icons in their natural habitat.

Bottom: When you hide icons, a small arrow appears in the notification area, pointing to the left (almost like a sleeve peeking out from under a bed). To uncover hidden icons, click the arrow and the icons reappear (with the arrow now pointing to the right). To hide the icons again, click the arrow.

Figure 2-18. Below Current Items, select the program you want to hide or display. A drop-down menu appears to the right of the program name, letting you choose to hide the program's icon when it's inactive, to always hide the icon, or to always show it. Select the option you want and click OK, then OK again.

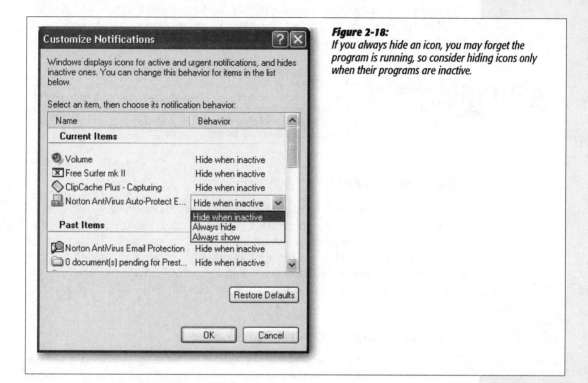

Figure 2-18:
If you always hide an icon, you may forget the program is running, so consider hiding icons only when their programs are inactive.

Note: If you're a cleanliness freak, you may want to hide all of the icons in the notification area, not just a few of them. To do that, run the Registry Editor (page 328) and go to My Computer → HKEY_ CURRENT_USER → Software → Microsoft → Windows → CurrentVersion → Policies → Explorer. Create a new DWORD (page 330) called NoTrayItemsDisplay. Assign it a value of 1. (A value of 0 keeps the icons displayed.) Exit the Registry and reboot. The icons are gone.

2-17   The Quick Launch Bar

One of Windows XP's greatest time-saving features is the Quick Launch bar—the area of the taskbar just to the right of the Start menu (Figure 2-19). As its name suggests, the Quick Launch bar contains icons you can launch with one swift click.

Quick Launch is usually turned on in Windows XP, but if it's not, you can activate it by right-clicking the Start button and choosing Properties → Taskbar. Select Show Quick Launch, and then click OK.

Tip: For a faster way to turn on the Quick Launch bar, right-click the taskbar, select Toolbars, and turn on Quick Launch.

To delete an icon from the Quick Launch bar, right-click it and choose Delete. That doesn't delete the program itself, but simply removes the icon from the Quick Launch bar.

To add icons to the Quick Launch bar, drag them from Windows Explorer, the desktop, or the All Programs menu to your preferred spot on the Quick Launch bar. Choose your icons with care, however. If you put too many of them in the Quick Launch area, it can become a cluttered, not-so-quick launch pad instead.

Figure 2-19:
The Quick Launch bar puts your favorite programs just a click away. One of its most useful icons is the Show Desktop icon, pictured on the far right. Click it to minimize all open windows and return to the desktop without the hassle of minimizing each window manually.

The Control Panel

When you click the Start menu, your ultimate destination is often the Control Panel—a kind of central dashboard that lets you customize many aspects of Windows XP, from your network connections to the date and time display, to your mouse and keyboard. Most people think that when it comes to the Control Panel, what you see is what you get. But the Control Panel earns its name in more ways than you think. This section explains how to tap into your latent domineering instincts.

2-18   Accessing the Control Panel Faster

Getting to the Control Panel's menus and dialog can be an epic clickfest. You have to click the Start menu, then the Control Panel icon itself, and often several other icons and menus to get to the one you need. Your hand could fall off before you reach your destination.

You can speed up the time it takes to get to Control Panel *applets*—the programs where you actually tweak settings—by having Windows XP display them in a cascading menu when you choose Control Panel from the Start button, as shown in Figure 2-20.

To make Control Panel applets cascade, right-click the Start menu and choose Properties → Start Menu → Customize → Advanced. Under the Control Panel heading, choose "Display as a menu." Click OK, then OK again.

Tip: If you're a serious Control Panel jockey, place a toolbar for it on the taskbar. Hint 2-17 tells you how.

2-19   Cleaning up the Control Panel

The Control Panel has a bevy of settings you can manage. But the sheer number of icons makes it tough to find the ones you want. You can clean things up by hiding the Control Panel applets you rarely use. When you hide these applets, you don't actually delete them—you just hide their icons at the back of the closet. You can still run them if you need to (page 49).

To hide the Control Panel applets, you have to use the Registry. First run the Registry Editor (page 328) and then follow these steps:

1. Go to My Computer → HKEY_LOCAL_MACHINE → SOFTWARE → Microsoft → Windows → CurrentVersion → Control Panel.

   As you might guess from the key's name, it's the one that handles many aspects of the Control Panel.

Figure 2-20:
Save valuable time and energy by displaying Control Panel applets as a cascading menu. If there's a particular applet you use frequently, save yourself even more time by dragging it from the menu to the desktop or Quick Launch bar to create a clickable icon for the applet.

2. Create a new key called *don't load.*

   Note that the "don't load" key may already be in your Registry. If it is, don't create another one. This key lists all the applets you want to hide. (Full instructions on creating new keys are on page 330.)

NOSTALGIA CORNER

Bring Back Program Manager

If you long for the old Program Manager from the days of Windows 3.x–which let you manage and run Windows programs–your days of longing are over. Program Manager still exists in Windows XP; it's just hidden. To run it, type *Program* at the Run box or command prompt and press

Enter. The old Program Manager appears, although it won't display your programs; you have to add them manually. Adding them is simple: Just drag them onto Program Manager from the Desktop, or from Windows Explorer.

---

3. **Create a new string value whose name is the filename of the applet you want to hide.**

For example, to hide the Mouse Control dialog box, the string value would be *main.cpl*. See Table 2-1 for a list of Control Panel applets and their filenames.

Before hiding an applet, run it from the Control Panel so that you know exactly what it does and you're sure it's one you rarely use.

4. **Continue to create string values for all the applets you want to hide.**

There's no limit to the number of applets you can hide, so go crazy.

5. **Exit the Registry.**

The applets no longer appear in the Control Panel.

Table 2-1. *Control Panel Applets and their Filenames*

Applet	Filename	What It Does
System Properties	sysdm.cpl	Shows the System Properties dialog box, which has a wide variety of information about your computer. Worth keeping.
Display Properties	desk.cpl	Shows the Display Properties dialog box, which lets you change your display settings, screen saver, themes, and similar features. Worth keeping.
Network Connections	ncpa.cpl	Shows the Network Connections folder, which lets you look at all the network connections on your PC, such as America Online. Worth keeping.
Accessibility Options	access.cpl	Shows the Accessibility Options dialog box, which lets those with disabilities set options that make it easier to use their computers. If you don't have a disability, go ahead and hide this applet.
Add or Remove Programs	appwiz.cpl	Displays the Add or Remove Programs dialog box, which lets you add or remove programs. Keep this one.
Add Hardware Wizard	hdwwiz.cpl	Displays a wizard that lets you easily add hardware. Worth keeping.
Internet Properties	Inetcpl.cpl	Displays the Internet Properties dialog box, which lets you change a variety of browser and Internet settings. You can get to this window in Internet Explorer by choosing Tools → Internet Options, so consider hiding this applet.
Region and Language Options	intl.cpl	Lets you change your language or regional settings, such as whether to display money in dollars or pounds. If you live in the U.S., you might as well hide this one.
Game Controllers	joy.cpl	Lets you configure a joystick or other game controller. If you don't have one, hide this puppy.
Mouse Properties	main.cpl	Lets you change how a mouse works, by changing its pointer (for example). Keep this one.

Table 2-1. Control Panel Applets and their Filenames (continued)

Applet	Filename	What It Does
Sound and Audio Devices	mmsys.cpl	Lets you configure your sound card and other audio hardware. You probably won't use this applet much, but it's helpful when something goes wrong, so keep it.
User Accounts	nusrmgr.cpl	Manages your user accounts, by letting you do things such as add users or change passwords. Keep it.
ODBC Data Source Administrator	odbccp32.cpl	One of the most arcane applets in all of Windows XP, and only needed by database programmers. Feel free to hide it.
Power Options Properties	powercfg.cpl	Gives you ways to change how your computer uses power, such as turning off the screen after it hasn't been used for 10 minutes. Useful if you have a laptop; otherwise, consider hiding it.
Phone and Modem Options	telephon.cpl	A difficult-to-use applet that lets you control modems in ways you probably don't want to investigate. Consider hiding it.
Time and Date Properties	timedate.cpl	Lets you change your system date and time. Keep it.
Speech Properties	sapi.cpl	Lets you control how your computer talks to you. If you don't like having a conversation with your PC, hide it.

To run an applet you've hidden: At the Run box or command line, type its filename from Table 2-1. For example, to run the Internet Properties applet, type *Inetcpl.cpl* at the command prompt or Run box, and then press Enter. (This method won't work for every applet; see the next hint for another option.)

2-20 Bypassing the Control Panel with Keyboard Shortcuts

As you saw in the last hint, you can run many Control Panel functions using the command prompt or Run box. But that won't let you run every applet and dialog box. For some functions, you need to use the *control* command. For example, to run the Folder options dialog box, type *control folders* at the command prompt or Run box and press Enter.

Table 2-2 gives you a list of commands, and what each controls.

Table 2-2. Commands for launching Control Panel applets and dialog boxes

Command	Applet or Dialog Box It Launches
control	Control Panel
control userpasswords	User Accounts
control userpasswords2	Advanced User Accounts
control folders	Folder Options
control desktop	Display Properties
control printers	Printers and Faxes

Table 2-2. *Commands for launching Control Panel applets and dialog boxes (continued)*

Command	Applet or Dialog Box It Launches
control mouse	Mouse Properties
control keyboard	Keyboard Properties
control netconnections	Network Connections
control color	Display Properties/Screensaver
control date/time	Date and Time Properties
control schedtasks	Scheduled Tasks
control admintools	Administrative Tools
control telephony	Phone and Modem Options
control fonts	Fonts Folder
control international	Regional and Language

2-21   Recategorizing Control Panel Applets

Applets in the Control Panel are organized by category, depending on what they, well…control. For example, the Mouse Properties applet is in the Printers and Other Hardware category, and the option to change your screen saver is in Appearance and Themes.

But you're not stuck with Windows XP's categorization scheme—you can put any applet in any category you want. So if you want the Mouse Properties applet to show up in the Appearance and Themes category, move it there. Use any system that makes it faster and easier to spot the panel you're looking for.

To put an applet in a different category, you need two pieces of information: (a) the filename of the applet (for example, main.cpl for the Mouse Properties dialog box), and (b) the Registry value for each Control Panel category. For applet filenames, use Table 2-1 on page 48. To get the Registry value for each Control Panel category, use Table 2-3 later in this hint. With that information in hand, you can reorganize any Control Panel applets.

To move a Control Panel applet to a different category, run the Registry Editor (page 328), and then:

1. Go to My Computer → HKEY_LOCAL_MACHINE → SOFTWARE → Microsoft → Windows → CurrentVersion → Control Panel → Extended Properties → {305CA226-D286-468e-B848-2B2E8E697B74}2.

   A long list of keys appears, each of which corresponds to a particular Control Panel applet.

2. Find the Registry Key of the applet you want to move.

   The filename of the applet appears on the end of the key, for example, %SystemRoot%\system32\main.cpl is the Mouse Properties dialog box.

3. Find the filenames for the applet you want to move, using Table 2-1 on page 48.

4. **Edit the DWORD value of the Control Panel category where you want the applet to appear.**

   For example, if you want the applet to appear in the Performance and Maintenance category, give it a value of 5. The Registry then displays the value as 0x00000005(5).

   Use Table 2-3 for a list of Control Panel Categories and the corresponding values. You can edit as many applets as you want.

5. **Exit the Registry.**

   The applet appears in the new category.

Table 2-3. Control Panel Categories and their Registry Value Data

Control Panel Category	Value Data
Accessibility Options	0x00000007 (7)
Add or Remove Programs	0x00000008 (8)
Appearance and Themes	0x00000001 (1)
Date, Time, Language and Regional Options	0x00000006 (6)
Network and Internet Connections	0x00000003 (3)
Other Control Panel Options	0x00000000 (0)
Performance and Maintenance	0x00000005 (5)
Printers and Other Hardware	0x00000002 (2)
Sounds, Speech, and Audio Devices	0x00000004 (4)
User Accounts	0x00000009 (9)
No category	0xffffffff

Icons and Themes

You can make Windows XP into your digital alter ego by choosing your own icons, adding a screen saver, or picking a desktop theme. Read on for hints on giving Windows XP a dash of individuality.

2-22   Turning Your Photos into a Screen Saver

You may not be a star on the big screen but you *can* be the star of your computer screen, or more precisely, your screen saver. Simply create a screen saver using your own digital photos or pictures you've scanned.

First, put all the photos you want to display on your screen saver in Documents and Settings → [Your Account Name] → My Documents → My Pictures.

Right-click the desktop and choose Properties → Screensaver (Figure 2-21). From the drop-down list, select My Pictures Slideshow. In the preview screen, your photo slideshow begins to play.

Click the Settings button if you want to change the size of the pictures, how long each photo should display, and whether to use transition effects between pictures—say, fading to black after the last shot of your triumphant bike race finish. (Hey, no one needs to know you came in 837th place.) When you're done, click OK until you get back to the desktop. Your screen saver is ready to go.

Figure 2-21:
When you choose a folder to be the launching pad for your customized screen saver, Windows turns all the pictures in that folder into a slideshow. If you want to create several screen savers, with different pictures for each, save the photos for each screen saver in separate folders within My Pictures. Then designate each folder as a screen saver's launching pad.

2-23 Using Themes To Dress Up Your PC

Themes control just about every aspect of how Windows XP looks and sounds, including its background wallpaper, colors, icons, cursors, sounds, fonts, screen savers, and the style of its buttons and windows. Think of it as your computer's personality type, or rather, *your* personality expressed through your PC.

Say you're a Star Wars fan: You can get a Star Wars theme with scenes from the movie as your background and screen saver, audio outtakes of Darth Vader for your system sounds, and fonts with a Star Wars look. Figure 2-22 shows you another option.

The only problem is that Windows XP comes with just two personalities: the basic Windows XP theme (which some people call "Luna" because that was its code name during Windows XP's development) and Windows Classic, a more stolid-looking theme based on older versions of Windows, which uses rectangular windows and solid colors.

Two themes isn't exactly a whole lot to choose from. But if you want to find more, there are literally thousands of themes you can download for free from many Internet sites, as explained later in this hint.

To change your current theme, right-click the desktop and choose Properties → Themes. Choose the theme you want to use from the shortcut menu, as shown in Figure 2-23, and then click OK. Like a teenager in a school lunchroom, Windows XP instantly takes on a new personality.

Where to find more themes

You can find themes easily online. People with too much time on their hands have created their own themes based on a personal passion or hobby and offered them free to fellow obsessives. Companies distribute themes as a way to market products. And movies and TV shows make them available to fans.

Figure 2-22:
Ooh la la! Turn your PC into a celebration of Paris with the free Chagall-Paris theme, which you can find on www.topthemes.com. Not only does it turn your wallpaper into a Chagall painting, but it turns the cursor into one of Chagall's flying men, and plays Parisian music for system events. You can find hundreds of other themes online as well.

Popular theme sites include: *www.topthemes.com*, *http://cinemadesktopthemes.com*, *www.themeworld.com*, *www.screensandthemes.com*, *www.themesunlimited*.com, and the Themes section of *www.tucows.com*. Movie-related sites are also good places to find themes.

Warning: Some of the themes people create and post online could violate copyright laws by incorporating characters, sounds, or photos they don't have permission to use. Use them at your own risk.

Depending on the theme you download, you may have to go through different steps to install it. As a general rule, all you have to do is install the theme in the right folder: My Computer → C: → Windows → Resources → Themes. Typically, when you download a theme XP automatically installs it in that directory as a file with the extension .theme. All the associated art files, sound files, icon files, wallpaper files, and cursor files come in a subfolder. (If it doesn't install this way, check the download's accompanying files—like the Read Me file—for information on how to install it.)

Once you've installed the new theme, just choose it as outlined earlier in this hint. Voila! You've now made your desktop your own.

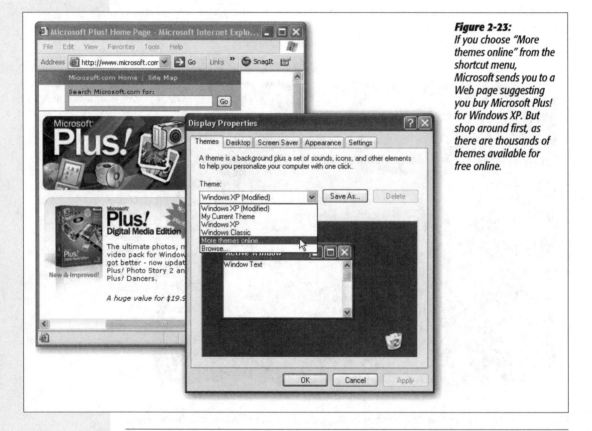

Figure 2-23:
If you choose "More themes online" from the shortcut menu, Microsoft sends you to a Web page suggesting you buy Microsoft Plus! for Windows XP. But shop around first, as there are thousands of themes available for free online.

Tip: A shareware program called Window Blinds lets you change your wallpaper, icons, and other facets of the Windows XP interface. See the box on page 33.

2-24 Creating Your Own Theme

Even though there are thousands of themes available online, you may find nothing more interesting than the one some guy in Philadelphia created to reflect his obsession with skateboarding. No problem—you can build your own. Here's how:

- **First, customize your desktop.** Right-click the desktop, choose Properties to open the Display Properties dialog box, and then adjust the following:

  - To swap in a new background, click the Desktop tab, choose one from the Background list, and then click OK.

  - To choose a new screensaver, click the Screen Saver tab, choose a new one from the menu, and then click OK.

  - You can pick new button styles, colors, and font size all from the Appearance tab. When you've got it all lined up, click OK.

  - To change the way your colors appear, click the Settings tab, pick a color quality from the menu, and then click OK. The settings tab is also the place to change your screen resolution. Move the Screen resolution slider to the left for a lower resolution, or to the right for greater resolution. Click OK when you're done.

- **Customize your mouse pointers** by typing *main.cpl* from the Run box and pressing Enter.

  The Mouse Properties dialog box appears, allowing you to choose a preset pointer scheme, or select individual pointers.

Note: An individual pointer is the pointer you see when you use your mouse. A pointer *scheme* includes a variety of pointers—one for when Windows is working (usually a spinning hourglass), one when you move your mouse across the screen, and so on.

  You can also create your own customized cursors, using a program such as Microangelo or CursorXP, as described in the box on page 56.

- **Customize your sounds** by typing *mmsys.cpl* from the Run box and pressing Enter. The Sounds and Audio Devices properties dialog box appears.

  Click the Sounds tab, and choose a preset sounds scheme, or select individual sounds for different system and program events—for example, when you shut down Windows. You can even record your own sounds and use those. For details on how to do that, see hint 1-13.

When you're finished customizing, go to the Themes tab of the Display Properties dialog box by right-clicking the desktop, choosing Properties, and then clicking the Themes tab. Then choose Save As, and save the theme to My Computer → C: → Windows → Resources → Themes.

Note: When saving themes, you don't have to save them in your My Documents folder. You can save them in any folder you want, but you'll have to remember where you saved them, or else there will be no way to call them up again.

Choose a descriptive name for the theme, so it's easy to remember when you want to use it. You can now use the theme as any other, as outlined earlier in this hint.

Making Your Own Cursors and Icons

If you're not wild about the cursors and icons Windows XP includes, don't settle—you can easily make your own using downloadable software.

A good program to help design your own icons is Microangelo, from *www.microangelo.us*. You can create animated icons as well as regular icons, in both the standard 32-pixel and large 48-pixel sizes. Even if you're not an artist, you can use the program to edit existing icons, shown below. You can also use this program to create cursors.

As you make changes in the main part of the Microangelo screen, on the left, you can see how they take effect in the Preview window. You can also add many kinds of special effects to your icons with the Paint Modifiers tool.

Microangelo is shareware and free to try, but if you continue using it, its creators ask you to pay $54.95.

If you want to make your own cursors, another option is CursorXP Free from *www.windowblinds.net*. It includes a host of free cursors and a variety of tools for customizing them, like changing their visual effects. It's free, as the name implies, but if you want a more powerful version, try CursorXP Plus from the same site, which costs $10. The Plus version lets you create cursor *trails* (ghost images of your cursor's track across the screen) and play with other special effects, like making your cursor appear transparent or change colors as it moves.

Windows Explorer and Searching

You probably spend approximately half your life browsing through your hard disk, copying, moving, deleting, and searching for files. On a computer, those tasks ought to be less time-consuming then rifling through paper files and folders, and indeed, Windows XP offers good basic tools for handling electronic paperwork. But that's all they are—basic tools.

The true power hound must master Windows Explorer, the utility that lets you navigate around your hard drive, as shown in Figure 3-1. This chapter teems with ways to turn this basic feature into a major workhorse. You'll learn the most efficient ways to find, open, rearrange, name, and display the files and folders on your PC.

The Windows Explorer Interface

You probably spend a lot of time using Windows Explorer, so why not make it work the way that *you*—rather than Microsoft's engineers—want it to work? As you'll see in this section, there are many ways to give Windows Explorer more power and efficiency, including keyboard shortcuts that can save you from mouse-related wrist strain.

3-1   Opening Explorer with a Keyboard Shortcut

Tired of clicking menus to get to Windows Explorer? Open it the fast way: Press the Windows key+E and Windows Explorer opens with just a flick of two fingers.

Note: The Windows key (the key with the Windows logo on it) resides in different places on different keyboards. On desktop computers, it often sits between the Ctrl and Alt keys. On a laptop, it could be almost anywhere.

Geeks can also open Explorer by typing *explorer.exe* at a command prompt or into the Run box and then pressing Enter. And if you want to open Windows Explorer to a specific folder, enter the name of the folder after the command, with the full path to the folder, like this: *explorer.exe C:\Windows*.

Figure 3-1:
To open Windows Explorer, right-click My Computer (either on the desktop or in the Start menu), and then choose Explore. If you don't see the list of folders in the left pane, choose View → Explorer Bar → Folders.

3-2 Speeding Up Windows Explorer with Keyboard Shortcuts

To speed up your pace in Windows Explorer, don't reach for the mouse. Instead, use keyboard shortcuts that let you handle common tasks without having to waste valuable time mousing around. Table 3-1 lists some of the most useful Windows Explorer shortcuts.

Table 3-1. *Windows Explorer Keyboard Shortcuts*

Keyboard Shortcut	What It Does
Alt+Enter	Displays the properties of the selected file or folder.
F2	Lets you rename the selected file or folder.
F3	Lets you find files in the selected folder.
F4	Displays a drop-down list of available disk drives.
F5	Refreshes the current folder display. (If you have Windows Explorer open, and you add a file to the folder using another program, that file might not show up in Windows Explorer until you refresh it using the F5 key.)

Table 3-1. *Windows Explorer Keyboard Shortcuts (continued)*

Keyboard Shortcut	What It Does
F6 (or Tab)	Cycles you between the top-most file or folder in the current directory and the little "x" icon that closes the left-side Folders pane. If you're in the File and Folder Tasks view (which has a pane on the left side with icons for common tasks), the F6 and Tab keys let you cycle between the top-most file or folder in the directory that's currently displayed and various file and folder tasks.
F10	Jumps to the menu bar.
Shift+F10	Opens the context menu when you've highlighted a file. This lets you perform actions like printing the file, copying it, or moving it. (You can also do this by right-clicking the file.)
F11	Toggles full-screen mode on and off. (In full-screen mode, Windows Explorer takes up your full screen.)
Delete	Deletes a file or folder.
Ctrl+W	Shuts down Windows Explorer.
Windows Key+E	Opens Windows Explorer.
Ctrl+X	Cuts the selected file or folder (Edit → Cut).
Ctrl+C	Copies the selected file or folder (Edit → Copy).
Ctrl+V	Pastes the selected file or folder (Edit → Paste).
Ctrl+Z	Undoes the last action.
Shift+Delete	Deletes the selected file or folder immediately, without moving it to the Recycle Bin. Use it when you're absolutely, positively sure you want to delete a file.
Home	Goes to the top of a folder list.
End	Goes to the end of a folder list.
Right arrow	Expands the current folder if it's collapsed; otherwise, moves your cursor to a subfolder or the next folder.
Left arrow	Collapses the current folder if it's expanded; otherwise, moves your cursor to a folder above the current subfolder.

3-3   Showing the Full File Path in Explorer

When you're using Windows Explorer, it's easy to become confused about exactly where you are. There are so many folders buried within folders buried within other folders, you can often find yourself wishing you had sprinkled some breadcrumbs along the way.

A simple trick can tell Explorer to show you the way—no breadcrumbs required. You can set Explorer to show you exactly where on your computer you are, and how to get where you want to go (Figure 3-2).

Tip: *Windows* Explorer is a cousin of *Internet* Explorer, the popular Web browser, which means you can navigate around them similarly. They both have address bars, and title bars, and you can use the back button in Windows Explorer much the way you do in Internet Explorer—click it to jump back to the previous frame.

To have Windows Explorer display its full file path, first open up Explorer and choose Tools → Folder Options → View. In the Advanced Settings pane, look under Files and Folders, and then turn on "Display the full path in the title bar" and "Display the full path in the address bar." Click OK. The full path now appears in the title bar.

Title bar

Address bar

Figure 3-2:
Displaying full path names on the Windows Explorer title bar and address bar helps keep you from getting lost on your own computer. The address bar is also useful for navigation: Type the name of one of your folders in it, and Windows Explorer takes you there. (Of course, it's up to you to remember your folders' names.)

Note: Depending on how you've set up Windows Explorer, the address bar may not be immediately visible. To make sure the address bar appears, choose View → Toolbars and select Address Bar.

FREQUENTLY ASKED QUESTION

Consistent Windows Explorer Views

Sometimes, Windows Explorer shows me a bunch of thumbnails in the right pane, but sometimes it shows me a list, or even a list with details. How do I get it to show me the same view all the time?

You can change the view for the *current* frame of Windows Explorer by choosing View and then selecting one of the six choices (from Filmstrip to Details) listed on the menu. Details is usually the most useful, as it lets you see a lot of tasty information about your files, including size, when they were last modified, and so on. (To choose your details,

right-click one of the existing details—like Name, Size, Type—and from the menu that appears, select the categories you want to add.)

If you want to set the view to be the same for every frame of Windows Explorer—the arrangement most people find easiest to deal with—first set your current window to the setting you prefer. Then choose Tools → Folder Options, click the View tab, and then click "Apply to All Folders." When XP asks if you want to reset all your folder views, click Yes, then OK to close the dialog box. You've just overcome Explorer's weird inconsistency.

3-4   Customizing Windows Explorer Toolbars

Besides the Address toolbar, there are two other toolbars that make working with Explorer easier: the Standard Buttons toolbar, which displays buttons across the top of Explorer for common tasks like searching, and the Links toolbar, which displays Internet links.

To choose which toolbars to display, open Windows Explorer, choose View →
Toolbars, and simply select the toolbars that appeal to you. The ones with check-
marks are the ones Windows is currently displaying. To hide a toolbar, return to
the Toolbars menu and click—that is, uncheck—the item you want to nix.

You can also customize the position and size of any toolbar by dragging its handles, as shown in Figure 3-3.

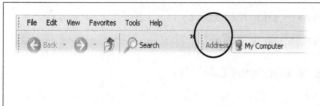

Figure 3-3:
*Drag a toolbar's handles to reposition and resize
it. In this figure, the handle is the dotted vertical
line to the left of the word Address. Drag the
handle down to move the toolbar to a new line. If
two toolbars share a line and not all the buttons
on each are visible, drag one toolbar to the right
to expose more buttons.*

Once the toolbars are where you want them, you can lock them in place. Choose
View → Toolbars → Lock the Toolbars. A checkmark now appears next to Lock the
Toolbars. When you lock the toolbars, their handles disappear. When you want to
move the toolbars again, you first have to unlock them by selecting View → Toolbars → Lock the Toolbars so that the checkmark goes away.

You can further customize the Standard Buttons toolbar by adding buttons,
removing buttons, changing the buttons' order, adjusting their size, and indicating how to display their text labels. To make any of these changes, choose View →
Toolbars → Customize. The Customize Toolbar dialog box, shown in Figure 3-4,
appears.

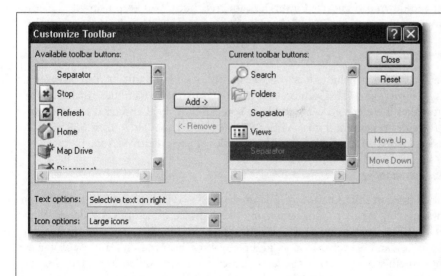

Figure 3-4:
*You can customize the
Standard Buttons
toolbar by adding or
deleting buttons. Be
careful not to add too
many, or there won't be
room to display all of
them. A little-known
option that's great for
anyone who likes to see
files and folders in all
their expansive glory is
the Full Screen button:
When you click it,
Windows Explorer takes
up your entire screen,
without even menus to
get in the way. Press the
Full Screen button to go
from full screen back to
normal size.*

You can use the Customize Toolbar dialog box to customize the Standard Buttons toolbar in the following ways:

- **Add a button** by selecting it in the left column, and choosing Add.

- **Delete a button** by selecting it in the right column, and choosing Remove.

- **Move a button** up or down by selecting it and clicking Move Up or Move Down.

- **Alter the size of buttons** by using the "Icon options" drop-down menu.

- **Change how text labels appear** by using the "Text options" drop-down menu.

3-5   Alternatives to Windows Explorer

Windows Explorer is *pretty good* at letting you view and manage your files and folders, but what if you don't want to settle for that?

Fortunately, Windows Explorer isn't your only option. You can download other programs that offer more power and a wider variety of features than Explorer. Here are three popular alternatives. Simply download and run them as you would any program.

PowerDesk

This program may be the most powerful file manager you can find. It includes a built-in file viewer for viewing more than 200 different types of files, a very powerful file searcher, and MP3 management tools. PowerDesk also lets you attach sticky notes to your files and customize your folders using colors, so you can easily distinguish them. For example, you could use blue for work and red for family stuff. You can download and try PowerDesk for free, but if you keep using it, the company expects you to pay $29.95. Find it at *www.v-com.com/product/pd_ind.html*.

Turbo Browser

This file manager includes lots of powerful utilities, like a built-in Web browser, an image viewer, an HTML editor, and a variety of Internet utilities (including one that makes it easier to download files). You can download and try it for free, but if you decide to keep it, it costs either $39.95 (for a basic version) or $89.95 (for a version loaded with bells and whistles). Find it at *www.filestream.com*.

Total Commander

One of the best things about this file manager is that it offers side-by-side file windows, making it easy to move and copy files between directories and drives. It also has built-in compression tools for shrinking your files (so they take up less hard disk space), and file comparison and directory synchronization features (so you can check whether two files with the same name in different folders are in fact the exact same file). You can also download this program for a free trial, but if you continue using it, the developer wants you to pony up $28. Find it at *www.ghisler.com*.

Working with Files and Folders

Isn't it amazing how today's powerful computers have turned people into...their own personal file clerks. Computers were supposed to *eliminate* this drudgery. Fortunately, Windows Explorer comes with a few built-in tools that give you better ways to manage your files and folders. This section reviews a handful of particularly useful tricks.

3-6   Instantly Jumping to a File or Folder

Using Windows Explorer to navigate to a particular file or folder can be tedious. Here's a better way to get exactly where you want to go. If you're in the left pane of Windows Explorer (also called the Folder pane), type the first letter or letters of the name of the folder you want to access. Windows transports you immediately to the correct place. If you're inside a folder, type the first few letters of the name of the file you need.

You can also jump quickly to the top or bottom of a list of folders or files. To go to the beginning of a list, press Home; to go to the end, press End.

3-7   Copying and Moving Files Faster

Hardly anyone knows about one of the most useful features in Windows Explorer: the Send To command, which is like an expressway for moving files. Here's how it works. When you right-click a file in Windows Explorer, one of the shortcut menu options that pops up is Send To. Selecting this option lets you copy or move the file to a list of destinations like your floppy drive or CD burner (Figure 3-5). This method is immeasurably faster than dragging a file across your desktop or mousing through menu commands.

Note: If you use the Send To menu to send a file to a folder or program on the same drive, the file *moves* to the new location. If you're sending it to a different drive, Windows makes a *copy,* so you'll still have a version in the original location. But there's a way to override these conventions: If you hold down the *Ctrl* key while sending to another location on the same drive, Windows creates a new copy instead of simply moving it. If you hold down the *Shift* key while sending a file to a different drive, Windows moves the file instead of copying it.

You can really amp up the power of Send To by adding programs or locations to the menu or deleting ones you don't need. To make these changes, go to Documents and Settings → [Your Account Name] → SendTo. (If you're having trouble finding this folder it may be among the folders that Windows keeps hidden; see hint 3-12, "Displaying Hidden and System Files and Folders," for instructions on how to make these folders visible). The SendTo folder is filled with shortcuts (links to other folders and locations), all of which appear on the Send To menu. In other words, if you put a shortcut to a folder called "Great American Novel" in the SendTo folder, you have a quick way to send a document to that folder—simply right-click the document and choose Send To → Work Backups.

To add a shortcut to SendTo, head to the SendTo folder in Windows Explorer and then choose File → New → Shortcut. Simply follow the instructions to create a shortcut. Add as many new shortcuts as you like. To keep the Send To menu from getting out of control, delete from this folder the shortcuts you don't need. As soon as you close the SendTo folder, the new menu settings go into effect.

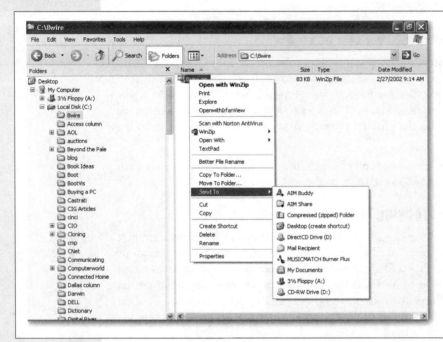

Figure 3-5:
The Send To feature saves time when you're copying or moving files in Windows Explorer. Although there are a limited number of destinations listed on the Send To menu, it's easy to add destinations and make it a much more useful tool.

3-8   Customizing the File Details Displayed in Explorer

Windows Explorer can tell you a lot about each file on your system without your even opening the file. Typically, you can see the file's name, its size, and the last time it was modified, but you can also tell Explorer to show the date it was created, when it was last viewed, who the author is, and other details depending on the file type (the artist or album title for audio files, for instance).

In any open Explorer window, choose View → Choose Details, and then select the details you want to display from the Choose Details dialog box (Figure 3-6). When you're done, click OK.

Tip: If you can't remember the name of a document, showing a file's size and the date it was last modified can help jog your memory about what's inside it.

3-9   Adding Images to Your Folders

In Windows Explorer's standard configuration, each and every folder looks exactly the same. If you want to make an individual folder stand out, you can apply images to the folder icons that appear in Explorer's thumbnail view, making it easier to distinguish your tax documents folder (with a graphic of Uncle Sam, perhaps?) from your collection of downloaded audio files (with a digital photo of your favorite Red Hot Chili Pepper).

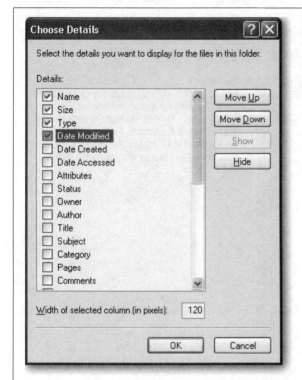

Figure 3-6:
You can choose from nearly a dozen types of details to display about your files, but the details show up in Windows Explorer only if you choose View → Details. Otherwise Windows shows you icons (or the file name) for each file, but not the details you've selected.

To add an image to a folder, open Windows Explorer and right-click the folder you want to decorate. From the menu displayed, choose Properties → Customize → Choose Picture. Navigate to any image you want to use and then click Open to see a preview of the picture inside the folder icon, as shown in Figure 3-7. If you're satisfied, click OK; if not, pick another image.

3-10   Showing File Name Extensions

Every file in Windows has a *file name extension,* typically a period followed by three letters, that identifies what type of file it is. For example, in the file name UnreportedIncome.doc, the extension is .doc, which indicates it's a Microsoft Word document.

It's important to know a file's extension before you open it so you know what kind of file you're dealing with (see the next tip). But Windows doesn't normally show file name extensions, so if you want to view this information you have to tell your computer to display it.

Tip: Displaying file names is more than a matter of convenience—it can also help you avoid getting infected with a computer virus. Viruses are sometimes transmitted by files with the extension .exe, which indicates the file is actually a program that runs when you double-click it. Sneaky virus writers can create a file that *appears* to be named readme.txt but is actually an .exe file with its file extension hidden. You won't know the true file name is readme.txt.exe unless you've chosen to display file name extensions. So check the actual extension, and if the file name ends in .exe, don't open it.

Figure 3-7:
Adding pictures to your folders can make it easier to spot the folder you want in Windows Explorer. If you store digital photos on your PC, for example, you can put all the pictures from your Caribbean vacation in one folder, and then identify the folder by adorning it with your favorite beach shot.

To make this change, open Windows Explorer and choose Tools → Folder Options → View. In the Folder Options dialog box that appears, turn off "Hide file extensions for known file types," and then click OK. Now you can view file extensions when using Windows Explorer and all your other programs, too. (You can also see the extensions in programs like Word when you open or save files.)

3-11 Renaming Groups of Files in One Fell Swoop

There are times when you have a group of related files you'd like to rename, but doing so one at a time can be a pain. For example, when you have pictures you want to transfer from a digital camera to your PC, they often have names with random numbers—not much help when you're trying to find the shots you took at the Harley convention. You can replace the random numbers with descriptive names, like Harley Pics.

To rename a group of files at once, select the ones you want to rename by Ctrl-clicking to highlight each file. Then right-click the first file and choose Rename. Type in the new file name—for example, *Harley Pics.jpg*—and then press Enter. Windows names the first file Holiday Pics.jpg, the next Holiday Pics(1).jpg, the one after that Holiday Pics(2).jpg, and so on. (If you want to get more specific, distinguishing the 1974 hog from the 1984 model, you have to resort to the old-fashioned method of changing one file name at a time.)

Tip: Here's a quick way to select groups of files. If the files you're highlighting are next to one another, click the first file in the group, then hold down the Shift key and click the last file in the group. Windows automatically highlights the entire group of files.

If you want a more powerful way to rename files, download Better File Rename from *www.publicspace.net/windows/BetterFileRename*. This program offers a mind-boggling number of options for renaming groups of files. For example, you can add time and date stamps to the beginning and end of names, or automatically replace or remove characters, as shown in Figure 3-8. (The time and date stamp feature are helpful if, for example, you're creating a time-lapse photo project.)

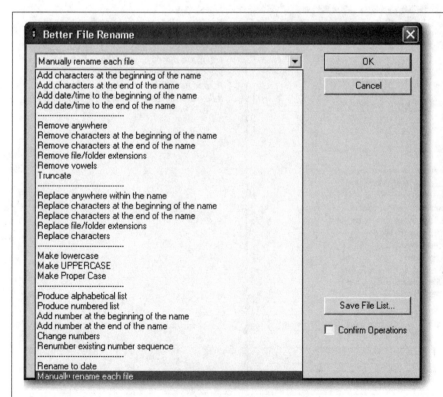

Figure 3-8:
Better File Rename is a shareware program that gives you a lot of control over renaming files. It can be a bit confusing at first, but once you get the hang of it, you can rename files in just about any way you want. You can even do things like find-and-replace phrases that recur in a bunch of different file names. Activate the program by selecting the photos you want to rename and then right-click on any photo in this group.

Better File Rename is shareware and free to try, but if you continue to use it, the developers ask you to pay $14.95.

3-12   Displaying Hidden and System Files and Folders

Windows Explorer is designed to help you view and manage all the files and folders on your computer, so you might expect that when you use it, you'd be able to see everything on your hard drive. No such luck.

Windows Explorer doesn't show you certain system folders and other special files Windows needs in order to function properly. Microsoft's engineers set up things this way to protect you from yourself, worrying that if you saw these so-called *hidden* files, you might accidentally delete or change something important.

But you may need to see these files and folders from time to time—like when you want to reorganize your Internet Explorer Favorites or try many of the other hints in this book.

Here's how to gain access to all the files on your computer:

1. **In a Windows Explorer window, choose Tools → Folder Options → View.**

   The Folder Options dialog box appears, as shown in Figure 3-9.

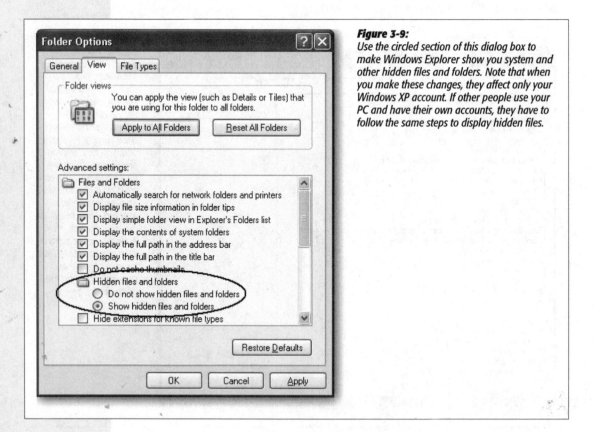

Figure 3-9:
Use the circled section of this dialog box to make Windows Explorer show you system and other hidden files and folders. Note that when you make these changes, they affect only your Windows XP account. If other people use your PC and have their own accounts, they have to follow the same steps to display hidden files.

2. Under Advanced Settings, scroll to the Files and Folders section, and then select "Display the contents of system folders."

You've just forced Windows Explorer to show you the contents of all system folders. But there are still more hidden files and folders you can't see yet, so go on to the next step.

3. Under Advanced Settings, in the "Hidden files and folders" section, turn on "Show hidden files and folders."

Now you're forcing Windows Explorer to show you all your hidden files and folders.

4. Under Advanced Settings, turn off "Hide protected operating system files."

A warning from Microsoft asks if you're sure you really want to make them visible. You do, so click Yes, and then click OK. All changes take place immediately, so now you can see all the files and folders that were previously out of sight.

WORKAROUND WORKSHOP

Viewing Hidden Folders on a Case-by-Case Basis

If you'd prefer to keep most hidden files and folders out of view but display others on a case-by-case basis, you can. For example, you might like to keep Windows Explorer uncluttered as a general rule, but view files in hidden folders when you want to accomplish a particular task (like performing many of the tricks in this chapter).

Start by leaving everything hidden, as described in Figure 3-9.

Then, when you're using Windows Explorer and you come across the warning shown below, simply click "Show the contents of this folder" to see what's inside; other files and folders meanwhile remain hidden.

Of course, don't modify files in any hidden folder without knowing exactly what you're doing—you could unknowingly damage the operating system.

> ## These files are hidden.
>
> This folder contains files that keep your system working properly. You should not modify its contents.
>
> Show the contents of this folder

3-13 Changing Where Windows Stores Documents

Windows and most programs automatically store files in the My Documents folder, which is actually a shortcut to My Computer → Documents and Settings → [Your Account Name] → My Documents. But what if you want to store files in another folder, like a folder you keep right on your desktop? You can change this option, but you have to use a Registry trick.

First, run the Registry Editor (page 328). Navigate to My Computer → HKEY_CURRENT_USER → Software → Microsoft → Windows → CurrentVersion → Explorer → User Shell Folders. Change the Personal string value to the folder where you want your files automatically stored, for example, *C:\Files*. When you exit the Registry, the change goes into effect immediately.

3-14   Making it Easier to Open Files

When you're using one of the utilities that comes with Windows, like Notepad, and you open a file with its File → Open menu, you see a very useful pane on the left side of the window that contains a list of icons, including My Computer, My Documents, or Desktop. Clicking one of those icons changes the list of files and folders that appears in the main area of the window. For example, selecting My Documents reveals that folder's contents, making it easier to select the file you want to open. The same folders appear when you choose the Save As command.

But you might regularly need a different set of folders than the ones that Windows comes preset to display in these cases.

Rather than live with the choices Windows has made, you can change the icons displayed on the left side of the File Open and Save As dialog boxes, as shown in Figure 3-10. Choose folders you use frequently, making opening and saving files easier.

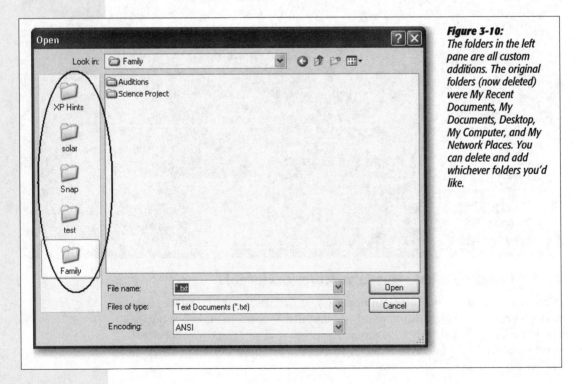

Figure 3-10:
The folders in the left pane are all custom additions. The original folders (now deleted) were My Recent Documents, My Documents, Desktop, My Computer, and My Network Places. You can delete and add whichever folders you'd like.

Note: This Registry hack only affects Windows XP applications that use Windows XP's Open and Save dialog boxes, such as Notepad and Paint. However, it doesn't affect Microsoft Office programs and other various and sundry applications that don't use Windows XP's common dialog boxes. Given that both Windows and Office are from Microsoft, you would think they'd use the same dialog boxes…but they don't. This mystery remains unsolved.

If you want to change the frequently used folders in dialog boxes for Microsoft Word, try Woody Leonhard's Place Bar Customizer, one of many useful utilities from *www.wopr.com*. It costs $29.95. For more limited options to customize these folders, try the free Tweak UI utility, described on page 28.

Here's how to make the change:

1. **Run the Registry Editor (page 328) and go to My Computer → HKEY_ CURRENT_USER → Software → Microsoft → Windows → CurrentVersion → Policies → comdlg32. If the key comdlg32 does not exist in the Policies folder, create it by right-clicking the Policies folder and choosing Edit → New → Key. Name this new key comdlg32.**

   The comdlg32 key controls common dialog boxes such as File Open or Save As. You can create a subkey underneath it that will let you put any folder you want in the dialog box, as discussed on page 330.

2. **Underneath the comdlg32 key, create a new key called *Placesbar*.**

   Right-click the comdlg32 key and choose New → Key. Name this new key Placesbar.

3. **Create a string value of Place0 for the Placesbar key.**

   Right-click the Placesbar folder and choose New → String Value. Set the new String Value to Place0.

4. **Enter the file path of the folder you want to appear in the Open dialog box.**

   Double-click the Place0 subkey. The Edit String dialog box appears. In the Value data box, enter the location of the folder you want to appear in the Open dialog box—for example, *C:\Projects*. Make sure to include the full path to the folder, including the drive letter (*C:* or whatever). Then click OK.

   Whatever folder you entered now appears at the top of the list of folders in the File Open window and similar dialog boxes.

5. **Create another string value for Placesbar called Place1.**

   Give it a value of the second folder you want to appear in the list of icons in the Open dialog box—for example, *C:\Budget*.

   You can put up to five icons inside the Open dialog box, so create new string values up to Place4, and give them values as outlined in the previous steps.

6. **When you're done, exit the Registry.**

   You don't have to reboot for the changes to take effect.

3-15 Setting the Program Used to Open a File Type

When you double-click a file, Windows launches the program it needs to open that file. But how does Windows know which program to launch? Simple: All files have an extension—like .doc—that Windows *associates* with a particular program. For example, Windows associates the .doc extension with Microsoft Word, and therefore uses Word to open any file ending in .doc.

But sometimes, programs can hijack your file associations. For instance, you may install a music program, and from then on whenever you double-click an .mp3 or .wma file, that new program launches, rather than Windows Media Player or whatever you *prefer* to use to listen to audio files.

What to do? You can control file associations yourself, overruling the settings various programs have made, and even the file associations Windows has set up. To make changes to file associations:

1. **Launch Windows Explorer and choose Tools → Folder Options → File Types.**

   After a second or two, the Folder Options dialog box fills with a list of all the file extensions on your computer.

2. **Select the file type whose file association you want to change.**

   For example, if you want to change the association for MP3 files, highlight the MP3 entry.

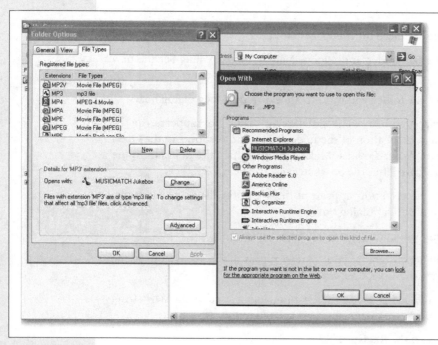

Figure 3-11:
When changing file associations, be careful that the program you select can actually open up the file type you're associating it with. For example, don't associate music files with a word processor like Microsoft Word— that's like asking a Brazilian to help you with your Japanese translation project. Before you make any changes, it's a good idea to first run the program to make sure it can handle that file type.

3. Click Change.

The Open With dialog box appears, as shown in Figure 3-11.

4. **In the Open With dialog box, click the program you want to use to open the file type, click OK, and then OK again.**

If the program you want isn't on the list, click the Browse button, and then navigate through your files to find the program you want to use. Highlight it and click OK, and then OK again.

To test your handiwork, double-click a file that ends in the extension you just edited—for example, an MP3 file. It now opens with the new program.

3-16   Displaying Cascading Folders on the Start Menu

If you frequently use a particular folder, it can be frustrating to have to open Windows Explorer and navigate to that folder each time you want to open a file inside.

There's a quicker way. You can display a folder as a *cascading menu* on the Start menu, one of a series of menus that opens to the right of the Start menu as you make a selection, as shown in Figure 3-12. (A *cascading* menu is a menu that leads to another menu, which in turn leads to another menu, in a cascading fashion.)

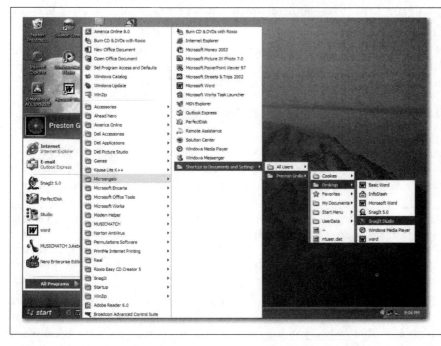

Figure 3-12:
Placing a folder on the All Programs portion of the Start menu gives you instant access to its contents. To delete a folder from the menu, right-click it and choose Delete. Don't worry— you're not deleting the actual folder from your hard drive, just the shortcut from the Start menu.

Suppose you keep most of your documents in a folder called Personal. The trick is to put Personal (or any folder you want to display on the Start menu) in the All Programs folder. Then when you want to open any of the files in it, simply choose

Start → All Programs → Personal. Another cascading menu appears with the contents of that folder, giving you faster access to your files.

To display a folder as a cascading menu on the Start menu:

1. **Open Windows Explorer, find the icon for the folder you want, drag it to the Start menu, and hold it there while the Start menu opens.**

   The Start menu pops up as if you had clicked it.

2. **After the Start menu fully opens, drag the icon for the folder to All Programs.**

   Keep holding down your mouse button as the All Program menu opens.

3. **Drag the folder icon to the place on the All Programs menu where you want the folder to appear, and then release the mouse button.**

   The icon for the folder is now on the All Programs menu, so you can open it quickly from the Start menu.

Compressing Files and Folders

No matter how large your hard disk is, it's never big enough. Sooner or later, you're going to run out of space, which means constantly pruning files or installing an extra hard disk—both of which can seriously carve into your Solitaire time.

Good news: you can create extra hard disk space without spending a penny or deleting files. Simply compress your files so they're much smaller than their normal size. This section offers hints on saving space with compression.

3-17   Getting Extra Disk Space by Using NTFS Compression

A simple way to get more disk space is to use Windows XP's built-in *NTFS compression*—a scheme that only works with hard disks that use the NT File System (NTFS). (The steps later in this hint explain how you can find out if yours does.)

Note: NTFS, besides being an intimidating technical-looking acronym, merely stands for the disk-formatting system that Microsoft developed for Windows NT back in 1993. It represented a departure and improvement over the earlier DOS and its descendant, FAT, a system that previous versions of Windows ran on. Windows XP, advanced and versatile, can run on either a FAT or NTFS drive.

NTFS compression can shrink the size of individual files and folders or entire drives. Once you've compressed any of these items, Windows XP automatically decompresses them when you use them, and then compresses them again when it saves them. (Unless you have a slow computer, you won't even notice this process.)

But be careful about *which* files you compress, because you can slow down your system if you choose the wrong ones, and you may not save much space on your hard disk in return. Here are some tips to keep in mind when deciding which files to compress:

- Music files in MP3 and WMA formats are already compressed, so compressing them won't yield benefits—but it *can* retard your system.

- GIF and JPEG graphics files are already compressed as well.

- Bit-mapped graphics file formats (like .bmp and .tif) are not compressed, so you can save a lot of space compressing those.

- Microsoft Word files and database files are great candidates for slimming down.

- Don't compress system files and .log files like those found in your Windows folder: If you do, your system can take a very severe performance hit.

- If you compress a file, you can't encrypt it. For more information about encrypting files and folders, see page 298.

Compressing a folder

Here's how to use NTFS compression for a particular folder:

1. **Make sure your hard disk uses the NTFS file system.**

    To find out, right-click the icon for your hard disk in Windows Explorer. Choose Properties → General and next to "File system," see whether it reads NTFS, as shown in Figure 3-13.

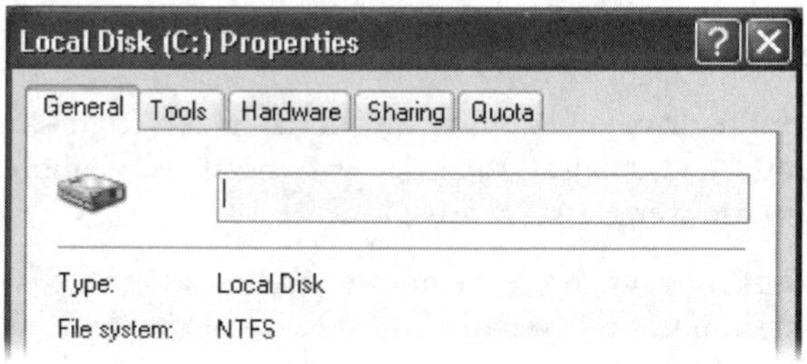

Figure 3-13:
Before you can use NTFS compression, you have to make sure your hard disk uses the NTFS file system. Even if you don't plan to use NTFS compression, it's a good idea to convert your file system to NTFS because it also allows you to encrypt files. For information on converting to NTFS, see page 74.

2. **In Windows Explorer, right-click the folder you want to compress, and then choose Properties → General → Advanced.**

    The Advanced Attributes dialog box appears, as shown in Figure 3-14. This dialog box also lets you control other folder features, such as indexing the folder for faster searches. (When you've *indexed* a folder, Windows keeps track of its files, so you can find them more easily.) For details about indexing and searching, see page 85 later in this chapter.

3. Turn on the box next to "Compress contents to save disk space" and click OK. When the Properties dialog box appears, click OK again.

Windows compresses the folder and all of its contents.

Figure 3-14:
The Advanced Attributes dialog box for a folder lets you do more than compress the folder's contents. You can also encrypt the folder so only you can see what's inside. But you can't compress a folder and also encrypt it. As you can see here, when you turn on compression, the encryption feature is unavailable (grayed-out). So if you have a folder whose contents you want to keep secret, better to encrypt it rather than compress it.

Tip: As you use Windows Explorer, you can tell which files are compressed and which aren't —compressed folders should be blue. If yours aren't, and you want them to appear in color, choose Tools → Folder Options → View. Scroll down and select "Show encrypted or compressed NTFS files in color."

Compressing an entire drive

If you want to compress an entire drive, and not just individual folders, right-click the drive in Windows Explorer and choose Properties → General → "Compress drive to save disk space." (You can compress any drive.)

After a prompt asks you to confirm your choice, Windows compresses every folder and file on the drive, one after another. Depending on the size of the drive, this process can take several hours, but you can continue to use your PC while the compression takes place. Just be aware that during that time, you may be prompted to close a file you're working on so Windows can compress it.

3-18   Getting Extra Space by Using Zip Folders

For files you frequently use, NTFS compression is a great bet because you can quickly open and then recompress 'em. But Windows XP helps you save disk space another way—by using *Zip* files. Zipped files use a type of file compression technology that smushes files and entire folders much more effectively than NTFS file compression. Plus, Zip files work on any kind of file system, not just NTFS. But zipped folders are slower to close and open—which can be a significant drawback.

Here's when you'd use Zip files instead of NTFS compression:

- **When you need to send a large file or files to someone via email.** You can Zip all the files into a single archive (folder) and send it without taxing your Internet connection—because you've shrunken the files, they take less time to transfer.

- **Storing files you rarely use.** You can create Zip archives to store the files, and then delete the originals. You can usually save anywhere from 10 to 90 percent of the original file sizes.

- **Gaining the maximum amount of disk space.** If hard disk space is at a premium, you'll save much more space with Zip files.

- **When you want to compress and also encrypt files.** Although you can't encrypt files that have been compressed using NTFS, you *can* encrypt files that have been zipped. So if you have sensitive files that are also very large, use Zip compression.

There are two different ways to create a zipped folder. If you want to create an empty folder that automatically zips files as you add them to the folder, follow these steps:

1. **In Windows Explorer navigate to where you'd like to create the zipped folder.**

   You'll create the folder in the right-hand pane.

2. **Choose File → New → "Compressed (zipped) folder" and type a name for the folder you're creating.**

   You can also create a zipped folder by right-clicking and choosing New → "Compressed (zipped) Folder." If you use this right-click shortcut, be careful not to click a file or folder because you'll just compress those items (rather than creating a new, empty zipped folder).

3. **Copy your files into the zipped folder.**

   Copy your files into the folder as you would with any folder. The zipped folder automatically compresses the files. To save disk space, delete the original files after you've copied them.

FREQUENTLY ASKED QUESTION

Compression Size

I turned on NTFS file compression. When I checked Windows Explorer it looks like my files still take up the same number of megabytes. Did I do something wrong?

Not at all. When you compress a file or folder, and then examine it in Windows Explorer, its size appears to be the same as it was before compression—the computer equivalent of losing ten pounds and having the bathroom scale register the same weight.

In fact, you have saved space by compressing the file. But for reasons known only to Microsoft engineers, Explorer normally only shows you the original uncompressed size, even if the file is compressed. Fortunately, there's a way to see the new, trimmer size (if you care about how large your files are). Right-click a compressed file or folder in Windows Explorer, and choose Properties → General. You'll see two listings for the file size: "Size" (before compression) and "Size on disk" (after compression).

Alternatively, if you have a folder with files in it and you want to zip up that folder, you can do so in a single step: From Windows Explorer, select the folder you want to zip and right-click it. Choose Send To → Compressed (zipped) Folder. (The original, unzipped folder remains, so delete it if you no longer want it.) Windows creates a new Zip file, with a .zip extension, containing the compressed folder.

Note: When you compress files using Zip, Windows Explorer won't show that you've saved any space, indicating instead only the uncompressed file size. To view the compressed size, see the box on page 77.

3-19   Using WinZip for More Compression Features

If you only zip files occasionally, Windows XP's built-in tools for that purpose work fine. But if you find yourself using compressed files more frequently—or wish Windows XP offered more zipping options—get yourself a copy of WinZip. This superb program allows you to choose from several levels of compression, lets you zip a file and email it in a single step, and offers a host of other features to make zipping and unzipping a snap.

Following are just some of WinZip's basic features:

- It creates *self-extracting* archives, so you can send the folder to someone as an .exe file, and when the recipient runs the file, it automatically unpacks itself, revealing all of the files. This is handy when you want to send a lot of files to someone, but don't want to clutter his email with many different attachments.

- It works with a wide variety of compression standards, not just Zip.

- It can span disks, so if you have a very large Zip file that won't fit on a single disk, you can split that file among several disks, and then easily reassemble it.

- It lets you add files to Zip folders using wildcards like *. This way, you won't have to manually add many files. Instead, you can automatically add dozens of files at a time. For example, you can add all of the MP3 files in a folder in one fell swoop, instead of adding them one by one.

And those are just a few of WinZip's better qualities. You can download a free trial copy from *www.winzip.com*. A full version costs $29.

POWER USERS' CLINIC

Make WinZip and Zip Folders Coexist

When you install WinZip, it takes over the .zip association and becomes the primary program Windows uses to handle Zip files and folders. But what if you *like* the way Windows handles Zip files, yet you still want access to all of WinZip's extra features? You can get the best of both worlds. All you need to do is tell Windows to handle your Zip files, instead of having WinZip handle them.

In Windows Explorer, choose Tools → Folder Options → File Types. Select Zip in the Extensions column and click Change. In the Open With dialog box that appears, choose "Compressed (zipped) Folders." With this change, XP is now associated with the .zip extension, but you still get to use all of WinZip's features by right-clicking a zipped folder.

3-20   Automatically Compressing and Emailing a Photo

When you send digital photos via email, you can go gray waiting for your Internet service provider to stuff the pics through the pipe. To save time, people often compress their pictures before hitting the send button.

But selecting a picture, compressing it, running your email program, attaching the compressed file, and then sending it can also cut time off your life span. Here's how you can compress the process:

1. **Open Windows Explorer and highlight the photo or photos you want to send.**

   Make sure you're in the File and Folder Tasks view, which has a pane on the left side with icons for common tasks. If you're not in that view, get to it by clicking the Folders icon in the Windows Explorer toolbar. To select multiple pictures, hold down the Ctrl key as you click each file.

2. **Click "Email the selected items" in Explorer's left-hand pane (it will say "Email this file" if you've selected only one file). The Send Pictures via E-Mail dialog box opens (Figure 3-15).**

   You may only see the top portion of the dialog box, and not the bottom, which lets you choose your exact picture size. If you don't see the whole dialog box, click "Show more options."

3. **Choose "Make all my pictures smaller," and select the size you want for the pictures you're sending.**

   The smaller the picture, the smaller the file, and the more quickly it travels. But balance file size against picture quality: if you make the file too small, your recipient may not be able to print a good copy of the family photo you send her.

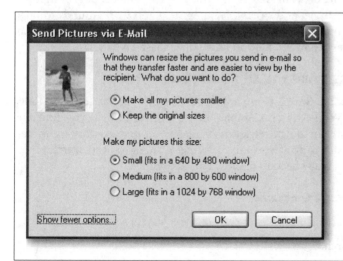

Figure 3-15:
When you compress files to send them via email, Windows converts the files to the .jpg format and sizes them according to the choices you make in this dialog box. The amount of space you'll save varies according to how large your original file is; the larger the file, the more space you'll save. For example, an 850 KB file can shrink all the way down to about 40 KB. But a 15 KB file hardly shrinks at all.

4. **Click OK. Your email program opens and attaches the compressed pictures to
a message, as shown in Figure 3-16.**

Fill out the address for the email and send it.

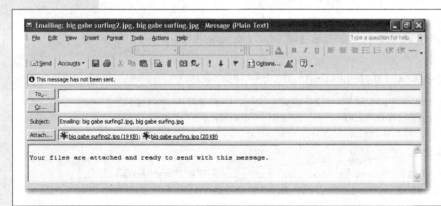

Figure 3-16:
*XP automatically
attaches the
compressed files to an
email message. If you
use Outlook, as shown
here, you can see the
file sizes of the
shrunken pictures
before you send them—
which gives you a hint
as to how long it will
take to send them.*

Tip: If you want to make sure your recipient can see your photo in all its original, multi-megabyte glory
but you also want to reduce the file size, compress the file using Windows XP's built-in Zip compression or
WinZip (page 78). Then attach that zipped file to an email message. This way, your compressed photo will
quickly email and download, but when your lucky recipient opens it, the photo will retain all its original
quality and resolution.

Searching Your Computer

Sometimes, finding a file on your disk is like hunting for a lost robot on Mars—
time-consuming, often futile, and sweaty. Here are tips and workarounds to help
you find what you need fast—whether you're looking for a budget document from
last year or an MP3 Martian music file you downloaded last week.

3-21   Customizing Windows XP's Basic Search Tools

Windows XP's search tool, Search Companion, offers some very basic search tools
for finding lost files. While Search Companion isn't going to help you find the
Holy Grail, it's not bad for quick retrievals of files you *know* are lurking somewhere on your computer. And if you mix in some of the advanced search tools,
described later, you can really beef up your search capabilities.

Four ways to launch Search Companion

You can launch the Search Companion in any of these ways:

- Choose Start → Search.

- From anywhere, press Windows key+F.

- In an Explorer Window, press F3.
- In an Explorer Window, choose Search.

Selecting or deleting an animated helpmate

Many people find the animated canine companion—dubbed Rover by his creators—more annoying than comforting. To turn off Rover, choose Change Preferences → "Without an animated screen character." If you're a fan of animated characters, but Rover skeeves you out, choose Change Preferences → "With a different character," and then choose from a list of other animated alternatives.

Types of searches

Search Companion offers four types of searches. You can choose one to limit the files Windows searches, potentially speeding up your search:

- Pictures, music, or videos
- Documents (word processing, spreadsheet, and so on)
- All files and folders
- Computers (on your network) or people (in your address book)

These search options all have wizards that can be tedious to click through. The advanced search option is a lot quicker and more effective, since it lets you search directly for all or part of a file name or a word or phrase in the file, rather than walking you through the wizard's multiple steps.

Advanced search

The advanced search feature is pretty straightforward, and it lets you look for files in useful ways. For example, you can search by typing in file names. You can also use *wildcards* like an * when searching for files. (A wildcard is a character you can use to search for multiple variations of a file name.) Thus, if you can't remember whether you called a file AfricaProject or AfricaReport or AfricaHoeDown, type *Africa** to search for multiple variations.

To use advanced search, from the Search Companion choose Change Preferences → "Change Files and Folders Search Behavior" → Advanced.

See Figure 3-17 for a view of the search window both with and without Rover and the wizard interface.

Tip: When you conduct a search, Windows doesn't normally search through system folders or hidden files and folders (page 68). If you want your searches to look in those places, too, first select the type of search you want to perform, then click "More advanced options." Turn on the "Search system folders" and "Search hidden files and folders" boxes. (Turn on "Search subfolders" too if you want your search to run through the folders that are contained within the folders you're searching through.) Now, whenever you use the Search Companion, it searches through system and hidden files and folders as well.

3-22   Finding Music and Picture Files

Finding the exact picture or song you want on your PC can be a nightmare. Unlike documents, music and photos typically don't have a lot of text you can search for, other than the file's name. Say you're looking for an MP3 file of Franz Schubert's Symphony #8, also known as the Unfinished Symphony. If you can't remember whether you called it Franz8, Schubert Symphony, Unfinished Business, FSS8AKAUS, or something else altogether—and it's nestled among thousands of other media files on your hard drive—you might be tempted to declare it the Unfound Symphony.

But you have another option. A little-known feature of the Search Companion looks not only for file names, but also for details embedded in a media file known as *metadata*. Metadata is descriptive information about a file, and it varies according to the type of file. For example, metadata for music files in the WMA and MP3 formats can include the artist's name, the album title, the musical genre, and even the lyrics. (Metadata for graphics files doesn't offer as much descriptive information, but does include the file's resolution and, if you've taken the photo with a digital camera, even the camera model.)

Metadata gets added to a file when somebody creates the file, so how much information appears mostly depends on the information grabbed at that time. For example, if you've recorded an MP3 file from a CD, the metadata for the MP3 includes whatever information your music recording software copied from the CD, such as the kind of music it is, the CD title, and the song title.

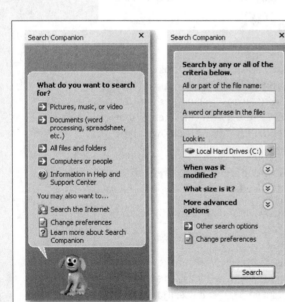

Figure 3-17:
Left: The default Search Companion window forces you into a wizard-like interface that takes you through several extra steps when performing a search. It also includes an animated dog that many people would like to curb.

Right: The advanced Search Companion interface lets you search without an animated character and without wizards.

Searching for metadata

You don't have to do anything special to tell Windows XP to search through metadata—the Search Companion does it automatically, in both the normal and advanced modes. You just need to know what kind of metadata you can look for.

To see the metadata for any media file, right-click the file, and then choose Properties → Summary. (Sometimes you have to choose Properties → Summary → Advanced.) Figure 3-18 shows the metadata associated with an MP3 file of Schubert's *Unfinished Symphony*.

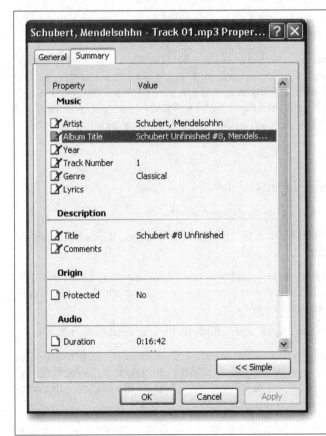

Figure 3-18:
The metadata for music files can contain a lot of hidden information about the file, including its genre, the CD title, song title, track number, the year it was recorded, and comments from the person who recorded the track. Often, not all the metadata fields contain information. What's available depends on the software used to record the music—or info that someone added later.

Once you know what you can look for, launch the Search Companion, go to the box that says "A word or part of the file name," and type whatever you want to find. For example, if you type *Classical*, the Search Companion looks for any music in that genre. (If you have about 3,000 classical music files on your drive, consider typing something more specific, like *Schubert* or *Unfinished Symphony* to narrow the field.)

Graphics files don't contain as much information, but you can search for the resolution of the file. For example, type *800×600* in the box that says "A word or part of the file name." If you've taken a picture with your digital camera, you can type in the camera name. (This trick works only if your camera was smart enough to put metadata in the file—not all cameras are.)

Note: For the media files you can see already, you can edit or add to the metadata. The editing process can be tedious, but the more information you put in the metadata field, the easier it will be to find that file when you're searching for it later on. From the Summaries tab shown in Figure 3-18, click any metadata field and you can add, edit, or delete at will (say, if the comments about the band don't match your opinion).

3-23 Saving a Search for Future Reference

If you frequently perform the same search—like looking for Word files that contain the phrase "outrageous things my mom said"—you don't need to retype those words every time you go hunting. Instead, you can save your search. Saved search files are a godsend if you do advanced searches, like looking by file size or date, and often perform the same search over and over, like doing a monthly search for memos you've written.

To save a search:

1. **Enter the search criteria and perform the search as usual.**

   You first have to run a search before you can save it.

2. **Choose File → Save Search from the Search Companion, then choose where you want to save the file.**

   Windows XP normally saves the search in your My Documents folder, but you can save it anywhere. In fact, if you plan to save a lot of searches, you might want to create a separate folder for them.

3. **When you want to run the search again, find the file and double-click it.**

   When you save a search, Windows XP creates a file named after the main criteria of your search. For example, if you search for all .doc files that contain the phrase "To Do list" and which have been modified in the past month, Windows names the file "Files containing text To Do list.fnd."

   You can rename the file, as long as it ends in the .fnd extension—for example, "To do list finder.fnd." You can't edit the actual search by changing the file name, though. So even if you renamed the original file "Vacation ideas finder.fnd" it would still search for the phrase "to do list," not "vacation ideas."

Tip: If you perform a search particularly often, consider creating a shortcut to it on your desktop. That way, you can just double-click it from the desktop to run it. Just create the search and then drag the .fnd file from Windows Explorer to your desktop.

3-24   Using the Indexing Service to Speed Up Searches

The Search Companion is useful, but for power searchers, it leaves much to be desired. For example, if your PC is stuffed to the gills, searches can take quite a long time. And the kinds of searches the Search Companion can perform are fairly limited. For example, it can't find files based on properties like when a file was last printed or its word count.

Windows XP's Indexing Service is a far more powerful tool. It can perform searches literally hundreds of times faster than the Search Companion and offers a sophisticated query language you can use. The service works by indexing the files on your disk—creating the equivalent of an index in a book. Then when you do a search, it looks in the index (called a catalog) rather than searching your entire hard disk.

But the Indexing Service has some drawbacks, too. Here's what you should know before deciding whether to use it:

- **The Indexing Service takes up a lot of disk space.** The index it creates requires anywhere from 15 to 30 percent of a typical drive, according to Microsoft. That means giving up a lot of gigabytes.

- **The Indexing Service can't do case-sensitive searches.** If you need to search by upper or lower case, use the Search Companion instead. For example, if you want to find a file named cookiemonster.doc, but not CookieMonster.doc, the Search Companion can help you but the Indexing Service can't.

- **The Indexing Service searches only certain file types.** These types include HTML files, text files, and Microsoft Office documents. If you want it to search other file types, such as graphics files, you have to get a third-party filter, and there aren't filters for all file types.

Note: For more information on where to find these filters, use Google or your favorite search engine to look for "indexing service filters."

- **There are times when you won't be able to use the Indexing Service.** While XP is indexing your hard drive, either initially or when updating (which it can do several times a day), you won't be able to use the Indexing Service. But you can still use the Search Companion at those times. The initial index usually takes a few hours; after that, most updates usually last only a few minutes.

The bottom line? If you search your hard drive a lot and can spare the disk space, it's worth using the Indexing Service—the speed alone is a major benefit, even if you don't take advantage of its sophisticated query language.

Turning on the Indexing Service

Ordinarily, the Indexing Service isn't turned on, so you have to activate it. First, launch the Search Companion, then choose Change Preferences → With Indexing

---

Service. (If you see Without Indexing Service instead, it means the Indexing Service is already turned on.)

After you activate the Indexing Service, building an index for the first time can take awhile, especially if you have a slow computer and lots of files. In any case, it's a good idea to start the Indexing Service and leave your computer on overnight.

You submit a search to the Indexing Service the same way you do to the Search Companion (it's the same interface), so you don't need to do anything special to use it once you turn it on.

Turning off the Indexing Service

To turn off the indexing service, run the Search Companion and choose Change Preferences → Without Indexing Service. The index remains intact (and still takes up space on your hard disk), but when you do a search, you won't be searching the index. You can always turn the index back on later.

If you decide that you'll never use the indexing service, you can save hard disk space by deleting the indexes that it created. To do so:

1. **At the Run box (Start → Run), type ciadv.msc and press Enter.**

   The Indexing Service Microsoft Management Console launches, which lets you manage a number of aspects of the indexing service, including deleting indexes.

2. **A list of catalogs appears. Right-click on the catalog you want to delete and choose Delete from the menu. Then click Yes from the dialog box that appears.**

   Each catalog is a different index. For each index, you'll be shown a variety of information, such as the size of the catalog in megabytes. If you're not using the Indexing Service, you should delete all the catalogs because you won't need any of them. In many instances, there will only be a single catalog.

POWER USERS' CLINIC

Downloading Better Search Software

Windows XP's search tools can usually help you find what you need, but if you want the most powerful search tools available, you need to download add-in software. One of the best search tools around is Sleuthhound, which indexes your hard disk on a folder-by-folder basis, and lets you search the index it creates. The results show up in a browser interface, much the way Google works.

The basic version of Sleuthhound indexes most common file types, while the Pro version even indexes Adobe Acrobat PDF files and other hard-to-index file types. Both versions are free to download from *www.rosecitysoftware.com,* but

if you decide to keep using them, the company charges $20 for Sleuthhound and $34.95 for Sleuthhound Pro.

Another program that can find a needle in the haystack of your hard drive is X1, which, like, Sleuthhound, indexes your hard drive when your first install it. It then lets you search for anything: emails, email *attachments,* contact, files, you name it. Even better, this powerful program lets you organize your stuff through its window; want to reply to an email or move an old message in Outlook or Outlook Express to a new folder? You can do it within X1—even if your email program isn't open. ($74.95 from *www.x1.com.*)

Built-In Utilities

Sometimes the things you notice least in life—your toothbrush, a knife and fork, your shoelaces—play an important role. They're not flashy or earth shattering, but you'd be hard pressed to get through the day without them.

Windows XP's built-in utilities are similar. These often overlooked little programs, like Notepad, Clipboard, and the Backup utility, perform key functions you use all the time—even if you're barely aware of them.

This chapter tells you how to get the most out of these programs, as well as some others you might not even know about, like the utility that sends faxes straight from your computer. You'll also learn about some inexpensive alternatives—perfect for when Windows needs a little more oomph than its built-in tools can provide.

Better Backups

Backing up is like buying insurance: you don't need it until you need it. And then you *really* need it. Unfortunately, most backup programs are not only expensive, they come with phonebook-sized manuals scary enough to make lost data seem like an appealing alternative.

Windows jumps into the breach: its backup software is free. And while the program is not the *easiest* to use, the following hints will help get you started. (If you're interested in spending a little bit of money for backup software that's slightly friendlier, skip ahead to hint 4-3 for tips on two alternatives to the Windows backup utility.)

4-1 Installing the Backup Program in Windows XP Home Edition

If you use Windows XP Home Edition, you may be wondering why you can't find the Windows backup program that came with previous versions of Windows. There's a simple reason: It's not there.

To make matters worse, the Windows XP CD's Welcome screen doesn't give you a chance to install the backup program even if you select "Install optional Windows components." The backup program is nowhere on the list.

Note: Windows XP Professional installs the backup program automatically.

But the phantom program is available, and if you have the Home Edition, you can easily install it manually. To do so, pop the Windows installation disk into your PC, navigate to My Computer → D: → Valueadd → Msft → Ntbackup, and double-click the file NTBACKUP.MSI. An installer launches and installs the backup program.

Note: If your CD drive is a letter other than the D drive, use that letter when looking for the backup program. For example, if your CD drive is your E drive, you'd find the backup program in My Computer → E: → Valueadd → Msft → Ntbackup.

MICROSOFT MYSTERY

The System Recovery That Doesn't

The backup program in Windows XP Home is not only tricky to install, it's also missing an important feature: the ability to recreate your PC's complete setup using Automated System Recovery. Unlike a standard backup, which restores only your data and programs, ASR restores your *entire* hard disk, including partitions and system settings, which is what you want when you have a total system failure—but you can't use it in Windows XP Home.

Bizarrely, the program in the Home Edition lets you *create* an ASR backup—but doesn't let you use it. The Home Edition can't use that backup to *restore* your system in case of a crash. Only the programmers at Microsoft know the reason for this paradox.

So when you launch the backup program in the Home Edition, don't bother clicking the Automated System Recover option (in the backup's wizard mode [page 89] it's the choice labeled "All information on this computer")—because it's worthless. Fortunately, you can still use the program to back up your key folders and files. Windows XP Pro *does* let you restore your system from an ASR backup.

4-2 Backing Up Your Goods

Installing Windows XP's Backup program is one thing; using it effectively presents a whole other set of challenges. This hint leads you through the fog.

Tip: You've heard it before, but it bears repeating: Back. Up. Your. Data. It's not a question of *whether* your system will crash, but *when* it will. Losing data is painful, recovering it is time-consuming, tedious, and often impossible. Depending on the amount of work you do on your computer, schedule backups at least weekly and possibly daily or semi-daily. Step 6 in this hint gives you tips on scheduling.

To set up the Backup program:

1. **Open it by choosing Start → All Programs → Accessories → System Tools → Backup. The program automatically launches a wizard.**

   On the Welcome page of the wizard, you can switch to Advanced mode for juicy tasks like viewing reports of previous backups.

2. **Click through the first two wizard screens until the What to Back Up screen appears (Figure 4-1). Choose *which* files you want to back up, and then click Next.**

   The first two options—"My documents and settings" and "Everyone's documents and settings"—back up the My Documents and Favorites folders, each account's desktop settings, and each account's Web browser's cookies. (See page 133 for more details on cookies.) This option is a good one if you're primarily concerned about preserving your *files*. In this mode, the program does not save your *programs*, so it uses a lot less space and goes a lot faster. If you think you may need to restore the whole system sometime, and you've lost the original XP and other program CDs, try the second or third choice.

   The next option is "All information on this computer." As described in the box on page 88, this option creates a system restore disk, but unless you sprang for the Pro edition of Windows XP, that disk won't restore squat.

   If you keep important files in places other than the My Documents or Favorites folder, select the third choice, "Let me choose what to back up." When you do, a new window launches that lets you pick and choose which folders and files on your hard disk to back up.

3. **Choose the drive and folder where you want to save your backup files, type in a name for your backup, and then click Next.**

   Backup lets you store your data on tapes, floppy disks, a network location, or your hard drive. Thing is, your hard drive may be the only option of those four that's practical for you…but when the computer crashes, you'll lose your hard drive, and thus all your carefully backed up data. If you fit this model, the box on page 90 explains a workaround for storing your backups on CDs.

4. **Select the type of backup you want to perform, and then click Next.**

   After you choose which files to back up and where to save them, you come to the wizard's final screen, which says you only need to click Finish to start the backup. Rather than finishing at this point, though, you should click the Advanced button, which gives you control over the type of backup to make. The box on page 91, "Five Ways to Back Up Your Files," explains your choices in detail.

5. **Select any verification, compression, and shadow copy options—they're all described by the wizard—and then click Next.**

   Some of these options may be grayed out depending on your computer's capabilities.

6. **Choose whether to append or replace your backups, and then click Next.**

If you have a huge storage drive, you can append your backups—a bulky system, but one that will leave you with archives of your files as they change over time. On the other hand, if your storage space is limited, replacing your backups takes up far less space and still leaves you with the most recent version of everything. The exception is Incremental backups; if you've chosen this type, *append* your data in order to keep a cumulative cache of your changes.

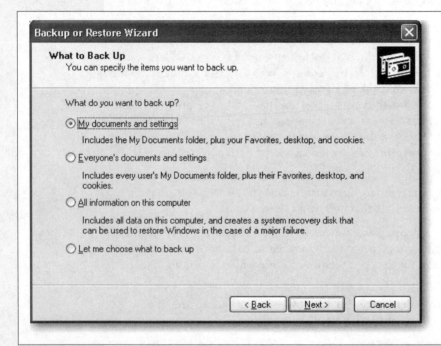

Figure 4-1:
When you select "Let me choose what to back up" from this page, a new window appears letting you back up not just programs and data, but also what the backup wizard calls your PC's "System State," which includes Registry information, boot files (files needed to start your computer), and other vital data.

WORKAROUND WORKSHOP

Backing Up to a CD

The Windows backup program lets you store your data on a tape drive, a network location, or even a measly floppy disk—but not on a CD. This omission is a serious drawback, considering how convenient and inexpensive CD-Rs and CD-RWs are.

However, there is a way to store your backups on CDs. Following the procedure in hint 4-2, select your hard drive as your backup destination by clicking Browse and choosing

a location on your computer. (If Windows prompts you to "insert a disk into drive A:" click Cancel). Then, after you've finished the steps in the backup process, you can copy the backup file to a CD-R or CD-RW.

If your backup is larger than the amount of data a CD can hold (typically, 650–700 MB), create two or more different backups, each smaller than 650 or 700 MB (depending on your CD's capacity), and then copy each resulting file to a different CD.

---

7. **Choose when to back up, and then click Next.**

Select Now to immediately run the backup. Select Later to schedule a backup; if you pick this option, you can set a regular schedule for automatic backups. The program gives you a lot of choices for scheduling. For most people, weekly backups are a reasonable *minimum* schedule, but daily backups are better. If the thought of losing a day's worth of work makes you queasy, back up every day.

UP TO SPEED

Five Ways to Back Up Your Files

Deciding backup type is important since it offers you a way to speed up the backup process by skipping over files that you've already backed up. You have five options here: Normal, Copy, Incremental, Differential, and Daily.

Normal. This option backs up the files you've selected and keeps a list of the files. Then, when you make subsequent backups using either the Incremental or Differential backup options (see below), the program backs up only newly added or changed files.

Copy. This option copies the files you've selected regardless of whether or not you've backed them up before. Choose it if you want to make copies of certain files without interfering with your normal backup routine.

Incremental. This quick 'n' dirty option backs up only the files you've selected *if they've changed* since the most recent Incremental or Normal backup. The Backup Wizard then adds these files to the list of files it's backed up. It doesn't touch any unchanged files or files backed up using the Normal mode, because they don't need to be backed up. Incremental backups are much faster than Normal backups. However, it takes longer to *restore* Incremental backups because you first have to restore the normal backup, and then restore every subsequent Incremental backup.

For example, if the first backup you ever made was a Normal backup one particular Friday, you'd at that point have one large normal file to restore from. Then, say the next time you got on your computer was Monday and the only thing you did was create one new file. An Incremental backup performed Monday night would back up only that lone new file. And on Tuesday if the only thing you did was create *another* new file, then when you performed an Incremental backup Tuesday night, you'd only be backing up Tuesday's new file. Finally, when it came time to restore, first you'd restore the Normal backup, followed by the Monday Incremental backup, and then the Tuesday Incremental backup.

Differential. Like the Incremental backup described above, this option backs up only the files you've selected that are new or that you've changed since the most recent Normal backup. The only difference is, it *doesn't* add these files to the list of files it's backed up. The next time you do a Differential backup, it will *again* copy all the files that have changed since the most recent Normal backup, as if the most recent Differential backup never existed. Because there are more files to back up, a Differential backup takes longer than an Incremental backup. But on the plus side, when you restore files, you only need to restore the Normal or most recent Incremental backup, and the latest Differential backup.

For example, if you did a Normal backup two weeks ago, and a Differential backup five times since then, to restore your data you would first restore the Normal backup, and then restore only the most recent Differential backup.

Daily. This spur-of-the-moment option backs up only files you've created or changed on the current day. It's best suited for backups that are outside your normal backup routine; for example, if you've just finished a major project you want to copy, but your normal weekly backup won't take place for several days.

---

8. **Click Finish to complete the backup.**

The backup runs as scheduled.

Restoring your backup

Say the worst has happened: Your hard disk goes on the fritz, and you need to restore your files. If you've followed the steps for creating backups, you're in luck. Start Windows XP's Backup program in Wizard mode, and then choose Restore Files and Settings. The program walks you through a simple series of prompts for restoring individual files, or for restoring an entire backup set.

4-3   Better Backup Programs

You can't beat the free price of Windows XP's built-in backup program, but after using it a few times, you might get the feeling that Microsoft hired the IRS to design the thing. The good news is that if you're willing to pony up a little bit of money, you can get a fairly decent backup program. Two reasonably priced, well-designed options are Backup Plus and InfoStash.

Backup Plus

One of the strengths of this program is its simplicity, particularly when restoring backups. Even though Backup Plus saves its backup file with a .bac extension, behind the scenes, the backup files are plain old .zip files. So if you want to restore files or folders, all you have to do is rename the backup file with a .zip extension, and then open the file with an unzipping program, such as WinZip or the zip program built into Windows (page 77). Your files are then waiting for you, ready to be used.

Backup Plus also lets you schedule backups, and unlike Windows' own backup program, Backup Plus can save files to any media, including CD-Rs and CD-RWs. Figure 4-2 shows how easy it is to add files to a backup set.

Backup Plus, available at *www.backupplus.net*, is free to try. It costs $39.95 if you decide to keep it.

InfoStash

InfoStash is another easy-to-use backup program. In addition to backing up your ordinary documents and settings, InfoStash comes with one major hallelujah-option: it can also back up your emails and your address book. Backups are stored as zip files, so restoring lost files is as easy as opening up a regular zip file (page 77).

And InfoStash lets you set your level of compression, from 1 to 9. With less compression, the backup is faster, but the resulting file is larger.

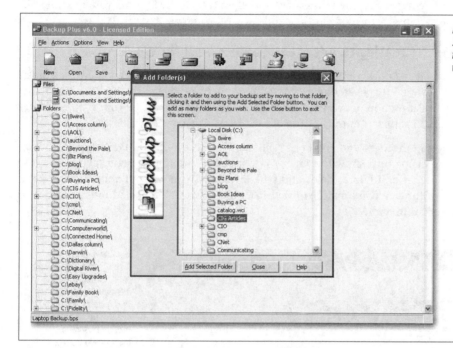

You can download and try InfoStash for free from *www.permutations.com*. It costs $29.95 if you decide to keep it.

Notepad and Clipboard

Windows XP's two most popular utilities are Notepad and the Clipboard. In fact, you use the Clipboard countless times every day without even knowing it: every time you cut, copy, or paste something, Windows stashes and retrieves the goods from its trusty Clipboard. And if you edit a lot of text files, you may use Notepad, which is faster and simpler than Word for editing small files. Both programs are more powerful than they appear; the following hints help you tap into their hidden abilities.

4-4   Inserting a Time and Date Stamp with Notepad

When using Notepad, you may want to put a time and date stamp in a file—for example, if you're adding comments to a document and want to show when the notes were made. To insert a time and date stamp at any point in a Notepad file, simply Press F5.

Notepad can also automatically insert a time and date stamp in a file every time you open it. This trick is especially useful if you're using a file to keep a journal or work record: Each time you open your file to compose a new entry, Notepad inserts a fresh time and date stamp. Simply create a blank text file with *.LOG* as the first line in the file, then press Save and close the file. Every time you open the file, Notepad inserts the current time and date. All you have to do is type away.

4-5   Creating Headers and Footers with Notepad

Notepad includes a little-known feature that lets you automatically insert *headers* and *footers* into your documents when you print them. (A header is text that appears at the top of every page in a document, like the title or your name; a footer is text that appears at the bottom of each page, like a page number.)

To create headers and footers in Notepad, choose File → Page Setup. The Page Setup dialog box, shown in Figure 4-3, appears. In the Page Setup dialog box, use the Header and Footer fields and type in the text you want to appear—or type in any of the key combinations listed in Table 4-1 for Notepad's built-in header or footer commands.

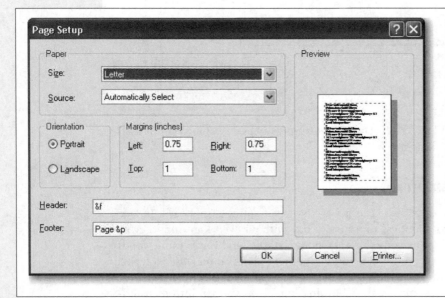

Figure 4-3:
Like many fancy word processors, Notepad lets you insert headers and footers. You can't see the headers and footers onscreen, though; they show up only in the printed document. Here, the settings in the dialog will create a header containing the file name, and a footer containing the page number, preceded by the word "Page."

Table 4-1. *Header and Footer Commands for Notepad*

Function	Key Combination
Inserts the file name (the word "Untitled" appears if the file doesn't have a name).	&f
Inserts the date.	&d
Inserts the time.	&t
Inserts page numbers.	&p
Inserts an ampersand (&).	&&
Aligns the header or footer to the left, center, or right.	&l, &c, or &r

You can use more than one command for the header or footer. For example, to insert a header that displays the file name and page number *and* aligns the header to the right, type this command into the Header box:

&f &p &r

Make sure to leave a space between each item so the header or footer is easy to read. You can also combine text with header and footer commands. For example, the command *Page &p* in a header or footer prints *Page 1* on the first page, *Page 2* on the second page, and so on.

4-6   Better Notepads

Notepad is great for plain text files, but if style's what you're after, you'll find the program a bit skimpy on formatting features. Furthermore, Notepad isn't so hot for creating HTML pages, because it doesn't include any HTML-specific help or commands. The more powerful WordPad, also built into Windows XP, offers some formatting features, such as tools for coloring text and inserting tabs, but not much else.

But there are plenty of Notepad alternatives that can handle text formatting, HTML coding, and programming. NoteTab Light and EditPlus are two of the best options available.

NoteTab Light

If you're budget conscious but want an excellent, all-around text editor, NoteTab Light is a good choice. For starters, it's free. It includes a souped-up Clipboard that lets you save boilerplate text for later use, and it also lets you open multiple documents at the same time. If you're a power hound, NoteTab Light lets you create macros—mini-programs that automatically perform a series of operations—or pull from its library of built-in macros. Creating HTML files is a snap thanks to a set of tools that lets you quickly insert HTML code.

NoteTab Light also comes in two premium versions (NoteTab Standard, which costs $9.95, and NoteTab Pro, which costs $19.95). These versions include features like a spell checker and an outline creation tool. All three programs are available from *www.fookes.com*.

EditPlus

If you create HTML pages and you're looking for an excellent text editor with lots of HTML shortcuts, EditPlus (Figure 4-4) is a good bet. It includes an HTML toolbar that lets you quickly insert common HTML tags, choose Web-safe colors and characters, build tables, and view Web pages within the program.

For programmers, EditPlus offers syntax highlighting for PHP, ASP, Perl, C/C++, Java, JavaScript, VBScript, CSS, and HTML. (You can also create your own syntax files for other languages.)

EditPlus is available at *www.editplus.com;* it's free to try and costs $30 if you decide to keep it.

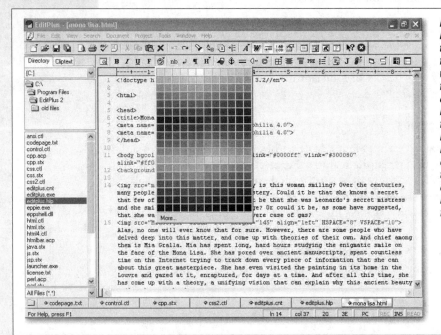

Figure 4-4:
If you use a text editor to create or edit HTML files, EditPlus comes with a handful of HTML-friendly tools, including a color picker, shown here, which saves you from having to memorize or look up HTML color codes. Just choose the color from the palette and EditPlus automatically adds the right HTML code to your file.

4-7   Viewing the Contents of Your Clipboard

The Windows Clipboard holds a single chunk of information at a time. If you copy a phrase, a paragraph, a graphic, or the entire contents of a Word file, Windows saves that information on the Clipboard and then pastes it from the Clipboard to a document when you select the Paste command. A lot of the time, you cut or copy something to the Clipboard and paste it right away. But if you forget what's on the Clipboard, how do you view it?

Enter an obscure little Windows XP utility called the ClipBook Viewer, which lets you see the current contents of your Clipboard or save individual clips as files you can use later. To run the ClipBook Viewer, type *clipbrd* at the command prompt or in the Run box (page 103). The Viewer opens and displays the contents of your Clipboard, as shown in Figure 4-5.

Note: When you run the ClipBook Viewer for the first time, your current clip may appear in a minimized window at the bottom left corner of the Viewer window. To see the clip, maximize it by clicking the middle button on the minimized bar.

You can use the ClipBook Viewer to save individual clips as files. Choose File → Save As, name the file, and save it to a folder. Windows XP saves the file with a .clp extension, but you can't open it just by double-clicking. When you want to open the clip, you have to run Clipbook Viewer, choose File → Open, and then browse to the correct file. After you've re-opened a file in Clipbook Viewer, you can then paste it anywhere you'd normally paste something.

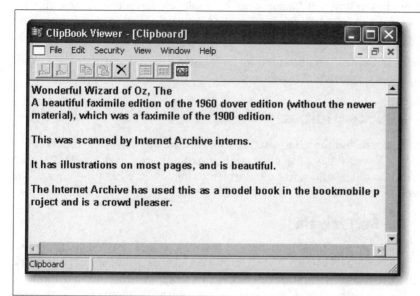

Figure 4-5:
Running the ClipBook Viewer doesn't affect the Clipboard; you can still copy and paste items as you normally would. When you copy a new clip to the ClipBoard, the old clip vanishes from the ClipBook Viewer and gets replaced by the new one.

4-8   A Better Clipboard

Windows XP's Clipboard is about as basic as it gets. It holds one clip at a time, and as soon as you save a new clip, the previous one vanishes. There's no way to save

Figure 4-6:
ClipMate lets you save hundreds of clips—not just one—providing you ready access to text and graphics clips that you may want to reuse at some point. It's handy if you have items you use regularly—for example, different versions of your company logo.

boilerplate text or other frequently used files, and once a clip is gone, it's gone (unless you've saved the clip as a file, as described in the previous hint).

For a much better Clipboard, get ClipMate, shown in Figure 4-6. It lets you save libraries of clips in different folders, combine multiple clips into one large clip, see thumbnail previews of your clips, and control how individual applications capture clips, essentially turning the clipboard into the useful tool it always should have been.

ClipMate is shareware. You can try it for free, but it costs $20 if you decide to keep it. Download it from *www.thornsoft.com*.

Other Built-In Utilities

Backup, Notepad, and the Clipboard are probably the best-known Windows utilities, but Windows XP has a few other gems stored in its utility closet. This section covers them and highlights a few tricks worth trying, like the Fax program and the Calculator.

4-9   The Fax Program

Although faxes seem archaic in the era of instant messages and email, *paper* was supposed to become obsolete, too. Reality check: faxing remains a part of life (those perpetual-motion machine sketches are tough to describe in an email). When you're hit with the need to send or receive a fax, Windows XP can come to the rescue. One of its least-known but most useful utilities is the Fax program.

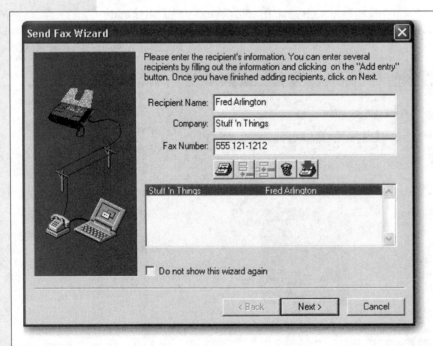

Figure 4-7:
Once you've installed Windows XP's Fax utility, you can fax a document directly from your computer. Using the Fax Wizard shown here, you can either type the name and fax number of the recipient or grab it from your Windows Address Book. To use your address book, click on the small Rolodex-like icon and choose a recipient.

Note: Your computer has to have a modem connected to a normal phone line in order to use the Fax utility. It can't send or receive faxes over a cable or DSL modem. And you can't *talk* on that phone line while you send or receive faxes.

Despite its obvious benefits, Fax isn't automatically installed with Windows XP, so you'll need to dig out your Windows XP installation CD. Once you pop the CD into your computer and the opening screen appears, choose Install Optional Windows Components → Fax Services. That's all there is to installing it.

If you want to fax a document that's on your computer already (for example, a Word document), simply open it, then select File → Print. In the Print dialog box, swap your normal printer for the Fax tool by clicking the drop-down list next to Name, and then choosing Fax. A wizard launches and takes you step-by-step through the process of sending a fax using your modem, as shown in Figure 4-7.

If you have a printed document you want to fax, you first have to scan it into your computer, open the scanned file using a graphics program, and then fax the file using the Print command as described earlier.

If you simply need to shoot a note to somebody and a fax cover sheet alone will do the job (with no document attached), try this trick. Choose Start → All Programs → Accessories → Communications → Fax → Fax Console. Once the console opens, choose File → Send a Fax. Fill out the form, including the name of the person you're sending the fax to and the phone number, and Windows sends your fax.

Note: For a quicker way to open the Fax Console, at the command prompt or in the Run box (page 103), type *fxsclnt.exe* and then press Enter.

You can also receive faxes with the Fax program. To accept an incoming fax as it's ringing, open the Fax Console (Start → All Programs → Accessories → Communications → Fax → Fax Console), and then choose File → "Receive a fax now." To read the fax, select your inbox in the Fax Console, and then double-click the document you want.

ALTERNATE REALITIES

Receive Faxes Without a Phone Line

When you receive faxes using Windows XP's fax utility, you need to make sure the program is open (or leave it running all the time). You also need to make sure your phone line isn't busy—if it is, incoming faxes won't come through. An alternate way to receive faxes is to use the free Internet fax-receiving service at *www.efax.com*.

When you sign up, you're assigned a phone number that you can give out to anyone who wants to send you a fax (eFax picks the number). When someone sends a fax to that number, eFax automatically converts it to a graphics file and emails it to you. Using a special viewer, you can then read and print the fax. If you want to *send* faxes using eFax you have to pay $12.95 per month, and you have to pay a fee for every long-distance fax you send.

Tip: The Fax program lets you send only one document at a time, not a group of documents. But you can combine several documents into one large document and fax that file.

If you want a more sophisticated program, WinFax Pro in a good choice, available from *www.symantec.com* for $99.95. It includes other features as well, such as integration with email programs and the ability to add a signature to outgoing faxes.

4-10   A Better Calculator

Windows XP's Calculator is good for basic calculations. To run it, choose Start → All Programs → Accessories → Calculator. Or, at the command prompt or in the Run box (page 103), type *calc.exe* and press Enter.

But if you need a more powerful calculator, say, for something geeky like financial, engineering, or scientific calculations, this built-in utility isn't up to the task. There is, however, an excellent free calculator called Calc98 that you can download from *www.calculator.org*. Calc98 lets you perform lots of sophisticated calculations, including statistical functions and metric unit conversions. And it can also operate using different number bases, like binary and hexadecimal. If you're in the mood to go really old school, it'll even let you calculate using Roman numerals.

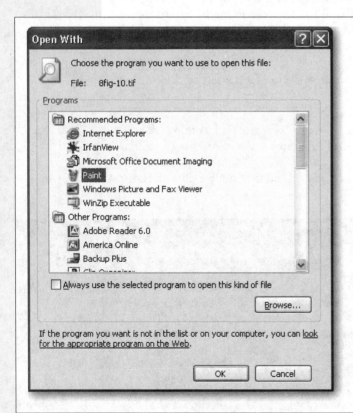

Figure 4-8:
Use this dialog box to tell Windows XP to open graphics files with Paint, not the Windows Picture and Fax Viewer. That way, you can edit Paint files, rather than just view them.

Tip: You can also do some seriously sophisticated calculating in the Google search box (*www.google.com*), which recognizes an amazing array of equations. Just type your calculation into a Google search box, and then press Enter. For more on the Google calculator, check out *www.google.com/help/features.html#calculator*.

4-11 Opening Graphics Documents in Paint

When you double-click a graphics file you've created using Windows XP's Paint utility, you'd expect it to open in Paint so you can work on it again. But for some reason, Windows XP opens the file with the Windows Picture and Fax Viewer instead. If you want to open the file in Paint, you have to use a workaround: Right-click the file, and then choose Open With → Paint.

To avoid having to do this every time, right-click an image you created with the Paint utility, and then choose Open With → Choose Program. The Open With dialog box, shown in Figure 4-8, appears. Choose Paint from the list, turn on "Always use the selected program to open this kind of file," and then click OK. From now on, whenever you double-click a file created with Paint, it'll open in Paint.

Tip: For third-party photo-editing software you may like even better than Paint, see the box on page 102.

4-12 Inserting Special Characters

There's a simple way to insert special characters into a document, including inverted question marks, capital letters with accents, or the symbol π—use the Character Map.

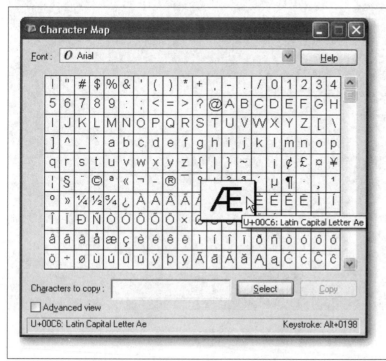

Figure 4-9:
The Character Map lets you paste special characters into any program. To search for a specific character, turn on the box next to "Advanced view," then type a search term in the box that appears. For example, to see all Greek letters and characters, type "greek".

Note: If you're using Word, you can first try the Insert → Symbol command, which may be quicker.

Open the Character Map by selecting Start → All Programs → Accessories → System Tools → Character Map. Choose a font from the Font box, and then click the character you want to place in your document. Windows XP displays a magnified version of whatever character you've chosen, as shown in Figure 4-9. Choose Select, and Windows copies the character to the Clipboard. From there, you can paste it into any program.

Tip: For a quicker way to get to the Character Map, at the command prompt or in the Run box (page 103), type *charmap* and then press Enter.

ADD-IN ALERT

Image Editing

These downloads help bring out your inner photo editor:

- **Paint Shop Pro.** This program is probably the most popular shareware graphics program of all time—and with good reason. It's a great photo editor with a full suite of special effects and editing tools that help you handle tasks like automatically cleaning up red eye, adding backgrounds, cropping photos, changing color schemes, and more. You can also use it to create graphics that are optimized for the Web, so they look their best when viewed online, as well as animated graphics using the program's "Animation Shop." ($74 shareware; Jasc Software; *www.jasc.html.*)

- **Picasa.** If you're looking for an excellent way to organize your pictures, try this program. It lets you organize all your photos in albums, create slide shows, and edit, print, and share photos. ($29.99 shareware; Picasa; *www.picasa.com.*)

- **FlipAlbum.** This unique program lets you create multimedia albums with your digital photos. The pictures appear in a virtual photo album that looks like the real thing, and the pages flip while music plays. Once you put your pictures in an album, FlipAlbum automatically creates thumbnails for the photos, a

table of contents, and indexes, making it easy to view your pictures later on. ($24.95 shareware; *www.ebooksys.com.*)

- **ACDSee PowerPack.** This suite of tools includes a picture viewer, photo editing software, and a slideshow program. It's an ideal set of tools for touching up photos taken with a digital camera, creating multimedia slideshows, and editing and viewing photos. It's not as powerful a picture editor as Paint Shop Pro, but it offers a better collection of all-around tools, like one that lets you create slideshows. ($79. 95 shareware; ACD Systems; *www.acdsystems.com.*)

- **Easy Thumbnails.** If you need to perform batch operations on a group of graphics files, or need to create thumbnails of them, try this free program. It automatically creates thumbnails out of graphics files in any folder, and it lets you apply special filters and do other kinds of editing to batches of files. (Freeware; Fookes Software; *www.fookes.com.*)

- **Adobe Photoshop Elements.** This stripped-down (and less expensive) version of Photoshop is ideal for doing touch-ups and other editing on digital photos. It's powerful and easy to use for tasks like eliminating red eye, adding special effects and filters, and more. ($99; *www.adobe.com.*)

4-13   Shortcuts to Open Windows XP Applications and Utilities

Often, the quickest way to open a built-in Windows XP application or utility is to use the command prompt or Run box, instead of clicking through a series of menus. (To get to the Run box, choose Start → Run. To get to the command prompt, choose Start → Run, type *command,* and press Enter.) For example, to open Notepad, at the Run box or a command prompt, type *notepad.exe* and press Enter.

You can run dozens of Windows XP utilities and programs this way. Table 4-2 lists Windows XP's built-in programs and utilities and their executable file names. (An *executable file name* is the name of the file required to run a particular program.) At the command prompt or in the Run box, type any of these file names for a quicker way to open various wizards, programs, and utilities.

Table 4-2. *Filenames of Windows XP's Built-In Applications and Utilities*

Application, Component, or Utility	Executable Filename	Purpose
Accessibility Options	access.cpl	Runs the Accessibility Options dialog box, where you can adjust settings for special-needs features like StickyKeys and Show-Sounds.
Accessibility Wizard	accwiz.exe	Runs the Accessibility Wizard, which helps those with special vision, hearing, and mobility needs customize their computer.
Active Connections Utility	netstat.exe	Lets you view information about your current network settings.
Add Hardware Wizard	hdwwiz.cpl	Helps you set up new hardware.
Add or Remove Programs	appwiz.cpl	Lets you add or remove programs.
Address Book	wab.exe	Launches the Windows Address Book so you can keep track of contacts.
Attrib	attrib.exe	Shows you information about files' attributes, such as whether they have been backed up.
Backup	ntbackup.exe	Launches the Windows backup program (page 88).
Cabinet (CAB) Maker	makecab.exe or diantz.exe (Both launch the same program.)	Launches a program that lets you compress and decompress files.
Calculator	calc.exe	Launches the Windows Calculator.
Character Map	charmap.exe	Launches the Windows Character Map (see Figure 4-9).

Table 4-2. *Filenames of Windows XP's Built-In Applications and Utilities (continued)*

Application, Component, or Utility	Executable Filename	Purpose
Chkdsk	chkdsk.exe	Launches a utility that checks your hard disk for problems and errors.
Chkntfs	chkntfs.exe	Tells you whether a hard disk uses the NTFS file system (see hint 3-17).
Clipbook Viewer	clipbrd.exe	Runs the Clipbook Viewer for viewing the Clipboard (see hint 4-7).
Command Prompt	cmd.exe or command.exe (Both options do the same thing.)	Launches a window that lets you enter MS-DOS commands.
Control Panel	control.exe	Launches the Control Panel.
Date and Time Properties	timedate.cpl	Lets you change the computer's date and time.
Device Manager	devmgmt.msc	Launches the Device Manager, which controls hardware settings.
Disk Cleanup	cleanmgr.exe	Launches the Disk Cleanup utility, which deletes unneeded files from your hard disk.
Disk Defragmenter	defrag.exe	Launches the Disk Defragmenter, which makes your computer run more quickly by organizing the files on your hard disk.
Display Properties	desk.cpl	Runs the Display Properties dialog box, which lets you change how your desktop looks.
Fax Console	fxsclnt.exe	Runs the Fax Console (see hint 4-9).
Fax Cover Page Editor	fxscover.exe	Runs a utility that lets you create simple cover pages for faxes.
Folder Options	control.exe folders	Launches the Folder options dialog box, which lets you customize how your folders look and behave in Windows Explorer.
Fonts Folder	control.exe fonts	Opens the Fonts folder. Double-click any font to see a page of sample text.
FreeCell	freecell.exe	Launches the game FreeCell.
FTP	ftp.exe or tftp.exe (Both options do the same thing.)	Runs a File Transfer Protocol utility that lets you transfer files over the Internet.
Game Controllers	joy.cpl	Launches the Game Controllers dialog box, which lets you change settings for joysticks and similar devices.
Hearts	mshearts.exe	Runs the Hearts game.
Help and Support Center	helpctr.exe	Launches the Help and Support Center (Figure 6-20).

Application, Component, or Utility	Executable Filename	Purpose
HyperTerminal	hypertrm.exe	Launches the HyperTerminal communications program, which lets you connect to Telnet sites.
Internet Backgammon	bckgzm.exe	Launches the Internet backgammon game.
Internet Checkers	chkrzm.exe	Launches the Internet Checkers game.
Internet Explorer	iexplore.exe	Launches Internet Explorer.
Internet Hearts	hrtzzm.exe	Launches the Internet Hearts game.
Internet Options	inetcpl.cpl	Launches the Internet Properties dialog box, which lets you control security, privacy and other settings for Internet Explorer.
Internet Reversi	rvsezm.exe	Launches the Internet Reversi game.
Internet Spades	shvlzm.exe	Launches the Internet Spades game.
Keyboard Properties	main.cpl keyboard	Lets you change your keyboard's properties.
Logoff	logoff.exe	Lets you log off Windows XP.
Microsoft Magnifier	magnify.exe	Launches a program to magnify parts of your screen.
Microsoft NetMeeting	conf.exe	Runs the Microsoft NetMeeting conferencing program.
Minesweeper	winmine.exe	Runs the Minesweeper game.
Mouse Properties	main.cpl	Lets you customize mouse properties.
MSN Explorer	msn6.exe	Launches the MSN Explorer browser.
Network Connections	ncpa.cpl	Opens the Network Connections folder.
New Connection Wizard	icwconn1.exe	Launches the New Connection Wizard, to help you create a new network connection.
Notepad	notepad.exe	Launches Notepad (see page 93).
On-Screen Keyboard	osk.exe	Launches an onscreen keyboard that lets you input text without typing.
Outlook Express	msimn.exe	Launches the Outlook Express email program.
Paint	mspaint.exe	Launches the Paint graphics program.
Phone and Modem Options	telephon.cpl	Lets you set options for your modem and telephone.
Pinball	pinball.exe	Runs the Pinball game.
Ping	ping.exe	Runs the Ping utility, which lets you check to see whether Web sites are up and running.
Power Options	powercfg.cpl	Lets you control how your computer uses its power.
Printers and Faxes	control.exe printers	Opens the Printer and Faxes folder.

Table 4-2. *Filenames of Windows XP's Built-In Applications and Utilities (continued)*

Application, Component, or Utility	Executable Filename	Purpose
Registry Editor	regedit.exe	Lets you edit the Registry.
Scanners and Cameras	wiaacmgr.exe	Lets you control a scanner or camera.
Send a Fax	fxssend.exe	Lets you send a fax (see hint 4-9).
Shutdown	shutdown.exe	Lets you shut down your PC.
Solitaire	sol.exe	Launches the Solitaire game.
Sound Recorder	sndrec32.exe	Lets you record sounds.
Sounds and Audio Devices	mmsys.cpl	Lets you control your sound and audio devices.
Speech Properties	control.exe speech	Lets you control speech recognition.
Spider Solitaire	spider.exe	Launches the Spider Solitaire game.
System Properties	sysdm.cpl	Launches the System Properties dialog box, which lets you examine and control many key settings for your computer, like Automatic Updates and System Restore.
System Restore	rstrui.exe	Launches System Restore, which lets you restore your computer to a state it was in previously.
Task Manager	taskmgr.exe	Runs the Task Manager.
Volume Control	sndvol32.exe	Lets you control the volume of your sound system and speakers.
Windows Explorer	explorer.exe	Launches Windows Explorer.
Windows Media Player	mplay32.exe wmplayer.exe	Runs Windows Media Player.
Windows Messenger	msmsgs.exe	Runs Windows Messenger.
Windows Movie Maker	moviemk.exe	Runs Windows Movie Maker, for making movies.
Windows Update	wupdmgr.exe	Runs Windows Update, which checks whether there are Windows updates available.
WordPad	wordpad.exe	Runs the WordPad text editor.

Microsoft Office

If you've been living on Mars for the past decade or so, you may never have heard of the software bundle called Microsoft Office. But more likely, you have an intimate relationship with at least one of the programs in the package: Microsoft Word (for creating text documents), Microsoft Excel (spreadsheets), and Power-Point (presentations). Some versions of Office also include programs such as Access (for creating databases) or FrontPage (for creating Web pages).

This chapter offers a grab bag of hints for maximizing the many benefits of Office 2003. It also tells you how to secure a fully working—and fully free—software suite that handles most of the same tasks as Microsoft Office.

General Office Advice

The hints in this section apply to *all* the Microsoft Office programs.

5-1   Killing Clippy

Microsoft's infamous "Clippy"—an overly eager animated paperclip (Figure 5-1) that pops up when it thinks you need help—may well be the single most reviled computer feature of all time. The character is *supposed* to provide useful tips as you work. Instead, it slows down your work, and even though it's a *paperclip,* it makes an array of obnoxious facial expressions. You can bump off Clippy from within any Office program by choosing Help → Hide the Office Assistant.

5-2   Turning Off the Office Clipboard

Even if you never use the Office Clipboard, which pastes text into Office files, it may still pop up occasionally, like if you press Ctrl+Insert twice in a row by accident. While some people like using the Clipboard, others find it intrusive. If you're among the annoyed, you can turn off the Office Clipboard so it never pops up. A simply Registry edit is the way to go.

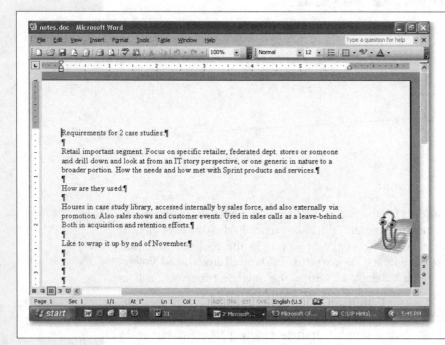

Figure 5-1:
Microsoft has come up with a lot of brilliant, incredibly useful tools over the years. Clippy is not one of them.

Close all Office applications and Run the Registry Editor (see page 328). Go to My Computer → HKEY_CURRENT_USER → Software → Microsoft → Office → 9.0 → Common → General and create a new DWORD value called AcbControl. Assign it a value of 1 and exit the Registry.

The Office Clipboard no longer pops up, but if you change your mind and want it to appear again, head back to the Registry, and either delete AcbControl or change its value to 0.

5-3   Finding Files Faster

If you want to find an Office file, Microsoft XP's generic search function (accessible by pressing the Window key+F) is *not* your best bet, because it's designed to search through your *entire* hard disk. If you're looking for Office-specific files, a better option is Office's powerful built-in Advanced Search function, pictured in Figure 5-2. To use Advanced Search in any Office program, choose File → Search and then in the window that appears, click the link at the bottom labeled Advanced Search.

You can fine-tune your search by specifying a word or phrase, a file type, a file name, the subject of the document, its size, which template you used to create it, the number of characters it contains—even the total time spent editing the document. With Advanced Search, you also can combine criteria. For example, you can search for a document that you created in a specific template, that has more than a certain number of characters, and that you created after a certain date.

To fine-tune Advanced Search, first choose the Property you want to search for or exclude—text, size (of the file), comments, creation date, and so on. Depending on the Property you choose, the Condition changes, offering you choices like "is," "includes," "today," or "tomorrow." After selecting the condition, enter a word or number in the Value box, then click Add to make your criteria part of the search. For example, if you want to find all your files that contain the words "Trump" and "egomaniacal," head to the Property menu and select "Text or property," then set the Condition to "includes" and type *Trump* in the Value box. Then click Add and repeat the process using the word *egomaniacal*. (Make sure the And button is checked if you want to find both "Trump" and "egomaniacal." If you check the Or button, you'll find documents containing either word.) Finally, click Go to perform the search.

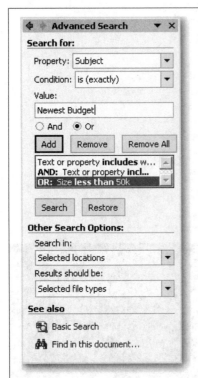

Figure 5-2:
Office's Advanced Search gives you some useful options you can't find in Microsoft XP's general search feature. To remove the search information, highlight it and click Remove. If you have multiple searches, click Remove all to remove them all.

Microsoft Word

No doubt you've already used Microsoft Word. Love it or hate it, you really can't avoid it; *air* is less ubiquitous.

But no matter how much you've used Word, you probably don't know all the cool stuff it can do for you. The following section explains a few handy tricks, like how to turn on or reveal text using "invisible ink," use Word as a personal translator, insert special characters, and create keyboard shortcuts for menu commands.

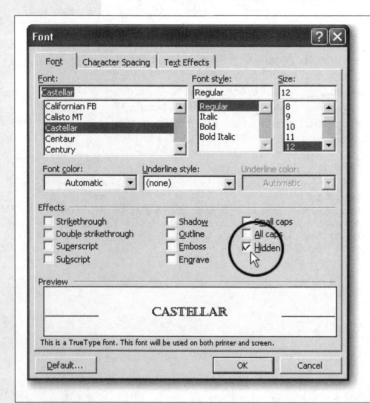

Figure 5-3:
You can hide text using this dialog box. To delete hidden text, you first have to make it appear, then you can delete it as you would any other text.

5-4   Using Invisible Ink

Unbeknownst to many people, Word has a feature that acts like invisible ink—text you can see onscreen, but that doesn't appear on paper when you print. This option is useful if you have a document chock full of comments and notes that you wish to distribute on paper—minus the personal notes. To make selected text disappear in a Word document, first highlight the passage you want to make like Houdini, and then choose Format → Font. In the dialog box that appears, under Effects, select Hidden (see Figure 5-3). The text disappears entirely—in fact, you can't even see it on your screen.

If you want the text you've hidden in a Word document to reappear onscreen, choose Tools → Options → View. Under "Formatting marks," select "Hidden text." The text now appears on your screen, with a dotted line beneath it to indicate it's hidden. Again, this means that even though you can see it on your screen, it won't appear on paper when you click Print.

5-5   Inserting Special Characters

At some point, you've probably wanted to use a special character in a Word document—perhaps the symbol for trademark (™), or copyright (©), or pounds (£). While these babies are fun to use, they're usually hard to find. But insiders know the real deal: while using symbols in Word isn't obvious, it *is* easy.

First, make sure your cursor is wherever you want the symbol to appear, then choose Insert → Symbol. A dialog box appears with a few dozen characters to choose from (Figure 5-4). Select the one you want, and click Insert.

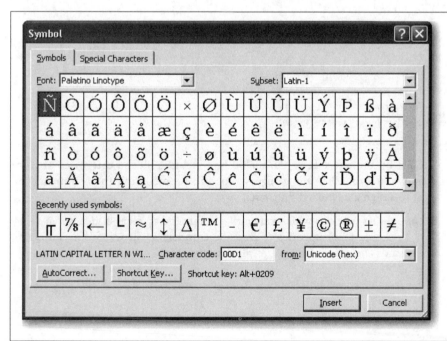

Figure 5-4:
Select the symbol you want to insert into a Word document. To save time, check the ones listed under "Recently used symbols" first. This list reveals the last 16 symbols you've used. Now just double-click any one to insert it.

5-6   Creating Your Own Keyboard Shortcuts

Performing basic tasks in Word can take many clicks and a lot of navigating through menus—if you're a novice. Power hounds go for the convenience and speed of keyboard shortcuts. And you can create them for every Word command out there. If you constantly count all the words in a document, for example, simply assign a keyboard shortcut, like Alt+C, to the Word Count command. Then you can just press two keys to get your answer.

Here's how to create a keyboard shortcut in Microsoft Word:

1. **Choose Tools → Customize → Keyboard.**

   The Customize Keyboard dialog box, shown in Figure 5-5, appears.

Figure 5-5:
When creating a shortcut key, choose a feature you use frequently. An example might be Word Count, or if you often translate text, the translate pane.

2. **The list on the left side of the dialog box includes all the categories of commands in Word. Click the category most likely to contain the command you want to assign a keyboard shortcut.**

   It's not always obvious which category a command appears under, so you may have to click a few categories to find the command you want—or choose All Commands and scroll through the alphabetized list.

3. **From the list of Commands on the right side of the Customize Keyboard dialog box, choose the command you want to assign a keyboard combination, and then press the keys you want for your shortcut.**

For example, choose ToolsWordCount, and press Alt+C to assign the Word Count feature to the Alt+C key. Whatever keyboard combination you typed appears in the "Press new shortcut key" box.

4. **Click Assign, then Close.**

From now on, whenever you type that keyboard combination, Word executes the command you've assigned this shortcut.

5-7   Turning Word into Your Personal Translator

You don't need to be a master linguist to translate a Word document into a foreign language or vice versa. You just have to be the proud owner of a computer outfitted with Word. Thanks to its amazing Translate feature, Word can translate a word, a phrase or an entire document for you automatically.

Like all digital interpreters, Word can mangle a phrase faster than you can say *quel dommage*. That tendency makes it a decent choice for small tasks, like translating a word or very short note. If you're going for a long document, however, proceed with mucho caution: Word's translation skills are not much better than a slow second grader's.

POWER USERS' CLINIC

Frequently Used Symbols

If you frequently use the same symbol, here are a couple ways to simplify the insertion process.

Assign a keyboard combination to your favorite symbol. Instead of mousing through menus to insert the © symbol, assign it a keyboard combo, such as Ctrl+Alt+C (or whatever you prefer—just be sure to use the Alt key, the Ctrl key, or a combination of the two in any shortcut you create). To do so, in the dialog box shown in Figure 5-4, click the symbol you want, then select Shortcut Key. A new dialog box appears. Type the key combination you want to assign to that symbol—such as Ctrl+Alt+C—then click Assign, then Close, then Close again. From now on, when you type that key combination the symbol you've assigned it to will appear.

Create an AutoCorrect command. You can also have Word automatically turn a certain sequence of text you type into a symbol. For example, whenever you type (c), you can have Word turn it into the © symbol using its AutoCorrect feature. To make the change, in the dialog box shown in Figure 5-4, select the symbol you want, then click Auto-Correct. In the new dialog box that appears, type the text you want Word to AutoCorrect—in this case, (c) —in the box that says Replace. Finally, click Add and OK. Whatever you do, just don't choose a word or series of characters that consistently appears in text, such as "the," or else AutoCorrect will become your own private Frankenstein.

Translating a word or phrase

To translate a single word in a document, select Tools → Language → Translate. The Translate pane appears to the right of your document, as shown in Figure 5-6. Type the word you want translated, and then from the "Look up in dictionary" menu, choose the appropriate languages (for example, English to French). Click Go, and the translation appears in the Results box.

Translating a document

To translate an entire document, you have to download a separate program from the Web. With a Word document open, select Tools → Language → Translate; the Translation pane appears. Choose "Entire document" at the top of that pane, then click the Go button near the bottom.

Figure 5-6:
You say "potato," I say "pomme de terre." To translate a single word, type it and click Go. Another method: Highlight the word you want translated in your Word document, choose "Current selection" in the Translate pane, and click Go.

The tool sends you to a Web page with a map of the world. Click the United States to trigger a page titled "Translation Services by WorldLingo." Download the free software and follow the installation instructions.

Next, close the document you want to translate, and then reopen it. You can now choose the languages you want to translate from and to.

5-8 Inserting Your Digital Signature into Word Documents

It's a fact of life: You can't do anything official without paperwork. Or course, that little chore is getting easier nowadays as more and more organizations accept signed documents via fax or email. What most people don't realize is that there's a way to *sign* files electronically.

Using Word's AutoText feature, you can easily insert your signature whenever and wherever you want. Here's how:

Tip: You can use this technique for other graphics or text as well. For example, if you frequently type a particular sentence or paragraph, create an AutoText entry for that passage by following these same steps. For example, if you always end your letters with "See you later, alligator," you can create AutoText for that phrase and quickly pop it in at the end of your letters.

---

1. **Sign a piece of paper, scan your signature, and save the image as a digital file.**

   If you don't have a scanner, you can go to a copying business such as Kinko's to use one. Save the scanned image of your signature on your computer, noting the file's name and where you saved it.

2. **Open the Word document you want to sign, and select Insert → Picture → From File, then browse to the file with your digital John Hancock and click Insert.**

   If you're not happy with the signature—if it's the wrong size, for example, or the quality isn't great—just rescan your autograph, then repeat the steps to insert it into a Word file.

3. **To save your signature for reuse in future documents, highlight the signature graphic, and then choose Insert → AutoText → New.**

   The Create AutoText dialog box appears. Type a word or phrase to name your signature, such as mysig, and click OK. Word automatically creates a new Auto-Text entry, which you can use to automatically insert text or a graphic into a Word document. Now, to insert your signature in the future, just type the word *mysig* (or whatever) and press Enter. Presto! Word drops in your digital signature—no ink necessary.

Tip: For a faster way to open the AutoText dialog box, highlight your signature graphic and then press Alt+F3.

5-9 Using the Word Count Toolbar

One of Word's most useful features is Word Count, which, as the name implies, counts the exact number of words in a selection of text or a whole document. Using this command is pretty simple: With a Word document open, choose Tools

→ Word Count. A box then appears telling you the number of words you've written, plus how many pages, characters, paragraphs, and lines are in your document.

But for those who live and die by such numbers (such as writers paid by the word), mousing up to the Word Count menu may not be easy enough. You can get a quicker fix by displaying Word Count as a floating toolbar. Figure 5-7 tells you how.

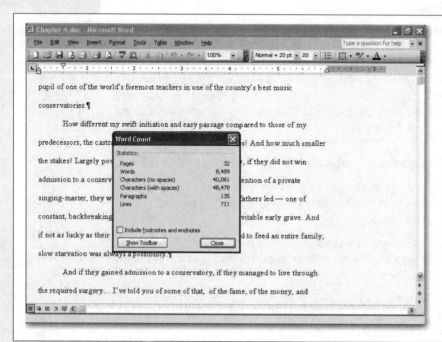

Figure 5-7:
If you frequently need to know the exact number of words in a document, turn on the Word Count toolbar and leave it displayed. To display the Word Count toolbar, choose Tools → Word Count, then click the Show Toolbar button. Click Cancel to close the Word Count dialog box (the Word Count toolbar stays open). To find out how much you've typed, click the Recount button.

Excel

Spreadsheet programs make it easy for anyone—even the number-phobic—to create everything from simple budgets to sophisticated financial analyses. This section explains how to get the most out of the most popular spreadsheet program on the planet: Microsoft Excel.

5-10 Automatically Importing Data from the Web

The Internet, as you know, is chock-full of astounding amounts of data—stock prices, population figures, environmental statistics, and more. But if you need to work with these numbers on a regular basis, the thought of cutting and pasting them into your own document may be enough to cause spasms in your mousing arm.

Fortunately, you can import data from the Internet directly into Excel. In fact, you can even tell Excel to update certain data automatically—sort of like having a personal statistician at your beck and call.

To import data into an Excel file, you have to be online. Then:

1. **Choose Data → Import External Data → New Web Query.**

   The New Web Query dialog box appears. In the address bar at the top, type the URL of the Web site that contains the data you want.

2. **In the Web page that appears, click the yellow arrow next to the data you want to import.**

   A thick blue box appears around the data you've chosen to import, and the arrow turns into a checkbox (see Figure 5-8).

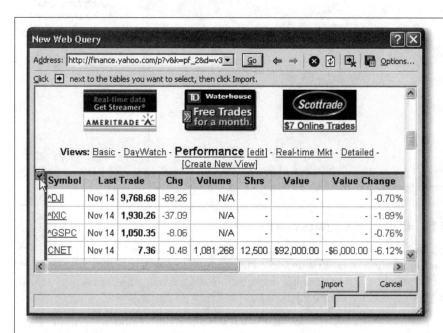

Figure 5-8:
When you tell Excel to import data from the Web, it doesn't know precisely what you want. To expedite the process, Excel identifies a large section of data on a page that it can import. From this data, you can choose what you want imported. (Most likely you don't want everything it selects, so be careful when choosing.)

3. **Click Import.**

   Excel's Import Data dialog box opens, asking where you want to place the data on your spreadsheet. Choose a location and click OK. The data appears in your spreadsheet, in separate cells, as shown in Figure 5-9. You may have to do a bit of cleanup, as sometimes Excel mistakenly identifies words or numbers and imports them along with the real data you want.

4. **To update the data in your Excel spreadsheet with the latest information from the Web, place your cursor in any of the cells whose data you imported and select Data → Refresh Data.**

   Excel updates the information, assuming it's still available online. You don't need to have your browser open, although you do need to be connected to the Web.

Tip: You can instruct Excel to automatically extract the latest information from the Web, without manually updating the data yourself. Open your Excel file and choose View → Toolbars → External Data. Then place your cursor in any cell with data you want Excel to automatically update from the Web. On the External Data toolbar, click the Data Range Properties button, and then check the box next to "Refresh every…minutes." Finally, from the drop-down box, choose how often you want the data refreshed.

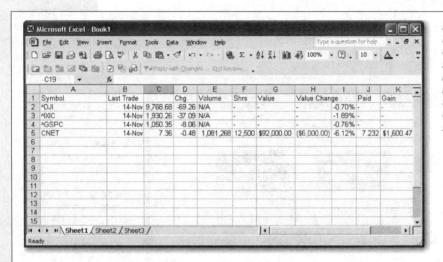

Figure 5-9:
Excel efficiently pastes data into your spreadsheet after you import it from the Web. However, only the data transfers—not any corresponding spreadsheet formulas.

5-11   Creating a Watermark

Excel files often contain sensitive information—staff salaries, next year's budget, home phone numbers for big-name clients, and so on. Some files simply aren't meant for public viewing, so it's important that everyone who sees a copy knows that the document is confidential.

One way to make that clear is to put a *watermark* stamped "Confidential" in the background of the report. Similar to an old-fashioned red stamp on printed stationery, this noticeable imprint doesn't obscure anything you've typed into the cells (Figure 5-10).

Here's how to add a watermark to an Excel file:

1. **Display the WordArt toolbar by choosing View → Toolbars → Word Art, then click the Insert WordArt button.**

   It's the leftmost button in the toolbar, and it looks like a slanted, three-dimensional letter A.

2. **In the WordArt gallery that appears, click the style of WordArt you want to use and click OK.**

   While it may be tempting to get creative here, keep in mind that it's a lot easier to read horizontal text than vertically stacked letters.

3. In the WordArt Edit Text dialog box, type the word *Confidential* (or any other word you want), select the font and the font size, and click OK.

Whatever you typed appears in your spreadsheet, blocking out other text, as shown in Figure 5-11.

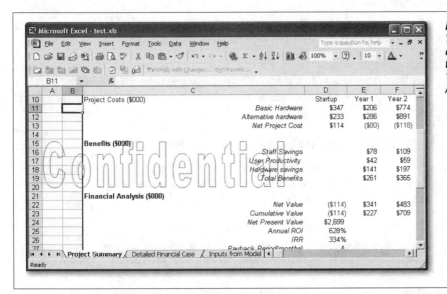

Figure 5-10:
You can, of course, type anything you want into the watermark: "Draft," "1999 Data," "No Dogs Allowed," and so on.

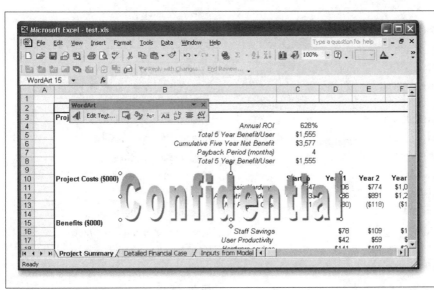

Figure 5-11:
A font size of 36 or higher is probably easiest to read.

4. **Right-click the WordArt you've just inserted, and choose Format Word Art → Colors and Lines.**

   For color, select No Fill. That makes the body of the WordArt transparent. For Line Color—the outline of the letters—select a light gray or a medium-intensity color. Click OK.

5. **Resize the WordArt so it fits on the spreadsheet and doesn't obscure any of the data.**

   Even though the watermark is transparent, its outline might make some of your data difficult to see. You can move or resize a watermark by selecting it (click around it until you see little boxes at its edges, as in Figure 5-11) and then dragging its corners.

5-12   Speeding Up Excel with Keyboard Shortcuts

When you're typing in numbers and working with formulas, a mouse just slows you down to a snail's pace. Speed up your work in Excel by using keyboard shortcuts. Table 5-1 lists shortcuts for common Excel tasks.

Table 5-1. Excel Keyboard Shortcuts

Shortcut Key	Purpose
Ctrl+Z	Undo
Ctrl+Arrow	Move to edge of region
Ctrl+*	Select current region
Ctrl+A	Select all cells
Ctrl+Home	Select A1
Ctrl+End	Select last cell in used range
Ctrl+Shift+End	Select from active cell to last cell in used range
Ctrl+Shift+Home	Select from active cell to A1
Ctrl+Page Up	Move to the previous sheet
Ctrl+Page Down	Move to the next sheet
Ctrl+Tab	Move to the next open workbook
Ctrl+N	Open new workbook
Shift+F11	Insert new worksheet
Shift+F3	Open the paste function window
=+FunctionName+Ctrl+A	Insert a new function
Ctrl+F3	Define name
F3	Paste name
Ctrl+Space bar	Select columns
Shift+Space bar	Select rows
Ctrl+1	Format cells

5-13   Quickly Add New Data to a Chart

It's a breeze to create charts in Excel using the Chart Wizard, which walks you through the process step-by-step. In an Excel file, highlight the data you want to put into a chart, click the Chart Wizard button, and follow the simple instructions.

But if you've already created a chart and merely want to include new data from your spreadsheet, there's no need to bother with the entire wizard process again.

Here's how to add new data to an existing chart:

1. **Click the chart you want to update.**

   A colored box appears around the chart's source data in the spreadsheet.

2. **Move your cursor over the corner of the colored box closest to the data you want to add to the chart. When the cursor becomes a double-headed arrow (Figure 5-12), drag that edge of the box to include the new data.**

   When you release the mouse, the new data appears in the chart.

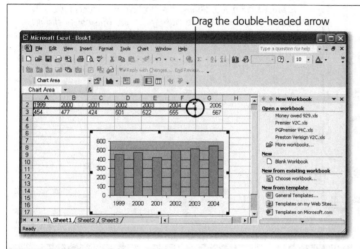

Drag the double-headed arrow

Figure 5-12:
If the cursor becomes two intersecting double-headed arrows, like a cross, keep moving it slightly until it becomes one double-headed arrow. (It won't work in the cross mode.)

PowerPoint

Looking to put more power into your PowerPoint presentations? Here are a few pointers.

Tip: For a hilarious spoof of what the Gettysburg Address would look like if President Lincoln had used PowerPoint, head to *www.norvig.com/Gettysburg*.

5-14   Saving Fonts with Your Presentation

When you distribute a PowerPoint presentation electronically, you can run into a serious problem: The fonts you used in your slides might not be available on the computers used by your readers. The result? PowerPoint substitutes different fonts for those that you carefully selected, and your presentation can appear out of whack.

To overcome this potential glitch, simply save the fonts with your presentation, making them accessible to anyone who opens the file.

Note: This technique only works with TrueType fonts, which are a family of fonts that ship with Windows. So if you went a little wild and dipped into your own esoteric font collection, you won't be able to save them with your presentation.

To save the fonts you used in a PowerPoint presentation, choose File → Save As, and then click the Tools button in the upper-right corner of the dialog box. Then choose Save Options → Embed TrueType fonts, as shown in Figure 5-13. Click OK, and then Save.

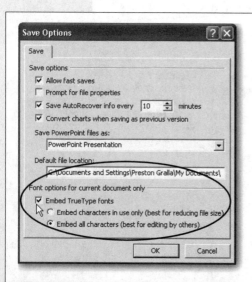

Figure 5-13:
When you save your fonts along with your presentation, choose the "Embed all characters" option if you need others to work on the presentation, too. Choose the "Embed characters in use only" option if no one else will be making changes (this option shrinks the file size of the presentation).

Viewing Presentations Without PowerPoint

Even if you don't have PowerPoint on your PC, you can still view PowerPoint presentations. And if you do have PowerPoint, but your colleagues don't, you can easily share your presentations with them.

All you need is Microsoft's PowerPoint viewer, which you can download for free from *www.microsoft.com/downloads* (on this page, search for "PowerPoint viewer").

After you install the viewer, you can open PowerPoint presentations and show them off. (You won't be able to create or edit presentations, though.) To run the PowerPoint viewer, browse to wherever you installed it and double-click its icon, then open the presentation you want to see or display. And if you need to send a PowerPoint presentation to someone who doesn't have the program, she can download the viewer to see your work.

5-15 Copying Your PowerPoint Settings to Another Computer

People like to customize PowerPoint. For example, you can include certain tool-bars and exclude others, or have a certain template open when the program starts. In fact, you may end up investing the better part of a few work days changing and tweaking various settings so PowerPoint looks and works exactly the way you like.

If that's the case, it'd be a drag to have to recreate those settings when you buy a new computer, or if you use PowerPoint on more than one machine. Thankfully, there's a simple way to transfer your PowerPoint customizations to any computer you use.

Your customizations are found in the file ppt.pcb, located in My Computer → C: → Documents and Settings → Your Name → Application Data → Microsoft → Power-point. Simply copy that file to the equivalent folder on another computer, and all of your PowerPoint customizations show up on the new PC.

5-16 Putting Your Presentations on a Diet

It's entertaining—and sometimes even useful—to include pictures and videos in your PowerPoint presentations. But when you do, your files can become super-sized, eating up tons of disk space on your computer.

Fortunately, there's a simple technique for trimming the size of a presentation without eliminating pictures and videos: Include a blank slide as the first slide viewed.

This may seem odd, because you'd expect that an extra slide would *increase* your file's size, not *decrease* it. But PowerPoint displays the first slide of a presentation as the *preview image* when you select a file in the Open dialog box. So if that slide is blank, rather than full of formatting and graphics, the preview image that Power-Point stores as part of the presentation will be smaller—making the entire file smaller, too. And if the first slide is hefty, you could easily trim off a few mega-bytes of space—a significant savings.

Access

Untold legions enjoy the power of Microsoft's Access database. For you select speed freaks and efficiency experts, here are some hints that make Access even better.

5-17 The Express Route to Creating Tables

Creating a new Access table is about as much fun as watching C-SPAN reruns of federal hearings about the European corn borer. So here's a nifty way around the problem: Recycle existing tables instead of creating new ones from scratch.

The process is pretty simple:

1. **Decide what table you want to make a copy of.**

   Choose a table that has the same basic structure of the table that you want to create.

2. **Open the database that contains a table you want to copy, and then in the Database window, look under the Objects pane and click Tables.**

   When you do so, all the tables in your database appear in a list in the right-hand pane.

3. **In the right-hand pane, right-click the table with the structure you want to copy, and then choose Copy.**

   Access copies the database to the Windows clipboard.

4. **Choose Edit → Paste.**

   The "Paste table as" dialog box appears (Figure 5-14).

5. **Give the table a name by typing text into the Table Name box. Then, under Paste Options, choose Structure Only and click OK.**

   Access creates a new table that has the structure of your old table—but not the data. The table appears in the same pane as your existing tables; simply double-click it to open it and add new data.

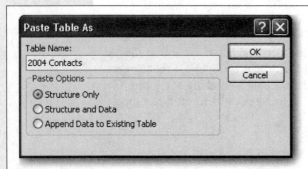

Figure 5-14:
If you're copying a table and you want to retain only the structure of your old table, not the data, choose Structure Only. If you plan on keeping some of the data, choose Structure and Data, and you can edit the existing data.

5-18   The Database Diet

Databases have a way of becoming fat and bloated, no matter how hard you try to keep them slim and trim. The problem is that when you delete a record, the database still retains the space that the record took up. Thus, over time, as you add and delete records, your databases get larger and larger—even though you think you're keeping them in check.

And super-sized databases tend to have data corruption problems.

The solution: Compact and repair your database regularly. This process removes all the empty space your deleted records left behind, and it keeps the database down to fighting weight. Simply choose Tools → Database Utilities → Compact and Repair Database.

But you may forget to run the compaction regularly. So here's better solution: Have Access do it for you *every time* you close the database. Open the database you want to compact automatically. Choose Tools → Options, and then click the General tab. Turn on Compact on Close, and then click OK. That's it. Access automatically compacts that puppy every time you close it.

Note: You have to do this process for each of your databases; there is no way to tell Access to compact all of them automatically.

5-19 Hiding Top Secret Tables

Say you're a CIA agent, and you have tables with sensitive data in them that you don't want anyone to see; here's a quick way to hide them.

Right-click the table you want to hide and choose Rename. Type in a new name, but make sure the first four letters are *usys*. That tells Access to turn the table into a *system object,* which are elements of the database that you can't see.

To make the table visible again, choose Tools → Options and click the View tab. Under Show, turn on System objects, and click OK. Presto—your table is visible. Make it invisible again by turning off the box next to System objects, and clicking OK.

FrontPage

FrontPage helps you roll your own Web pages. The tips in this section help you get more out of FrontPage.

5-20 Flowing Text Around a Picture

When you place a picture on a Web page you're designing, text appears above it and below it, but not to the right of the graphic or the left. The result? Amateurish pages that have vast empty spaces.

You can instead have FrontPage flow the text around the picture, either to the right or to the left:

1. **Right-click the image.**

   The Image Properties dialog box appears.

2. **Choose Picture Properties.**

   Here you can control how the picture will appear on the page. Click the Appearance tab.

3. **In the Wrapping style section, choose either Left or Right.**

This choice *should* be straightforward, but it's actually quite confusing. When you choose *left,* the text wraps around the right edge of the picture. When you choose *right,* the text wraps around the left edge.

The deal is that in the dialog box, *left* or *right* refers to where the picture will appear—not the text—as you can see if Figure 5-15.

4. **Click OK**

The text now wraps around the picture the way you want.

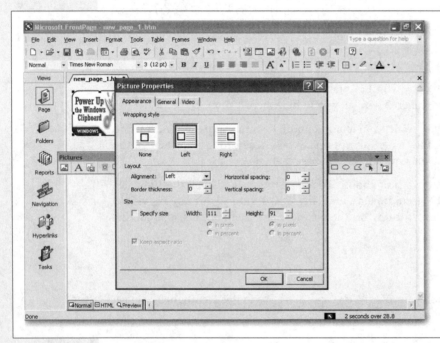

Figure 5-15:
When choosing to wrap text around a picture, you can also add a border to the graphic by choosing a border size from the border thickness drop-down box.

5-21   Watermarks

You've probably come across Web pages where the background doesn't scroll when you scroll the page. In other words, the background always stays static. That's called a *watermark,* and you can easily create one in FrontPage.

First, choose a background for your page. To do so, right-click the page, and then choose Page Properties. Click the Background tab, and turn on "Background picture." Click the Browse button to find a picture you want to use as your page background. To make the picture a watermark rather than a normal background, simply turn on Watermark and click OK.

Note: Watermarks don't work with all browsers, so not everyone who visits your Web site can see the background as a watermark. If someone visits your site with a browser that doesn't support watermarks, they'll see the background but it'll scroll along with the page.

5-22 Creating an Online Photo Gallery

If you have photos you'd like to share with the world (6,000 shots of your baby learning to eat his toes, say), an online photo gallery is a great option. But trying to arrange all those photos manually can be deadly. Instead, turn to FrontPage for easy, tidy picture galleries. Here's what to do:

1. **Put your insertion point at the spot on a page where you want to place a gallery, and then choose Insert → Web Component.**

   The Insert Web Component dialog box appears.

2. **Click Photo Gallery, and from the right-hand pane, choose the style of gallery you want to create.**

   You'll see a thumbnail view of what each style of gallery will look like, and a description of each.

3. **Click Finish.**

   FrontPage opens the Photo Gallery Properties page, which lets you place your pictures in the gallery.

4. **Click Add, and then choose Pictures from Files.**

   The File Open dialog box appears. Browse to the pictures you want to put into the gallery, and select them. (To choose more than one, hold down the Ctrl key while you select multiple pictures.) Then click Open, which takes you back to the Photo Galleries Properties page, where you can see a listing of all the photos you've chosen.

5. **Change the order of the photos by highlighting a photo and clicking the Move Up or Move Down button.**

   When you move a photo up, it moves closer to the front of the gallery. When you move it down, it moves closer to the end of the gallery.

6. **When you have everything arranged to your satisfaction, click OK.**

   After a few seconds, FrontPage imports your photos. You can still change the order of your photos. Just right-click the gallery, and then choose Photo Gallery Properties. The Photo Gallery Property page appears. Move the photos as described in the previous step. Once you're satisfied with your gallery, continue building your Web page as you would normally, and then post it online as you would normally.

The Internet

For many people, getting online is the main reason to have a computer these days. And in Windows XP, you surfers have a partner: The Internet has become so integrated with the operating system that it's often hard to tell where one begins and the other one ends.

This chapter gives you the skinny on the Internet and XP, with hints teaching you how to surf faster, keep yourself safe online, kill ubiquitous pop-up ads, and use instant messenger programs.

Note: Don't see what you're looking for here? Chapter 7 covers Web browsers, Chapter 8 gives you email tips, and Chapter 9 goes into detail on networking and WiFi.

Internet Speed Tricks

If you're like most folks, when you log on to the Internet, you're only interested in three speeds: fast, faster, and fastest. This section explains how to rev up even the slowest connection.

6-1 Faster Surfing I

Pictures are often worth a thousand seconds—or more. Many Web sites are full of logos, obnoxious banner ads, and other annoying graphics. You can surf faster by turning off the picture display—a particular boon to dial-uppers.

To tell Internet Explorer not to display graphics, choose Tools → Internet Options → Advanced. Scroll down to the Multimedia section, and turn off "Show pictures." An X now appears in place of each graphic you encounter while surfing. If you change your mind and want to display graphics again, simply return to this dialog box, and turn on "Show pictures."

ADD-IN ALERT

Managing Dial-Up Internet Access

If you have no plans to upgrade to cable or DSL, try letting DUN Manager brighten your dial-up existence. This program manages dial-up network connections by scheduling automated dial-up times, performing diagnostics on your connection, displaying a graph of your connection speed, or blocking connections at certain times—say, when your kids are supposed to be doing their homework. (£25 shareware [$45 based on the exchange rate at this writing]; *www.magsys.co.uk.*)

6-2   Faster Surfing II

Here's another easy-bake recipe for speedier surfing: set your browser to launch with a blank page rather than loading your home page each time you open up a new window.

To start Internet Explorer with a blank home page, choose Tools → Internet Options → General. The Internet Options dialog box, shown in Figure 6-1, appears. Click Use Blank and then OK. From now on, Internet Explorer starts with a blank slate.

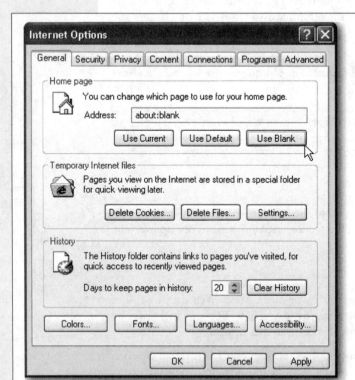

Figure 6-1:
When you start Internet Explorer, it goes immediately to the page listed in the Address box, which is called your home page. If you haven't chosen a home page yourself, Explorer may use a Microsoft site or the home page of the company that made your computer. To speed up your browsing, start with a blank page instead.

6-3   Caching Up

As you move around the Web, your browser *caches* the pages you visit, which means it saves them to a folder on your PC. Then, when you visit those Web pages again, your browser grabs the text and pictures from your PC's cache rather than the Web, so it doesn't have to repeatedly download the same information—the happy result of which is more efficient browsing.

Note: How can your browser tell what's new? It examines each element on the page, compares them to what's in your cache, and downloads only the ones that have changed.

The size of your cache is important. If your cache is too small, your browser can't save very many Web pages, and you lose the benefit of the system. But a big cache eats up a lot of disk space.

To optimize your cache setting for faster browsing in Internet Explorer, select Tools → Internet Options → General → Settings. The dialog box in Figure 6-2 appears, which lets you change the amount of disk space allocated to your Temporary Internet files folder (another name for your cache). If the amount is less than 2 MB, it's probably too small. Consider making it at least 5 MB, and possibly more if you have space to spare. To increase the cache, drag the slider to the right (drag it to the left if you want to decrease the file's size). Click OK twice.

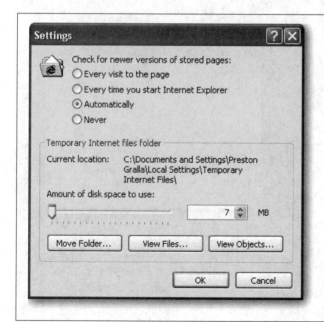

Figure 6-2:
You can speed up your Web browsing by allocating more space to your Temporary Internet files folder, also known as your cache. Depending on the size of your hard drive, you might want to let it save many tens of megabytes of data.

Note: For more tips on managing your cache, turn to page 186.

Reach Your Favorite Sites on the Double

A second may not *sound* like a long time, but it *feels* like a life sentence when you're waiting to reach a Web page. Here's how you can shave off a sliver of time.

Each time you visit a Web site, a complicated electronic transaction takes place between your computer and the site you're visiting. After you type in an address, such as *www. oreilly.com* (called a host name), the Internet translates those letters into corresponding numbers it can understand (for example, 208.201.239.37). This set of numbers is known as an *IP address* (for Internet protocol).

The Internet translates the words into numbers by using the *Domain Name System* (DNS), a network of servers that matches URLs (*www.oreilly.com*) to the corresponding IP address. In other words, when you type an address in your browser, your computer contacts a DNS server, and that server sends your browser the IP address—which your browser then uses to visit the site you're trying to get to. (The term geeks use for the process of matching a host name to its proper IP address is *resolution* or *name resolution*).

It takes time to send your request to a DNS server, wait for the server to look up the proper IP address, and then wait for it to send the IP address back to your PC. You can eliminate this delay and accelerate your browsing a bit by editing the *HOSTS file* on your PC (or creating one if you don't have one already). The HOSTS file contains host names and their corresponding IP addresses. When you're surfing, XP first looks at this file to see if it has an entry for the Web site you're trying to visit. If XP finds an entry, it resolves the address itself and passes it along to your browser, bypassing the DNS server and letting you reach your destination a split second faster. Which can feel significant.

Before you dive into your HOSTS file, you need the IP address of any site you want to jump to on the double. The simplest way to learn them is with XP's built-in *ping* utility, which sends a stream of data to a Web site. To use the ping utility, go to a command prompt (page 136) and type *ping sitename*—for example, *ping www.oreilly.com*—to get a response saying

something like *Pinging oreilly.com [208.201.239.37] with 32 bytes of data.* The number in brackets is the IP address. (For more information about *ping*, see page 143.)

Now you're ready for the HOSTS file, which is a plain text file you can create or edit with a text editor like Notepad. In most cases you can find an existing HOSTS file in My Computer → C: → Windows → System32 → Drivers → Etc → HOSTS. (The file has no extension at the end of its name—it's just called HOSTS.) If your Etc folder appears to be empty, in Notepad's Open file dialog box, try selecting "All Files" from the "Files of type" pop-up menu. If it's still not there, simply create a new file in the Etc folder and call it HOSTS.

Open HOSTS in Notepad and enter the IP addresses and host names of the Web sites you frequently visit, as shown here. You can have as few or as many entries in your HOSTS file as you like.

Put each Web site on its own line, with the IP address in the first column and the corresponding host name in the next column. At least one space should separate the two columns. When you're finished editing the file, save it to the same location.

If you later find you can't reach a Web site on your list, make sure the IP address is up to date. If it has changed, and your HOSTS file still has the old address, your browser won't be able to find the site.

6-4   Speeding Up Downloads

The Internet is full of tremendously useful files—like many of the programs rec-ommended throughout this book. But even if you have a fast Internet connection, downloads can take a sputteringly long time to transfer to your PC.

You can speed things up with a free program called Download Accelerator Plus, avail-able at *www.speedbit.com*. (Of course, you have to download it before you can use it.) The program, which works with most of the leading browsers, including Internet Explorer, Netscape, and Mozilla, takes over the duties of your browser's download manager (the utility that manages the files you download from the Internet).

When you download a file using Download Accelerator Plus, the program automat-ically connects to multiple sites and downloads pieces of the file simultaneously, sig-nificantly accelerating the process. (Because the program has been designed to work alongside your browser, you still download files the same way: by clicking links on Web pages.) You can also schedule Download Accelerator Plus to download files at specific times by right-clicking the file and choosing a download schedule (handy when you want a whopper of a file to transfer in the middle of the night).

UP TO SPEED

Understanding IP Addresses

Every location on the Internet, including your computer, has an IP address, a series of four numbers separated by dots, like this: 207.11.234.11. Web sites you visit, such as Yahoo! or *www.oreilly.com*, rarely change their IP addresses. The same doesn't hold true for personal com-puters, though.

Unless you request otherwise, most Internet service provid-ers (ISPs) assign you a new IP address each time you con-nect, known as a *dynamic* address. That's because ISPs don't

have enough IP addresses to assign one to every customer. Instead, ISPs have a pool of IP addresses they can assign customers whenever you connect—assuming that not all their customers try to hop online at the same time.

If you want to run a Web site from your own computer, you need a *static* IP address (i.e., one that doesn't change), so other computers can reliably find you. Many ISPs offer this service, though they may charge more for it.

Pop-Ups and Cookies

Pop-up windows—those pesky ads that "pop up" in front of Web sites every-where—are threatening to suck all the fun out of browsing the Web. Fortunately, you can employ some seriously effective pop-up exterminators to stamp them out. This section gives you a few options.

Cookies can also make waves as you surf. In the digital world, cookies are bits of data left on your hard disk by Web sites you visit, sometimes keeping track of pref-erences you've set up at a site, like your user name and password. But Webmasters can also use them to track your online activities in more Orwellian ways. This sec-tion explains how to manage cookies so they're under your control—not some-body else's.

6-5   Software that Stops Pop-Ups

For all its sophistication, Internet Explorer has no built-in way to stop pop-ups. Fortunately, you can download software to catch the ads before they spring. Here are two good, free choices.

EMS Free Surfer not only kills pop-ups, but it can also shut down every open Internet Explorer window with a single click, including your main browser window, and it includes an add-in tool that cleans your system cache as well as your list of recently visited sites. You can get EMS Free Surfer at *www.emsproject.com/ FS/Support.htm*.

Another option is the Google Toolbar, which adds a *very* handy Google search box to Internet Explorer. It includes an excellent pop-up killer. You can download the Toolbar from *http://toolbar.google.com*. For tips on installing and using it, see page 178.

6-6   Alternative Browsers that Stop Pop-Ups

Although Internet Explorer doesn't automatically delete pop-up ads, other Web browsers include built-in pop-up killers. Netscape, Opera, Mozilla, and Firefox are all good options. (Chapter 7 is all about alternative browsers.)

- **To use Opera's pop-up killer,** choose File → Preferences → "Refuse pop-up windows." Another choice you have in Opera is permitting pop-ups to open only in the background (behind your main browser window).

- **To tell Netscape to zap pop-ups,** select Edit → Preferences → Privacy & Security → Popup Windows, and choose "Block unrequested popup windows" (see Figure 6-3). Then click OK.

ADD-IN ALERT

Speeding Up Your Internet Connection

Windows XP has many settings you can tweak to speed up your Internet connection, but changing all these settings yourself can eat up more time than it saves. For a quicker fix, try one of the following software downloads. (Deciding which of these programs to use to quench your thirst for faster Internet is kind of like choosing between Coke and Pepsi—it's somewhat a matter of personal preference.)

Internet Turbo. This program offers a host of features for speeding up your connection, whether you use cable, DSL, or dial-up, by tweaking all kinds of hidden Registry and other settings. It can also prevent your Internet Service Provider (ISP) from disconnecting you every time your connection goes idle. ($19.95 shareware; *www.clasys.com.*)

.NETSpeedBoost. This program, similar to Internet Turbo, makes the most of your bandwidth by fine-tuning your connection settings. .NETSpeedBoost can also stop your ISP from disconnecting you, and includes a special utility that makes sure America Online doesn't sign you off. ($24.95 shareware; *www.appwalk.com.*)

Netscape also lets you accept pop-ups from selected sites, which is great if you often visit sites that have *legitimate* pop-ups, like forms you might need to fill out. From the screen shown in Figure 6-3, choose Allowed Sites and enter the address of any sites whose pop-ups you want to allow. (Some sites use pop-ups to ask your user name and password when you log in, for example; you may want to allow pop-ups on those sites.) Then click OK twice.

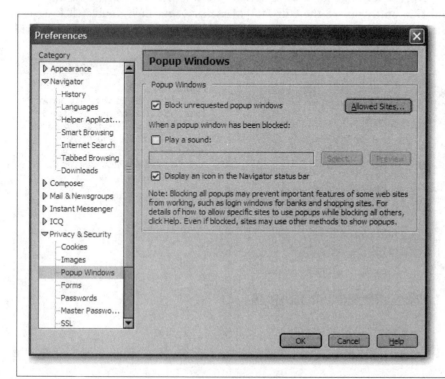

Figure 6-3:
You can instruct Netscape to play a sound every time it deletes one of these little pop-up critters. Check the box next to "Play a sound," and then browse to the sound you want to hear. The sounds are built into Netscape, but you can also use any sound that you have stored in a file on your hard drive.

- **To block pop-ups using Mozilla,** choose Edit → Preferences → Advanced → Scripts & Windows, and turn off "Open unrequested windows."

- **In Firefox,** go to Tools → Options, and click Web Features. At the top of that dialog box, make sure "Block Popup Windows" is turned on. Like Netscape, Firefox lets you accept pop-ups from some sites. In the Web Features dialog box, click Add Site, and in the little window that opens, type in the address you want to allow pop-ups for, then click OK.

6-7   Shooting the Windows Messenger

A new kind of obnoxious pop-up has emerged in the past year: ads that pop up even when you're not surfing the Web. These pop-ups use XP's Windows Messenger Service, which isn't related to the Windows Messenger instant messaging program. Instead, Windows Messenger Service was designed to send messages over a local area network. It lets a network administrator, for example, alert employees that a server will be down for maintenance. Hardly anyone uses it these days—except resourceful spammers.

Fortunately, it's easy to turn off. At the Run box or a command prompt, type *services.msc* and press Enter to run the Microsoft Management Console. (To get to the Run box, choose Start → Run. To get to the command prompt, choose Start → Run, type *command*, and press Enter.) In the console, scroll down on the right-hand side until you see the entry for Messenger, and then double-click it. The screen pictured in Figure 6-4 now appears. Next to "Startup type" select Disabled and then click OK.

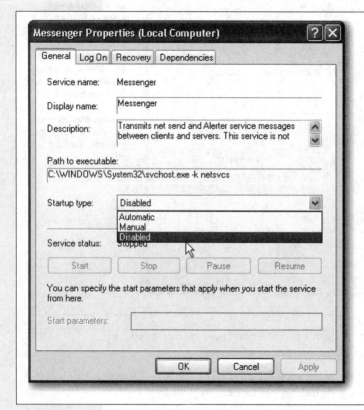

Figure 6-4:
Turn off the Windows Messenger Service by selecting Disabled from the "Startup type" menu. Early versions of Windows XP shipped with the Messenger Service automatically turned on, but in more recent versions of XP you may find it's already killed.

To reactivate the Windows Messenger Service, follow the same path and choose Automatic as the Startup type.

Tip: If you'd prefer to use downloadable software to turn off the Messenger service, there's a free program, called Shoot the Windows Messenger, available from Gibson Research at *http://grc.com/stm/ shootthemessenger.htm*. This program lets you turn the Windows Messenger on and off without having to navigate down into Windows' innards.

6-8   Crumbling Cookies

Because cookies can be used for both good and evil, Internet Explorer provides a way to block the ones you don't want to let in. In Internet Explorer choose Tools → Internet Options → Privacy; the screen in Figure 6-5 appears. To change how Internet Explorer handles cookies, move the slider between the various levels of privacy settings, from Accept All Cookies to Block All Cookies (see below to learn how to decode the levels). Click OK when you're done.

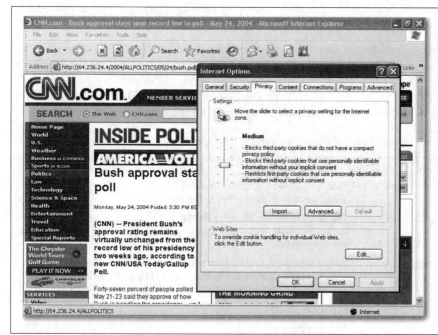

Figure 6-5:
The slider in this dialog box lets you choose from six levels of privacy settings to indicate how you want your browser to handle cookies. If you turn off all cookies, many Web sites may not function properly, so it's best to choose a less restrictive setting.

Internet Explorer's cookie settings can be difficult to decipher. You need to know both cookie jargon and what the various settings will do. Here's the jargon low down:

- **First-party cookie.** A cookie created by the site you're currently visiting. These cookies are often used by e-commerce sites like Amazon to let you log on without retyping your user name and password, or to let you customize how you use the site. First-party cookies don't usually invade your privacy and are generally considered safe.

- **Third-party cookie.** A cookie created by a site other than the one you're currently visiting. Advertisers or advertising networks often use these cookies to identify you and track your surfing activities. Thus, some people consider third-party cookies invasive.

- **Compact Privacy Statement.** A policy that describes how cookies are used on a site, such as explaining why and how they're used and how long they'll stay on your PC. (Some cookies are automatically deleted when you leave a Web site, while others are saved on your computer until a specified date.)

- **Implicit Consent vs. Explicit Consent.** Explicit consent means you've told a particular site it can use personally identifiable information about you. (This type of consent is sometimes referred to as *opting in* since you usually have to choose an option that says something like "Yes, please send me marketing fluffery.") Implicit consent means you haven't told a site *not to* use personally identifiable information, or that you haven't *opted out*. Sites that use an opt-out approach sneakily present you with an already filled in "Yes, please send me marketing fluffery" box, hoping you won't notice.

Table 6-1 gives you the inside dope on the cookie settings. When making your choice, keep in mind that some sites won't function well or at all at the higher privacy settings, particularly if you choose to reject all cookies. Medium High is a decent compromise between protecting your privacy and letting Web sites offer you some personalized features (like Amazon's book recommendations).

Table 6-1. *Internet Explorer's Cookie Settings and What They Mean*

Setting	How the Setting Affects Cookies
Block All Cookies	Blocks all cookies, without exception. Does not allow Web sites to read existing cookies.
High	Blocks cookies from all Web sites that don't have a compact privacy policy. Blocks all cookies that use personally identifiable information without your explicit consent.
Medium High	Blocks third-party cookies from sites that don't have a compact privacy policy—a policy that describes how cookies are used on the site. Blocks third-party cookies that use personally identifiable information without your explicit consent. Blocks first-party cookies that use personally identifiable information without your implicit consent.
Medium (Default)	Blocks third-party cookies from sites that don't have a compact privacy policy. Blocks third-party cookies that use personally identifiable information without your implicit consent. Accepts first-party cookies that use personally identifiable information without your implicit consent, but deletes them when you close Internet Explorer.
Low	Blocks third-party cookies from sites that don't have a compact privacy policy. Accepts third-party cookies that use personally identifiable information without your implicit consent, but deletes them when you close Internet Explorer.
Accept All Cookies	Accepts all cookies, without exception. Allows Web sites to read existing cookies.

When you surf along and Internet Explorer blocks a cookie, it displays a small cookie-blocking icon in the lower-right portion of the status bar (the section at the bottom of the Internet Explorer screen), as shown in Figure 6-6.

Note: Other browsers, such as Netscape, Mozilla, Opera, and Firefox, also let you control cookies. Look for Privacy settings.

6-9   Custom Cookie Settings

If you don't like the pre-set levels Internet Explorer uses to handle cookies, you can customize your browser to act the way you want. For example, you can tell Internet Explorer to reject all cookies except those from certain sites, reject cookies from specific sites you identify, or reject all first-party and third-party cookies. (For details about first-party and third-party cookies, see hint 6-8.)

Figure 6-6:
Gotcha! Whenever Internet Explorer blocks a cookie, it displays this icon in the lower-right portion of the status bar. Double-click it to see a list of all the cookies that have been blocked.

To accept or reject all cookies from a specific site, choose Tools → Internet Options → Privacy → Edit. The "Per Site Privacy Actions" dialog box appears, as shown in Figure 6-7. Type the name of the site you want to accept or block cookies from, and click either "Block" or "Allow." Now click OK.

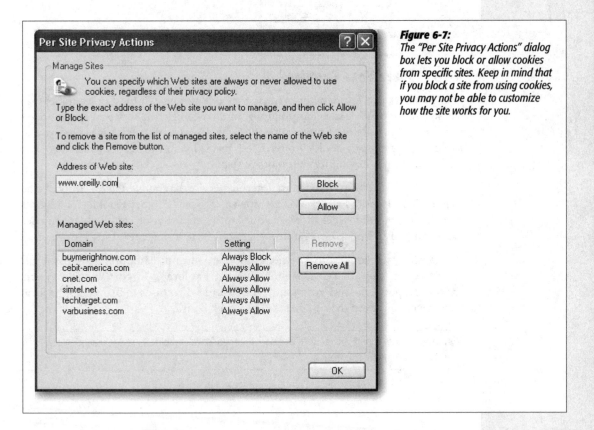

Figure 6-7:
The "Per Site Privacy Actions" dialog box lets you block or allow cookies from specific sites. Keep in mind that if you block a site from using cookies, you may not be able to customize how the site works for you.

To customize how you handle first-party and third-party cookies, choose Tools → Internet Options → Privacy → Advanced. Turn on the "Override automatic cookie handling" box, as shown in Figure 6-8. You can accept or reject all first-party or third-party cookies, or instruct Explorer to ask you whether to accept them (the "Prompt" option).

Figure 6-8:
The Advanced Privacy Settings dialog box lets you override how Internet Explorer handles cookies. You can also decide to allow "session cookies"–cookies that last only as long as you're on a specific Web site. These cookies are then deleted once you leave the site.

6-10 Share Your Cookies

While cookies can invade your privacy, they can also be helpful. For example, they can log you into Web sites automatically and customize the way you use and view some sites. So when you buy a new PC, why re-enter all the settings that you've saved in your existing cookie preferences? Instead, you can *export* your cookies to your new computer with just a few quick steps.

To export or back up cookies in Internet Explorer, choose File → Import and Export. The Import/Export Wizard opens. Choose "Export Cookies" and click Next. Browse to the folder or drive you want to export your cookies to, then click Next and Finish. The wizard exports your cookies to a single text file.

To transfer your cookies to another computer, you must import the file you just exported. On the other PC, launch Internet Explorer's Import/Export Wizard, choose "Import Cookies," and follow the wizard's directions to browse to the location where you saved the cookie file. Then click Finish.

Tip: You can also export your cookies and back them up for safekeeping in case you accidentally delete ones that contain useful information.

6-11　Examining and Deleting Cookies

If you have the time—and patience—you can examine every cookie on your system in order to decide which ones you want to delete. Since Internet Explorer stores each cookie as an individual text file, you can read and delete those text files like any other file on your PC.

To look inside your cookie jar, open Windows Explorer and go to My Computer → Documents and Settings → [Your Name] → Cookies. (Your Name refers here to your Windows XP account name.) XP displays a list of individual cookies in a format like this:

```
your name@abcnews.com[1].txt
```

Not every cookie file name follows this exact format, however. For instance, you may not see your name, and the Web site that created the cookie might not be identified either. Each cookie's creator typically appears after the @ sign, but sometimes only a number appears. If the Web site isn't identified in the file name, then opening the cookie file will sometimes reveal the site's name in the first line or two of the cookie. (Open it simply by double-clicking it in Windows Explorer.)

If you want to delete a cookie, delete it in Windows Explorer as you would any other file.

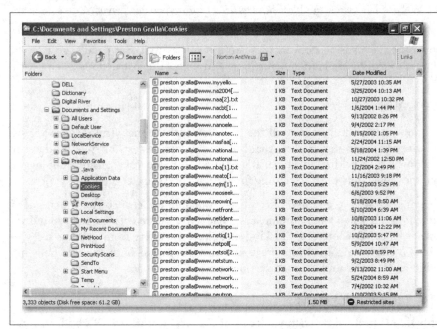

Figure 6-9:
When you open Windows Explorer and view your cookie list, you may be amazed at the number of cookies on your hard disk.

6-12   Managing Cookies with Add-On Software

If your cookie management needs are really complex, you may want to use a program specifically designed to deal with these morsels. Cookie Pal, available from Kookaburra Software (*www.kburra.com*), is one really good option.

Cookie Pal lets you easily identify the sites you want to accept cookies from, and also includes a cookie manager that lets you read and delete cookies. Furthermore, it lets you accept or reject cookies on a case-by-case basis as you browse the Web. Cookie Pal is shareware and free to try, but if you plan on using it continuously, it'll cost you $15.

6-13   Keeping Advertisers Away from Your Cookies

Online ad networks can build a comprehensive profile of all your Web travels and personal interests simply by placing a single cookie on your computer that tracks you across multiple sites. If that prospect troubles you, you can fight back by *opting out* of some of the biggest ad networks. (Opting out means declaring that you don't want them tracking your activities.) When you opt out, the network places a special cookie on your hard disk that tells various sites not to track what you're doing.

To opt out of the DoubleClick online advertising network—one of the biggest on the Web—visit *www.doubleclick.com/us/corporate/privacy/privacy/ad-cookie* and click the "Ad Cookie Opt-Out" button.

Some other advertising networks let you opt out as well. For details, go to *www. networkadvertising.org/optout_nonppii.asp* and follow the instructions listed.

Firewalls

No doubt you've heard about all the evils that lurk online: viruses that wipe out data on your computer, hackers that break into your system, or spyware that surreptitiously tracks what you type. It's enough to make you consider unplugging from the global network and settling for Solitaire on your PC.

A better option is to employ a firewall—a valuable piece of software that guards your computer when you're online. Essentially, firewalls erect a barrier around you while you surf the Internet, blocking malicious intruders from gaining access to your PC. Here are some hints on how to use firewalls—both the one built into Windows XP and a sophisticated version you can download.

6-14   A Basic Firewall

For basic PC protection when you're on the Internet, turn on XP's built-in Internet Connection Firewall (ICF). ICF provides nuts-and-bolts security by stopping any inbound Internet traffic you didn't request. In other words, if you want to visit a Web site, check email, or download a file, the firewall lets that data through; but if a hacker tries to sneak onto your system, the firewall makes like J-Lo's personal bodyguard and blocks the way.

Be forewarned that ICF has one very serious drawback: It doesn't protect you against *Trojans*, which are programs that let someone else take control of your PC. Using a Trojan, a hacker could copy your files or use your PC to launch attacks against other computers. (XP's built-in firewall can't stop Trojans since it only blocks *incoming* Internet traffic, and Trojans work by making *outbound* connections from your PC. To stop Trojans, you need to download a firewall like ZoneAlarm, page 146.)

Note: If several computers are sharing an Internet connection through a single PC, only the PC that directly accesses the Internet should run ICF. If you do run ICF on the other computers, you can cause connection problems that could block your Internet access or prevent your computers from communicating.

To turn on XP's built-in firewall:

1. **Right-click My Network Places and choose Properties.**

   You may have a My Network Places icon on your desktop, but if you don't, you can access it by opening Windows Explorer. My Network Places is near the bottom of the screen.

ADD-IN ALERT

Tracing and Monitoring Internet Traffic

If you want to find out what path your communications take when you connect to a Web site, or figure out where an email message actually came from, here are a few utilities that let you trace your electronic steps across the Internet (when you visit a site, you actually get there via a series a *routers*, devices that carry Internet traffic). Aside from impressing your geek friends at parties, you can use this info to figure out why Internet communication sometimes takes longer than snail mail.

VisualRoute. VisualRoute traces the path of data on a world map, so you can see the geographical journey your connection is making. It can also identify the geographical location of any Web site, telling you, for example, that your favorite Italian cooking site is actually based in Beijing. VisualRoute also includes a tool for troubleshooting email problems. ($50 shareware; *www.visualware.com.*)

NetScan Tools. This suite of tools includes a variety of enhanced Internet utilities for handling commands like Traceroute (which traces the path data takes over the Internet) and Ping (which checks whether an Internet server or Web site is up and running). It can also help you find the names of people who run any Web site. Best of all, NetScan Tools lets you accomplish all this by clicking friendly icons. ($25 shareware; at *www.netscantools.com.*)

Internet Toolbox. This program lives up to its name—it provides a full kit of network tools. Besides Traceroute, Ping, and similar utilities (described above), Internet Toolbox also has a feature called Connections Watcher, which lets you see who has connected to your computer (either from the Internet or a local network), and what machines you're connected to on the Internet. Other network monitoring tools include Host Monitor, which maintains a log of which machines and servers on your network are working (or not). ($24.95 shareware; *www.idylesoftware.com.*)

2. In the Network Connections folder that appears, right-click the Internet connection you want to protect with XP's firewall and then choose Properties → Advanced.

If you use more than one Internet connection, you need to set up a firewall for each of them.

3. In the Advanced tab of the dialog box shown in Figure 6-10, turn on "Protect my computer and network by limiting or preventing access to this computer from the Internet." Click OK.

That's it. The firewall is now at its post protecting your PC.

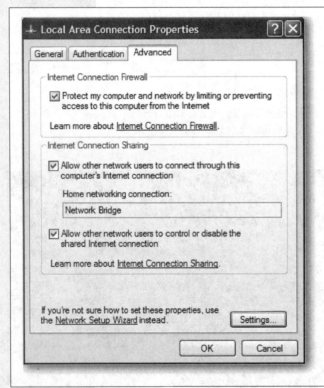

Figure 6-10:
Activate XP's built-in Internet connection firewall by checking the top choice in this dialog box. The firewall stops unsolicited Internet traffic from getting through to your PC.

6-15   How to Bypass XP's Firewall

If you want to run a Web or email server and also use XP's Internet Connection Firewall, you need to tweak some settings because ICF doesn't automatically allow inbound Internet traffic to reach those servers.

Thankfully, there's a way to bypass the firewall and let your Web or email server do their work, while still blocking other kinds of inbound Internet traffic. The solution is fairly straightforward: You can tell ICF to allow only specific types of traffic, such as a Web server, email server, or FTP server. Meanwhile, all unwanted traffic remains blocked from reaching your PC.

To trigger this feature, right-click My Network Places, and choose Properties. Then right-click your Internet connection and choose Properties → Advanced → Services. (Make sure the connection already uses XP's firewall, as described in the previous hint.) The Advanced Settings dialog box, shown in Figure 6-11, appears. Select the services you want and click OK.

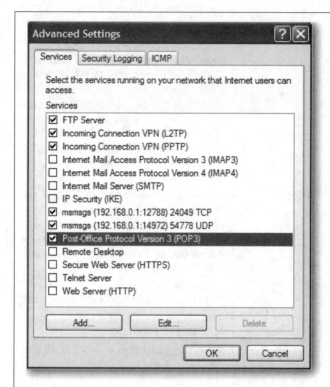

Figure 6-11:
You can allow specific services and traffic to bypass the firewall using this dialog box; just select the ones you want to grant the right of way. For maximum, the-Pope-is-coming-to-your-town security, only allow those services you absolutely need (see Table 6-2 for advice).

Table 6-2 lists the services you can let bypass the firewall, and describes what each service does. Note that "msmsgs"—which refers to Windows Messenger—may or may not appear in the dialog box. If you've used Windows Messenger or Outlook Express (which uses some Messenger components), it should appear. Unlike all the other services listed, Windows Messenger is turned on by Microsoft. All the others are turned off until you decide to turn them on.

Table 6-2. *Services that Can Bypass the Firewall*

Service	What it Does
FTP Server	Allows others to connect to an FTP server on your PC.
Incoming Connection VPN (L2TP)	Allows access to a Virtual Private Network (VPN) using the L2TP tunneling technology. A VPN is a secure way of connecting to a network over the Internet. L2TP is a specific security technology for VPNs.

Table 6-2. Services that Can Bypass the Firewall (continued)

Service	What it Does
Incoming Connection VPN (PPTP)	Allows access to a Virtual Private Network using the PPTP tunneling technology.
Internet Mail Access Protocol Version 3 (IMAP3)	Allows others to connect to an IMAP3 email server on your PC to retrieve email.
Internet Mail Access Protocol Version 4 (IMAP4)	Allows others to connect to an IMAP4 email server on your PC to retrieve email.
Internet Mail Server (SMTP)	Allows others to use a Simple Mail Transfer Protocol (SMTP) server on your PC to send email.
IP Security (IKE)	Allows use of the Internet Key Exchange security technology. Only turn this on if you use software that specifically requires it.
msmsgs	Allows use of Windows Messenger, plus any software that uses its components, such as Outlook Express.
Post-Office Protocol Version 3 (POP3)	Allows others to connect to a POP3 email server on your PC to retrieve email.
Remote Desktop	Allows others to connect to your PC and take control of your desktop using XP Professional's Remote Desktop feature. (This is only available in XP's Professional edition.)
Secure Web Server (HTTPS)	Allows others to connect to a Web server on your PC that uses the HTTPS security protocol.
Telnet Server	Allows others to use a Telnet server on your PC to use your PC's resources.
Web Server (HTTP)	Allows others to connect to a Web server on your PC.

You can allow any service to bypass XP's firewall, not just the ones that first appear on ICF's Services list. To add a new service to the list, click the Add button on the screen shown in Figure 6-11. Enter the name of the service you want to bypass the firewall, the IP address of the PC on your network that hosts that service, and the port number the service uses. If you're not sure what ports the service requires, you can find a complete list of port numbers and what they're used for at *www.iana.org/assignments/port-numbers*. For more information about ports, jump to page 148.

6-16   A Better Firewall: ZoneAlarm

XP's built-in firewall has one very serious deficiency: It can't monitor and block outbound traffic from your PC to the Internet. And since Trojans do their damage by installing themselves on your system and allowing others to take control of your PC, XP's firewall doesn't protect you against these surreptitious invaders.

However, there is a firewall that blocks Trojans: ZoneAlarm. Available from ZoneLabs (*www.zonealarm.com*), this firewall comes in three delicious flavors: a free version and two for-pay versions with different levels of protection.

- **ZoneAlarm,** the free version, offers excellent protection against inbound threats, stopping Trojans and alerting you when someone is probing your computer. It also provides specific information about the intruder.

- **ZoneAlarm Plus** also protects you against email-borne worms and viruses, and offers far superior intruder tracking and reporting. Cost: $39.95.

- **ZoneAlarm Pro** does everything its brothers do, plus it gives you control over cookies, stops pop-up ads, and controls rogue ActiveX Controls and JavaScript applets. Cost: $49.95.

At a minimum, try ZoneAlarm. But if you really want more control in protecting your PC from would-be attackers, it's worth paying for one of the more robust versions. Figure 6-12 displays a record of activity that ZoneAlarm Pro has monitored and blocked.

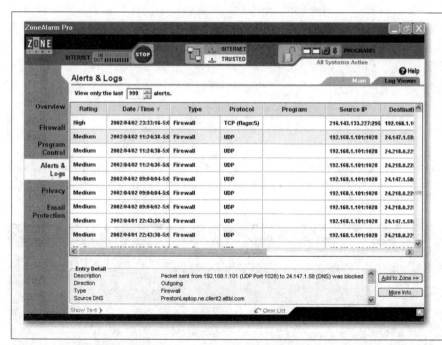

Figure 6-12:
Besides keeping your PC safe by blocking certain kinds of Internet traffic, ZoneAlarm Pro also keeps a log of potential intruders and of all activity between the Internet and your PC.

6-17   Testing Your Security with Shield's Up

Do you *really* know how secure your PC is? Probably not. But there's a free online tool that probes your PC for online security vulnerabilities: Shield's Up. Offered by the Gibson Research Corporation, Shield's Up tests your computer to see if it can make connections to some of the most well-known and exposed elements of your PC.

To test your computer using Shield's Up, go to *www.grc.com* and click the Shield's Up link. Once the site runs its tests, it shows you the results and explains what the reports mean—where you're vulnerable (see the box below), and how serious those vulnerabilities are. Figure 6-13 shows the results of probing one particularly well-guarded machine.

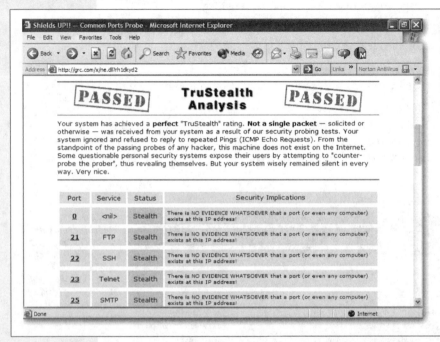

Figure 6-13:
Shield's Up reports that this PC is operating in "stealth mode," meaning it's not vulnerable to most Internet-based attacks.

Gibson Research Corporation's Web site also has lots of useful information about Internet security, as well as free and for-pay software you can download to help block your Internet ports.

UP TO SPEED

Vulnerable Areas: NetBIOS and Internet Ports

Your PC has a couple of areas that are particularly tempting to hackers: the NetBIOS and the Internet ports. While security software ought to help you protect these things, you'll be better prepared to deploy protection if you understand what you're guarding.

Your PC's NetBIOS (Network Basic Input/Output System) is software that allows your computer to work with other computers on a network. Needless to say, it's important to guard your NetBIOS from unauthorized visitors. If someone did reach the NetBIOS, they would have crucial access to many areas of your PC, including your programs and files.

Internet ports aren't physical objects; they're virtual connections your computer uses to send and receive data over the Internet. Different Internet services use different ports. For example, you use port 80 to communicate with Web servers when you surf the Web. And the infamous Back Orifice Trojan, which can give malicious hackers complete control over your PC, uses a variety of ports, including 31337 and 31338.

Tip: Once you've seen your vulnerabilities, install a firewall and do another round of tests to see if the firewall makes a difference.

Online Safety You May Not Have Considered

Installing a firewall and controlling your cookies are smart ways to protect yourself when you're online, but they're not the only security measures you should consider. This section gives you several additional strategies for safeguarding your computer and your personal information as you surf the Web.

6-18   Controlling Your Internet Security Levels

In the real world, it's usually obvious which are the seedier, more dangerous parts of town. But that isn't always true on the Web. An attractive, respectable-looking home page may actually be disguising a site intent on harm.

To help protect you from potential menaces, Internet Explorer categorizes Web sites and other places you may visit online (for example, an intranet) and places them into a handful of different *security zones,* each of which applies different levels of protection to your computer. The four security zone levels are as follows:

  • **Internet** (medium security)

  • **Local Intranet** (medium-low security)

  • **Trusted Sites** (low security)

  • **Restricted Sites** (high security)

Table 6-3 explains which security settings are applied for each zone. Any sites on your company's network or intranet are automatically added to the Local Intranet zone. All other Web sites are automatically added to the Internet zone. You can move sites from the Internet zone to the Trusted Sites or Restricted Sites zones manually. For example, if you know from experience that you can unequivocally trust *www.catster.com*, go ahead and put it in the Trusted Sites zone.

To assign a Web site to a particular zone, open Internet Explorer and choose Tools → Internet Options → Security. The Internet Options screen appears; Figure 6-14 tells you how to use it.

Table 6-3. Internet Explorer's Security Settings

Security Zone Level	How the Setting Affects Security
High	Disables many of Explorer's features, including ActiveX controls, Java and Java applets, and downloads.
Medium	Asks whether you want to run an ActiveX control before running signed ActiveX controls; disables unsigned ActiveX controls and certain other ActiveX controls; enables downloads and Java applets; prompts before downloading potentially unsafe content. (Note: Unsigned ActiveX Controls are those that have not been digitally "signed" by a site, so you can't know for certain who created the control.)

Table 6-3. *Internet Explorer's Security Settings (continued)*

Security Zone Level	How the Setting Affects Security
Medium-Low	Most settings are the same as Medium, except Medium-Low runs certain content such as ActiveX controls without first displaying a message asking your permission.
Low	Runs all content, such as ActiveX controls; offers the minimum number of safeguards and prompts, so, for example, you won't be asked whether you want to run an ActiveX control.

Note: *Java applets* and *ActiveX controls* are two kinds of programs that you can download to your PC and run inside your Web browser. They're frequently used to add interactivity to Web sites and are usually safe, but sometimes they're programmed to do your computer harm.

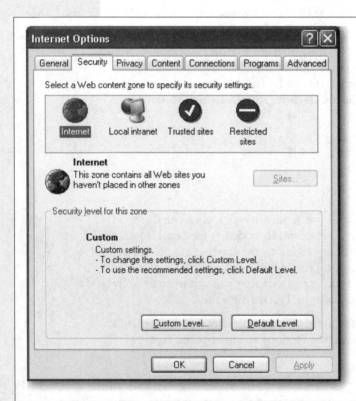

Figure 6-14:
Use this screen to assign Web sites to different security zones. For example, to assign a Web site to the "Trusted sites" zone, select "Trusted sites" and then click the Sites button. Enter the Web site's address in the dialog box that launches.

Adjusting the security level of each zone

If you're not happy with the security level that Microsoft has assigned to a particular zone, you can pick a different level. To change a zone's security level, open Explorer and choose Tools → Internet Options → Security. Click the zone whose security setting you want to change and then select Default Level. A dialog box appears; move the slider to the security level you want that zone to have, and click OK.

For even greater control, Internet Explorer lets you customize the settings *within* each security level. For example, you can enable Java applets in the High setting, or disallow ActiveX Controls in the Low setting. To customize the settings for any level, choose Tools → Internet Options → Security. Click to select a zone, and then click Custom Level. In the Security Settings dialog box that appears, you can enable, disable, or customize up to two dozen security settings for that level.

6-19   Beware of AutoComplete

Internet Explorer's AutoComplete can be a great time-saver. It remembers things like Web sites you've visited, passwords and user names you've entered, and your shipping address, and then it recalls that information the next time you start entering the same data. For example, AutoComplete might automatically fill in the rest of a form once you've entered your first name or even prompt you with a list of words it knows will be helpful to you.

AutoComplete's convenience does, however, come with some privacy and security downsides. Namely, anyone using your computer can easily gain access to things like password-protected Web sites because AutoComplete can automatically input user name and password information.

To protect your privacy, you can turn off AutoComplete altogether, or you can use it to remember only certain information. For example, you can tell it *not* to remember passwords. To make these changes, open Internet Explorer and choose Tools → Internet Options → Content → AutoComplete. The AutoComplete Settings dialog box appears (Figure 6-15).

Figure 6-15:
The AutoComplete Settings dialog box lets you decide which items AutoComplete should remember, and which it should forget. For absolute safety, turn off all boxes, which means it won't remember anything. Of course, this now means you have to remember all the information you're telling Internet Explorer to forget.

Turn on the items you want AutoComplete to keep track of, and turn off the settings you'd prefer it didn't remember. Your passwords are the most sensitive information AutoComplete remembers, so you should strongly consider turning this option off.

To delete all the entries AutoComplete already has in its database, click Clear Forms to delete all forms-based information, such as your name and address. Then click Clear Passwords to delete your passwords.

Note: AutoComplete works in conjunction with Windows XP's user accounts feature—in which information is kept separate for each person who uses your PC. So, for example, if you've logged out of your XP account and your sister is logged in, she won't be able to use your AutoComplete information—and vice versa. Therefore, another way to protect yourself, even while using all of AutoComplete's functions, is to log out of XP whenever you're not at your PC.

6-20   Don't Let the Web Bugs Bite

Web bugs are invisible bits of data (sometimes called *clear GIFs*) that follow you around on a Web site and track what you do. Unfortunately, they're surprisingly common.

You can avoid these spies by using a free program called Bugnosis, which identifies Web bugs on any site you visit, and alerts you whenever you encounter one. It doesn't, however, possess the ability to eliminate the bug. But, hey, at least you'll know *when* you're being bugged, so you can leave the site before you're spied on.

To download Bugnosis, visit *www.bugnosis.org*. After you install the program, a small "bug" image appears whenever you visit a site that has a Web bug.

6-21   Protecting Yourself Against Spyware

Spyware is software that watches your Internet activity without telling you, and reports back to an ad server about where you've been and what you've done. It frequently piggybacks on other free programs, such as the file-sharing software Kazaa. Companies then use the information they've gleaned about you to deliver advertising to your PC, frequently through the free program you downloaded. Even when you delete the program the spyware piggybacked on, the snooping software may still remain on your PC, watching your every step. It may also continue to deliver ads to you whenever you're online.

Some spyware's even more intrusive, doing things like changing your browser's home page without telling you or redirecting you to a competitor's site when you're about to make a purchase. Fortunately, you can eliminate spyware with a program called AdAware.

AdAware is a free anti-spyware program available from Lavasoft at *www.lavasoft-usa.com*. It scans your PC for spyware, gives you a report on what it finds, and offers to delete any of the spyware it uncovered. As a safety precaution, AdAware backs up everything you delete through it, so if you ever nix something you later need, you can easily restore the copy—and your sanity. Figure 6-16 shows AdAware in action.

Note: When deleting spyware, you may also disable software you still want to use. For example, if you find and remove the Cydoor spyware program from your PC, Kazaa's file-sharing stops working. So consider creating a Restore point before deleting any spyware, in case you change your mind. (See page 303 for the scoop on Restore points.)

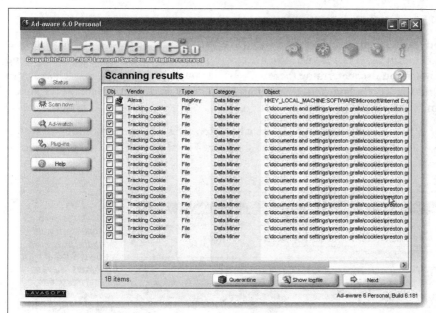

Figure 6-16:
AdAware lets you review each piece of potential spyware it finds before it deletes anything. It also keeps backups of the spyware it deletes, so you can restore any file that you might decide you want. For good measure, you can also delete those backups.

6-22 Protecting a Public Wireless Connection

If you wirelessly connect your laptop to a *hotspot* at a coffee shop, airport, hotel, or similar public location, you face a serious security risk. (A hotspot is a public location that offers *WiFi* access to the Internet; WiFi is just a fancy term for wireless Internet access.)

Typically, hotspots offer virtually no security. That means other people using the same hotspot can easily snoop on your Internet activity, possibly stealing your passwords as you type them. What's more, others can even gain access to your computer if you have file sharing turned on.

To keep yourself secure, it's a good idea to use a *Virtual Private Network* (VPN) specifically designed for hotspots. A VPN is a piece of software that lets you make secure connections over the Internet by encrypting your data. VPNs are most commonly used by businesses with employees who are not all in the same location. But they're useful—and advisable—for hotspots, too. (For more on VPNs, see pages 145–146.)

If you're surfing the public airwaves, HotSpotVPN, available at *www.hotspotvpn.com,* is an excellent option. It's simple to set up and use, and costs only $8.88 a month. To use it, simply go to the Web site, sign up, and follow the instructions. The service runs over the Internet, so you don't need to download any software to use it.

Note: For information about how to find and connect to hotspots, see page 238.

6-23   Surfing Anonymously

You might be surprised learn how much a Web site can glean about you each time you stop in for a quick visit. Web sites can figure out what operating system and browser you use, determine the last Web site you visited, grab the contents of your Windows XP clipboard, decipher your IP address, and in many cases even determine your general geographic location.

For a better understanding of just what Web sites can unearth about you, visit *www.anonymizer.com/privacytest*, as shown in Figure 6-17. The site's privacy test is a real eye-opener.

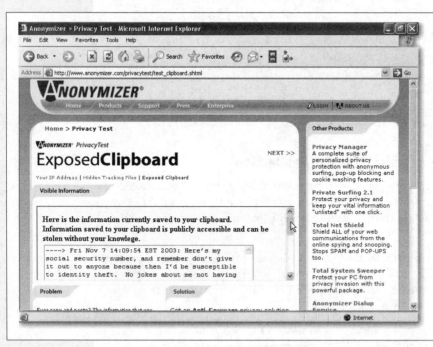

Figure 6-17:
Any Web site can grab the contents of your clipboard, as you can see here. But that's just for starters. They can find out much more as well, such as your geographic location and the Web site you previously visited.

The best way to ensure that Web sites can't gather personal information about you and your computer is to surf anonymously—by using an *anonymous proxy server,* which acts as a kind of cloak by sitting between you and the Web sites you visit. When you use an anonymous proxy server, your browser doesn't contact any Web sites directly; instead, it tells the proxy server which sites you want to visit. The proxy server then contacts the Web site, accesses the page you want, and displays it for you. Sites you're viewing don't get any information about you because the proxy server—not the Web site itself—delivers the pages to you.

Note: When you use anonymous proxies, your surfing will be slower than usual. Still, many security experts believe the trade-off in speed is worthwhile.

Several Web sites provide this service for free, including Anonymizer (*www. anonymizer.com*), the Cloak (*www.the-cloak.com*) and Surfola (*www.surfola.com*). Some charge extra fees if you want other services, such as blocking pop-up ads or deleting cookies.

Tip: Many shareware programs let you surf the Web with anonymity. See the box on page 166.

Evaluating and Troubleshooting

There's nothing more maddening than not being able to connect to the Internet when you absolutely, positively *have* to check your email or pay a quick visit to *mary-kateandashley.com* for some quick fashion advice. Fortunately, unless a backhoe has cut through an Internet backbone or a major power outage has left half the country in the dark, there are usually ways you to troubleshoot virtually every Internet connection problem. This section offers a few hints on what to do and how to fix minor glitches when the Internet misbehaves. (For more help and shareware options, see the box on page 143.)

6-24   Peering into Your Internet Connection

Here's how to discover everything you ever wanted to know about your current Internet connection: open the Local Area Connection Status box. It reveals your IP address, how long you've been connected, how much data you've sent and received, and a whole lot more. This information is vital when troubleshooting a connection problem, or when communicating with technical support.

To access this box, right-click My Network Places (either on the desktop or from the Start menu) and choose Properties to open the Network Connections folder. If you double-click the connection you want to investigate, the Local Area Connection Status box appears, as shown in Figure 6-18.

Click the Support tab for even more details about your connection, such as your IP address. If you click the Details button, you can find other goodies, like your network adapter's *MAC address,* which is usually labeled Physical Address. (A MAC address is not an Apple thing. It's actually a number that uniquely identifies a network adapter; MAC stands for Media Access Control.) You might need the MAC address because many cable companies ask for it to establish your Internet connection.

Even more useful than just getting details about your connection is a simple, one-step solution built into Windows XP that often solves Internet woes such as not being able to send and receive email or browse the Web. It's the mighty Repair button, and it works by resetting a few key connection settings (including your IP address). To use this button, go to the Network Connections folder by right-clicking My Network Places and choosing Properties. Then right-click the connection that's broken, and choose Repair. Frequently, XP can solve the problem and you're good to go.

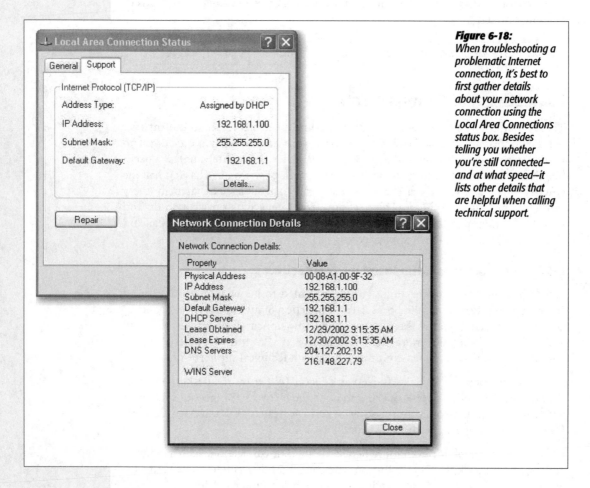

Figure 6-18:
When troubleshooting a problematic Internet connection, it's best to first gather details about your network connection using the Local Area Connections status box. Besides telling you whether you're still connected—and at what speed—it lists other details that are helpful when calling technical support.

6-25 Your Real Internet Connection Speed

No matter what speed your ISP promises, your *actual* connection speed is almost always lower—regardless of whether you use dial-up, cable, or DSL to connect to the Internet.

You can test your true current Internet connection speed at the Bandwidth Place Web site (*http://bandwidthplace.com/speedtest*), which is pictured in Figure 6-19. The evaluation is instantaneous. To run it, click through "Start a personal test."

Note: Many things can affect your Internet speed. For example, if you use a cable modem, and many people in your neighborhood are also online, the heavy traffic can slow you down.

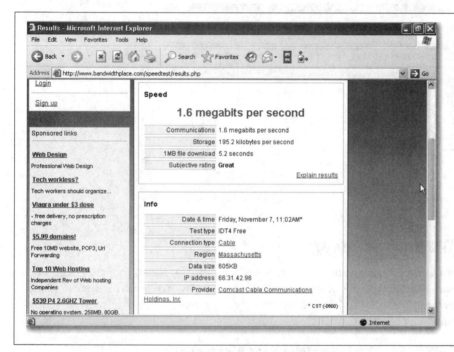

Figure 6-19:
To get a true sense of your connection speed, try the test several different times during the day, as speeds can vary from moment to moment.

Tip: For shareware that can help manage and speed up your Internet connection, see the box on page 134.

6-26 Diagnosing a Broken Internet Connection

Here's something you can try if your Internet connection seems to be dead and you're waiting on hold for your ISP's tech-support: Windows XP's built-in network diagnostics tool tests basic settings and network functionality, then diligently reports on what it finds (which can often be helpful information for the ISP's tech people once you finally reach them).

To use the diagnostics tool, choose Start → Help and Support → "Networking and the Web" → "Fixing Networking or Web Problems" → "Diagnose network configuration and run automated networking tasks." Next, click "Scan your system." After several minutes, the diagnostics tool produces a report like the one pictured in Figure 6-20.

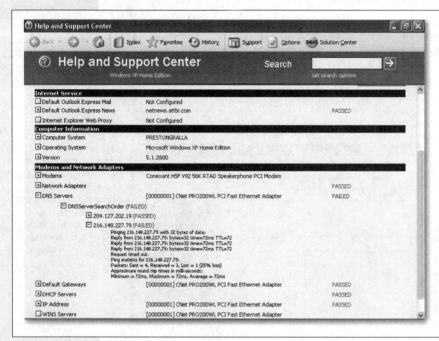

Figure 6-20:
The network diagnostics tool scans your system and reports on any network problems it finds. It's good information to have when you call tech support for help.

Windows Messenger

Instant messaging is the new email: it's a trendy but useful tool that lets you chat with other people instantly. Windows XP boasts its own built-in instant messaging program called Windows Messenger. Here are hints on how to make the most of this cool program.

6-27 Are You Using Windows Messenger or MSN Messenger?

Windows Messenger and MSN Messenger are both instant messaging programs from Microsoft. They look alike and work similarly, but they're not the same program. The main difference: Windows Messenger is built into Windows XP (you can run it by choosing Start → All Programs → Windows Messenger) and MSN Messenger isn't (you have to download it from the Microsoft Network at *www.msn.com*).

How can you tell which messenger program you're using? There's an easy way to find out: Open the program and click Help. "About Windows Messenger" appears if you're using Windows Messenger, and "About MSN Messenger" appears if you're using MSN Messenger. There are, of course, other instant messaging programs you can use, such as AOL Instant Messenger and Yahoo! Messenger, but those aren't built into XP.

Note: Windows Messenger and MSN Messenger are not related to XP's Windows Messenger Service, which you can use to send and receive messages on a local area network. (For example, a network administrator might need to send a note to everyone on the network, warning that a printer is not working). One drawback of the Windows Messenger Service is that it's sometimes used to send spam. For advice on stopping this pesky intrusion, see page 135.

6-28   Protecting Your Privacy in Windows Messenger

When using Windows Messenger, you sacrifice some privacy in exchange for instantaneous communications. For example, when Windows Messenger is up and running, other folks using Windows Messenger can usually see when you're online. Plus, people can easily view personal information about you, such as your name and phone number, that you provide when you first start using Windows Messenger. As a counter measure, you can customize Messenger to protect your privacy.

Blocking others from knowing you're online

When you log on to Windows Messenger, anyone who's put you on her Windows Messenger contact list receives a notification that you're online. Fortunately, there's a way to prevent messenger buddies from knowing you've logged on. Open Windows Messenger and choose Tools → Options → Privacy to bring up the screen shown in Figure 6-21.

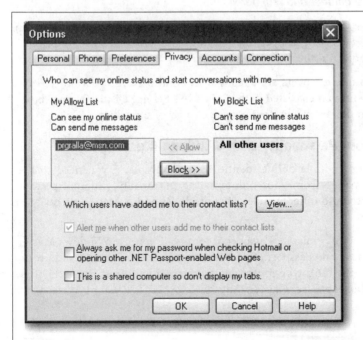

Figure 6-21:
If you don't want certain people to know when you're online, add them to your Block List. Keep in mind, though, that anyone you block won't be able to send you instant messages. (You can still send them messages, however.)

The Allow list on the left lists all of your contacts, while the Block list on the right lists those you want to hide your presence from. To add someone to the Block list, highlight that person's address on the left and click Block. (Someone must be listed as a contact before you can block him, but that person can't tell that you've blocked him out.) You can also block everyone *except* your contacts by choosing "All other users" in the Allow list, and then clicking Block.

Protecting your password

Messenger can automatically sign you into *.NET Passport* Web sites, such as Hotmail. This may be convenient, but it also means that anyone using your computer can check your email or gather other personal information from other Passport-enabled sites.

Note: .NET Passport is a Microsoft technology developed to let you sign on to a multitude of Web sites or services without entering your user name and password for each one separately. Once you sign up for a .NET Passport (which happens when you first use Windows Messenger, or sign up for a Web site such as HotMail), each time you log into one Passport service, you're automatically logged into other Passport services. (By the way, people pronounce this technology "dot Net.")

To ensure that no one uses your account to automatically log into Passport-enabled Web sites, open Windows Messenger and choose Tools → Options → Privacy. Then turn on the option that says, "Always ask me for my password when checking Hotmail or opening other .NET Passport-enabled Web pages."

Hiding your phone number and real name

To check whether you're unintentionally sharing your phone number and name by using Windows Messenger, open the program and choose Tools → Options → Phone. If your phone number is listed there, you may want to delete it.

To make sure no one discovers your real name, choose Tools → Options → Personal, and see if your name is listed in the "My .NET Service Display Name" box. If it is—and you'd rather be incognito—choose an alias of some kind.

6-29   Split Your Personality with Windows Messenger

Some people want multiple online identities. For example, if you need to keep your work life separate from your online dating personality, different accounts help you show the world different sides of yourself. Windows Messenger easily lets you set a few yous.

First you need to set up separate Passport accounts. If you use Windows Messenger, you already have one Passport. To create another one, at a command prompt or the Run box (page 136), type *control userpasswords2* and press Enter. The User Account dialog box appears. Choose Advanced → .NET Passport Wizard, and follow the directions to create a Passport. Create as many as you want; each Passport can have a different identity (for instance, a different address and name).

To switch to a different Passport identity, log out of Messenger by choosing File → Sign Out. Then log in again by selecting "To sign in with a different account, click here." The sign-in screen shown in Figure 6-22 appears. Choose a different Passport account to sign in with that identity.

Figure 6-22:
Choose which identity you want by selecting an email address from the drop-down list. If you'd like to sign in to Passport automatically when you use that account, select "Sign me in automatically."

6-30   Yes, You Can Skin Messenger

For fans of "skinning"—techie jargon for changing a program's look and feel—Messenger offers you one way to alter its appearance: Change the background graphic it uses.

To choose a different graphic, first go to My Computer → C: → Program Files → Messenger and rename the current graphic file (lvback.gif) with a new name (like oldlvback.gif). Then create or find the image you want to use as Messenger's background graphic. (If you're creating it, make sure it's in .gif format and make it 160 pixels wide by 140 pixels high.) Name it lvback.gif and copy it to My Computer → C: → Program Files → Messenger.

Now the next time you open Messenger, your new background graphic will be there to greet you. To return to the original graphic, delete the file you created, and rename the old file (oldlvback.gif or whatever you called it) lvback.gif.

6-31   Turning Off Messenger's Tabs

Messenger launches with several tabs on the left-hand side, which take up a lot of space. To turn off the tabs, choose Tools → Options → Privacy and select "This is a shared computer, so don't display my tabs." Then click OK.

6-32   Save a Messaging Session to a Text File

Windows Messenger doesn't automatically keep copies of your instant messaging conversations, which is why some people prefer an IM chat to the recorded volleying of an email exchange. But if you suddenly decide you're in the midst of an instant messaging session that you can't bear to see disappear, there is a way to save it to a text file.

At any point while you're messaging with someone, choose File → Save to save the entire conversation as a text file—even the part before you decided to save. On the downside, you can't save conversations that have already ended.

Note: You can't tell whether your chat partner has saved a conversation, so if you *want* the record to disappear, use ESP instead of IM.

6-33   Windows Messenger Add-Ons

Luckily, you don't have to use Windows Messenger strictly the way Microsoft shipped it. To enhance its capabilities, you can easily download a variety of cool add-ons. One option, Global Incognito Chat, lets you encrypt your messages so no one can snoop in on them. This user-friendly add-on is available for free at *www.globalincognito.com*.

Another program, BlastIM, adds a number of time-saving features, including broadcasting messages to multiple contacts, and forwarding conversations to other Windows Messenger users. It's shareware and free to try out, but if you decide to keep it, you're expected to pay $20. Get it from PowerHouse Programming at *www.powerhouseprogramming.com/blastim.html*.

Other Instant Messengers

Windows Messenger is just one of the many free instant messaging programs out there. This section tells you where to get the others and how to use them.

6-34   Downloading Other Instant Messengers

Windows Messenger suffers from the same problem as its competitors: You can pretty much only use it to communicate with other people who use the same instant messenger program (Windows Messenger does also let you chat with folks who use MSN Messenger). To communicate with the broadest range of people, one option is to download multiple instant messengers. You can run several IM programs simultaneously without worrying about technical conflicts. These are the ones with the biggest audiences; the last one runs across *all* the messenger programs:

- **AOL Instant Messenger (AIM).** Using AIM, you can communicate with America Online subscribers, as well as anyone who uses the standalone AOL

Instant Messenger. There are more people who use AIM than any other instant messenger, and it works pretty much the same way as Windows Messenger. (AIM also lets you chat with any Apple-loving friends who use iChat.) Get AIM at *www.aol.com*.

- **Yahoo! Instant Messenger.** This popular instant messenger, which works similarly to Windows Messenger, is run by Yahoo!. Get it at *www.yahoo.com*.

- **ICQ.** This instant messenger is particularly popular internationally. It offers a wider range of features than other instant messengers, but tends to be more confusing to use (for tips, see page 165). You can download ICQ at *www.icq.com*.

- **Trillian.** Another way to keep in touch with friends who use a different instant messaging program is by using a program called Trillian, which can communicate with ICQ, Windows Messenger, Yahoo! Messenger, and AOL Instant Messenger, making it the best choice for people with contacts on many systems.

You don't need to run the other programs—just Trillian, which is shown in Figure 6-23. In fact, you don't even need to have the other instant messenger programs; Trillian does all the communicating for you. It has most of the features the other programs offer and displays a buddy list identifying which contacts use each of the other services. You can download Trillian for free at *www.ceruleanstudios.com*.

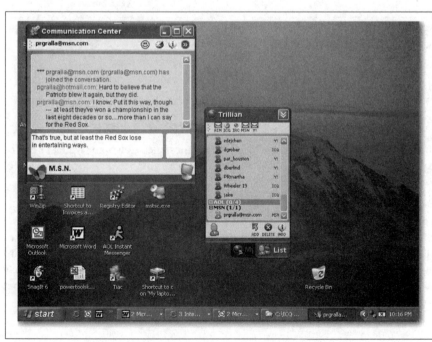

Figure 6-23:
The universal messenger Trillian can communicate with all the major instant messenger programs. Trillian also lets you apply different themes to your messenger, and if you like transparent windows, you can make its windows various shades of "clear."

6-35   Turn Off the AIM Today Window

Every time you log into AOL Instant Messenger (AIM), an AIM Today window appears, filled with advertising and news stories. But if you're like most people, you use an instant messenger to have quick online conversations, not to read the news or click an ad.

To stop the AIM Today window from appearing when you sign on, click the Preferences icon in the Buddy List bar, select the Sign On/Off category in the pane on the left, and turn off "Show AIM Today window at sign on." The next time you open AIM, the AIM Today window is blessedly gone.

6-36   Stopping Online Harassment in AIM

The beauty of instant messengers is that anyone can send you a message instantly; the downside is that sometimes those messages are obnoxious or annoying. With AOL Instant Messenger, you can easily issue a warning to anyone who's hassling you.

Although this may sound a bit like blowing a whistle at a playground, it can still be rather effective. For example, other AIM users can see how many warnings someone has received (akin to a rating on a site like eBay), lending a certain amount of community shame to the offender. And when the offender accumulates too many warnings, he receives a "time out": AOL blocks him from the service for a certain time period.

Warning: Don't use this feature lightly. Warnings tend to beget other warnings, so if you overreact, you could find yourself in the penalty box, too.

To issue someone a warning, click Warn in the window displaying whatever message you found offensive.

6-37   Sending Text Messages with Yahoo! Messenger

You don't need to use a cellphone to send text messages—also known as SMS, for short message service—to friends' phones. You can just send them with Yahoo! Messenger. To send a text message, open Yahoo! Messenger and choose Tools → Send → Start a Mobile Conversation.

If you've never sent a text message to a particular phone, you first have to fill out a form with the recipient's phone number and any contact information you want to include, such as an address. As you're typing the message, Messenger alerts you to how many characters you have left. (Depending on the phone service, there may be a character limit per message.) After you send your note, a window opens that displays your friend's response—if there is one.

6-38   Spicing up Yahoo! Messenger

Like quirky, colorful graphics? You don't have to stick with the dull screens and icons Yahoo! Messenger comes with. Instead, you can spice things up by downloading free add-ons for your messenger, including dancing characters, games, company logos, and more. Get them from *http://messenger.yahoo.com/messenger/ imv/*. After you've downloaded a picture, just click on the IMVironment button in Yahoo! Messenger to apply it to Yahoo! Messenger. Boom! Instant makeover.

6-39   ICQ on the Desktop

If you want fast access to ICQ and all of your ICQ contacts, you can "float" them so they sit as icons on your desktop. Then, when ICQ is running, you can double-click a contact to send a message. To float ICQ on your desktop, right-click the ICQ flower in the System Tray and highlight Status "Floating" On.

6-40   ICQ Shortcut Keys

ICQ is a complicated program, bristling with confusing menus and icons. Consequently, you sometimes have to navigate through scores of menus just to find the command you want. Luckily, you can speed up the process by using any of the ICQ keyboard shortcuts, as shown in Table 6-4.

Table 6-4. ICQ Keyboard Shortcuts

ICQ Function	Shortcut combination
Activate/Deactivate ICQ Window	Ctrl+Shift+A
Create an ICQ Note	Ctrl+Shift+N
Activate WebSearch	Ctrl+Shift+S
Copy Browser's URL to the Search function	Ctrl+Shift+D
Check for New Mail	Ctrl+Shift+C
Send Mail	Ctrl+Shift+E
Search Contact List	Ctrl+Shift+F3
Advanced Find	Ctrl+Shift+F
Bring ICQ Notes to front	Ctrl+Shift+M
Create a new reminder	Ctrl+Shift+R

6-41   Protecting Yourself Against Instant
Messaging Dangers

Increasingly, malicious hackers are using instant messengers to attack other people's computers, or to steal private information such as passwords and user names.

To protect yourself against this high-tech piracy, be sure to check out ZoneAlarm IM Secure, from ZoneLabs, the same company that makes the ZoneAlarm firewall (page 146). This helpful safeguard protects your instant messaging programs by making sure no one can spy on your conversations, steal your passwords, or send malicious code to harm your PC. Download it for free from *www.zonealarm.com*. For even further protection, you can buy ZoneAlarm IM Secure Pro for $19.95.

ADD-IN ALERT

Protecting Your Privacy Online

Logging onto the Internet doesn't have to mean that your life—or at least your PC—is an open book . There are lots of downloads you can get that protect your privacy online; here are a few worth checking out:

- **Anonymity 4 Proxy.** This unique program uses anonymous public *proxy servers* to shield your identity from any Web site you visit. (Proxy servers sit between you and the sites you visit, so the publisher can't glean any information about you or your PC.) Anonymity 4 Proxy lets you choose from hundreds of public anonymous proxy servers available on the Internet. ($35 shareware; *www.inetprivacy.com.*)

- **SurfSecret Privacy Protector.** This online safety tool cleans out your cached Internet files, destroys your history trail, and uses a variety of methods to wipe away all traces of where you've surfed. You can tell it to automatically clean your tracks at any interval you choose—every day, say, or every month. ($39.95 shareware; *www.surfsecret.com.*)

- **Window Washer.** Like SurfSecret, Window Washer cleans up traces of your Internet activity so no one can spy on you or figure out where you've been online. It also includes a slew of extra features, like the ability to clean out instant messenger files. ($39.95 shareware; *www.webroot.com.*)

- **AT&T Privacy Bird.** This clever little add-in examines the privacy policies of sites you visit, and like a little birdie, tells you whether they meet your privacy standards. (Freeware; *www.privacybird.com.*)

Web Browsers

For many people, PCs are *for* surfing the Web. And while using a browser may seem straightforward, Internet Explorer (which comes installed on nearly every Windows XP machine) and similar programs have all kinds of hidden features and fancy tricks that you've probably never tried.

This chapter outlines nearly three dozen hints on better browsing, like changing Internet Explorer's title bar, searching the Web more efficiently, and making better use of your Favorites list. It also gives you a few good alternatives to Internet Explorer.

Smarter Surfing

Whether you spend twenty minutes a week online or twenty hours a day, a few tricks can help you surf more effectively. This section shares surf-master secrets, and they apply to pretty much all browsers. Those that work only with Internet Explorer say so.

7-1   Address Shortcuts

Want to save a few keystrokes when opening a Web site? When you type a URL in the Internet Explorer address bar, type only the domain name (for example, if the URL is *www.dogfancy.com*, type only *dogfancy*) and press Ctrl+Enter. Explorer figures out the missing info and heads right to the site.

Note: This technique works only for URLs that end in *.com.* If you want to visit a Web site that ends in .net, .org, .edu, or any other extension, it won't work. So, for example, if you wanted to visit the University of Cincinnati Web site, and typed *uc* then pressed Ctrl+Enter, you would end up at *www.uc.com*, not *www.uc.edu.*

7-2 Getting the Big Picture

Many Web pages—maybe most—take up more space than a single browser window. To see more at once, you can make Web pages fill your whole screen and eliminate Internet Explorer's toolbars. With Internet Explorer open, just press F11 and the page expands, as shown in Figure 7-1. Press F11 again and the normal view returns—complete with toolbars.

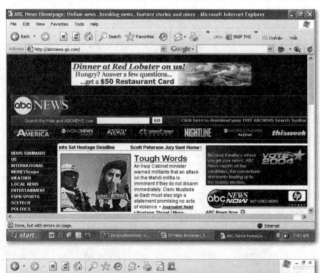

Figure 7-1:
Top: The normal display.

Bottom: Full-screen mode lets you see more of a page, but it's not exactly a practical way to surf because Explorer's address bar and navigation buttons disappear—as you can see here—and you can't type in URLs or click the Back button. But it's a great way to read Web pages when you only need to scroll down or over.

Tip: If you like full-screen mode so much that you want Internet Explorer to always open that way, you can force it to do just that, using the Registry. First, run the Registry Editor (see page 328) and go to My Computer → HKEY_CURRENT_USER → Console. Find the "fullscreen" value and change the value from 0 to 1. Then go to My Computer → HKEY_CURRENT_USER → Software → Microsoft → InternetExplorer → Main. Find the "fullscreen" value and change its value from no to yes. Exit the Registry and reboot. The next time you open Internet Explorer, it launches in full-screen mode.

7-3 Making Web Fonts Easier to Read

You can't always rely on Web designers to build pages that are easy to read—sometimes the fonts are too small, sometimes they're too big, and sometimes they're just ugly. Happily, you aren't stuck with the size of the fonts you come across on the Web.

There are two ways to change font size. If you have a wheel mouse—a mouse with a wheel in its center you can use to scroll through pages—you can decrease the font size by holding down the Ctrl key while you move the mouse on the wheel forward; to increase the font size, hold down the Ctrl key while you move the mouse on the wheel backwards. There are five font sizes you can choose—Figure 7-2 shows the smallest and largest.

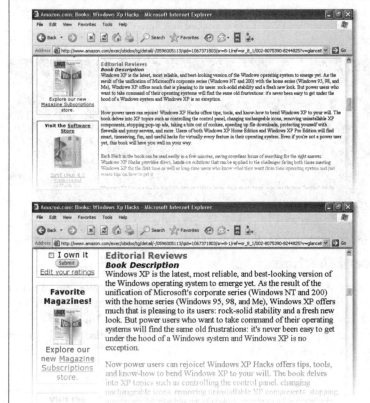

Figure 7-2:
Top: When you make the font size on a Web page smaller, the text may be harder to read, but you can see more text on the page at once.

Bottom: When you make the font size larger, the text is easier to read, but not as much information fits on your screen without scrolling.

If you prefer keystrokes, in Internet Explorer, choose View → Text Size, and from the list that appears, select the size you prefer. (In other browsers, look for similar options in the View menu.)

Note: Not *all* Web sites let you change font size. Occasionally, designers set pages so you can't adjust them—an irritating control.

7-4   Opening a New Web Page in Its Own Window

Click a link on a Web page, and your browser whisks you away to a new destination—perhaps never to find your way back to your starting point. But what if you want to see *both* the original page and the new page at the same time? Or what if you simply want to retain the original page? Good news: you can have more than one browser window open at a time.

To open a new page in its own window, simply right-click the link when you select it (instead of clicking the left mouse button as you normally would), and then choose Open in New Window. A new page opens at the new location, and your original page remains on screen (though perhaps hidden behind the new window).

Note: Sometimes when you click a link on a Web page, it opens in a new browser window even when you didn't choose that command. Web designers can control what happens when you click a link—whether it opens in a new window or no—and some dictate that links open new pages.

FREQUENTLY ASKED QUESTION

Taming Internet Explorer

When I'm working in Word or Outlook, and I click a link, Internet Explorer jumps to that page—which means I lose whatever page I had open. Can I change this reaction?

Yes!

If you find this behavior disconcerting, you can tell Internet Explorer to quit it. In the browser, choose Tools → Internet Options → Advanced. Scroll down to the Browsing section and uncheck the box next to "Reuse windows for launching shortcuts." Click OK.

From now on, when you click a link in an email message or a Word document, the site will open in a new Internet Explorer window, and you won't lose track of the page you had open.

7-5   Keyboard Shortcuts

One of the best ways to speed up your surfing is to lay off your mouse and use your keyboard instead. Most browsers let you do nearly everything without ever lifting your hands from the keys. Table 7-1 lists keyboard shortcuts in Internet Explorer that can make your browsing more efficient. For keyboard shortcuts in other browsers, see pages 195, 198, and 200.

Table 7-1. *Internet Explorer Keyboard Shortcuts*

Shortcut	What It Does
Browsing the Web and viewing Web pages	
F5 or Ctrl+R	Refreshes the Web page you're viewing—if it has a different time stamp than the latest version on the Web.
Ctrl+F5	Refreshes the Web page you're viewing, even if it has the same time stamp as the latest version on the Web.
F11	Switches Internet Explorer to full-screen view—and makes the address bar, title bar, and menu disappear. If you're already in full-screen mode, it switches to the regular view.
Esc	Stops the current page from downloading
Page Up	Moves up the page for approximately the length of one screen.
Page Down	Moves down the page for approximately the length of one screen.
Home	Goes to the beginning of the page.
End	Goes to the end of the page.
Tab	Moves forward through all the items on a Web page, including links. If you're filling out a Web form, it moves to the next part of the form.
Shift+Tab	Moves back through all the items on a Web page, including links. If you're filling out a Web form, it moves to the previous part of the form.
Alt+Home	Opens your home page.
Alt+Right arrow	Moves forward one page.
Alt+Left arrow or Backspace	Moves back one page.
Alt+Up arrow	If you're in the Favorites pane, it moves an item up in the Favorites list.
Alt+Down arrow	If you're in the Favorites pane, it moves an item down in the Favorites list.
Ctrl+Tab or F6	Highlights the address bar, or if you're in the address bar, moves the focus of your cursor to the Web page.
Ctrl+A	Selects every element on the current page.
Ctrl+B	Opens the Organize Favorites screen.
Ctrl+D	Adds the current page to your Favorites folder.
Ctrl+E	Opens Internet Explorer's search pane so you can search the Internet.
Ctrl+F	Opens the Find dialog box so you can search for text on the current page.
Ctrl+H	Opens the History pane.
Ctrl+I	Opens the Favorites pane.
Ctrl+N or Ctrl+R	Opens a new copy of Internet Explorer.
Ctrl+O or Ctrl+L	Runs the Open dialog box.
Ctrl+P	Prints the current page.
Ctrl+S	Saves the current page to your hard disk.
Ctrl+W	Closes the current window.

Table 7-1. Internet Explorer Keyboard Shortcuts (continued)

Shortcut	What It Does
Using the Address Bar	
F4	Opens the Address Bar history.
Up arrow	When an AutoComplete list is displayed, it moves forward through the list.
Down arrow	When an AutoComplete list is displayed, it moves backward through the list.
Alt+D	Selects the text in the Address bar.
Ctrl+Enter	Enters *http://www. .com/* in the Address Bar.
Ctrl+Left arrow	In the Address Bar, it moves the cursor left to the next "." or "/" in the address.
Ctrl+Right arrow	In the Address Bar, it moves the cursor right to the next "." or "/" in the address.

7-6   Filling Out Forms Faster

Most browsers have an incredibly great feature for filling out online forms—Auto-Complete, which as the name implies, automatically completes whatever you're typing. When you type a few letters in a form, like *pre*, Explorer guesses what you're going to type next based on how you've filled out forms in the past, and fills it in (in this case, *preston@gralla.com*). If you the browser thinks more than one possibility could complete your entry, it displays your choices in a small pop-up window. Select the one you want, rather than retype your address, your email, your name, or whatever.

This system is a terrific time-saver. But if you've ever mistyped an entry in a form, or typed information that's no longer valid, like an old email address, that pops up, too.

If you find those outdated or mistyped entries irritating, there's an easy way to kill them. In Internet Explorer, just double-click an empty box in a Web form (or single click and press the Down Arrow key) and your entire list of AutoComplete entries appears. Scroll to the one you don't want to appear anymore and press Delete. Repeat as needed. In other browsers, you may have to clear *all* your form entries in order to delete just one or two pesky mistypes. For example, in Firefox (page 194), choose Tools → Options → Privacy, and under Saved Form Information, click the Clear button.

7-7   Revisiting History

There was a Web site you visited an hour ago…or was it this morning, or maybe last night, or yesterday morning, or…you can't remember. Not the site's name, not its address, not even when exactly you visited. But you want to go back. And you don't know where to start.

Fortunately, browsers have a built-in time machine: the history list. This handy feature keeps track of your past travels on the Web, making it easy to revisit a site you gave up for lost.

Here's how to use the history list in Internet Explorer; other browsers have very similar features. Head to the toolbar and click the History button, shown in Figure 7-3 (top). A pane appears on the left side of your browser (Figure 7-3, bottom); it lists all the sites you've visited in the last 20 days. Simply click the name of any site to go back again.

Tip: You can also open the History pane by choosing View → Explorer Bar → History or by pressing Ctrl+H.

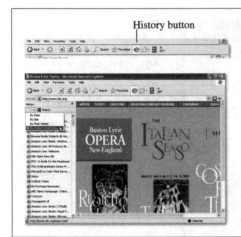

History button

Figure 7-3:
Top: Click this button to open a pane with your browsing history.

Bottom: You can change the order of the History pane to view sites alphabetically or by how recently you visited. If you want to delete any site from the list, right-click it and choose Delete. To close the History pane, click the History button again.

If 20 days isn't enough of a breadcrumb trail for you (or if it's too much), you can adjust Internet Explorer's memory. A history of up to 90 days or so can save you surprisingly often, but the farther back the history goes, the more disk space it sucks up. To pick your perfect span, choose Tools → Internet Options, and on the General tab, look for History and then adjust "Days to keep pages in history."

Tip: If other people share your PC, and you don't want them to know what sites you've visited, you can clear your history. Do it by choosing Tool → Internet Options and clicking Clear History and then OK. Explorer erases your tracks.

7-8   Printing a Wide Web Page

Sometimes when you print a Web page, particularly one that has wide margins, the right-hand side of the page gets cut off. There's a simple solution: change your printer's orientation from portrait (the normal, vertical layout) to landscape (a horizontal layout with the wide edge at the top of the page).

In your browser, choose File → Print → Preferences to open the Print Preferences dialog box, shown in Figure 7-4 (in browsers other than Internet Explorer, the menu path may be File → Print → Properties). Choose the Landscape button and Press OK.

Note: From now on, anything you print appears in landscape mode, so you have to change your setting back to Portrait when you want to print a normal page again.

Many Web sites have a "Print this Page" button or a similar link that displays a new page reformatted so it fits on an 8.5×11 sheet of paper (often, without the clutter of advertisements or the site's navigation tools). Choose this option whenever possible to get the cleanest printout. Usually, you still have to click your browser's print button as you would with any Web page.

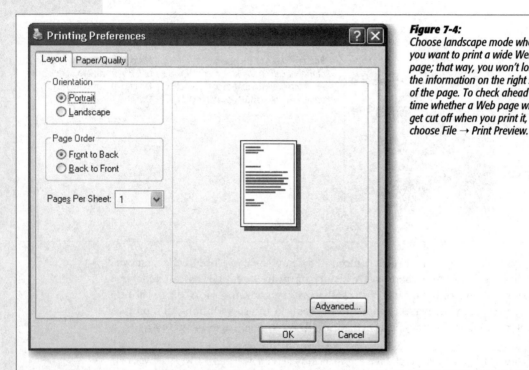

Figure 7-4:
Choose landscape mode when you want to print a wide Web page; that way, you won't lose the information on the right side of the page. To check ahead of time whether a Web page will get cut off when you print it, choose File → Print Preview.

7-9   Saving Web Pages on Your PC

It's probably happened to you dozens of times: You find a page on the Web that you'd like to read later when you're not connected to the Internet (say, when you'll be on a plane, in a waiting room, or at a ballgame).

There's a simple solution to the problem: browsers let you save any Web page to your own computer. You can then read the page whenever and wherever you want.

To save a Web page, choose File → Save As. Browse to the folder where you want to save the file, rename the file (if you want), and choose what format you want to save it in. You have several choices for saving the files (the choices may vary slightly depending on your browser):

- **Web Page, complete (*.htm, *.html)** This saves the page in its normal HTML (hypertext markup language) format. With this option, Internet Explorer saves all of the Web page's graphics in a folder inside the folder where you saved the page.

- **Web Archive, single file (*.mht)** This saves the page in a single file in a special compressed format known as Multipurpose Internet Mail Extension HTML. It doesn't create any folders, and saves all the graphics in a single file. If you don't have any plans to use the page's HTML code, it's better to save the file in this format (rather than Web Page, complete), because it keeps all the files in a single, tidy location.

Tip: If you plan to send the Web page to someone via email, save it in the .mht format. That way, you can easily attach the file to an email message, without worrying about pieces of the page getting lost along the way.

- **Web Page, HTML only (*.htm, *.html)** This saves only the HTML portion of the page, but not any graphics, so it doesn't create a new folder. When you open the saved page, though, it might be difficult to read, because graphics are sometimes used to hold the pieces of a Web page together, or for information that doesn't appear in the text. Choose this option if you're planning to reuse the HTML in a page you want to create.

- **Text File (*.txt)** This saves only the text from the page. This is a good choice if you want to save only text from a page, and you don't care about the pictures.

To read a Web page after you've saved it, open your browser and choose File → Open, then browse to the folder where you saved the page.

POWER USERS' CLINIC

Fancy Printing Options in Internet Explorer

When it comes to printing, Internet Explorer can do a lot more than just print the Web page you're currently viewing. Among the little-known tricks up its sleeve: the ability to print a list of every link on a Web page, or to print the current page plus all linked pages. You can also customize how Explorer prints a Web page that uses frames, which divide Web pages into separate sections.

To print a list of all the links on a page, choose Print → Options and select "Print table of links." When you click Print, Explorer prints the page you're viewing, then a list of links that appear on the page, including the address and

shortcut text (the text you see underlined on a Web page for a link).

To print the page you're viewing, as well as all the pages it links to, choose Print → Options and select "Print all linked documents." (Beware: This choice could suck up a lot of paper and ink.)

If you want to print a Web page designed with frames, choose Print → Options, then select whether you want to print each frame separately on its own page, just the frame currently selected in your browser, or the page exactly as it appears on screen.

7-10 Saving Web Pages with SurfSaver

If you save a lot of Web pages to your PC (as outlined in the previous hint), pretty soon you end up with the same problem you started with: How can you find the information you need fast?

If you use Internet Explorer, here's a good solution: SurfSaver, software that lets you save pages to your PC, and then search the text on the pages, or keywords associated with each page. SurfSaver integrates right into Internet Explorer, so you can save pages easily as you surf the Web.

When you want to find a page you've saved, you launch a search, as shown in Figure 7-5. (The left pane opens in your browser only when you use SurfSaver.) You can search for keywords you've created as you save each page, the full text, the title of the page, and other criteria. SurfSaver is free to try, but costs $29.95 if you continue using it. Get it at *www.surfsaver.com*.

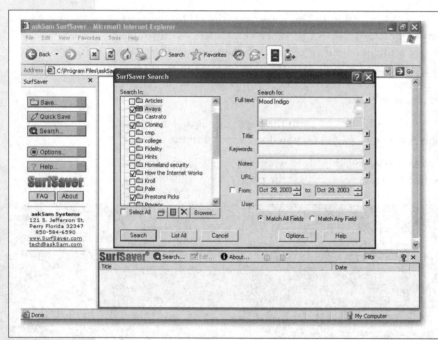

Figure 7-5:
SurfSaver lets you search the full text of a Web page, the page's title, or keywords you input when you saved the page. You can also organize your saved pages in folders, so it's easy to browse to the pages you want.

7-11 Saving Frequently Updated Web Pages Automatically

Some Web pages don't age well. For instance, on news sites, pages go stale faster than Pecan Sandies left out in a humid kitchen. If you want to save a Web page that changes frequently, and you use Internet Explorer, you just have to tell your browser to visit the site on a regular schedule and save the latest update to your PC.

Say you commute to work every day on a bus or a train. You can tell Explorer to grab the latest headlines from your favorite news sites each morning while your PC is online at home, then you can read those pages with your morning coffee on the train. Here's how:

1. **Go to the Web site you want to have "delivered," and save it as a Favorite.**

   You can press Ctrl+D, or choose Favorites → Add to Favorites.

2. **Right-click the site in your Favorites list and choose Make Available Offline.**

   The Offline Favorite Wizard appears. Click Next. If you want to skip the introductory screen the next time you use the wizard, turn on "In the future, do not show this introduction screen."

3. **The screen shown in Figure 7-6 appears. It lets you decide whether to save only the page itself, or also any pages it links to.**

   If you just want to save that one page, click No. If you also want to save the pages it links to, click Yes and then choose the number of links deep you want to save—in other words, indicate how many levels of links Explorer should follow and save. Be careful if you choose to save linked pages, because your hard disk can fill up quickly with more pages than you have time to read. (A good choice is to save a single level of links.) Click Next when you're done.

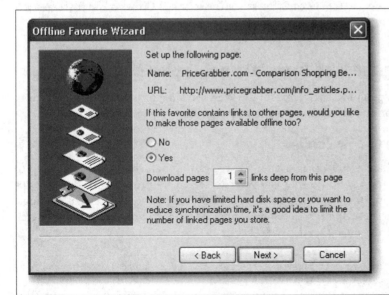

Figure 7-6:
When you tell Internet Explorer to save the latest version of a Web page on your PC, you can also save other pages it links to—but saving too many pages can take a long time and fill up your hard drive.

4. **In the dialog box that appears, choose whether to save (i.e., synchronize) the page only when you tell it to, or automatically on a schedule—kind of like buying the newspaper from a newsstand when you want it, or having it delivered.**

   If you choose to synchronize the page on your command, you have to open Internet Explorer and select Tools → Synchronize when you want to get the latest version from the Web. If you choose to synchronize on a schedule, Internet

Explorer saves the page on whatever schedule you choose. After you make your choice, click Next.

5. **If you choose to synchronize on a schedule, a new screen appears, letting you choose how often and at what time you want Explorer to save the page.**

   You can also tell your PC to connect to the Internet automatically at the time of synchronization if you're not online. To have it connect automatically, turn on the option at the bottom of the screen. If you don't select this option, and your computer isn't connected when it's time to synchronize, your browser won't be able to update the file.

6. **Complete the wizard.**

   If the site you're saving requires a user name and password, you have to type them in the wizard's final screen. (If you don't, Explorer won't be able to access the site to save the page.) When you're done, click Finish.

To view the page on your PC after you've synchronized—and when you're not connected to the Internet—open Explorer and choose File → Work Offline, then click the site on your Favorites list that you want to view.

Note: After you've chosen File → Work Offline, Internet Explorer starts in Offline mode when you open your browser. The next time you want to go online, click Work Offline again and clear the check mark next to it.

Searching the Web from Internet Explorer

Most people spend half their time on the Web *searching* for stuff they want to read, watch, play, or download. Here're a few tips to help you search smarter.

7-12   The Google Toolbar

If you use Google 400 times a day, you're wasting valuable time by surfing to Google's home page every time you want to search. Improve your efficiency 80-fold by bringing the Web's most popular search engine to you: install a Google toolbar in Internet Explorer. The super-handy add-on lets you run a Google search no matter where you are on the Web (Figure 7-7).

Note: The Google toolbar works only with Internet Explorer. If you use Mozilla, Netscape, or Firefox, try the Googlebar, described on page 195.

Google toolbar—

Figure 7-7:
You get all the power of Google, packed into this tiny toolbar. Using it is the single best thing you can do to improve your surfing experience.

To add the Google toolbar to your browser, go to *http://toolbar.google.com* and click the "Download Google Toolbar" button. The toolbar installs itself in Internet Explorer. When you want to do a search, just type your keywords in the search box and press Enter. Google displays the results in your open browser window as if you did the search at *www.google.com.*

That's not the only thing the Google Toolbar can do. Here are just a few of the other ways it can make your surfing easier:

- **Kill pop-ups.** If you can't stand the pop-up ads that seem to be everywhere on the Web, the Google Toolbar can save you the annoyance—it automatically nips them in the bud. To allow pop-ups on a specific site, or all the time, click the popup button. (For more about stopping pop-ups, see page 134.)

- **Fill in forms.** Click the AutoFill button to have the Google Toolbar fill in online forms for you, providing information such as your name, address, and email address. (You, of course, have to fill in the information one time, and after that, the Google toolbar remembers.)

- **Search the site you're visiting.** Not all Web sites offer a way to search their own pages—and those that do often don't work very well. For better results, you can use the Google Toolbar to search the Web site you're viewing; simply click the "Search this Site" button.

Note: For more a full rundown on the Google toolbar and deskbar (next hint)—and everything else Google—check out *Google: The Missing Manual.*

7-13   The Google Deskbar (Not just for Internet Explorer)

Using the Google toolbar can speed up your searching dramatically. But there's another shortcut you can take to Google—and it doesn't even require you to have a browser open (though you do have to be connected to the Internet). Try the Google *deskbar*, which lets you search Google from the Windows XP taskbar along the bottom of your screen and then view your results in a special window (Figure 7-8). It looks weird at first, but it can be surprisingly useful.

You can download Google's deskbar for free from *http://toolbar.google.com/deskbar.* It automatically installs itself as a toolbar on the Windows XP taskbar, but you have to turn it on by right-clicking the taskbar and choosing Toolbars → Google Deskbar.

Note: To make the search box bigger or smaller, drag the small vertical bar on the left edge of the search box as far left or right as you want to go.

The Google deskbar is particularly handy when you're in a program like Microsoft Word and you need to look up something on the Web. Rather than switch to (or open) your browser, just press Ctrl+Alt+G to move your cursor to the deskbar search box and run Google from there.

You can also use the Google deskbar to do specialized searches. For example, type your search terms, and then press Ctrl+N when you want to search only news sites. To search for images, press Ctrl+I, or to search for dictionary definitions Ctrl+D. (Google finds the definitions in an online dictionary.)

Tip: You can find additional features of the deskbar by pressing the little arrow button at the far right edge. A menu pops open, with a slew of choices, including an entry for Options, which opens a dialog box that lets you customize the deskbar.

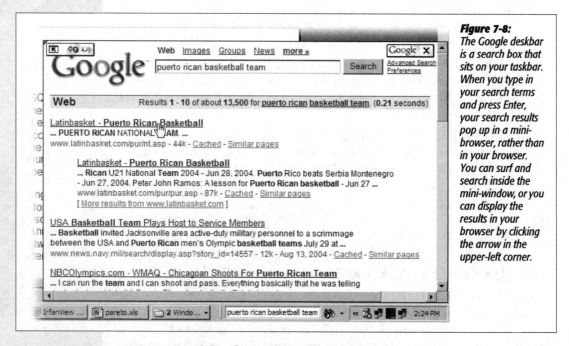

Figure 7-8:
The Google deskbar is a search box that sits on your taskbar. When you type in your search terms and press Enter, your search results pop up in a mini-browser, rather than in your browser. You can surf and search inside the mini-window, or you can display the results in your browser by clicking the arrow in the upper-left corner.

7-14 Searching from the Address Bar

Internet Explorer's address bar—the place where you type in URLs you want to visit—also serves as a *search* box. If you type in search terms instead of a Web address, Explorer takes you to the MSN search site and shows you a list of relevant results. It's a nifty trick.

But if MSN is not your search engine of choice, you change the underlying search service with a tool called TweakUI. (For details about TweakUI, see page 28.)

Note: If you've installed the Google toolbar, you can make Google your underlying search engine without TweakUI. On the Google toolbar, click the Options button (or, on the right edge, choose Google → Options) to open the Options dialog box. Click the More tab, and under Search Options, choose "Use Google as my default search engine in Internet Explorer." Click OK.

Here's the TweakUI method:

1. **Download and install TweakUI from** *www.microsoft.com/windowsxp/pro/ downloads/powertoys.asp.* **If you've already installed TweakUI, skip to the next step.**

   Installation is straightforward; there's nothing you need to do beyond following the instructions.

2. **Choose Start → All Programs → Power Toys for Windows XP → TweakUI for Windows XP.**

   TweakUI opens. If you've already got a TweakUI icon on your desktop, you can double-click it to run it instead.

GEM IN THE ROUGH

The Google Calculator

When you need a calculator on the fly, don't waste your time hunting for Window XP's version (which is buried on the Start menu). Instead, jump to Google's toolbar (page 178) or deskbar (page 179) to do calculations for you. (You can also run calculations from Google's home page, though that's not as convenient.)

Type any calculation in a Google search box—for example 9+5784, and then press Enter to have Google display the answer. Google can solve a wide variety of math problems, including basic arithmetic, complicated math (like trigonometry functions), and units of measure and conversions.

You don't even have to know math jargon to get answers; Google can interpret some plain English requests. For example, if you type *feet in three meters*, Google returns the answer *three meters = 9.84251969 feet.* But it doesn't understand all questions. For example, if you type *how many inches in a meter?* it gives you an answer. But it doesn't understand the more elaborate question, *how many inches are there in a meter?*

For a nice rundown of Google's calculator features—which are amazingly sophisticated—check out *www.googleguide.com/ calculator.html.*

---

3. **Go to Internet Explorer → Search, and then click Create.**

   The Search Prefix dialog box, shown in Figure 7-9 appears. In the Prefix slot, type in a word you'll use to trigger searches. (That is, what you type in the prefix box is what you'll have to type in your address bar before your search terms.)

   For example, to search using Google, type *Google* in the Prefix box. You don't have to use the site's full name. For example, if you want to type *gl* to search using Google, enter *gl* in the Prefix box.

Note: You can only type one word in the prefix box, or else the search won't work. So, for example, when you set up Internet Explorer to search from the address bar using the Ask Jeeves site, you'd have to use a single word in the address box—for example, *Ask*. That way, when you want to search using Ask Jeeves, you'd type *Ask* and then your search term in Explorer's address bar.

In the URL box, type this URL, exactly as you see it, for a Google search: *www.google.com/search?q=%s.*

This URL depends on the search engine you want to use. For a list of the URLs you should use for Alta Vista, Yahoo, Lycos, Ask Jeeves, and Google, see Table 7-2.

Table 7-2. *Search URLs for Search Sites*

Search Engine	URL
Google	*http://www.google.com/search?q=%s*
Yahoo!	*http://search.yahoo.com/search?p=%s*
Alta Vista	*http://www.altavista.com/sites/search/web?q=%s*
Lycos	*http://search.lycos.com/default.asp?query=%s*
Ask Jeeves	http://web.ask.com/web?q=%s

4. **Click OK and then Apply.**

You can now search from Internet Explorer's address bar by typing *Google* and then your search term, like this: *Google Bartoli*.

Tip: When searching, you can use more than one search term—for example, *house cat*—just as you would when you're doing a search at *www.google.com* or any other site.

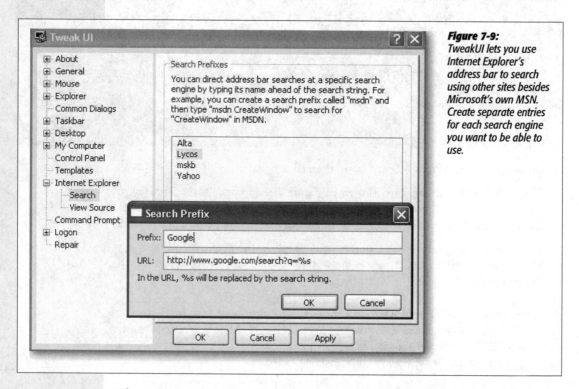

Figure 7-9:
TweakUI lets you use Internet Explorer's address bar to search using other sites besides Microsoft's own MSN. Create separate entries for each search engine you want to be able to use.

If you want to be able to search from Internet Explorer's address bar using other search engines, like Yahoo!, Alta Vista, Lycos, or Ask Jeeves, repeat steps 3–6 for each service.

Managing Your Favorites

In Internet Explorer, URL bookmarks are called *Favorites*. They're crucial tools for power surfing—but if you have a lot of them, your list can get unruly and hard to use. This section helps you tame the beast.

Note: The tips in this section apply specifically to Internet Explorer, but all browsers have similar features.

7-15   Finding Favorites Fast

Favorites lists tend to bloat up, making it hard to find the sites you want to visit—and negating the point of *having* Favorites. Here's a quick remedy.

Your Favorites list is really only a folder on your computer, saved in My Computer → Documents and Settings → Your Name → Favorites. To find a site that's missing, right-click that folder in Windows Explorer, choose Search, and then type the name of the site you're looking for, or a word you think is part of the site's name. Windows Explorer displays a list of matching results. Double-click the one you're looking for, and Internet Explorer takes you there.

WORKAROUND WORKSHOP

Launching Outlook from Within Internet Explorer

You're browsing the Web when you hit a golfing site that reminds you you have an appointment with the physical therapist—but you can't remember when you're supposed to be there. So you go through all the pointing, clicking, and menu maneuvering to find Outlook, launch it, and then open the Calendar.

Here's a better way. Use the Internet Explorer's address bar to launch the Calendar or any other Outlook feature.

To open your Outlook calendar, type *Outlook:Calendar* in your browser's address bar and press Enter—before you can say, "I'm late!", the calendar opens in Outlook. This trick also works for your Outlook contacts (type *Outlook:Contacts*), Outlook Today (*Outlook:Today*), Outlook Tasks (*Outlook:Tasks*), Outlook Notes (*Outlook:Notes*) and any Outlook folder, such as your email inbox (*Outlook:Inbox*).

7-16   Organizing Favorites from A to Z

Finding favorites can be tough if they're not organized in any particular order. You may have to scroll past a site about fly-fishing, your Amazon Wish List, and a site that features cats in Halloween costumes just to get to your brother's divorce party photo album…or did that come after the Web site for your parking garage?

It's much easier to find a site you want if your list is alphabetized. To put them in alphabetical order, choose Favorites and right-click any site on the list; on the menu that appears, choose "Sort by name." Your browser rearranges the whole Favorites list alphabetically.

If you organize your Favorites in folders and want the contents of each folder alphabetized, you have to go through the process for each one. Select a folder, right-click one of the sites within the folder, and choose "Sort by name." Lather, rinse, repeat.

7-17 Copying Favorites to Another Computer

Once you've gone to the trouble of compiling a killer Favorites list—maybe even organized into categories like "annoying loud music," "vintage videogame t-shirts," and "bipartisan political blogs"—it would be heart-breaking to start over just because you bought a new laptop. Or perhaps you have such an enviable Favorites list you want to share it with a friend or a co-worker. Whatever the reason, it's easy to transfer your Favorites list from one computer to another. Here's how:

Tip: You can also follow these steps to export your cookies (for more about cookies, see page 133 in Chapter 6).

---

1. **In Internet Explorer, choose File → "Import and Export."**

   The Import/Export Wizard appears.

2. **Click Next and choose Export Favorites, then click Next again.**

   Choose which folder you want to export *from* (Figure 7-10).

   If you want to export all of your Favorites, choose the Favorites folder. But you can also export just one folder within your Favorites list (say, your news sites), by selecting a specific folder.

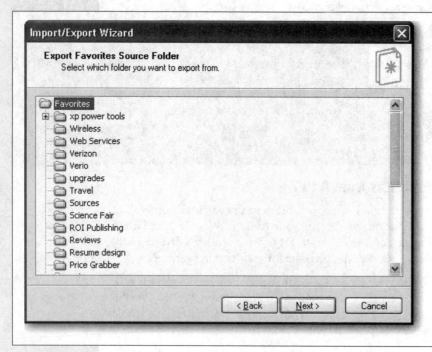

Figure 7-10:
If you just want to export one folder from your Favorites list, choose that folder, rather than Favorites, when you get to this screen. You can only export one folder at a time, though, so you have to run the Wizard twice to export two separate folders.

3. **Click Next and browse to wherever you want to export the Favorites.**

   If you're sharing your Favorites with someone over a network, browse to a folder on that person's computer, so he can easily import the file. You can also save your favorites on a removable disk or CD-R, or save the file on your hard disk and then email it as an attachment.

4. **Click Next, and then Finish.**

   Your Favorites are ready for importing.

5. **On the computer you want to transfer your favorites to, find the export file, and then import it to Internet Explorer on *that* computer.**

   Choose File → Import and Export. Run the wizard again—except this time, choose Import Favorites, and follow the wizard's directions. Explorer adds the favorites you've imported to the existing Favorites list.

7-18   Creating Favorite Files and Folders

It's a fact of modern life: sometimes you're surfing eBay—at work—and, suddenly, your boss pops in. You've probably perfected the small talk to make while you furtively switch out of Internet Explorer, find the folder that has the document your boss wants, double-click the file you need, and wait for Word to open it.

You can save time—and maybe your job—by adding files or folders you use frequently to your Internet Explorer Favorites. That way, you can open the file or folder as you would any other Favorite—with just a flick of the mouse.

Note: If you save a file to Favorites, the program you used to create it opens—for example, Microsoft Word. And if you save a folder, Windows Explorer pops up with the contents of that folder.

The Favorites list is just a folder, just like any other folder on your PC; you can find it in My Computer → Documents and Settings → Your Name [Your XP user name] → Favorites. Any files or folders you copy to the Favorites folder show up as Favorites in Internet Explorer.

Your best bet is to copy *shortcuts* to the files or folders, rather than move the actual files or folders themselves. That way, the files and folders stay where they are on your hard disk in whatever way you like them organized, but you can get to them via Internet Explorer. To copy a shortcut to your Favorites file, open Windows Explorer and highlight the file or folder you want to create a shortcut to, and choose File → Create Shortcut. Then go to My Computer → Documents and Settings → Your Name → Favorites, and choose File → Paste Shortcut.

To create a shortcut to a folder, right-click the folder, and from the menu that appears, choose the folder name. From the menu that cascades off that, choose Create Shortcut. Then go to My Computer → Documents and Settings → Your Name → Favorites, and choose File → Paste Shortcut.

Cache Flow

As you surf the Web, your browser keeps a copy of everything you download, including pages, graphics, Java applets, and sound files. The copies wind up in a folder known as your browser's *cache*, which just refers to a bunch of stored files.

Note: Many Web sites include interactive features such as games you can play online. Often, these features are actually small programs that run inside your browser, called *Java applets*. Java is a programming language that lets developers write programs that can run on many different operating systems, including Windows XP, the Mac, and Linux. An applet is a little program.

When you visit a Web page, your browser first looks at its cache to retrieve whatever it's saved on your own computer before downloading items from the Internet. This process speeds up browsing, because your browser doesn't have to download the same images, text, or other files over and over again. But it can also clog up your hard disk, and some people worry that snoops can peek into their cache and know what sites they've visited—which is in fact possible.

Windows XP lets you customize the size of your browser's cache, its location, and how they system uses it.

Note: The hints in this section apply specifically to Internet Explorer, but all browsers have similar features.

7-19   Customizing the Cache

The first thing you should probably do is decrease the amount of disk space Windows XP devotes to the cache. Internet Explorer typically uses about three percent of your hard disk for its cache, which on many PCs can add up to hundreds of megabytes of space—and possibly more than a gigabyte. That's overkill. Here's how to reduce the cache.

First, open the Settings dialog box in Internet Explorer by choosing Tools → Internet Options → General → Settings. Figure 7-11 explains what to do next.

While you're in the Settings dialog box, you can adjust an important feature: how frequently and when you want Internet Explorer to check your cache for stored Web pages. This setting involves a trade-off between your browser's response time and ensuring you see the most current version of a Web page. Here's what each option means and how you should decide:

- **Every visit to the page.** If you choose this option, when you re-visit a Web site, Internet Explorer first checks the site to see whether anything has been updated since your last visit, and then displays the updated files. If the files haven't been updated, it displays them from the cache. If you use a dial-up connection, this can slow down your browsing, though it ensures that the pages you display are always up to date. This setting is a good bet for broadband surfers—those who have high-speed connections such as cable or DSL—since they generally don't have to worry about download times.

- **Every time you start Internet Explorer.** If you choose this option, Internet Explorer checks each Web site you visit for updates only once per session, no matter how many times you drop by. So the first time you visit a site during a browsing session, Explorer checks for new files; but if you go back to that site during the same Internet session, Explorer displays the files from its cache. This speeds up browsing, but you risk seeing outdated Web pages, especially on sites that are updated more than once a day.

- **Automatically.** This setting offers a good compromise between speedy browsing and getting the latest information. When you use it, Internet Explorer calculates how frequently the Web pages you visit are updated, and based on that, determines how frequently to check the Web site instead of the cache.

- **Never.** When you choose this option, Internet Explorer displays the files in its cache, and never checks the Web site for new information. While this leads to the fastest Web browsing, it also means you'll frequently see outdated information when you surf, so it's generally not a good choice unless you're a dial-upper and you frequently visit pages that rarely change.

Figure 7-11:
Shrink the amount of space devoted to the cache by dragging the slider to the left, or by entering a specific number in the edit box. (If you want to increase the cache size, drag the slider to the right.) Depending on how much space you have on your hard disk, you might make the size 50 megabytes or more.

7-20 Viewing Your Cache

You can view and open all the files in your Explorer cache. This trick is handy when you remember seeing a picture on a Web page recently, but you can't remember *where* you saw. If you sift through your cache, you may just be able to hit on it. Simply open Internet Explorer and choose Tools → Internet Options; then, on the General tab, look for the Temporary Internet Files section, and choose Settings

→ View Files. Windows Explorer opens your cache folder so you can see what's inside.

Tip: The quickest way to view your Internet Explorer cache is to open Windows Explorer and go to Documents and Settings → [Your Name] → Local Settings → Temporary Internet Files. ([Your Name] is your XP user name.)

Your Temporary Internet Files folder (same thing as your cache) most likely contains a mix of graphics, cookies, HTML files, Java applets, and other objects from Web sites you've visited. To open any of them, just double-click the icon as you would any other file. XP asks, "Running a system command on this item might be unsafe. Do you wish to continue?" Click Yes to open or run the file.

7-21 Cleaning Out Your Cache

Every once in a while, you should clean out your cache and delete all the files there. Doing so frees up hard disk space and makes sure no one can peer into your cache and see what Web sites you've been visiting. (To snoop, all someone would have to do is sit at your PC and follow the directions in the previous hint to examine your cache; hackers may be able to reach your cache, too—see page 281.)

To clean out your cache, open Internet Explorer and choose Tools → Internet Options; in the Temporary Internet files section, click "Delete files." If you'd like Explorer to automatically delete these files every time you close your browser, choose Tools → Internet Options → Advanced. In the Security section, select "Empty Temporary Internet Files folder when browser is closed." This option may make your browsing a little slower when you turn on your computer in the morning and first open Internet Explorer.

Customizing Internet Explorer

Internet Explorer is by far the most popular browser on the planet. But just because a lot of people use it, that doesn't mean everyone knows how to get the most out of it. This section gives you tips on making your browser work the way *you* want.

7-22 Browser Windows the Size You Want

Internet Explorer has the unfortunate habit of opening at odd sizes—sometimes short and squat, sometimes long and narrow, sometimes too big, and sometimes too small. The same thing may happen when you open a link in a new window—the size may not be exactly what you want, so you have to waste time resizing the window yourself. Before you do that dance again, read on: You can force Internet Explorer to open whatever size window you prefer.

First, close all Internet Explorer windows you have open on your desktop, and then re-launch your browser. Right-click any link and choose "Open in New Window." Make the new window your ideal size by dragging its sides (mouse over the window edge until you see the double-headed arrow, then drag). When you have the window just right, hold down the Shift key and click the X icon in the top-right corner to close it. Resize and close the original Internet Explorer window that remains.

The next time you open your browser, you won't have to tug and pull corners: Explorer should open at exactly the size you want.

Note: You may need to remind Explorer of your preference from time to time by going through this process again.

7-23 Rolling Your Own Toolbar

If you're not happy with Internet Explorer's toolbar buttons, changing them is a snap. In fact, you can add and delete features or rearrange the toolbar any way you want.

Simply right-click the toolbar and choose Customize; the Customize Toolbar dialog box, shown in Figure 7-12, appears. You can customize Internet Explorer's toolbar in three ways:

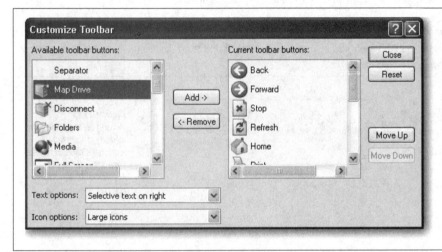

Figure 7-12:
Using this screen, you can customize your toolbar by choosing which icons to display, the size of the icons, their placement, and whether to include text labels. If you want to revert to the toolbar's original layout, click the Reset button.

- **Change the icon size.** Choose whether to display small or large buttons using the "Icon options" menu.

- **Change how icon text is displayed.** You can display descriptive text underneath the icons on the toolbar, hide the text, or just display it to the right of selected icons. Choose which option you want from the "Text options" menu. If you don't use text labels, you can fit more buttons on the toolbar, but you may not remember what each one does. A good compromise is to display text labels for some buttons.

- **Choose which icons to display on the toolbar.** The current toolbar buttons are displayed on the right side of the dialog box. To delete a button, highlight it and choose Remove. To move an icon to the left or right on the toolbar, highlight it and choose Move Up or Move Down. (Move Up moves the icon to the left; Move Down moves it to the right.) To add a button to the toolbar, highlight it in the "Available toolbar buttons" section and select Add.

When you're finished reorganizing, click Close. The changes take effect immediately.

7-24 Changing the Toolbar Background

If you're a stickler for design details, you may be tired of looking at the same dull gray toolbar across the top of Internet Explorer. Then again, you may never have even noticed that Explorer's toolbar *has* a background color. Either way, here's a news flash: You can use any image you want for the toolbar's background.

Note: When you change the background image on Internet Explorer's toolbar, that same image appears on the Windows Explorer toolbar as well.

First, find an image you want to use in lieu of the gray stripe. Make sure it's small, and don't worry if it's very small —Internet Explorer will "tile" the image by displaying it as a repeating pattern if it's smaller than the toolbar. The image has to be in bitmap format, so save it with a .bmp extension.

Tip: If there's an image you want to use for your Internet Explorer toolbar but it's not in .bmp format, don't fret—you can easily convert any graphic to .bmp format using the free IrfanView program from *www. irfanview.com*.

Figure 7-13:
When you're placing an image on Internet Explorer's toolbar, make sure it's small—and choose a design that doesn't obscure the toolbar's icons and menus like this one does.

Save the image on your hard disk—and note where you save it—then close Internet Explorer. Run the Registry Editor (see page 328) and go to My Computer → HKEY_CURRENT_USER → Software → Microsoft → Internet Explorer → Toolbar. Create a new string value called BackBitmap. For its value, enter the name and location of the image you just saved (for example, *C:\Backgrounds\leaves.bmp*). Exit the Registry Editor and open Internet Explorer.

Your toolbar now has a new look. But be careful what image you put on the toolbar, because a busy design can obscure the toolbar's icons and menus (see Figure 7-13). A good source of images to experiment with is *http://images.google.com*.

7-25 Changing Internet Explorer's Title Bar

Look at the title bar in Windows Explorer—the bar at the very top of the screen. What does it say? The name of the site you're currently visiting, followed by "Microsoft Internet Explorer." Accurate, but dull.

You can change "Microsoft Internet Explorer" to say anything you want—*My World Wide Web,* for example, or *Browse at Your Own Risk,* or *Eat Here, Get Gas.*

To give the title bar your own twist, first close Internet Explorer, and then run the Registry Editor (see page 328). Go to My Computer → HKEY CURRENT USER → Software → Microsoft → Internet Explorer → Main. Create a new String Value called Window Title, and for its value, type the name you want to appear in the title bar. (If the Window Title value is already in your Registry, you only need to edit it by typing a new name for the title bar.) When you start Internet Explorer, your handiwork debuts on the title bar, as you can see in Figure 7-14.

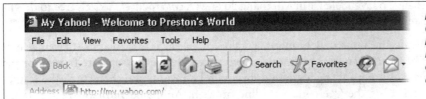

Figure 7-14:
Customize your browser by changing Internet Explorer's title bar. Go crazy—you can name it anything you like.

If you change your mind later, you can edit your title using the same registry trick, or revert to the title "Microsoft Internet Explorer," by deleting the Window Title value you created.

7-26 Changing Internet Explorer's Logo

If you're tired of staring at Microsoft's dull animated logo in the upper-right corner of Internet Explorer, you can change that graphic to anything you want—your company logo, a tiny photo of your kids, a pic of your friendly neighborhood postal carrier. The sky's the limit.

Note: When you change the logo in Internet Explorer, you automatically change the logo in Outlook Express, too.

Before you can make the change, however, you need to know a bit about browser logos. Internet Explorer has both a static logo and an animated logo: the static logo is what you see when the browser is inactive, while the animated logo appears when your browser is doing something—for example, downloading a Web page. Both logos come in two sizes: small and large. (You can specify which size Internet Explorer displays by choosing View → Toolbars → Customize; in the Customize Toolbar dialog box that appears, head to the Icon Options menu and select either Large icons or Small icons.)

When you create your own logo for Internet Explorer, you have to make two sets of two icons: small and large versions of the animated and static logos. The static logos should be 22×22 pixels for the smaller size and 38×38 pixels for the larger size. The animated logos have to be *animated* bitmaps (.bmp format), and each should have a total of ten frames. (An animated bitmap is a graphic that displays an animated series of frames.) Internet Explorer cycles through those ten frames, which is how it creates an animated effect. The smaller animated bitmap should be 22 pixels wide and 220 pixels high. The larger animated bitmap should be 380 pixels wide and 38 pixels high. (Because each bitmap is animated, and you're making ten of them, the width will be ten times the height of the finished animated bitmaps.)

You can create the static bitmaps with any graphics program, including the version of Paint that comes with Windows XP. (To run it, choose Start → All Programs → Accessories → Paint.) Although Paint lets you create bitmaps, it's really not the best tool for the task. So unless you're a pro at doing this kind of thing, use an icon creation program to create your icons hassle-free. An excellent choice is Microangelo, available from Microangelo at *www.microangelo.us*. It's free to download and try out, but if you keep using it, you're expected to pay $54.95.

To create the animated bitmaps, you need special tools. Again, Microangelo is your best bet. If you prefer, though, you can create the ten separate frames for the animated bitmaps using a graphics program like Paint, and then stitch the frames together using the free command-line program Animated Bitmap Creator, available from *http://accesscodes.hypermart.net/download.html*.

Now that you've created new icons, you're ready to use them in Internet Explorer. If you have Windows XP Professional, you can change the logos using the all-purpose Group Policy Editor, a tool that lets you make many kinds of changes to XP without mucking around in the Registry.

Run the Group Policy Editor by typing *gpedit.msc* at a command line or the Run box and pressing Enter. When it opens, go to User Configuration → Windows Settings → Internet Explorer Maintenance → Browser Interface. Double-click "Custom Logo" and in the dialog box that appears fill in the locations of the four new logos you created (the large and small sizes for the static and animated images).

If you have Windows XP Home, here's how to make the switch:

1. **Run the Registry Editor (see page 328) and then go to My Computer → HKEY_ LOCAL_MACHINE → SOFTWARE → SOFTWARE → Microsoft → Internet Explorer\Main.**

   This key contains many important Internet Explorer settings. You have to create new settings to tell Internet Explorer to display the new static logos.

2. **Create two string values named SmallBitmap and BigBitmap.**

   These values tell Internet Explorer to display the static logos that you've created. For the SmallBitmap's value data, give it the file name and full location of the small bitmap you created, for example, C:\Windows\IEsmalllogo.bmp. For the BigBitmap's value data, give it the file name and full location of the big bit-map you created, for example, C:\Windows\IEbiglogo.bmp.

3. **Now it's time to tell Internet Explorer to use your animated logos. Go to HKEY_LOCAL_MACHINE\SOFTWARE\SOFTWARE\Microsoft\Internet Explorer\Toolbar. Create two string values named SmBrandBitmap and BrandBitmap.**

These values tell Internet Explorer to display the animated logos. For the SmBrandBitmap's value data, give it the file name and full location of the small animated bitmap you created, for example, C:\Windows\IEsmallanimat-edlogo.bmp. For the BrandBitmap's value data, give it the file name and full location of the big animated bitmap you created, for example, C:\Windows\IEbiganimatedlogo.bmp.

4. **Exit the Registry.**

You have to restart Internet Explorer for the changes to take effect. To go back to the Internet Explorer's original logos, simply delete the Registry values you created.

Alternative Browsers

Henry Ford once said he'd be happy to manufacture cars in any color that people wanted—as long as that color was black. You might think that a similar aesthetic holds true for Web browsers: You can use any one you want, as long as it's Internet Explorer.

In fact, Internet Explorer isn't the only browser in existence. Several other great ones are available as well, free for the download. This section tells you how to get them, and once you've gotten them, how to get the most out of them. They all have one feature that Internet Explorer doesn't: *tabs*. A browser window can hold multiple tabs, and each tab corresponds to a different Web site (Figure 7-15), which is a serious boon for power surfers.

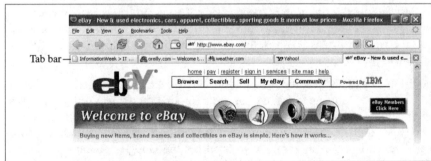

Figure 7-15:
Tabbed browsing is a configuration that lets you open multiple Web pages within one browser window—a major screen-space conservation initiative.

When it comes to alternative browsers, Netscape, Mozilla, Firefox, and Opera are among the best known. They're all free, although Opera displays ads (to get a version that doesn't include ads, you have to pay $39).

Mozilla, Netscape, and Firefox, meantime, are cousins. All three browsers are based on the same stable technology, known as Gecko. Here's how to tell them apart.

Mozilla vs. Netscape

Mozilla 1.6 and Netscape 7.1—the latest versions of each, as of this writing—look similar and act nearly the same. The most obvious difference is that Mozilla installs with different themes. (A *theme* describes the way a program looks—things like the colors and shape of the buttons, icons, and other interface elements.) But the two browsers are typically used by different types of people.

Mozilla is popular with programmers and other geek types because it comes with a seemingly infinite number of settings you can tweak, and because it always has a test version that's slightly more advanced than Netscape's latest version. Netscape, on the other hand, is owned by AOL. So while it comes with the same basic features Mozilla has, it includes AOL Instant Messenger, a shopping button, and a few other extras that make it appealing to civilians.

But Netscape also has a few notable problems. It harbors windows that crop up regularly, exhorting you to join the Netscape Network, whatever that is. And it installs extra programs, like Rediscover AOL, and desktop icons, even if you don't ask for them. Even more important, AOL is dithering about whether to keep coming out with new versions of Netscape. Possibly, they will let the Netscape browser fade into the sunset, so this is probably not the best time to adopt it.

Firefox

If Mozilla is too complicated, and Netscape is too clogged up with AOL clutter, a third option, Firefox, created by the fine folks at Mozilla, might be juuuust right. Unlike Mozilla and Netscape, which come loaded with an email program, a Web page composer, chat tools, and tons of features that only a few people use, Firefox is a standalone browser that incorporates only the most popular tools and settings. Not only does this arrangement make Firefox easier for the average person to use, but it also means the program is speedier and it takes up less room on your hard drive. (If you want email or many other features, Firefox offers dozens of *extensions*, otherwise known as add-ons, that you can easily install; hint 7-31 tells you all about them.

In addition to its lightweight configuration, Firefox has a sleek interface, state-of-the-tech security, pop-up blocking, tabbed browsing, and many other tasty features, including a built-in Google search box (which also lets you search for a term on the page you're currently viewing). For fancier features, you can add the Googlebar (see next hint)—a feature that emulates the Google toolbar—to Firefox. And if you type a search term into the address bar, it automatically runs a Google "I'm Feeling Lucky" search.

Firefox's underlying technology is the same as Mozilla's, so problems tend to show up in things like the occasional misspelled menu item or a cookie setting that includes the observation, "Cookies are delicious delicacies," inserted by an engineer with a raging sense of humor.

Note: Sometime during 2004 or so, the Mozilla honchos plan to come out with version 1.0 of Firefox, which will probably include a couple more features and fewer misspellings. At that point, Firefox will be the organization's primary offering for everyday browsing, while Mozilla will likely remain a favorite of geeks who like its extra components and eight jillion settings.

For a nice set of answers to frequently asked questions about Firefox, see *http://texturizer.net/firefox/faq.html*. To download it, head over to *www.mozilla.org/products/firefox/*, choose your operating system, and let 'er rip.

Opera

Some people favor Opera because it takes up less hard disk space than Mozilla or Netscape. Fans also like the wide-open feeling it gives to pages as you surf. To get Opera, go to *www.opera.com*.

7-27 A Google Toolbar for Netscape, Mozilla, and Firefox

Hint 7-12 describes the stunningly great Google toolbar, which lets you search the Web using Google's search engine without visiting *www.google.com*. There's just one problem: Google created the toolbar for Internet Explorer only.

If you use Netscape, Mozilla, or Firefox, however, you're in luck. You can get the Googlebar, a version of the Google toolbar that mimics the original nicely. You can download the Googlebar for free from *http://googlebar.mozdev.org*.

Tip: If the Googlebar doesn't appear after you install it and restart your browser, press Ctrl+F8, which turns the Googlebar on and off. Firefox has no menu item for turning the Googlebar on and off, so this shortcut can be important.

As with the Internet Explorer version, the Googlebar toolbar integrates directly into your browser. Just type your search term into the search box on the Toolbar and press Enter, and you get the same results as if you did the search at Google's Web site.

7-28 Speeding Up Netscape with Keyboard Shortcuts

You can browse the Web faster with Netscape by using keyboard shortcuts. Table 7-3 lists keyboard shortcuts for many of Netscape's menu commands, so you can get where you need to go without lifting your fingers from the keyboard.

Table 7-3. *Netscape Keyboard Shortcuts*

Key Combination	What It Does
Ctrl+B	Opens the Manage Bookmarks window.
Ctrl+H	Opens the History window.

Table 7-3. *Netscape Keyboard Shortcuts (continued)*

Key Combination	What It Does
Ctrl+R	Reloads the current Web page.
Alt+Home	Opens your Home page.
Ctrl+L	Selects all the text in the location bar.
Ctrl+Shift+L	Launches a window that lets you type whatever URL you want to visit.
Ctrl+Q	Closes the browser.
Ctrl+N	Opens a new Navigator window.
Tab	Moves to the next link on a Web page, or the next input box in a form on a Web page.
Shift Tab	Moves to the previous link on a Web page, or the previous input box in a form on a Web page.
F11	Makes Netscape take up the entire screen. Press it again to return Netscape to normal size.
Ctrl- (minus sign)	Makes all text on the page smaller.
Ctrl+ (plus sign)	Makes all text on the page larger.
Ctrl+T	Opens a new Navigator tab.
Ctrl+Page Down	Switches to the next tab.
Ctrl+Page Up	Switches to the previous tab.
Ctrl+W	Closes the current tab (or the browser window if only one page is open).
F9	Opens/closes My Sidebar, which is a pane on the left of the screen with links to frequently used features, such as instant messaging.
Alt+Page Down	Switches to the next sidebar panel.
Alt+Page Up	Switches to the previous sidebar panel.

7-29 Dressing Up Netscape with Themes

Don't like the way Netscape looks? No problem—you can change it. Netscape lets you use different themes, which have unique color schemes, types and sizes of buttons, and so on.

To switch from your current theme in Netscape, choose View → Apply Theme and then choose the theme you want to use. Netscape comes with two themes, Modern and Classic, which you can see in Figure 7-16. To have your new theme take effect, close Netscape and restart it.

If Netscape's Modern and Classic themes don't appeal, you can find plenty of themes for free online. To see some other options, choose View → Apply Theme → Get New Themes; Netscape takes you to its "Theme Park" Web page. You can browse through the themes until you find one that suits your style, then choose Import Theme and follow the directions to import it into your browser.

7-30 Filling in the Blanks with Netscape

Netscape's Form Manager is like a personal assistant, keeping track of details such as your name, address, email address, shipping information, billing information, credit card number and more. Then it pops all that data into Web forms for you, so you don't have to retype it over and over.

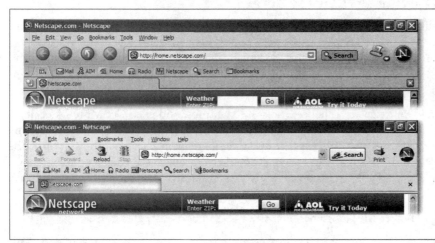

Figure 7-16:
Top: Netscape's Modern theme, shown here, has large, rounded buttons and a metallic feel.

Bottom: Netscape's Classic theme has a more staid look, which hasn't changed much since Netscape came out in 1994. Note how the buttons and colors are dramatically different in the two themes, although the screen layout is similar.

To use it, choose Tools → Form Manager → Edit Form Info. The Form Manager appears, shown in Figure 7-17. Enter whatever information you want the Form Manager to pass along and click OK. Then when you come across a Web page with a form you have to fill out, choose Tools → Form Manager → Fill In Form, and Netscape does the work for you. If you don't want to submit certain details Netscape can fill in, you can edit the information on the form, picking and choosing what you want to automate.

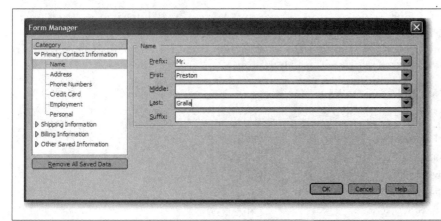

Figure 7-17:
The more information you put into Netscape's Form Manager, the better it will work for you. But think twice about entering your credit card details, because then anyone who uses your PC can use your credit card to buy whatever they want.

Tip: If you're too lazy to enter all your information into the Form Manager, it can harvest that data from a form you've already filled out. Fill out a form on the Web and choose Tools → Form Manager → Save Form Info. The Form Manager gathers the information from the form you've already completed and saves it for future use, so you don't have to tax yourself with any extra keystrokes.

7-31   Adding Firefox Features

Much of Firefox's appeal is that it's a simple, speedy browser. So what if you want something fancy? Firefox has a very cool system for letting you add features à la carte. These add-ons are called *extensions*, there are dozens of them, and they run from the hugely helpful (the Googlebar, described on page 195, is actually an extension) to the whimsical (the CuteMenus extension adds icons on your menus).

To add an extension, choose Tools → Extensions, and click Get More Extensions. Firefox jumps to a Web site with a list of extensions, organized by category, and by top-rated and most popular (*http://extensionroom.mozdev.org/* shows you a the whole list at once). When you find one that intrigues you, click it to open a page that describes the extension and lets you install it (click Install Now). You may have to restart Firefox for the extension to work.

In addition to the Googlebar, here are a few other useful extensions:

- **Ieview** lets you right-click a page and then open it in Internet Explorer. This feature is useful when you're visiting a page that doesn't display properly in Firefox (an occasional occurrence).

- **Single Window** opens a new page in a tab rather than in a separate Firefox window.

- **Tabbrowser Preferences** lets you control more tab behavior.

7-32   Mozilla Firefox Shortcuts

Firefox fans, Table 7-4 lists the keyboard shortcuts that'll prevent you from reaching for the mouse during a surfing session, a few of which you might not have thought of (like automatically completing a .com address). Check out *http://texturizer.net/firefox/keyboard.html* for more.

Table 7-4. Mozilla Firefox Keyboard Shortcuts

Command	Keyboard Shortcut
Add Bookmark	Ctrl-D
Back	Backspace
Bookmarks	Ctrl+B
Close Tab	Ctrl+W
Close Window	Ctrl+Shift+W
Complete .com Address	Ctrl+Enter
Complete .net Address	Shift+Enter

Table 7-4. *Mozilla Firefox Keyboard Shortcuts (continued)*

Command	Keyboard Shortcut
Complete .org Address	Ctrl+Shift+Enter
Copy	Ctrl+C
Cut	Ctrl+X
Decrease Text Size	Ctrl+-
Find on page	Ctrl+F
Forward	Shift+Backspace
Full Screen	F11
History	Ctrl+H
Increase Text Size	Ctrl++
New Tab	Ctrl+T
Next Tab	Ctrl+Tab
New Window	Ctrl+N
Open File	Ctrl+O
Previous Tab	Ctrl+Shift+Tab
Reload	F5
Reload (override cache, page 186)	Ctrl+F5

7-33   Rewinding Your Opera Session

Surfing the Web is generally a long and winding road—and you're often far from where you started after you've been clicking around for hours. Opera offers a nice feature to help you get back to your starting point: you can "rewind" your surfing session to return to the first site you visited when you launched your browser.

To find your way back, just click the Rewind button, or press Shift-Z. This feature works separately for each tabbed window you have open, so when you rewind one window, it doesn't affect the other ones.

7-34   Waving the Opera Wand

Think of all the Web sites you log into—all those user names, all those passwords. It's tough to remember whether you used your childhood nickname for your password, or the name of your favorite basketball star. And even if you can remember all of your user names and passwords, typing them over and over is a chore.

Solve both problems with Opera's Wand. Whenever you log into a site, Opera asks whether you want to save your user name and password. Tell Opera to save it. The next time you log into the site, click the Wand button and Opera automatically fills in those blanks for you.

7-35 Speeding Up Opera with Keyboard Shortcuts

Opera is a fast browser, but you can surf even more efficiently by using your keyboard instead of your mouse. Rather than point and click your way around the screen, save time using the Opera keyboard shortcuts, listed in Table 7-5.

Table 7-5. Opera Keyboard Shortcuts

Key Combination	What It Does
Alt+P	Opens the Preferences dialog box, which lets you change all of your preferences for using the program.
F12	Opens a short list of frequently changed Opera preferences, for example, controlling pop-ups.
X Ctrl+Right Alt+Right	Goes to the next page in your history list.
Z Ctrl+Left Alt+Left Backspace	Goes to the previous page in your history list.
Ctrl+Space	Opens your home page.
G	Toggles loading and display of images in the active page—which can stop all images from loading on a page, then display those images when you press the key again.
0 + (Numeric)	Zooms in 10 percent.
9 - (Numeric)	Zooms out 10 percent.
6 * (Numeric)	Restores a zoomed page to normal (100 percent).
Ctrl+N	Opens a new browsing window.
F1	Displays Opera help screen.
Ctrl+B	Displays the Keyboard Shortcuts page.

7-36 Nota Bene Opera

Wouldn't it be nice to be able to jot down notes as you browsed the Web, easily copying text from the sites you visit to your virtual notebook?

Opera lets you do just that—and it's an outstanding feature. You can take notes, write reminders to yourself, or cut and paste text from Web sites using Opera's Notes tool. And when you double-click text you've pasted into a note from the Web, Opera takes you back to the site where you copied the text. For researchers, it's one of the all-time greatest features built into a browser.

To take notes in Opera, make sure the Hotlist (also called the Panel) shows in the left-hand pane. If it's not displayed, click the Hotlist icon on the top toolbar, or press F4. When the Hotlist is showing, click Notes. A list of any notes you've made in the past appears. To create a new note, click "New note," and type whatever you want—or copy text from a site you're browsing. You can also create folders to organize your notes. Figure 7-18 shows Opera's Notes feature in action.

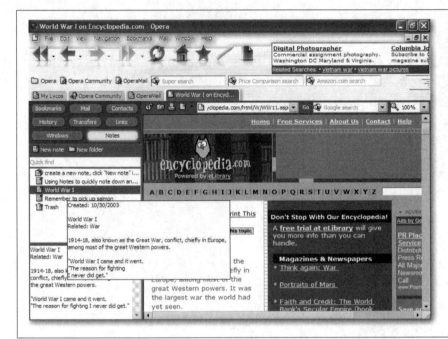

Figure 7-18:
When you hover your mouse over a note in Opera, a balloon appears displaying the first part of the note, as you can see here. Opera lets you create an unlimited number of notes.

Email

If you're like most people, you live and die by email, the greatest time-saver and time-waster known to humankind. It helps you stay in touch with friends and family around the globe—and it helps spammers stay in touch with you, whether you like it or not.

Chances are, you use one of two email programs from Microsoft: Outlook or Outlook Express. While they share a number of similar features, including their name, they're actually quite different pieces of software. Outlook Express comes with Windows XP; Outlook, the more powerful and complicated of the two programs, comes with Microsoft Office (or you can buy Outlook on its own). This chapter explains dozens of ways to add power to both of these juicy programs; it also gives tips on other email software such as Eudora.

Note: As you make your way through these hints, remember that what you see on your computer may differ somewhat from what you read here. Microsoft is notorious for changing Outlook every time it releases a new version, so your menus and features may vary a bit from what you see in this book. Outlook 2003 is a prime example, as it's dramatically different in some ways than previous versions, most notably in the way that it handles spam (page 217).

Sending and Receiving Email

Email is super easy to use, but there are actually a bunch of cool tricks to it you may not know about. This section tells you how to send a message more quickly, how to create your own personalized mail schedules, how to clean up those annoying > characters that litter forwarded email, and more.

8-1   Email in a Hurry

You can easily speed up your email composition by creating a desktop icon that automatically opens a new email message. Then, when you want to send a message, all you have to do is double-click that icon, type your message, and shoot it off.

To set up an email desktop icon, right-click your desktop and choose New → Shortcut. In the Create Shortcut box that appears, type *mailto:* and click the Next button. Type a name for the shortcut, like *Send an Email,* then click Finish. From now on, whenever you double-click that icon, your email program immediately opens a brand new message.

You can also create a shortcut that opens a new email message and addresses it to a specific person—which is useful if you frequently email a particular person. Just create the shortcut as described above, but type an email address next to *mailto:* like this—*mailto:johnjacob@jingleheimerschmidt.com.* When you name the shortcut, you may want to mention the recipient, as in, Email JJ. That way you'll remember who you're emailing.

ADD-IN ALERT

Checking Web-Based Email with a Desktop Email Program

When you use a free email service like Hotmail (*www. hotmail.com*) or Yahoo! mail (*www.yahoo.com*), you typically have to check your email on the Web, rather than with a desktop email program like Outlook or Eudora. That's because the free services don't let you use the normal *POP3* or *IMAP* email servers. (POP3 and IMAP are protocols that email servers use to handle the receipt and distribution of mail; email programs that live on your hard drive, like Outlook, use these protocols to exchange mail with the world, while Web-based email uses different standards.)

However, two free programs have figured out clever technological workarounds for the problem, letting you use your favorite email software to send and receive all your email without ever hitting the Web. Here are the details about each program:

- **YahooPOPs!** Normally, if you want to use your email software to get mail from Yahoo!, you have to pay extra. But if download and install the free YahooPOPs! program from *http://yahoopops.sourceforge.net,* you

can do it without paying a penny. After you install the program, you have to enter information about your Yahoo! account, such as your account name and password, then configure your email program to treat YahooPOPs! as if it were ISP-based email (just create a new account in your regular email program as you would normally). Voila! You can now use your email software to retrieve Yahoo! mail.

- **Hotmail Popper.** The only email software that lets you retrieve mail from Hotmail is Outlook Express. If you use Outlook or any other email program, you're out of luck…or are you? With Hotmail Popper, available for free from Boolean Dream (*www.boolean. ca/hotpop*), you can use any email software you want to send and receive mail from your Hotmail account. As with YahooPOPs!, after you install Hotmail Popper, you have to enter information such as your account name and password, then configure your email software to treat Hotmail Popper as if it were normal ISP-based mail.

8-2   Blind Carbon Copies

Sometimes, you want to send a copy of an email to someone without tipping off the message's other recipients. This arrangement is called a blind carbon copy, or Bcc. For example, if you're writing your boss to praise a co-worker, you might want to send a Bcc to the co-worker, so he can see your good deed.

But how do you send a Bcc? In Outlook and Outlook Express when you create a new message there doesn't appear to be any Bcc field. Here's what you need to do. After you create a new message, click the To: button. Choose a name from the list that appears, highlight it, and choose Bcc. If the person you want to Bcc doesn't show up, or you don't have any names in your address book yet, create a new contact by clicking the New Contact button. Now you can add that person to the Bcc list.

Tip: If you want the Bcc field visible *every time* you create a new message, both Outlook and Outlook Express let you add it. Open a new message, choose View and then look for All Headers or Bcc Field. Select either choice, and from here on out, your messages have a Bcc slot.

8-3   Checking Mail on Your Schedule

You may notice that Outlook and Outlook Express automatically check for mail every 30 minutes or so, whether you've told them to or not. The only problem is that this schedule can distract you from your work. A better option is to tell your email program to operate on *your* schedule.

Outlook

To change the mail-checking schedule in Outlook, choose Tools → Options → Mail Setup → Send/Receive. If you don't want Outlook to automatically check for mail, turn off the box next to "Schedule an automatic send/receive every _ minutes," click Close, and then click OK. Now Outlook only sends or receives mail when you click the Send/Receive button yourself. If you want Outlook to check mail on a particular schedule, check the box, and from the drop-down list, choose the schedule you want Outlook to follow.

Outlook Express

If you don't want Outlook Express to automatically check for new mail, choose Tools → Options → General, turn off "Check for new messages every _ minutes," and then click OK. To set a particular schedule, turn on this option and, from the drop-down list, choose how often you want Outlook Express to send and receive mail, as shown in Figure 8-1.

8-4   Allowing Time for Second Thoughts

Have you ever sent an email and immediately wished you could *unsend* it? Both Outlook and Outlook Express offer a way to *not* send your messages as soon as you

---

hit the Send button. Instead, your messages patiently wait in your outbox until the next time you *retrieve* your mail—then the messages get sent.

To have Outlook behave this way, choose Tools → Options → Mail Setup and turn off the box next to "Send immediately when connected." In Outlook Express, choose Tools → Options → Send and deselect "Send messages immediately."

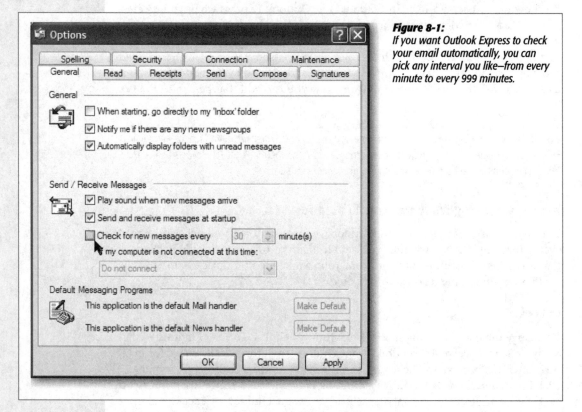

Figure 8-1:
If you want Outlook Express to check your email automatically, you can pick any interval you like—from every minute to every 999 minutes.

8-5   Cleaning Up Email Conversations

Email conversations can quickly fill up with "<" or ">" symbols, extra lines, or other extraneous characters, particularly when a message has been volleyed back and forth with multiple responses. You can automatically strip out all those symbols and make your message easy to read using the program eCleaner, available for free from *http://ecleaner.tripod.com.*

Once you've installed the software, start by opening eCleaner and then opening the email message you want uncluttered. Next, copy the text of the email to the Windows clipboard, run eCleaner, and press the F1 key or click the program's Smiley icon. Then return to your email program and paste the text into a message. Voila! The unnecessary symbols and characters are gone, though you might need to do a little bit of manual cleanup to completely finish the job.

8-6   Revealing Message Headers

When you receive an email, there's a lot of information about the message you don't see—like which mail server sent it, which servers the message passed through during its journey to you, and what time the message was sent.

Note: When you send an email to someone, a type of computer called a *mail server* makes sure your message gets to the proper recipient. A server that sends mail is an SMTP server, which stands for secure mail transfer protocol; one that *receives* mail is a POP3 server, which stands for Post Office Protocol.

Most of the time, you probably don't care about this hidden information. But there are times when you might want to see it. For example, you may want to find out which server has sent you a piece of spam, or if your mail seems to be arriving after some delay, you can learn when incoming messages actually left the launching pad.

This information is all buried in each message's *header*—details about the email that are typically hidden by Outlook and Outlook Express. Figure 8-2 shows you what's in a header.

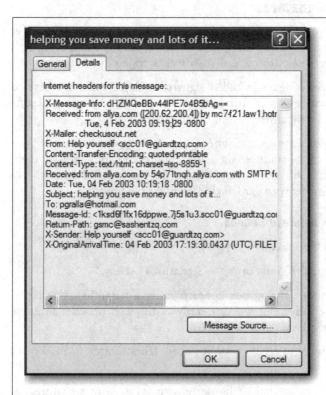

Figure 8-2:
Outlook Express, like Outlook, lets you look inside email headers.

To see header information in Outlook, right-click the message you want to view and choose Options. The header information appears at the bottom of the screen. You can scroll through this information, and also copy and paste it, just as you would any other text in XP. You can also view this information when you're reading a message by choosing View → Options.

Note: When you're reading a message in Outlook, choosing View → Message Header doesn't display the same details. Instead, it turns the To:, Cc:, and Subject: lines on and off in your email.

To reveal header information in Outlook Express, right-click a message and choose Properties → Details. A screen like the one shown in Figure 8-2 appears.

Sign-Offs

You can unleash your inner, digital John Hancock thanks to a few signature tools in email. As this section explains, you can end your messages with a custom signature, use homegrown art, or even include a digital business card.

8-7   Customized Signatures

Have you ever noticed how some emails feature a carefully constructed sign-off at the bottom of the message—either no-nonsense information like the sender's name and phone number, or a pithy (or not-so-witty) saying or quote?

These personalized blocks of text are called signatures. And you don't have to retype them every time you send an email. Instead, you can set up your email software to automatically add a signature to your outgoing mail.

Both Outlook and Outlook Express can append signatures to the bottom of your messages. You can even create multiple signatures, and then choose among them depending on the recipient of your email. Writing the president of a bank? Use your standard signoff. Writing your garden club buddies? Go flowery.

Setting up and using a signature in Outlook

To create a signature in Outlook follow these steps:

1. **Choose Tools → Options → Mail Format → Signatures → New.**

   The Create New Signature dialog box appears. Enter a name for your signature—something descriptive, so you can easily distinguish between multiple signatures, if you create them.

2. **Decide whether you want to create your signature from scratch or modify an existing signature.**

   Select one of the options beneath "Choose how to create your signature," as shown in Figure 8-3. If you haven't yet created a signature, you'll probably want to pick "Start with a blank signature" which lets you start with a blank canvas.

If you've already got a signature that you like, but you just want to create a slightly different version—for example, a signature that includes your mailing address in addition to your name—pick "Use this existing signature as a template:" and then select from the pop-up menu the name of the signature that you want to use as a model.

"Use this file as a template" lets you import a file created in another program, like Word or Notepad. If you select this option you first need to create and save the file, which can only be a text file (one that ends in .txt); then click Browse to select the file.

Once you've made your selection, click Next.

Figure 8-3:
When creating a new signature, you can start from scratch, customize an existing signature, or use a text file as a template.

3. **Create your signature.**

Regardless of which method you chose in the previous step, you'll create your signature in the "Signature text" box, as shown in Figure 8-4. You can also attach your own *vCard*—an electronic business card that some email programs recognize—to your signature (see hint 8-9 for more on vCards). Do so either by choosing a vCard from the pop-up menu or by selecting "New vCard from Contact."

Click Finish, then OK.

4. **Assign a signature to new messages and to replies and forwarded messages.**

You should be on the Mail Format tab of the Options dialog box. If not, return there by choosing Tools → Options → Mail Format. In the Signature section, use the drop-down list to select which signature you want to appear at the end of new messages and which signature you want for replies and forwards (you can choose the same for both). You can also choose None.

Tip: You can manually add or a change the signature in any email by choosing Insert → Signature and choosing from the list of signatures you've created.

Figure 8-4:
With signatures, you're not limited to the letters of the alphabet; you can use any character on your keyboard. So you might want to offset a quote with hyphens, as shown here.

Setting up and using a signature in Outlook Express

To create a signature in Outlook Express follow these steps:

1. **Choose Tools → Options → Signatures → New.**

   As you can see in Figure 8-5, Outlook Express automatically creates a blank signature, named Signature #1.

2. **Enter your signature in the Text box. You can rename the signature by highlighting it, choosing Rename, and entering a new title.**

   Use a descriptive name for your signature so you can easily differentiate among the various signatures you set up.

3. **Click OK.**

   From now on, whenever you send an email, Outlook Express adds your sign-off to the bottom of the message.

Tip: If you have more than one email address, Outlook Express lets you assign different signatures to each one. Choose Tools → Options → Signatures and highlight the signature you want to assign to a particular email address. Then click Advanced, choose the email address you want the signature to adorn, and click OK. To assign a different signature to another email address, repeat the process.

Figure 8-5:
Create a new signature using the Edit Signature text box, or use the contents of a text file by selecting the File button and browsing to an existing file.

8-8   Fancy Signatures

In lieu of, or in addition to, regular text you can also use pictures made entirely with keyboard characters, for your signature, like this:

```
  '&`
   #
   #
  _#
 ( # )
 / 0 \
( === )
`---'
```

GuitarMania…Don't fret! We sell guitars—strings attached.

The guitar is an example of *ASCII art*. (ASCII stands for "American Standard Code for Information Interchange.) ASCII characters are plain text characters you can type using your keyboard.

A number of Web sites post what's known as ASCII art, pictures or images composed entirely of ASCII characters. What's really sweet is that you can copy this artwork for free. A few good sources are *www.chris.com/ascii, www.xs4all.nl/~svzanten/ascii/line_art,* and *www.ascii-art.com.* To transfer art from a Web site into your signature, first copy it to the clipboard, and then paste it into your signature, or into a file you create in Notepad (Figure 8-6).

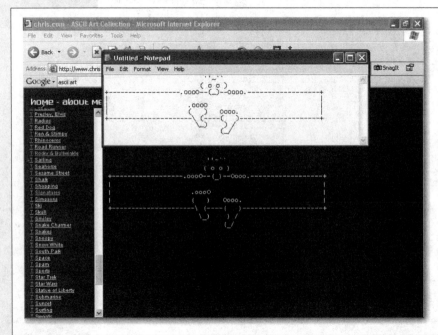

Figure 8-6:
Copying and pasting ASCII art from the Internet is an easy way to spruce up your email signature. Sometimes, the artist asks that you copy his or her initials with a drawing, although this site—http://chris.com/ascii/—doesn't require it.

You can also create ASCII art from a drawing you already have on your computer. Start by downloading the shareware program Email Effects from *www.sigsoftware.com.* Then import your drawing into the program. Poof! Email Effects automatically creates a piece of ASCII art from the drawing. Email Effects also includes tools that make it easy to create your own ASCII art from scratch. It's shareware and free to try, but if you continue to use it, you'll need to shell out $15.

8-9 Using Digital Business Cards

Time was, you'd get a business card from somebody and you'd have staple it to a page in your Rolodex or hand-enter the info into your address book. Now, thanks to *vCards*—electronic business cards that automatically input a person's details into most email programs' contact lists—the process happens faster than a speeding bullet.

vCards are attached to email messages as files with the extension *.vcd*. When you receive an email message with a vCard attached, just double-click the attachment, and your address book copies the information in the vCard—either creating a new entry or updating an existing one. You can use this feature with most email programs.

You can also attach your own vCard to outgoing email using either Outlook Express or Outlook.

Creating and sending vCards with Outlook

In Outlook, you can send your own vCard with every outgoing message or just the ones you specify. To attach a vCard to *all* your outgoing mail:

1. **Choose Tools → Options → Mail Format → Signatures.**

   This opens the same dialog box that lets you create signatures for your email. For more information about signatures, see hint 8-7.

2. **In the Create Signatures dialog box, click New.**

   Although you'd typically use this screen to create a new signature, in this case, you're creating a vCard.

3. **In the Create New Signatures dialog box that appears, type a name for your vCard and click Next.**

   Name it something descriptive, so you instantly recognize it when you choose it from a drop-down list. Also, it's a smart idea to include the word vCard in the name, so you remember the signature is associated with your vCard.

4. **In the Edit Signature dialog box that appears (see Figure 8-7), click "New vCard from Contact." Then choose the contact information you want to attach as a vCard, click Add, and then click OK.**

   In the Edit Signature dialog box, the address you're attaching as a vCard shows up in the vCard options section.

5. **Click Finish and then OK.**

   Outlook creates a vCard and automatically attaches it to all your outgoing mail.

Note: If you need to find your vCard in the future, Windows XP saves it in My Computer → C: → Documents and Settings → [Your Account] → Application Data → Microsoft → Signatures. (Your Account is your XP user name.)

If you want to attach a vCard to some messages and not others, rather than creating the card as outlined above, here's how. Open your contacts in Outlook, and highlight the contact information you want to use for your vCard. Then choose File → Save As; for the format, choose vCard Files (*.vcf). Browse to the folder where you want to save the vCard, and remember this location. Then when you're sending a message and want to include a vCard, attach it as you would any other file, by clicking the paper clip button near the top of the screen.

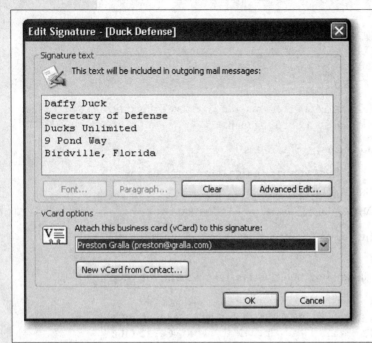

Figure 8-7:
In Outlook, you can include both a vCard and a signature at the bottom of your email.

Sending vCards with Outlook Express

As with Outlook, Outlook Express lets you automatically attach a vCard to every email you send, or just to specific messages.

To send a vCard with all your messages, choose Tools → Options → Compose. The dialog box shown in Figure 8-8 appears. In the Business Cards section, turn on the box next to Mail, and choose your name from the drop-down list on the right. If you want to edit your data, click Edit and a form appears that lets you edit the information. When you're done, click OK. Now, every time you send an email message to someone, Outlook Express attaches a vCard.

To attach a vCard to messages on a case-by-case basis, don't turn on the box on the screen shown in Figure 8-8. Instead, open the Address Book in Outlook Express, highlight the contact information you want sent as a vCard, and choose File → Export → Business Card (vCard). Save the file to your hard disk. Then, whenever you want to attach a vCard to an email message, click the Attach button, browse to where you've saved the vCard, and attach it. Then send the mail as you would normally—your vCard rides along as an attachment.

Slamming Spam

If you have a desire to enlarge certain body parts, want to make a mint at home in your free time, or expect Nigerian strangers to shower you with several million dollars in exchange for a modest investment, then you love spam. Otherwise, it's one of life's biggest annoyances.

The following section helps you to stanch the flood.

8-10   Hiding Your Email Address from Spammers

The best way to avoid unwanted mail is to keep your email address out of spammers' hands in the first place. There's no foolproof way to do this—no matter how hard you try, some spammers will track you down—but there are several things you can do to minimize the risk.

- **Opt out of mailings.** Web sites frequently ask when you register at them whether you want to receive email offers from the site's sponsors, or from the site itself. Just say no! Although some sites post privacy policies explaining how they use or share their email lists, often the best defense is to completely avoid sharing your address.

- **Use a different email address for registering.** Another strategy is to use a separate email address when you sign up for things online, so your main email account doesn't get overwhelmed with junk. (You can set up a free email address through sites like *www.hotmail.com* or *www.yahoo.com;* also, many ISPs let their customers use several email addresses on one account.) Use this alternative address when you register with a Web site, enter a contest online, or need to give your email address to a company you don't know. That way, if your address gets passed on to spammers, it won't affect your main email account.

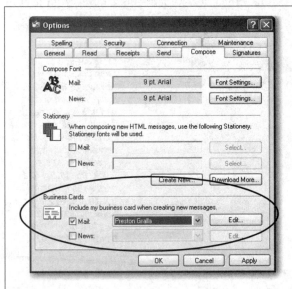

Figure 8-8:
You can attach vCards to all outgoing email, as well as any messages you post on Internet discussion boards. To leave your digital calling card with your discussion board posts, turn on the box next to News, and choose your contact information or name from the drop-down list.

• **Spell out your email address if you post it on a discuss group or display it on a Web site you've created.** Many spammers use "harvesting" programs to collect email addresses posted on Web pages (a favorite target is Internet discussion groups because posts remain online indefinitely). When these harvesting programs find email addresses, they add them to their spam lists. So if your email address is going to appear online, spell it out—for example, use "jay at lo dot com" rather than *jay@lo.com*. Real people can figure out how to reach you, but harvesting programs won't.

8-11 Built-In Spam-Fighting Tools

Your next line of defense is to use the anti-spam tools built right into your email program. These tools won't *completely* stop spam, but they can at least blast out an unhealthy chunk.

Spiking spam with Outlook

Some of the spam out there is enough to make a longshoreman blush. Outlook's reaction is similar: it can scan incoming messages and then display junk mail in gray and messages with adult content in maroon. To activate this spam patrol, select Tools → Organize and then click the Junk E-Mail button. Then click either (or both) of the buttons that say Turn On. Now you can easily scan your inbox for messages in either gray or maroon and delete them manually.

Note: This section covers versions of Outlook released before Outlook 2003; for Outlook 2003, see page 217..

You can also manually add domains and addresses to Outlook's anti-spam list as a more robust way of fighting spam. When you receive a message you consider spam, right-click it and choose Junk Email. From the menu, choose "Add to Junk Senders list" or "Add to Adult Content Senders list."

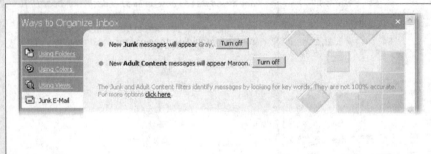

Figure 8-9:
From this screen, you can turn Outlook's spam filters on and off, and add new names to the junk mail list. Outlook differentiates between regular spam (which it considers "Junk" messages) and pornographic spam (which it calls "Adult Content"). So make sure to turn on both types of filters.

Note: When messages are labeled Junk–either by you or by Outlook–Outlook sends them to a Junk folder, and you can delete them from there. The advantage is that you can easily sift through the Junk folder and look for legit email, then delete the rest wholesale. It's a lot easier than picking through your inbox for the bad apples.

Another way to add senders to either list is to click the Organize button on the Outlook toolbar, and choose Junk E-Mail. The screen shown in Figure 8-9 appears. To add a sender to either list, click the link that says "For more options click here," then select Edit Junk Senders or Edit Adult Content Senders. Now add addresses to either list.

Canning spam with Outlook 2003

With Outlook 2003, Microsoft finally got spam-fighting right. As soon as you turn the program on, it starts fighting spam, and you don't have to do a darn thing. Whenever it encounters what it believes is spam, it promptly moves the offending email to the Junk Email folder. You can then delete it yourself by deleting mail from the folder.

You can, however, fine-tune its spam-fighting features. The program starts off using what it considers a low-filter level, which means it filters out most spam, but it also might miss some. On the other hand, the low-filter setting is less likely to filter out legitimate mail, so for most people it's the best way to go. However, if you want to really beef up your spam fighting, choose Tools → Options → Junk Email, select High, and click OK. This is Outlook's most aggressive setting.

You can also teach the spam filter to improve over time, by telling it when a particular piece of email is spam or legitimate. Right-click a message and choose Junk Email. To tell Outlook to treat a certain sender's email as spam, select Add Sender to Blocked Senders List. To tell Outlook to treat the sender as legitimate, choose Add Sender to Safe Sender List. And if you find a piece of legitimate email in the Junk Email folder, right click it and choose Junk Email → Mark as Not Junk.

Canning spam with Outlook Express

Outlook Express's spam-fighting tools are fairly rudimentary, but they can still keep some of the Viagra offers and get-rich-quick schemes from reaching your inbox. Its main drawback is that Outlook Express requires a little bit of effort on your part—at least to get the spam filter setup. Specifically, you need to add spammers' email addresses and/or *domains* to a Blocked Senders List. (A domain is the main part of an Internet address, or what comes after the @ sign in an email address—for example, moneysinkpit.com.) Then, every time a message comes in from a blocked address or domain, Outlook Express automatically sends it to the Deleted Items folder.

To add an address or domain to the list, choose Tools → Message Rules → Blocked Senders List. The screen pictured in Figure 8-10 appears. Type the email address or domain you want to block and click OK. From now on, messages from that sender or domain go straight to your Deleted Items folder without cluttering up your inbox.

Note: If you block spam this way, be sure to check your Deleted Items folder regularly, in order to confirm that no unwanted email accidentally ended up there.

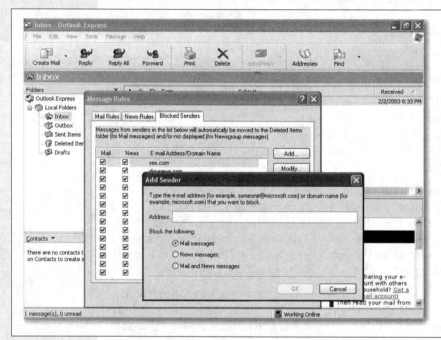

Figure 8-10:
Outlook Express fights spam by blocking mail from specific email addresses or entire domains (for example, Microsoft.com). When you block an address or domain, you have a choice of blocking it not only in email, but also when you participate in Internet newsgroup discussions.

8-12 Third-Party Spam-Killers

If you use a version of Outlook released before Outlook 2003, or any version of Outlook *Express,* you'll probably find their spam-fighting tools about as effective as a squirt gun aimed at a house fire.

You can always buy more robust software to stem the onslaught of junk mail, but that often means paying a monthly fee. If you're budget-conscious, another option is to download a free spam-fighting program. SurfSecret SpamDrop, available for free at *www.surfsecret.com/products/product-SDROP.html,* uses the collective effort of thousands of people to kill spam.

As each person uses the program to identify and delete spam from their own inbox, SpamDrop shares that information with everyone else using the software. As a result, the program can now kill the same spam in other people's mailboxes (by adding that sender to a blocked list in everyone's software).

SpamDrop also lets you add email addresses to a *whitelist* or a *blacklist*. A whitelist is a list of email addresses it's OK to receive email from, even if the software considers it spam. A blacklist is a list of email addresses you never want to receive email from, even if the software considers it legitimate mail. SpamDrop works with Outlook, and is free for personal use. It doesn't work with Outlook Express as of this writing, although its authors claim they're working on making it compatible.

Tip: Want to get revenge on spammers? Sign up for the free Spam Cop service at *www.spamcop.net.* The site teaches you how to trace spam information back to the sender, and then report on the sender to the Spam Cop site. Be forewarned that tracking spam is not for the faint of heart or time.

Naturally, there are several other effective spam killers besides SpamDrop. Among them is MailWasher, which works with any email program. Rather than operating inside your email program, MailWasher operates before your email so*ftware* kicks in, identifying spam so you can delete it before it hits your mailbox. You can download MailWasher from *www.mailwasher.net.*

Organizing and Handling Mail

If your inbox look like the computer equivalent of a bad hair day, you'll probably welcome some tools to tame mess. This section offers all kinds of hints for organizing and handling your mail, including nifty ways to force your email software to sort everything automatically for you.

8-13   Adding New Contacts in Two Seconds

Here's a super-quick way to add new contacts to Outlook and Outlook Express. If you use Outlook, when you receive an email from someone you want in your address book, open the message, right-click the From: or Cc: line, and then choose Add to Contacts. Outlook adds the sender's name and email address to your contacts. In Outlook Express, you don't even have to open the email; in your inbox, just right-click the message and choose Add Sender to Address Book.

WORKAROUND WORKSHOP

Outlook Express Address Book Bloat

Outlook Express has the very bad habit of automatically adding names to your address book. Every time you reply to an email message, the program enters the person's contact information in your address book without telling you.

As a result, your address book can quickly fill up with people you may not ever want to contact again. It also means

you can end up with duplicate entries. For example, if someone already in your address book sends you a message from a new or different email address, Outlook Express creates a separate entry for that person.

To stop this behavior, simply choose Tools → Options → Send, and turn off "Automatically put people I reply to in my address book."

8-14   Marking Messages Unread

Outlook and Outlook Express both mark new, unread emails in bold so they stand out from others in your inbox. But when you keep your cursor on a message for several seconds, the bold disappears—even if you haven't actually read the message. As a result, you have no way of telling which messages you've opened, and you can easily forget to go back and read the message as your inbox overflows with new mail.

It's a snap to return a message to its unread state: Right-click it and choose "Mark as unread" from the context menu. Now you won't forget to send your boss the spreadsheet she requested, or bid on that unicycle your friend saw on eBay.

8-15   Clearing Clutter

Email conversations can go back and forth for a *while*, generating a bunch of messages about the same subject scattered all over your inbox. Here's a terrific—and little known—trick for organizing that clutter: *threaded* conversations. When you thread your messages, Outlook or Outlook Express clumps together all the messages that are part of the same conversation. Figure 8-11 shows you what threading looks like.

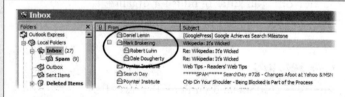

Figure 8-11:
When you thread your email, related messages appear indented below the first one in that conversation. It takes half a day to get used to this arrangement, and then it's hard to live without.

To thread your messages in Outlook 2003, when you're in your inbox, select ViewCurrent View → By Conversation Topic. That's it; you've just decluttered your inbox.

Note: In Outlook, this setting applies to one folder at a time. If you want to thread the messages in other folders, like Sent or Bar Mitzvah Invitations 2006, you have to repeat the process when you've got that folder open.

In Outlook Express, choose View → Current View → Group Messages by Conversation. The setting applies to all your folders.

Tip: If you've threaded the messages in a very full folder, and you want to sort by date or sender or attachment so you can find a particular message, it's often easiest to turn *off* threading when you search, and then turn it back on when you're done. Just follow the menus again to turn it off.

8-16   Taking Control of Mail Overload

If you're having a hard time sorting your mail manually, both Outlook and Outlook Express offer help. Although many people don't realize it, you can set these programs to automatically move incoming mail to a specific folder based on who sent the message (say, sort all the messages from people in your Dungeons and Dragons club to one folder), or based on keywords in the text (anything mentioning "dodecahedral dice" goes in the same folder) . They can also sound an alarm when a message from the big cheese in your department drops into your inbox, and they can do other helpful tricks to help you stay on top of your mail.

These actions are called *rules*, and they simply trigger different responses depending on instructions you've set. They're key to power email management.

Creating rules in Outlook

To create a rule in Outlook, choose Tools → Rules Wizard; the Rules Wizard appears, as shown in Figure 8-12. Now just follow the wizard's instructions to establish some organizational rules for Outlook to follow.

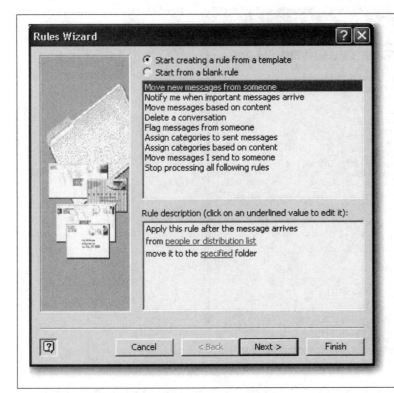

Figure 8-12:
The Rules Wizard lets you automate how Outlook handles your incoming email. Choose the rules you want to apply from the top part of the screen, and click the links near the bottom to finish. You may want to choose a destination folder, for example, after you click the link.

For some people, following the wizard's instructions is a no-brainer. Others find the process time-consuming—and error-prone. You can make the setup process feel less like you're training to become a computer programmer by starting with a message in your inbox that you want to create a rule around. That way, Outlook begins the rule-creation process by giving you some suggestions—many of which can turn out to be spot on.

Here's what you need to do:

1. **Select the message you want to base your rule on.**

   Find a message you want Outlook to handle in a particular way, like an email from your mother, whose missives you want to route to the "Mail from Mom" folder.

2. **Right-click the message, and choose Create Rule.**

   The screen shown in Figure 8-13 appears. To start with, the rule already contains certain information about the message, such as the sender and its subject. Each of these kernels of information appears next to a blank box. To incorporate these items into your new rule, select the box next to the factors you want (Outlook considers these factors *conditions*). Click Next.

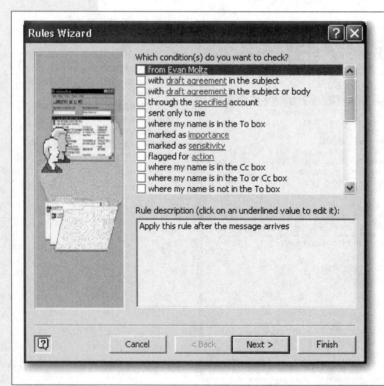

Figure 8-13:
One way to create a new rule is to select an existing email message, then choose the parts of the message you want to base the rule on—the sender's address, for example.

3. **Select the action you want Outlook to perform (when it encounters the conditions that you've identified).**

   In the screen that appears, select the action you want Outlook to take—say, transferring every message from a particular sender to a specific folder—and click Next.

4. **Specify any exceptions you want to add to the rule.**

In the following screen, you can create an exception to your rule; in other words, you can say when *not* to apply the rule. For instance, if the message is marked as having High importance, you may want to leave it in your inbox. Click Next.

5. **Name the rule.**

Now every time mail arrives matching the conditions you've specified, Outlook performs the actions you've chosen.

Note: You can edit or delete a rule you've created by choosing Tools → Rules Wizard. To edit a rule, highlight it and choose Modify. To delete a rule, highlight it and choose Delete.

Creating rules with Outlook Express

Here's how to create a rule in Outlook Express:

1. **Choose Tools → Message Rules → Mail.**

The New Mail Rule dialog box appears, as shown in Figure 8-14. If you've already created any rules, Outlook Express displays them in a list, which you can edit. Create a new rule by clicking New.

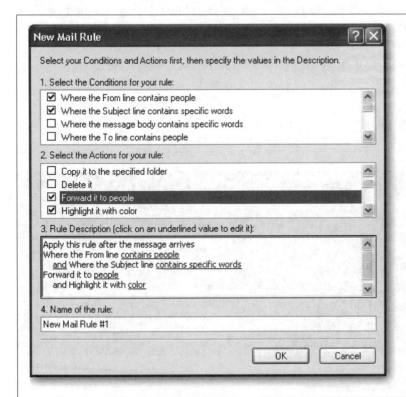

Figure 8-14:
To create a new rule in Outlook Express, follow the four steps depicted on this screen. When you click an underlined link in step 3, you must fill in specific pieces of data that are required to finish the rule (for example, by identifying which people you want to send a message to).

Note: You can also create rules by selecting a message as your starting point and, from the Outlook Express menu bar, choosing Message → Create Rule from Message. The New Mail Rule Dialog box appears, with information from that message already filled in

2. **In step 1 of the New Mail Rule dialog box, select the conditions you want to trigger the rule.**

   Conditions might include certain words in the subject line, or when the email is from a specific person. Note that you can combine several of these conditions. For example, if a message is from your car mechanic *and* the subject includes the phrase "new transmission needed," shoot it into your Crisis folder.

3. **In step 2 of the dialog box, select the actions you want Outlook Express to take.**

   You may ask Outlook Express to move the message to a specific folder, forward it to a particular person, or just delete it. Once again, you have the ability here to combine several actions. For example, you might want to automatically move those mechanic messages to your Crisis folde, *and* copy them to your Car Repair History folder *and* highlight them red.

4. **In step 3 of the dialog box, click the blue links for more information about the rule you're creating.**

   For example, if you've created a rule that looks for a particular word in the subject line and then moves the message to a specific folder, you would type the keyword Outlook Express should look for, and also choose the folder where you want the email moved to.

5. **In step 4 of the dialog box, type in a name for the new rule and click OK.**

   That's it. You're good to go.

Note: Your control over these rules doesn't end after you create them. You can always edit them, delete them, or change the order in which they're applied by choosing Tools → Message Rules → Mail.

POWER USERS' CLINIC

Import and Export Rules in Outlook

If you've got Outlook on more than one computer, or you go out and buy a new machine, you can save yourself the headache of having to recreate rules from scratch. You just need to transfer the rules from one PC to the other.

In Outlook, choose Tools → Rules Wizard → Options, and click Export Rules. Outlook creates a file that ends with a .rwz extension. Outlook sends the file to your My Documents folder, unless you tell it otherwise. When it's done, copy this file to your other computer and open Outlook. Then select Tools → Rules Wizard → Options → Import Rules, and open the .rwz file. That's it. Outlook automatically incorporates the mail-sorting rules you've imported. Using this method, you can also share rules with other Outlook users.

8-17 Opening Blocked File Attachments

Email-borne viruses are nasty. They can inflict serious harm on your PC and can also use your computer as a jumping-off point to attack other machines. As a service to us all, Microsoft has taken a draconian approach to protecting you from these dangers. If you use Outlook or Outlook Express, your email program may refuse to let you open a wide variety of file attachments, including those ending in .exe, .bat, and many other common file extensions.

Table 8-1 lists some of the files Outlook blocks you from opening (for a full list, check out *http://support.microsoft.com/default.aspx?scid=kb;en-us;829982*). When you receive a file with one of these extensions, Outlook is courteous enough to show you the message name and inform you that it was blocked.

Note: Depending on the version of Outlook you use, it may not block you from opening any files—or it may block only some of the files in Table 8-1.

Table 8-1. Blocked File Extensions in Outlook

Extension	File Type
.asx	Windows Media audio or video
.bat	Batch file
.cmd	Microsoft Windows NT command script
.cpl	Control panel extension
.crt	Security certificate
.exe	Executable program
.hlp	Help file
.hta	HTML program
.inf	Setup information
.js	Jscript file
.jse	Jscript encoded script file
.msi	Microsoft Windows installer package
.msp	Microsoft Windows installer patch
.mst	Microsoft Windows installer transform; Microsoft Visual Test source file
.ops	Office XP settings
.pcd	Photo CD image; Microsoft Visual compiled script
.prf	Microsoft Outlook profile settings
.reg	Registry entries

Opening attachments with Outlook

With the right coaxing, Outlook will let you open any type of file attachment with a simple Registry hack. First, quit Outlook if it's running. Then run the Registry Editor (see page 328) and go to My Computer → HKEY_CURRENT_USER → *Software* →

Microsoft → Office → 10.0 → Outlook → Security. Create a new String Value called Level1Remove. In the Value Data field, type the name of the file extension you want to open, for example, *.exe.* Separate multiple file extensions with a semicolon, like this: *.exe; .bat; .pif.* Use Table 8-1 as a guide to decide which blocked file extensions you want access to. (Warning: Be careful about allowing .EXE files through, because they can contain viruses.) Exit the Registry and reboot. You can now open the file extensions you specified.

Tip: Attachment Options is a free Outlook add-in program that lets you open email attachments—without having to edit the Registry. It's available at *www.slovaktech.com/attachmentoptions.htm.*

Blocked attachments and Outlook Express

Like its *software* compadre, Outlook Express also takes a heavy-handed approach by preventing you from opening a wide variety of email file attachments. Those ending in .exe, .bat, and many other common file extensions, are all off-limits.

Note: Depending on the version of Outlook Express you use, it may *not* block you from opening attachments. But if you've installed Windows XP Service Pack 1, Outlook Express Service Pack 1, or Internet Explorer 6 Service Pack 1, chances are Outlook Express does, in fact, prevent you from opening certain file attachments. Using a newer version of Windows XP may also limit your ability to open attachments.

With Outlook Express, you can't select which specific types of attachments you want to open; you must tell it to grant you access to all blocked file types, or none at all.

To open blocked attachments, choose Tools → Options → Security, and uncheck "Do not allow attachments to be saved or opened that could potentially be a virus," as shown in Figure 8-15. (You may have to close Outlook Express and restart it for the new setting to take effect.)

Figure 8-15:
When you deselect this box, Outlook Express lets you open any email attachment you receive. If this is how you want to proceed, make sure you always use anti-virus software when opening these attachments—otherwise, you're asking for trouble!

Uncheck box to let yourself open all
email attachments in Outlook Express

Getting Email to Play Nicely with Windows

Email and Windows XP don't always play well together. For example, XP often insists on needlessly launching Windows Messenger whenever you open Outlook. The following hints are designed to stop this incessant quarreling and keep you emailing smoothly.

8-18   Killing the "Unread Messages" Notice

Your Windows welcome screen tells you the number of unread messages you have in your email box, with one teeny-weeny caveat: It's usually wrong (Figure 8-16). No one, including Microsoft, seems to know why this happens. But there's no reason you need to keep seeing this useless information.

Figure 8-16:
The number of messages announced by your welcome screen can be waaaay off.

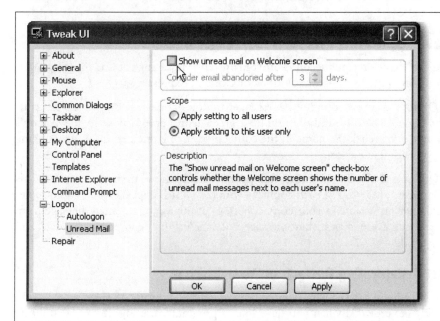

Figure 8-17:
TweakUI lets you stop XP from telling you on the Windows welcome screen how many unread email messages you have. The number is invariably inaccurate, so you might as well turn it off.

To make this change, you need to download and install a program called TweakUI, available for free at *www.microsoft.com/windowsxp/pro/downloads/powertoys.asp*. (For more about TweakUI, see page 28).

Once you've installed the software, choose Start → All Programs → Power Toys for Windows XP → TweakUI for Windows XP. Choose Logon → Unread Mail, and in the screen that appears (Figure 8-17), turn off "Show unread mail on Welcome screen" and click OK. From now on, Windows XP won't bother telling you how many messages it thinks you haven't read.

8-19   Killing the Windows Messenger

When you use Outlook or Outlook Express, Windows Messenger may open every time you use either program. If this bothers you, there's an easy way to keep Messenger from popping up.

In Outlook Express, choose Tools → Options → General, and deselect "Automatically log on to Windows Messenger." Depending on your version of Outlook Express, you may instead need to choose Tools → Windows Messenger → Options → Preferences, and deselect "Run this program when Windows starts." Now click OK.

Note: This change stops Windows Messenger from starting whenever you start Windows, not just when you start Outlook Express.

To turn off Windows Messenger in Outlook, choose Tools → Options → Other, and uncheck the box next to "Enable Instant Messaging in Microsoft Outlook. "Click OK.

8-20   Contacting Windows Messenger Buddies

You can shave precious seconds off your Instant Messaging routine by using Windows Messenger from within Outlook or Outlook Express.

In Outlook Express, Windows Messenger buddies appear at the top of the contacts pane. When a buddy is online, a green icon appears next to the person's name. Double-click the name in the contacts pane to launch an instant messaging session with that person.

In Outlook, if a buddy is online, that person's name shows up in the InfoBar. This bar appears at the top of each contact's window (which appears when you double-click a person's name in your contact list), or at the top of an email message from the contact. To send an instant message, click the InfoBar, compose a message, and click Send.

8-21   Relocating Outlook on Your Taskbar

The Windows XP taskbar—which runs along the bottom of your screen—can quickly get crowded when you have lots of programs running. If you're suffering from taskbar overload, you might want Outlook or Outlook Express to tuck itself into the *notification area* whenever you minimize either program. (The notification area, also called the *system tray*, is the right-hand portion of the taskbar, next to the clock).

To activate this change, you need to download and run a separate program: either HideOE (to hide Outlook Express), or HideOlk (to hide Outlook), both available for free at *www.r2.com.au.*

Note: You can also use a Registry hack to shift Outlook to the notification area when you minimize the program. Run the Registry Editor (page 328) and go to My Computer → HKEY_CURRENT_USER → Software → Microsoft → Office → 10.0 → Outlook → Preferences. Create a new DWORD value called MinToTray and assign it a value of 1. Exit the Registry; the change takes effect right away. To return Outlook to its normal behavior, either delete the MinToTray DWORD value, or give it a value of 0.

Outlook-Only Tips

Most people only scratch the surface of Outlook's capabilities. This section explains how to delve more deeply into its mysteries and realize more of its vast potential.

8-22   Opening Outlook in Separate Windows

If you use Outlook for your email, calendar, and contacts, you probably spend too much time flipping back and forth among these tools. Every time you want to switch between, say, your inbox and your calendar, you have to click the Outlook Bar—or in Outlook 2003, the Navigation Pane—then choose the feature you want. Here's a quicker way: Open your contacts, calendar, and email in their own windows. Now you can view them onscreen at the same time, or switch among them using the Alt-Tab key combination.

If you're reading email, say, and need to check your calendar, right-click the calendar icon in the Outlook Bar or Navigation Pane and choose Open in New Window. Your calendar opens in a separate window. You can now switch between your inbox and your date book by pressing Alt-Tab, or simultaneously view both onscreen by right-clicking the taskbar and choosing either Tile Windows Horizontally or Tile Windows Vertically.

8-23   Deleting Outlook Items Lickety-Split

Deleting anything in Outlook is normally a two-step process. When you delete an email message, for instance, Outlook doesn't actually get rid of it—it just moves the message to the Deleted Items folder. You must then manually empty your Deleted Items folder to permanently vanquish the message (or set Outlook to empty that folder every time you exit the program).

If you want to cut your deletion work in half, here's what to do: Hold down the Shift key when you delete an item to have Outlook delete it immediately, rather than moving it to the Deleted Items folder. You can also delete multiple items at once using this technique. First, select the items you want to delete by holding down the Shift key when you click them. Then, when they're all selected, keep pressing Shift when you press the Delete key; they all disappear from your screen without a trace.

8-24   Removing Outlook's Memorized Addresses

One of Outlook's niftier features is its ability to remember people you've sent mail to in the past. Whenever you open a new message and type a few letters into the "To:" field, a list pops up with names or addresses that begin with the same letters, as you can see in Figure 8-18.

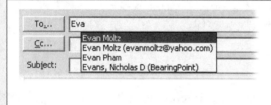

Figure 8-18:
Unlike the rest of us, Outlook never forgets a name, prompting you with a list of past correspondents whenever you type a few letters into the "To:" box in a new email message. If you don't want Outlook to display a list of past correspondents when you type the first few letters of an address, you can tell it to stop second-guessing you. Open Outlook and choose Tools → Options → E-mail Options → Advanced E-mail Options, and turn off "Suggest names while completing the To, Cc and Bcc fields." Then click OK three times.

But as neat as this feature is, it causes problems as well: Outlook has a memory like an elephant, so it never forgets an address. This means the pop-up lists grow longer and longer, and are frequently filled with outdated addresses—not to mention people you never plan to email again.

It's easy to kill any address from the pop-up list. Create a new email message, start to type an email address, and when the list of addresses pops up, use the up or down arrow keys to highlight the address you want to scratch. Then press the Delete key. Outlook stops displaying the name in its prompts, but doesn't delete that person's record from your contacts. In many cases, names on the pop-up list aren't in your contacts file, so if you don't want to cut the cord completely, create a new record before deleting the name from the pop-up list.

8-25   Backing Up Outlook

If you've become dependent on Outlook, it probably stores much of your digital life—all your email; contact information for your friends, family, and co-workers; and your daily schedule ever since you switched to a digital calendar. If you lose your Outlook data, you're sunk.

Avoid identity loss by backing up your Outlook data. One of the easiest ways to do so is by using a free program from Microsoft. Called Personal Folders Backup software, a precious program available from *www.microsoft.com/downloads/details.aspx?displaylang=en&familyid=8b081f3a-b7d0-4b16-b8af-5a6322f4fd01*. It lets you back up Outlook with just a few clicks and then easily restores your data if something goes awry.

Note: Personal Folders Backup only works with Outlook 2000 and later versions.

After you've downloaded the backup software, install it, and then run Outlook. Choose File → Backup. Outlook stores its important data in files with a .pst extension, such as Outlook.pst. You can choose where to back up your files (save them somewhere *other* than your PC for true security), and whether you want Outlook to remind you to tackle this chore. If you need to restore the files later, open Outlook, and choose File → Backup → Open Backup. Browse to the .pst file you saved and open it.

Note: If you use Outlook on an Exchange Server—which is frequently the case if your company provides you with an email account—there won't be any .pst files on your system. That means you won't be able to back up your messages, contacts, and calendar yourself. No worries, though: Your Exchange administrator should be doing it for you.

POWER USERS' CLINIC

Backing Up Outlook Manually

You don't have to use extra software to back up Outlook—you can do it manually. You just need to locate the .pst file that houses your Outlook information, and then copy that file to a different folder, or a removable disk such as a CD. When you want to restore the data, just copy the .pst file back to its original location.

Typically, Outlook keeps your email messages, calendar, and contacts in a file named Outlook.pst, which is located in My Computer → C: → Documents and Settings → [Your Name] → Local Settings → Application Data → Microsoft → Outlook folder. (Your Name is your user account name.) If the file isn't there, you can find it by

right-clicking the Outlook Today icon in Outlook, choosing Properties → Advanced and looking in the Filename box. If you archive your old email messages, there will also be a file named Archive.pst in the same folder as your Outlook.pst file. To back up Outlook, just copy these files to a disk or another computer. To restore them, copy them back to their original locations.

If you use the Windows Address Book instead of Outlook for your contacts, then your contact information is kept in a file with the extension either .pab or .wab. If that's the case then you also need to back up the .pab or .wab file, along with your .pst file, to create a backup of your contact data.

8-26   Sharing Outlook on Two Computers

Using Outlook on two computers—for example, a desktop at home, and a laptop you take with you on trips—can be tricky because there's no apparent way to share email between the two computers. The email you send and receive on your laptop stays on the laptop, and the email you send and receive on your desktop stays on the desktop. And never the twain shall meet…or so it seems.

It turns out, you can keep all your mail and contacts in synch, just by copying a single file between the two computers. In Outlook, email and contact information is stored in a file that ends with the extension .pst (typically, the file's called outlook.pst). You can find it in My Computer → C: → Documents and Settings → [Your Account] → Local Settings → Application Data → Microsoft → Outlook. To transfer all your email and contacts from one computer to another, simply copy the most recent outlook.pst file to the other machine.

So if all your email and contacts are on your desktop PC, but you're going to travel with your notebook, copy the outlook.pst file from your desktop to your notebook. (Save the file in My Computer → C: → Documents and Settings → Your Account → Local Settings → Application Data → Microsoft → Outlook.) Then use Outlook on your laptop when you travel, as you normally would. When you get back from your trip, copy the outlook.pst file from your notebook back to your desktop PC, so all your mail and contacts are in synch.

8-27   Using Outlook to Keep Up with the News

With help from an add-in called Newsgator, Outlook can keep you current on news from around the world—whether you're interested in international coverage from the *New York Times*, articles from *New Scientist* magazine, or postings from your favorite reptile-lovers Weblog.

Working inside Outlook, Newsgator gathers news using a system called *RSS* (Really Simple Syndication)—one of the biggest phenomena to hit Web publishing since graphics became commonplace. RSS lets Web publishers distribute information in a format certain *software* can read. Thousands of general interest news sites and specialized publications publish news feeds in RSS format, including the *New York Times*, O'Reilly, MTV, CNN, *Forbes*, the *New Yorker*, and many blogs.

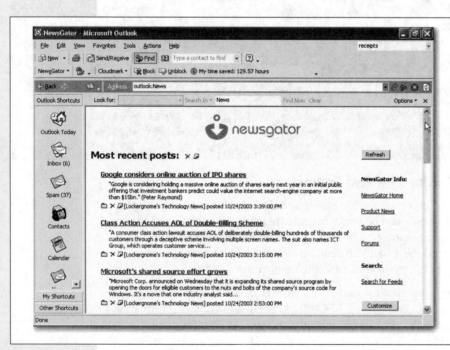

Figure 8-19:
Newsgator can gather news from thousands of different sources and let you read summaries of the articles it finds using Outlook. For the latest news, click the Refresh button.

You can download Newsgator for a free trial at *www.newsgator.com.* (If you decide to keep it, you'll be asked to fork over $29.)

Newsgator runs in Outlook as a toolbar across the top of the screen. The program checks for news on a schedule that you select, then , in the News folder, reports how many new articles it found from those sources. You can then read a synopsis of the article using Outlook (Figure 8-19).

To read the full article, click its link, and Internet Explorer opens the page with the article you want. To actually see the alerts, go to the News folder. You can search by keywords to find news feeds and then subscribe to the ones you want to receive. Also, when you're browsing the Web, if you come across a site that distributes a news feed, you'll see a small icon like that shown in Figure 8-20. To sign up for that feed, just right-click it and choose Subscribe; Newsgator adds it to your news roundup.

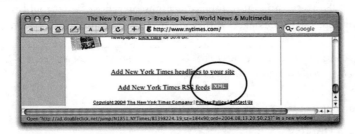

Figure 8-20:
If you're interested in receiving news feeds using Newsgator, look for a button that says XML or RSS on the sites you want to keep up with. Here, the New York Times site provides an XML button.

Tip: If you don't have Outlook, you can still read RSS news feeds using other programs, like NewsDesk (*www.wildgrape.net*) or SharpReader (*www.sharpreader.com*), both free to download. If you're interested in searching through RSS feeds, go to *www.blogdigger.com, www.daypop.com, www.feedster.com, www.newsisfree.com* or *www.syndic8.com* and enter a few words that describe the feed you're looking for.

Just for Outlook Express

For you Outlook Express fans out there, here're a few tips to make your software experience even more pleasing.

8-28   Killing the Outlook Express Startup Screen

If you hate wasting even a nanosecond on the way to your inbox every morning, you can set Outlook Express to take you there immediately. In your Folders pane, double-click the Outlook Express folder (if you don't have the Folders pane open, press Ctrl+Y and in the window that appears, double-click the Outlook Express folder.) At the bottom of the new screen, turn on "When Outlook Express starts, go directly to my Inbox." Ta da.

8-29   Renaming the Outlook Express Window

Outlook Express's window title (the name that appears at the top of its screen) is, not surprisingly, Outlook Express. But if you're feeling more creative, you can change the window title to any phrase you want.

To give Outlook Express your own title, first close the program. Then run the Registry Editor (see page 328) and go to My Computer → HKEY_CURRENT_USER → Identities → {UniqueIdentity} → Software → Microsoft → Outlook Express → 5.0. (Note: UniqueIdentity is a number such as {E46F102B-802C-4FF4-B1D3-B574483B2F75}.) Create a new String Value named WindowTitle. In the value field, type your own title for Outlook Express—say, *Everything That Matters*—then exit the Registry. When you open Outlook Express, your own handiwork greets you at the top of the program.

8-30   Backing Up Outlook Express

If you use Outlook Express and you're the kind of person whose worst nightmare involves losing all your email messages, you've got to back them up. Here's how.

Note: For more tips on backing up and restoring Outlook Express files, including your address book, see *http://support.microsoft.com/default.aspx?scid=kb;en-us;270670.*

To make a backup copy of your messages:

1. **Choose Tools → Options.**

   When the dialog box open, click the Maintenance tab.

2. **On the Maintenance tab, click Store Folder.**

   A little box opens showing the location of your message files.

3. **Highlight the whole folder path, and then press Ctrl+C to copy it.**

   Once you've got it copied, click Cancel twice to get out of the dialog boxes.

4. **Choose StartRun.**

   Put your cursor in the box and paste in your folder path (press Ctrl+V to paste). Then click OK to open Windows Explorer to the folder holding all your messages (they're labeled by folder, with the extension .dbx).

5. **In Windows Explorer, select all the messages (Ctrl+A), and then copy them (Ctrl+C).**

   Browse to the place where you'd like to copy your files—hopefully a folder you backup to a CD or external drive. But you can also choose your desktop or somewhere else obvious for now.

6. **Create a new folder (FileNewFolder) and name it something memorable.**

   Mail Backup will probably do the trick.

---

7. **Open the new folder and paste your mail files into it (Ctrl+V).**

That's it. You've got a backup copy that you can now copy somewhere else safe—ideally somewhere *not* on your PC. (See page 87 for more about backups.)

Tip: Various shareware programs can add even more features to Outlook and Outlook Express See the box below.

Adding Features to Outlook and Outlook Express

If you think your email program is a few features shy of perfection, there are plenty of downloads that can add more bells and whistles to both Outlook and Outlook Express. Generally, there are more downloads available for Outlook than its slimmed-down cousin, but here are a few options for both programs:

- **Outlook Express Backup and Outlook 2000/XP Backup.** These two programs, from the same publisher, make it easy to backup Outlook and Outlook Express. With these add-ins, you can backup all your data for multiple identities, set up an automated backup schedule, and view the backup file to see what email you've sent and received. With Outlook Express Backup, you can even copy text from a single backed-up message. That way, if you've accidentally deleted an important email message, you can easily retrieve it from the backup file, instead of having to restore every email you've ever sent and received. ($29.95 shareware; *www.genie-soft.com*.)

- **Fax4Outlook.** This add-in lets you send and receive faxes with Outlook (but not Outlook Express), keeping track of your incoming and outgoing faxes in folders

separate from the rest of your data. Fax4Outlook integrates with Windows XP's Fax Wizard, so it uses your phone line—you can't send faxes using an Internet connection. (For more about the Fax Wizard, see page 98.) Fax4Outlook is worth getting if you do a significant amount of faxing and don't want to waste precious desk space on a fax machine. ($29.95 shareware; *www.outlook4team.com*.)

- **Nelson's Email Organizer.** If you suffer from email overload, this program can help you get your digital act together—but only with Outlook, not Outlook Express. It automatically sorts your email into a variety of easy-to-use folders (both canned and ones you set up), does lightning-quick searches through your mail, notifies you when new messages arrive, and lets you sort your email into various views (such as mail sent in the past week). ($39.95 shareware; *www.caelo.com*.)

- **Annotis Mail.** If you're a fan of multimedia email, give this program a try. It lets you easily insert pictures, markers, sticky notes, sounds, and videos into your email, using either Outlook or Outlook Express. ($24.95 shareware; *www.annotis.com*.)

Beyond Outlook: Other Email Software

Of course Outlook and Outlook Express aren't the only email programs you can use. In fact, some people think other email software is superior to both—and the alternatives are often free. Here are three excellent options if you're thinking of straying.

Tip: If you have a Web-based email account like Hotmail or Yahoo!, see the box on page 204 for a cool way to access it in your favorite email program.

8-31 Eudora

Before Outlook and Outlook Express, Eudora was the email program of choice for power hounds everywhere. And it's still going strong today. Eudora has all kinds of cool features you won't find anywhere else. For example, it can check your email before you send it using its "MoodWatch" feature, which rates the message's level of aggression (based on a quick scan of the text), from an ice cube up to three chili peppers.

Eudora also lets you send voice mail via email, and displays all kinds of statistics about your email usage, including how many messages you've sent in a particular month, as well as your monthly average. You can download Eudora for free from *www.eudora.com*. While the program is free it does come with ads. If the thought of email sponsorship makes you cringe, you can buy an ad-free version of Eudora for $49.95, or use the "light" version, which lacks some of the main program's features (but none of the ones mentioned here).

8-32 Thunderbird

If you love Firefox, the zippy browser from the Mozilla team (page 194), consider trying Thunderbird, its email cousin. Thunderbird looks and works a lot like Outlook Express, making it a good choice if you're feeling out-Microsofted, but still want familiar features. You can download it for free from *www.mozilla.org/products/thunderbird/*.

8-33 IncrediMail

If you're the kind of person who likes animations, colorful picture backgrounds, sound effects, 3-D effects, special fonts, and other such things, this is the program for you. IncrediMail lets you add a bunch of email special effects so that, for example, when you delete a message, you see it being shredded. You can also add special effects to emails that you *send*, as well. Just imagine your librarian's glee when she receives a funky, multimedia spectacle instead of an ordinary black-and-white text message. You can download IncrediMail from *www.incredimail.com*.

Note: If you switch mail programs, you can usually bring your address book and messages over from your old program. On the old program, look for a feature that *exports* these items, and after you've done that, look in the new program for a feature that *imports* them.

Networking

In the Internet Age, no PC is an island. And Microsoft built Windows XP explicitly for these interconnected times. Compared to the dark days of Windows 95 and 98, Windows XP makes it a cinch to set up a home network, connect to the Internet or a company network, and surf the Web with or without wires.

This chapter offers tips on how to get the most out of XP's networking capabilities—not to mention valuable advice about security issues and troubleshooting.

Note: Setting up a network is getting easier all the time, especially as more of the big device manufacturers like Linksys, D-Link, and Belkin produce starter kits for networking newcomers. However, the setup process is still oftentimes a weekend-killer (or, at the very least, beyond the scope of an individual chapter) so the hints that follow assume you've already got either a wired or a wireless network up and running.

Wireless Networking

One of the most user-friendly things about Windows XP is that it includes built-in support for *WiFi*, the wireless networking system that has freed computer users from the chains of cables and phone lines. As WiFi's popularity has grown, it's now possible to surf the Internet from many hotel lobbies, check your email at the airport, and conduct Web research from the comfort of your own bathroom.

The hints in this section focus on maximizing your wireless experience and keeping your PC safe in a wireless world.

9-1 Zero Configuration WiFi Services

Windows XP makes it easy for you to find available WiFi networks by automatically running what it calls Zero Configuration WiFi Services (which French network administrators have been rumored to refer to as Zecows). Zero Configuration lets you automatically find WiFi networks without having to muddle through a time-consuming series of configuration steps.

Note: In order to actually connect to a WiFi network, you have to follow the steps in the next hint ("Connecting to Wireless Networks").

Verify that the Zero Configuration is running on your PC by choosing Start → Control Panel → Administrative Tools. Double-click Services, then scroll down to the listing for Wireless Zero Configuration and look in the Status field. If it says Started, you don't need to do anything. If it doesn't, then right-click the Status Field and choose Start, as shown in Figure 9-1.

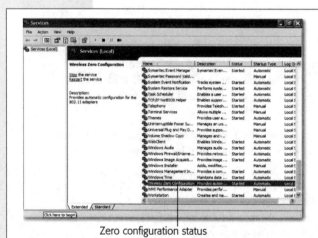

Figure 9-1:
After you turn on Zero Configuration WiFi Services, you won't notice even the slightest change in your PC because the feature works in the background.

Zero configuration status

9-2 Connecting to Wireless Networks

XP makes it easy to connect to any WiFi network. For example, there are many WiFi *hotspots* you can connect to in coffee shops, hotels, airports, restaurants, and other public places. Hotspots are public areas that provide a wireless Internet connection you can hook to via your WiFi-enabled computer—sometimes for a fee, sometimes for free, but always without worrying about cables and cords.

Note: Some hotspots are password-protected, which means, of course, that unless you know the secret password you can't use that hotspot.

To connect to a hotspot, or to your own WiFi network, here's what you need to do:

1. **Open your Wireless Network Connection Status dialog box by double-clicking the network icon in the notification area (the notification area is on the task-bar, just left of the clock).**

   The network icon looks like two screens, one on top of the other; if you see more than one such icon, mouse over each and wait for a little box to appear that tells you *which* network it's the icon for (you're looking for Wireless Network Connection).

2. **In the Wireless Network Connection Status dialog box, choose General →
   Properties. Then click the Wireless Networks tab.**

   The screen pictured in Figure 9-2 appears. In the Available networks area, you should see the name of any nearby wireless networks. If no WiFi network appears, but you know one is nearby, click Refresh. You may see multiple WiFi networks—perhaps set up by your neighbors.

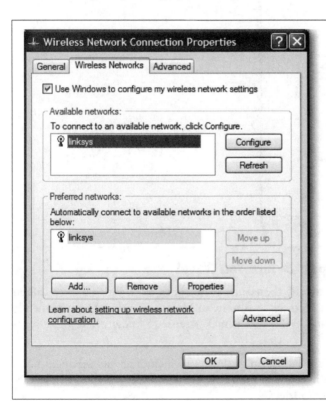

Figure 9-2:
Here, it's easy to choose which network to connect to, since there's only one network visible (called "linksys") in the Available networks section. If you've connected to other networks in the past, they'd be listed under "Preferred networks." Only currently live networks appear in the "Available networks" section.

3. Highlight the network you want to connect to and click **Configure**.

The "Wireless network properties" dialog box, as shown in Figure 9-3, appears. Leave the "Data encryption" and "Network Authentication" boxes turned off.

4. Click **OK**.

You should now be connected to the WiFi hotspot.

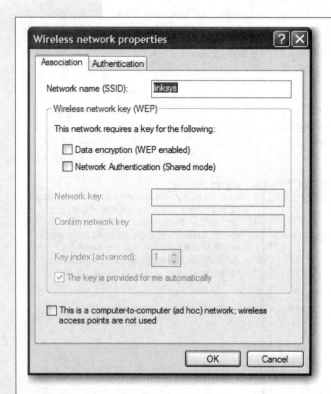

Figure 9-3:
Confirm that the WiFi network listed (in the "Network name (SSID)" box) matches the name of the WiFi network you want to connect to. Page 242, later in this chapter, explains how to turn on encryption in case you want a more secure network.

9-3   Finding Hotspots Before You Travel

The U.S. is dotted with literally thousands of hotspots, from the Sub Zero cafe in Anchorage, Alaska to the Four Seasons hotel in Miami, Florida. If you frequently travel with your laptop and WiFi card, it makes sense to know where these spots are *before* you hit the road.

There are lots of Web sites that list public hotspots, including *www.hotspotlist.com* (Figure 9-4) which lists hundreds of public hotspots in every state across the U.S. (and even in a few other countries).

Other useful WiFi hotspot directories are *www.jiwire.com*, *www.wifinder.com,* and *www.wi-fihotspotlist.com.*

Note: Not every list of hotspots is always current or exhaustive, so it's a good idea to check more than one.

Figure 9-4:
Hotspotlist.com tells you whether a hotspot is free or if you have to sign up with a wireless service provider in order to log on (fees for 24 hours of access typically cost $10 or less).

UP TO SPEED

Your WiFi Connection Speed

WiFi signals can often deteriorate if they're sharing the same airspace as other radio wave–using devices like microwaves and some cordless phones. To check the strength of your WiFi connection, double-click the network icon in your PC's Notification area. The "Wireless Network Connection Status" dialog box (shown here) pops open.

It indicates whether you're connected to the network, the maximum speed of the connection, the signal strength, how long you've been connected, and the number of packets of data sent and received.

Although the window contains a figure indicating your speed (in this instance, 11 Mbps), oftentimes your *true* connection speed is lower. To find out how to get a slightly more accurate measure of your real speed, see hint 6-25.

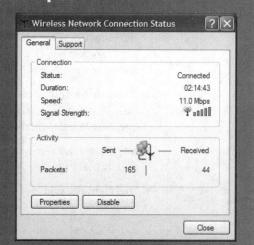

9-4   Protecting Your Wireless Network with WEP

The downside to WiFi's convenience is that it's less secure than its wired networking counterparts like Ethernet and even plain-old dialup. A really determined hacker can wheedle her way into a computer that's using WiFi and that you haven't properly protected.

You can minimize the chances of being spied by using *Wired Equivalency Privacy* (WEP), a technology that encrypts data traveling between your PC and your hotspot. WEP uses *encryption keys*—numbers or passwords that turn the data into gibberish—so that only those with the proper key can read it. The hotspot and each PC that connects to it must use the same key in order for encryption to work.

WEP is available in two flavors: 64-bit and 128-bit. 128-bit encryption is harder to crack, because it uses a longer key. But not all hardware supports 128-bit encryption, so check your documentation to see if yours does.

Note: The use of encryption slows down your network. Exactly how much depends on many variables, including the quality of the hotspot and the network cards being used, the exact placement of the devices, and any sources of nearby interference such as portable phones. Test your network with and without encryption to experience the speed difference, and then decide if the added security is worth the slow-down.

Before setting up WEP, confirm the level of encryption each computer on your network can support. You're looking for the lowest common denominator here: if even one computer can deal with 64-bit encryption only, your whole network will have to use that standard.

Once you've figured out the level you can use:

1. **In your router, turn on WEP.**

   This process varies from manufacturer to manufacturer, so check your documentation. The main step requires you to enter a password that XP then uses to generate an encryption key. Remember the password and the encryption level you choose; you'll need them when you configure your computers to use encryption.

2. **On each computer on your WiFi network, double-click the wireless network icon in the Notification area, and choose Properties → Wireless Networks to open the Wireless Network Connection Properties dialog box.**

   Any nearby wireless networks are listed under "Available networks." There's a chance that only one will be listed—the one you set up.

3. **Highlight the name of your network in the "Available networks" area and click Configure.**

   The Wireless Network Properties dialog box appears (Figure 9-5).

4. Turn on "Data encryption (WEP enabled)" and uncheck "The key is provided for me automatically." If you entered a value for a key index in step 1, choose that value in the Key index section. Type your password in the "Network key" box and then again in the "Confirm network key" box. Click OK.

Figure 9-5 shows the Wireless Network Properties dialog box filled out properly. When you click OK, your PC begins using encryption to connect to the network. Repeat the same steps for each computer connected to the network.

Figure 9-5:
When turning on WEP using this dialog box, it's critical that you type in the encryption key information precisely, including upper- and lower-case letters.

Note: An even newer encryption technology called *WPA* (short for WiFi Protected Access) is even more secure than WEP. But WPA only works with Windows XP, which means that if you have other non-XP computers on your WiFi network, you won't be able to use it. Furthermore, depending on the version of XP you have, you may need to download a patch from Microsoft to be able to activate WPA. Microsoft has a special Web page that contains more details: *http://support.microsoft.com/default.aspx?kbid=826942.*

9-5   Unplugging the Unplugged Icon

When using your wireless network, an icon may appear in the notification tray, warning you that your network cable is unplugged. What gives? After all, you're connected through a wireless network, and you probably don't even *have* a cable attached to your computer.

If this useless warning bugs you, you can easily kill it. Here's what you need to do:

1. **Open your Network Connections folder.**

   In the notification area, right-click the network icon that has an X through it and choose Open Network Connections. The Network Connections folder opens.

2. **Select your Ethernet network connection.**

   If you're not sure which connection is your normal wired connection, click each in turn and then look in the details area of the Network Connections folder (on the left side of the window). Here, you'll see information listed about the connection you've highlighted, including the name of the network adapter and its status. Look for one that's labeled "unplugged."

3. **Turn off the notification area icon.**

   Once you've found your wired connection, right-click it and choose Properties → General. Turn off the box that says, "Show icon in notification area when connected," as shown in Figure 9-6, then click OK. The icon should go away.

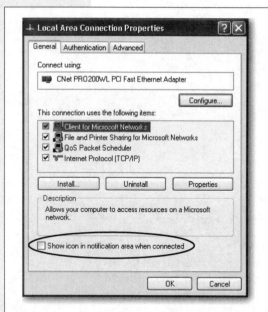

Figure 9-6:
Uncheck the highlighted box if you don't want the icon for your "unwired" connection to appear in the notification area. Don't turn off the icon for your wireless connection, though; if you do, you won't receive a notification when you've made a wireless connection.

Home Networking

Home networks—which can be wired, wireless or a combination—are ideal for sharing a high-speed Internet connection, using one printer with several PCs, or sharing files on multiple computers. This section offers tips on safe, hypersonic networking.

9-6   Desktop Shortcuts for Your Network Resources

Shortcuts on your desktop are the quickest way to access computers, drives, folders, or other resources on your network. To create a shortcut, just open My Network Places, and drag each frequently used folder or item to your desktop. Voilá! XP creates a desktop shortcut for each one. If you've created mapped network drives, as described in hint 9-10, drag those to the desktop from Windows Explorer. Then when you want to open any of these items, just double-click them.

9-7   Finding Another Computer on the Network

If you share a network with many computers—say, in a busy office—it can take a fair amount of hunting and clicking to locate a colleague's PC. Here's a quicker way to find another computer on a network—as long as you know its name or part of its name.

To start, press Ctrl+Windows key+F and conduct a search, just as you'd search for a file on your own PC. You can search for a name or even just a few letters. For example, if you search for "jus," XP finds all the computers whose names contain that string of letters (e.g., Justin, Justice, or AuJus). To connect to the computer you want, just double-click the correct one.

9-8   Stop Searching for Network Resources

When you connect to your network, XP checks to see if any new printers or folders that have been designated as shared resources have been added to the network. If XP does find any of these shared resources it adds shortcuts to them in My Network Places. (My Network Places lets you browse through the network.)

On a small network, this is a convenience; on a larger network, it can be rather annoying as new printers and folders continually appear or disappear. To turn off this feature, open Windows Explorer and choose Tools → Folder Options → View. In Advanced Settings, turn off the box next to "Automatically search for network folders and printers" and then click OK.

9-9   Speeding Up My Network Places and Network Browsing

When you open My Network Places or browse to another computer on your network, your network may seem to be working in super slo-mo. One reason for the pokey response is that when you connect to another computer, Windows XP checks for Scheduled Tasks on that computer, which can easily take 30 seconds or more. (Scheduled Tasks are tasks that a computer automatically performs, such as a weekly virus scan.)

For a quicker response, you can tell XP not to check other computers for scheduled tasks.

To do so, run the Registry Editor (see page 328) and go to My Computer → HKEY_ LOCAL_MACHINE → SOFTWARE → Microsoft → Windows → CurrentVersion → Explorer → RemoteComputer → NameSpace. Then delete the subkey {D6277990- 4C6A-11CF-8D87-00AA0060F5BF}. (The value for it is Scheduled Tasks.) Finally, close the Registry and reboot; you should now see a quicker response.

9-10   A Faster Path to Computers on Your Network

If you frequently need to access a drive or folder on another computer on your network, clicking there through My Network Places can wear out your wrist . For more direct access to another drive or folder on your network, consider this simple trick: mapping it as a network drive.

When you map a folder or drive, it appears on your PC as a normal drive, such as F:, even though it's actually still on another PC on the network. The advantage is that you can reach the folder or drive just as you would a drive on your local PC— with just a single click.

To map a file or folder as a network drive, run Windows Explorer (Windows key+E) and choose Tools → Map Network Drive. In the Map Network Drive dialog box, shown in Figure 9-7, use the menus to fill in a drive letter, as well as the drive or folder location.

Figure 9-7:
If you map a network folder as a drive on your PC, you can access that folder more quickly by using My Network Places. One potential glitch: if anybody renames the remote folder or drive, you won't be able to reach it anymore from your shortcut. Fortunately, you can just make a new shortcut.

To make sure the drive is available to you immediately whenever you log into XP, choose "Reconnect at logon." Then click Finish. The new drive now appears in My Computer and Windows Explorer.

9-11   Coaxing Your Network Card to Run Its Fastest

Most Ethernet network cards run at one of two speeds: 10 Mbps (known to geeks and hardware manufacturers as 10Base-T mode) or 100 Mbps (a.k.a., 100Base-T mode). The cards are set to automatically sense your network's speed and switch to the appropriate mode. But they don't always successfully make the leap, which means you have to give them a nudge.

To make your network card work at a higher speed:

1. **Run your PC's Device Manager by typing** *devmgmt.msc* **at the command prompt (choose Start → Run and type in** *cmd***).**

   The Device Manager is a tool that helps troubleshoot a variety of hardware problems. For more tips about using it, turn to page 257.

2. **Click the + button next to Network adapters, and highlight the adapter you want to force into 100Base-T mode.**

   If you have a wireless network card as well as a wired network card, make sure you choose the *wired* one (wireless cards *can't* run as fast as 100 Mbps).

3. **Choose Properties → Advanced to open the Adapter Properties dialog box.**

   Under Connection Type or Media Type, change the value from Autosense to 100 Mbps, and click OK.

   You should now get the higher connection speed on your network.

9-12   Optimizing Your Router

The heart of a home network is a *router*, an inexpensive piece of hardware that connects multiple PCs to each other and to a modem. Your router's out-of-the-box settings don't always offer you the best performance possible. For instance, what happens if somebody else has setup your network and forgotten to change the manufacturer's default password? You don't have to be the head of Homeland Security to know that's not a good thing.

Here're a few tweaks for happiest networking:

Keeping your connection alive

Some ISPs disconnect you from the Internet if you haven't used your connection for a certain amount of time. Fortunately there are a few ways to prevent this from happening:

- **Connect on Demand.** Turn this setting on to automatically re-establish your Internet connection if it drops.

- **Maximum Idle Time.** Set this setting to 0. Now your router maintains an Internet connection, regardless of how long it's been since you last used your PC.

- **Keep Alive.** Set this setting to "on." It's another way of maintaining a constant Internet connection, even if your PC is idle.

Changing your router's password

Most routers require a password in order to use the *Administrator* account, which gives you control over how the router works. Most routers come with a default password—for example, Linksys routers typically ship with the preset password "admin." Since that's not particularly tough to guess, and anyone who's bought a Linksys router now knows it, you should change the password by clicking the Password tab and following the directions there. Otherwise, someone else could take control of your router—and lock you out of your own network.

Note: If you have a DSL connection, the *MTU* (Maximum Transmission Unit) setting on your router is important. It determines the size of each *packet* of information sent to and from your network. (When you send data over the Internet, it gets broken into pieces called packets: these packets often travel separately and are then reunited when an email message, Web page, or file reaches its destination.) As a general rule, DSL users should use a value of 1492 for their MTU.

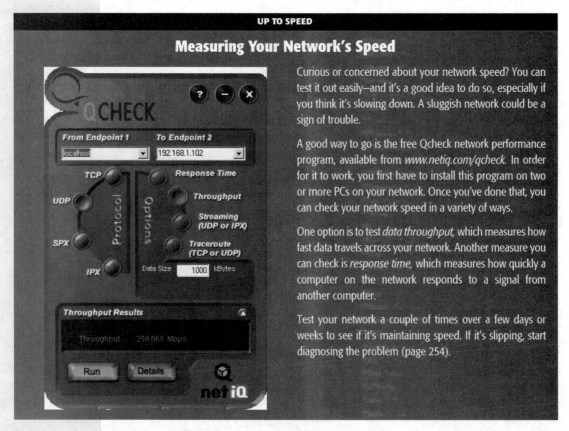

UP TO SPEED

Measuring Your Network's Speed

Curious or concerned about your network speed? You can test it out easily—and it's a good idea to do so, especially if you think it's slowing down. A sluggish network could be a sign of trouble.

A good way to go is the free Qcheck network performance program, available from *www.netiq.com/qcheck.* In order for it to work, you first have to install this program on two or more PCs on your network. Once you've done that, you can check your network speed in a variety of ways.

One option is to test *data throughput,* which measures how fast data travels across your network. Another measure you can check is *response time,* which measures how quickly a computer on the network responds to a signal from another computer.

Test your network a couple of times over a few days or weeks to see if it's maintaining speed. If it's slipping, start diagnosing the problem (page 254).

9-13   Sharing Files on a Network

One of the advantages of being on a network is that you can easily share files and folders with other people. Here's how:

Note: Sharing folders with others on a network is not the same as sharing folders with other people who use your computer. Your Shared Documents folder contains files and folders that other people with accounts *on your PC* can access. But people *on your network* can't access those files and folders unless you specifically designate the Shared Documents folder as a shared folder.

1. **Run Windows Explorer and right-click the folder you want to share.**

   Here're a few things to keep in mind when you're choosing files to share. First, when you share a folder, you also share any subfolders underneath it. Second, don't share any system folders, such as My Computer → C: → Windows, because someone may damage them and seriously harm your system. For the same reason, don't share an entire drive, such as the My Computer → C: drive. In fact, you may want to set up a specific folder that you share on the network. For example, you can give it the extremely creative name of Shared Network Folder, and then put files and folders in it that you want to share. That way, all other folders and files on your PC won't be accessible to other people.

2. **From the Properties dialog box that appears, click the Sharing tab and select "Share this folder on the network."**

   The dialog box shown in Figure 9-8 appears. If "Share this folder on the network" is grayed out, it means you're not currently on a network.

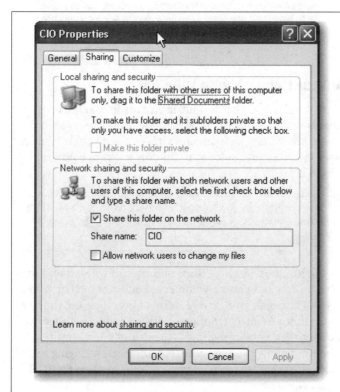

Figure 9-8:
This dialog box can be very confusing. The top portion–"Local sharing and security"–pertains only to your own computer, so use it only when sharing folders with other people who use your computer. For sharing files on a network, pay attention to the bottom section, "Network sharing and security."

3. **If you want the folder to have a different name on the network than it has on your computer, type the alternative name in the "Share name" box.**

Because others on the network probably aren't as familiar with your folders as you are, use a descriptive name for the folder they can understand.

4. **If you want others to be able to edit the files on your hard disk, select "Allow network users to change my files."**

As a general rule, you shouldn't turn on this option, since it lets other people alter the files (as well as delete them) on your computer without your knowledge. Unless there's a good reason to allow others to edit your files—like you're on a corporate network and your whole department works on the same files—don't select this option.

5. **When you're done, click OK.**

Other users on the network can now share the folder and files you've selected.

In Windows Explorer, the icon for a shared folders has a small hand holding a folder, as you can see in Figure 9-9 (the hand is actually pretty tiny, so you need to look closely). If a folder's not shared, it looks like any normal folder.

Figure 9-9:
Folders that can be shared with others on a network look as if hands are holding them (the bottom two here are shared); those that aren't shared merely look like regular old folders.

9-14   Chatting on Your Network with WinChat

Few people realize it, but Windows XP has a built-in instant messaging program, WinChat. It doesn't have as many features as instant messaging programs like ICQ or AOL Instant Messenger, but it's free of spam and viruses. Even better, WinChat is more secure than other IM programs, since you can only use it to communicate with people on your network.

Note: As with most instant messenger programs, you can only send messages to others who are running WinChat, and you can only deliver messages to people who are running the software at the same time you are.

To run WinChat, open the Run box (Start → Run) and type in *winchat* and press Enter. Next, click the dial button and choose whomever you want to chat with on your network. (When you click dial, you receive a list of everyone on your network, even if they're not running WinChat. So if you dial someone and they don't respond, it may not be that they're ignoring you—they simply may not be running the program.) If the recipient is running WinChat, she hears a ringing sound. When she clicks the Answer button, the two of you are free to chat. Figure 9-10 shows WinChat in action.

Troubleshooting Network Problems

Computer networks are moody. When they're working at their best, they're pure pleasure, seamlessly connecting PCs to one another and to the Internet. On the flip side, they break down for no apparent reason, and they act ornery just when you need them most.

This section offers tips for dealing with your network's temperamental side, helping you alleviate common frustrations and take action when things go awry.

9-15 Moving Your Laptop from One Network to Another

If you use a laptop at the office and at home, and you have different network set-ups for each, you can hit networking hell when you move from one to the other. Specifically, your settings may not work in both places, forcing you to constantly change them. Here's a quick fix: set up two *IP configurations*, and let Windows XP switch between the two as needed. (The IP configuration simply tells your computer whether to use the same IP address every session or to change it each time; see the box on page 133 for more on IP addressing.)

If you access the Internet, you already have one IP configuration. To find it, right-click Network Places on the Start menu or desktop and choose Properties; the Network Connections folder opens. Right-click your main network connection and choose Properties. In the dialog box that opens, select the Networking tab and highlight Internet Protocol (TCP/IP), then click Properties. The Internet Protocol (TCP/IP) dialog box appears, which contains all your IP information.

To create a configuration for a second network, click "Alternate configuration"; the Alternate Configuration dialog box, shown in Figure 9-11 appears. You have two choices here:

- If you use an IP address that never changes for your network, choose the User configured button, then fill in that static IP address. For the other settings in this section, check with your network administrator, or your ISP; they can tell you what settings you need to enter.

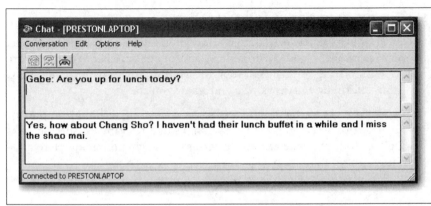

Figure 9-10:
If you frequently have top-secret chats with other people on your network, WinChat is a good choice because it's secure.

• If you get a new IP address every time you connect to the network, select "Automatic private IP address" instead. (You don't need to fill out any additional information in the dialog box.)

When you're done, click OK until all the dialog boxes have closed. You can now connect to either network automatically, without having to change any settings. You don't have to manually switch between the two settings, either—XP does that automatically when you connect.

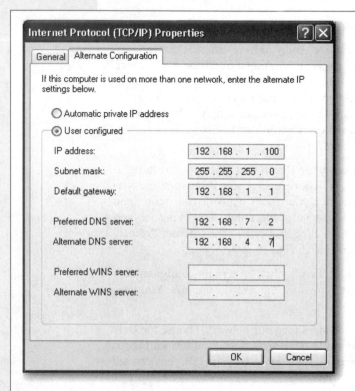

Figure 9-11:
Set up a second IP configuration if you have a laptop and use different IP configurations on different networks. If you only connect to networks that assign you IP addresses automatically, you most likely don't need to use a second IP configuration.

9-16   Finding Your Network Information

These days, knowing the network configuration information for your PC is almost as important as knowing your own address and phone number. Your network configuration information includes your IP address, host name, and MAC address—thus informing a network who and where you are.

Mostly, you need to know these numbers when contacting technical support or doing your own troubleshooting, but they can also be relevant for specific tasks like sharing files with someone else via an instant messaging program. Here are a few of the numbers you should keep handy:

- **Your IP address.** The numeric address that identifies every computer on the Internet. It's a series of numbers, such as 129.137.147.1, and whenever you do things like browse the Internet, other computers use it to locate you and send along information. You can find it manually by typing *ip config /all* at a command prompt. (To get to the command prompt, choose Start → Run, then type in *cmd* and press Enter.)

- **Your MAC address.** A MAC address is a unique number that identifies a piece of hardware, such as a router or the network card in a computer. (MAC has nothing to do with Apple computers; it stands for Media Access Control—obviously.) If you use your laptop on more than one network, the system administrators at any given place may need your MAC address to get you on their network. Here's how to find it.

  Choose Start → Run and type in *cmd,* then press Enter to open the command prompt window. At the prompt, type *ipconfig/all,* and then press Enter. The system shows you a screen full of connection numbers; the one you're looking for is the Physical Address, under the heading Ethernet adapter Wireless Network Connection. It's 12 characters, like this: 00-D0-B7-BD-40-F1.

- **Your host name.** The name of your computer in English; it's the name you assigned it when you set up XP.

POWER USERS' CLINIC

Release and Renew Your IP Address

One of the most common problems with network and Internet connections is a glitch with an IP address. An IP address may "time out" and no longer be valid, for example. Or, for some reason, two computers may somehow be given the same IP address, causing a spate of conflicts.

MAC address → Adapter Address 00-06-A1-00-9F-32
IP address → IP Address 192.168.1.102

Fortunately, Wnticfg.exe—an excellent utility from Microsoft, despite its name—can help solve these problems. Download it for free from Microsoft at *www.microsoft.com/ windows2000/techinfo/reskit/tools/existing/wntipcfg-o.asp.* (Previous versions of Windows had a built-in utility called Winipcfg.exe that provided essentially the same information Wnticfg.exe offers. As of XP, Winipcfg is history.)

Once you install it, look in My Computer → C: → Program Files → Resource Kit for Wnticfg.exe and open the program. It runs as a compact little screen, but if you want to see expanded information about your PC's network configuration, click More Info.

To fix an IP problem, try this. Click Release (at the bottom of the window) to clear your IP address, and then click Renew to get a new one. Taking this simple step often solves many stubborn connectivity problems.

9-17 The Network Diagnostics Tool

If you're experiencing a network or Internet connection problem, Windows XP's built-in diagnostics tool may be able to reveal the culprit. With just a few mouse clicks, it tests basic settings, a variety of network protocols, and whether your hardware is functioning properly.

To use the diagnostics tool, choose Start → "Help and Support" → "Networking and the Web" → "Fixing Networking or Web Problems" → "Diagnose network configuration and run automated networking tasks."

The next screen that appears offers two choices: "Scan your system" or "Set scanning options." The first option scans your system immediately for problems, while the second choice lets you customize what it scans—this is the option you want. Under Options, make sure you turn on Domain Name System (DNS), Dynamic Host Configuration Protocol (DHCP), default gateways, IP address, and Windows Internet Naming Service (WINS).

When you click "Scan your system," XP performs its magic. After several minutes, a report like the one pictured in Figure 9-12 appears, letting you know if anything is wrong.

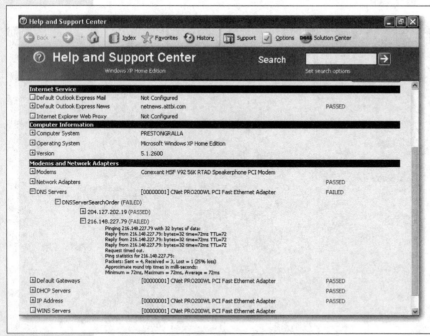

Figure 9-12:
This report can help you fix the problem yourself, or you can pass along the details to tech support. If you click Save to File, XP saves the report as an HTML file. To view past reports, click Show Saved Files.

9-18 Repairing a Broken Network Connection

Network connections break more often than highway repair crews. *TCP/IP* problems are among the most common network problems, and have to do with the underlying communications rules that control the Internet. (TCP/IP stands for

Transmission Protocol/Internet Protocol and is the standard for transmitting data over networks.)

Here's how to deal with TCP/IP attitude:

- **Release and renew your IP address.** Release the connection by going to the command prompt (choose Start → Run, then type in *cmd* and press Enter.), and then typing the command *ipconfig /release [adapter name]. [Adapter name]* is the name of the device whose connection is broken, for example, Broadcom Controller). Then renew the connection by using the command *ipconfig /renew [adapter name].* You can also release and renew an IP address using the Wntipcfg utility, as detailed in the box on page 253.

- **Try automated repair.** In the Network Connections folder, right-click the broken connection and choose Repair. (To access the Network Connections Folder, right-click My Network Places and choose Properties.) Frequently, XP can solve the problem for you by itself.

- **Run the Network Setup Wizard.** This walks you through TCP/IP and network configuration, helping you to correct any errors you may have inadvertently introduced. To run it, choose Start → Control Panel → Network and Internet Connections, and then click Network Connections. Under Common Tasks, click Network Setup Wizard.

- **Reset your router.** If you have a home network, the problem may lie with your router, or in the connection between the router and your broadband provider. Follow the directions in your router's documentation to reset it.

Tip: If you have a router at home, and you use a *Virtual Private Network* (VPN), or encrypted connection, to reach your corporate network from your bedroom office, one particular router setting can kill off the connection. Check your router settings (page 247) for something like "Block WAN Request," which can disable VPN access.

This setting usually comes turned on, and it stops certain kinds of Internet traffic from getting through to your home network. It also blocks access to many VPNs. You can usually change this setting by logging into your administrator's account and turning off any setting that prevents WAN requests.

- **Reset your cable modem or DSL modem.** If you have a broadband connection, there may be a problem with the assignment of your IP address by your ISP. Turn off your cable or DSL modem (it might have just a plug but no on/off button), unplug its Ethernet cable, and leave it off for five minutes. Now restart it. You can also try releasing and renewing your IP address (page 253) after you turn the connection back on, or resetting your router at the same time you reset your broadband modem.

- **Reset TCP/IP to its original configuration.** If all else fails, try to reset your TCP/IP configuration to the same state it was in when XP was first installed on the computer. To do that, use the NetShell utility by going to the command prompt and entering this command: *netsh int ip reset.* Now press Enter.

Hardware

Unless you're seriously into cables, you probably pay attention to your hardware only when something goes wrong—like when your machinery seems possessed by demons. The good news is that you can solve many glitches with just a little bit of tweaking and fiddling. And that's what this chapter is all about: hints for tackling some of the most common hardware problems.

Hardware Troubleshooting

Half the fun of having a computer comes from the gadgets you get to plug into it: digital cameras and MP3 players and printers. But these devices don't always get along with each other. Conflicts include intermittently working mice, printers that don't print, and extremely unhappy computer owners. This section explains how to peer deep into your hardware to see what's gone wrong, and how to fix problems once you find 'em.

Tip: One of the most persistent hardware problems is cable clutter. You can tame it with a *cable organizer* (also sometimes called a *cable tunnel*) which gathers together all your cables and hides them inside a plastic housing. There are several types, including boxes you can tuck cables into, or slotted guides specifically designed to keep cables from intertwining. They usually cost about $10 at office supply stores and sites like *www.cableorganizer.com*.

10-1   Getting Help from the Device Manager

If you've got a stubborn hardware problem—such as a mouse that's not responding, or a CD drive that doesn't seem to be reading CDs—XP's Device Manager can help. The Device Manager (Figure 10-1) not only supplies information about devices installed on your system, it can also troubleshoot hardware problems itself. This hint tells you how to turn the Device Manager into your peripherals' own Mr. Fixit.

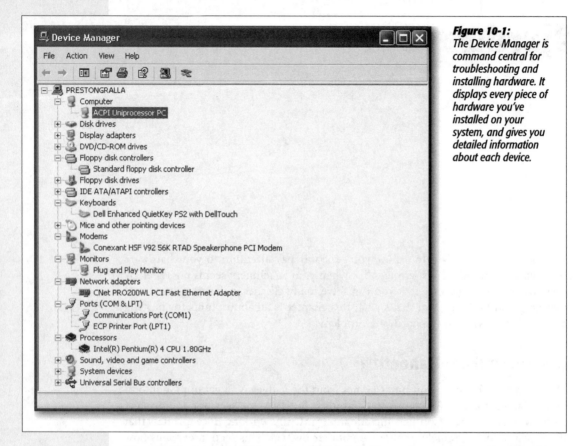

Figure 10-1:
The Device Manager is command central for troubleshooting and installing hardware. It displays every piece of hardware you've installed on your system, and gives you detailed information about each device.

Start the Device Manger by right-clicking My Computer, and then choosing Manage. From the new window that opens, select Device Manager, which displays a list of all the hardware on your system, organized into categories. (Different versions of XP display this information in slightly different ways.)

Tip: For quicker access to the Device Manager, at a command prompt or in the Run box, type *devmgmt.msc*. (To get to the Run box, choose Start → Run. To get to the command prompt, choose Start → Run, type *command*, and press Enter.) You can also select Control Panel → Performance and Maintenance → System → Hardware → Device Manager.

If XP detects any devices not working correctly, the Device Manager displays one of three icons next to the device's name.

- **A yellow exclamation point** means the device has a problem or conflict of some sort. For example, if your mouse is working intermittently, you may see this icon next to its name.

- **A red X** means the device is disabled and isn't working at all.

- **A blue i (for "information")** means the device's configuration has been altered using the Device Manager.

To see more details about a problem, double-click any device with a colored icon next to it. An error message and error code appear in the Device status section of the General tab. Unfortunately, these error messages tend to be vague and unhelpful (sample: "Your registry may be bad"). But Microsoft *does* offer more elaborate explanations, and even includes suggested remedies, on its Microsoft Developer Network (MSDN) Web site (*http://msdn.microsoft.com*).

Finding the right page on the MSDN site actually takes a bit of work since—surprise, surprise—Microsoft has lots of pages with error messages on them. Here's what to do: In the search box on the upper-right corner of the MSDN home page, select the MSDN Library button. Then, using quotation marks, enter this search: "Device Manager error messages." You'll see a link to a page with each error code listed and from there you can usually find straightforward remedies, like when to reinstall a driver or when to unplug a device and plug it back in. Obviously, if your PC is really on the fritz, you'll need to access this page from someone else's computer.

Tip: The Device Manager's General tab also includes a Troubleshoot button that launches a wizard to try and help you solve problems related to the device.

10-2   Resolving Conflicts

Even if you've removed a piece of hardware from your computer—an old printer or a network card, for example—XP may think it still exists, which can cause clashes with hardware that really exists. You can get these *phantom devices* to show up in the Device Manager so you can either eliminate them or use the tips explained in the previous hint to quash any conflicts.

There are two types of phantom devices:

- **Hidden devices** are attached to your computer, but XP can't see them. They're usually older model printers, scanners, and other peripherals that aren't *Plug-and-Play* (devices that XP automatically recognizes once you attach them).

- **Ghosted devices** are devices that were once attached to your PC, but aren't anymore (like an MP3 player), or that have been moved from one slot to another inside your computer's case (like a network card).

Displaying *hidden* hardware is a simple matter. Run the Device Manager (by right-clicking My Computer and choosing Properties → Hardware → Device Manager) and choose View → Display Hidden Devices; the devices appear immediately.

Displaying *ghosted* devices, on the other hand, takes a bit more work:

1. **At the command prompt or Run box (choose Start → Run and type in *cmd*), type *set devmgr_show_nonpresent_devices=1* and press Enter.**

   It may seem like nothing has happened (the command prompt appears blank), but XP is actually working behind the scenes.

2. **At the same command prompt or within the same Run box, type *start devmgmt.msc* and press Enter.**

   The Device Manager launches in a separate window. (Don't launch the Device Manager by any other method or this step won't work.)

3. **Choose View → Display Hidden Devices.**

   The Device Manager displays a list of devices attached to your PC. Ghosted devices appear gray; active devices appear in black, as shown in Figure 10-2.

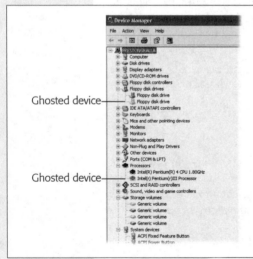

Ghosted device——

Ghosted device——

Figure 10-2:
In the Device Manager, ghosted devices—those are the ones that aren't currently on your PC—appear gray. In this figure there's a ghosted floppy drive and a ghosted processor.

Once you've revealed all of your computer's hidden or ghosted devices, examine the Device Manager to see if any of them conflict with your other hardware (see hint 10-1). If you do find conflicts, double-click the problematic device, and from the General tab, click Troubleshoot. You can also uninstall the device by right-clicking it and choosing Uninstall.

Tip: Use the Device Manager to print a comprehensive system summary that includes everything there is to know about your hardware. Just run the Device Manager and choose Action → Print.

10-3 Driver Magic

As power users know, if you run into a hardware problem, one culprit may be the device's *driver,* a piece of software that lets your PC communicate with a peripheral. Driver problems are likely to occur when you try to add an old device to a new computer (say, an antique scanner to your zippy new laptop), and the old driver doesn't work with the new system. In these cases, a new, updated driver (usually from the device manufacturer) may solve the problem—though in some cases, a new driver you've installed may actually have *caused* the problem. Switching back to an earlier driver is called *rolling back* the driver. You can also sometimes clear up trouble by uninstalling a driver, and then reinstalling it. All this magic happens through the Device Manager, on a device's Driver tab.

Note: Before updating, rolling back, or uninstalling drivers, it's a smart idea to set a *System Restore Point,* which lets you return to your PC's configuration at the moment you set it—just in case your driver work leads to serious trouble. (See page 303 for information on how to use System Restore.)

To access the Device Manager, in the Run box or command prompt (page 258) type *devmgmt.msc,* and then press Enter. Now right-click the device that's causing the dustup and choose Properties → Driver. The screen shown in Figure 10-3 appears.

Here's what you can do from this dialog box:

Update a driver

Before you can update a driver, you first need to obtain it (usually from the manufacturer's Web site; look in the Support or Downloads section).

UP TO SPEED

Hardware Installation Problems

XP is usually good about automatically recognizing and installing hardware. But there are times when its stubborn side emerges and the system simply doesn't recognize that you've installed a new piece of hardware on your PC. If that happens, try these troubleshooting hints:

Check the manufacturer's Web site for new installation software or drivers. The software that came on your installation disk could be outdated, so you may need a newer version to properly install the device. (For information on how to install and uninstall drivers, see hint 10-3.)

Use the Device Manager to check for conflicts. Check whether any other devices are causing problems with the installation. For information on how to troubleshoot using the Device Manager, and how to handle conflicts, see hint 10-1.

Check the connections, cables, and contacts. If you're installing an internal device that attaches to your computer via the slots inside its case, make sure the device is properly seated in the expansion slot. For all devices, check that the cables are connected properly, and all contacts are clean.

Check your ports. If you're installing a device to a particular port (the USB port, for example), use the Device Manager to check that the port is working properly (the Device Manager lists ports as well as hardware devices).

Sometimes, the driver includes a setup program that you need to run before you update the driver itself. You should also double-check that the driver you've downloaded is newer than the one you currently have. Here's how: using the Device Manager, look at the version number of your existing driver, and see if the README file of the new driver lists its version number. If no documentation is available, right-click the new driver file (it ends in a *.sys* or *.dll* extension) and choose Properties → Version. The version number of the new driver should be listed there.

Once you're ready to update your driver, click the Update Driver button. The Hardware Update Wizard appears. Follow its directions to update the driver.

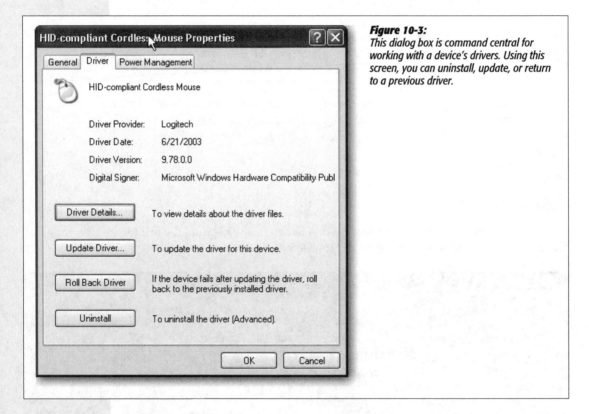

Figure 10-3:
This dialog box is command central for working with a device's drivers. Using this screen, you can uninstall, update, or return to a previous driver.

Roll back a driver

If you've recently updated a driver and suspect it may be butting heads with a device, try going back to the previous driver you were using. To roll back the driver, open the Device Manager, right-click the device that's acting cranky, and choose Properties → Driver. Click Roll Back Driver and follow the instructions in the wizard that appears.

Uninstall a driver

When you remove a piece of hardware (an old printer, for instance), the drivers don't simply vanish. Even after the hardware has been sent out to pasture, these old drivers may continue to load, occupying valuable system resources and potentially causing conflicts.

To get rid of a driver, open the Device Manager, right-click the device you're troubleshooting, and choose Properties → Driver. Click the Uninstall button and follow the directions in the wizard that appears.

Note: If you're uninstalling a driver for a Plug-and-Play device (see page 259), the device must be connected to your computer before you can begin the process.

ADD-IN ALERT

Analyzing Your Hardware

If you yearn to understand your hardware at the deepest level and even anticipate potential problems, the Internet is teeming with software that just might satisfy you. Here are some of the top options:

Sandra (System Analyzer Diagnostic and Reporting Assistant). This program is the best system information tool and system benchmarker you can find. It has dozens of modules—50 in the trial version, 75 in the paid version—that report on every aspect of your system you can imagine and many you can't. Sandra also benchmarks your system performance, so you can see how well it performs (a *benchmark* is a measurement of performance that becomes a point of reference for future measurements). ($29 shareware; *www.3bsoftware.com.*)

Fresh Diagnose. This diagnostics tool scans your system and gives a comprehensive report about its motherboard, peripherals, video system, bus, and more, telling you exactly what hardware you have installed, and how well that hardware works. It also benchmarks system performance for your CPU, hard disk, and CD and DVD drives. Best of all—it's free. Download it at *www.freshdevices.com/ freshdiag.html.*

Belarc Adviser. Like Fresh Diagnose, this free program scans your system and creates a detailed report about your hardware and software, including what's installed, what versions are available, and so on. (Freeware; *www.belarc.com.*)

Laptop Tricks

Nothing beats a laptop when it's time to hit the road and you need to keep working on a spreadsheet, a pile of email, or your Homer and Jessica Simpson genealogy Web site. This section offers advice on caring for these sometimes finicky contraptions.

10-4   Extending Your Laptop's Battery Life

No matter how many hours PC manufacturers promise, laptop batteries always seem to conk out a bit early (and usually during some vital research, like when you're trying to watch a DVD of some of Governor Schwarzenegger's favorite persuasion techniques).

Thankfully, there are a few ways to extend your laptop battery's life:

- **Turn off your wireless signal.** WiFi cards can use a substantial amount of power; turning yours off can save you up to 20 minutes of battery life. Turn it off by right-clicking its icon in the notification tray and choosing Disable.

- **Lower the backlighting on your screen.** Your screen takes up a substantial amount of electricity, and you often don't need it set to maximum brightness. Check your system documentation for how to change the lighting level, then reduce it to a comfortable level.

- **Use the correct power scheme.** XP includes a number of preset *power schemes,* which control settings like how quickly your computer goes to sleep and when your screen saver kicks in. You can change your power schemes by choosing Control Panel → Performance and Maintenance → Power Options. The dialog box shown in Figure 10-4 appears. For maximum battery life, choose "Max Battery" from the "Power schemes" drop-down list. "Low Power Mode" and "Portable/Laptop" are also good choices, although they don't preserve as much power as Max Battery. After you select a power scheme, click OK.

Figure 10-4:
Reduce your laptop's power consumption by choosing a juice-saving power scheme like "Max Battery." You can also customize any of XP's built-in power schemes by changing the settings in the bottom half of this screen. To create a new scheme of your own, choose your settings, click Save As, and give your power preferences a new name.

10-5   Helping a Fussy Laptop Enter Standby

Most laptops take the computer equivalent of a nap by going into *system standby*—an energy-saving state in which a laptop uses less energy—after they've been idle for a little while (page 1). But just like certain people simply can't snooze in the afternoon, some laptops can't enter standby mode, even when they're idle. Why? Because *USB polling* fools the computer's processor into thinking the laptop is active. (XP polls or sends a signal to USB ports to determine if there's any activity on the ports.)

To prevent your laptop from being fooled, simply increase the polling interval. Here's how:

Run the Registry Editor (page 328) and then go to Go to My Computer → HKEY_LOCAL_MACHINE → System → CurrentControlSet → Control → Class → {36FC9E60-C465-11CF-8056-444553540000} → 0000. Create the new DWORD value IdleEnable, and set the data value to a number between 2 and 5. This sets the polling interval, in milliseconds (the higher the number, the longer the interval). The default polling interval is 1 millisecond.

If there are additional subkeys for My Computer → HKEY_LOCAL_MACHINE → System → CurrentControlSet → Control → Class → {36FC9E60-C465-11CF-8056-444553540000} such as 0001, 0002, etc., repeat the procedure and create the IdleEnable DWORD in each of them. When you're done, exit the Registry and reboot.

Tip: Hibernate—a deeper sleep than Standby—is another good way to save laptop juice. Hint 1-2 tells you all about it.

10-6   Removing a Useless Warning

When you remove a PC card from a laptop, you receive a warning telling you that you've...removed a piece of hardware. Since you were the one who just removed the card, you already knew that. Want to reduce your daily helping of useless messages? The Registry Editor's ready and waiting.

To turn off the removed-card warning, run the Registry Editor (see page 328) and then go to My Computer → HKEY_CURRENT_USER → Software → Microsoft → Windows → CurrentVersion → Applets → SysTray. Create a new DWORD value called PCMCIAFlags. Set its value to 0. Then exit the Registry and reboot. To turn the warning back on, set the PCMCIAFlags to 1.

Printers and Printing

It's been more than a decade since pundits proclaimed the imminent arrival of the paperless office. That prediction has turned out to be about as accurate as the Dow Jones's topping 35,000. Since printers are still being asked to churn out piles of paper, you need to know how to keep them in shape. This section explains how to get the most bang for your page.

Tip: If you have a choice, use a printer's USB port rather than its parallel port. Parallel port connections use a substantial amount of your PC's microprocessor, slowing down all other programs. In fact, some programs may not respond at all during especially large print jobs sent through the parallel port. (New printers typically connect to PCs using USB ports; many don't even have parallel ports.)

10-7   Printing Font Samples

Windows XP features dozens of interesting and unique fonts. Some are fun, some professional, some downright funky. Problem is, when you use a program like Word, you have no real way to preview them. Sure, Word's got a drop-down list of font choices, but you can only see a few characters of each font. What you really need is a full preview of every single character in the font.

The system's built-in *font previewer* is one of those hidden XP gems that few people know about, and even fewer use. To view and print samples of a font on your system choose Control Panel → Appearance and Themes → Fonts. Windows Explorer displays a folder with a list of every font on your system.

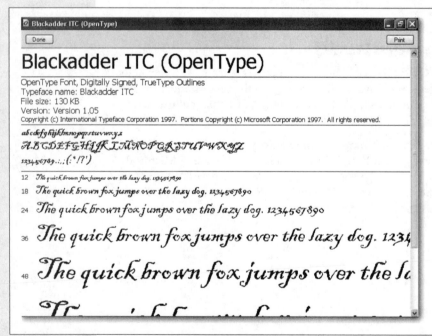

Figure 10-5:
When you preview a font, XP not only displays how every letter and character appears, but also lists the font type, version number, and the amount of disk space the font occupies on your system.

Tip: For a quicker way to access your fonts folder, open Windows Explorer and go to C: → Windows → Fonts.

When you double-click the font you want to view, a screen like the one pictured in Figure 10-5 appears. You can view the font onscreen or print a handy sample by clicking Print. (For future reference, you may even want to create a "font book" by printing a sample of every font on your system and filing them in a three-ring binder.) Once you're finished, click Done to close the window.

POWER USERS' CLINIC

Using the Command Line to View and Print Fonts

If you're a big fan of the command line (and who isn't?), you can view or print fonts without using menus or Windows Explorer. First you need to know the font name and its location, including its full path. (As a general rule, fonts are found in My Computer → C: → Windows → Fonts.) Once you know the file name and location, open up a command prompt. Then, to view a font, type *fontview [pathname] [filename]* ([pathname] should include the full path to the font, and [filename] includes the font name and exten-

sion, such as .ttf or .fon). For example, to print the Algerian font, named *alger.ttf,* you would type this command:

   fontview C:\Windows\Fonts\alger.ttf

To print the font, use the /p switch command, like this: *fontview /p filename*. For the Algerian example, the print command would look like this:

   fontview /p C:\Windows\Fonts\alger.ttf

10-8   Receiving a Message when Your Print Job Is Done

With a little bit of tweaking, you can program your printer to tell you (in the form of a pop-up message) when your print job is done. If you work in an office where the printer is out of eyesight, or if you share it with other people, this trick can save you a lot of checking up—especially when someone else's 300-page document is slowly churning out.

Note: Your printer uses the Windows Messenger Service (not related to the Windows Messenger instant messaging program) to alert you when your print job is done. If you turned off this service to block spam (page 135), you can't use this hint.

To set up a printer alert, run the Registry Editor (page 328) and then go to My Computer → HKEY_LOCAL_MACHINE → SYSTEM → CurrentControlSet → Control → Print → Providers. Find the DWORD value NetPopup. If the value isn't there, create it. To tell your printer to notify you when it finishes printing, set the value to 1. To disable the notification, set the value to 0. Exit the Registry and restart XP to trigger the change.

10-9   On-the-Road Printing Strategies

Unless you're the type of road warrior who carries a printer in his rucksack, you're facing the eternal laptop-in-transit dilemma: how do I print something? Fortunately, you've got a few options.

Kinko's

Kinko's has a nifty downloadable tool that lets you send a file over the Web and print it out at most Kinko's branches. Here's how: go to Kinko's Web site (*www.kinkos.com*) and from the Online Printing menu, select "Print to a FedEx Kinko's" (Kinko's is now part of FedEx). Then download and install the File Prep Tool, following the instructions listed on the site. Once you've got the tool installed, you can print from almost any program. Printouts cost anywhere from 10 cents per page on up, depending on the paper stock you choose.

Print workaround: fax it

What if you're not near a Kinko's? If you happen to be near a fax machine, you have another good option. Before you hit the road with your laptop, install XP's fax program (it lets you fax any document from your PC). To install the program, insert the XP installation CD into your CD drive; when the opening screen appears, choose Install Optional Windows Components → Fax Services. (For more help installing and using the fax program, see page 98.)

Then, when you're ready to print, open the file and fax it (choose File → Print and select the fax icon from the print screen).

Tip: If you're faxing to a hotel, be sure to check to see whether the hotel charges guests for receiving faxes; many hotels do.

Print Like a Pro

Here're some downloads that can bump you from printing layperson to printing pro.

Fine Print. This handy piece of software gives your printer a slew of capabilities that go beyond a simple 8.5 x 11 page. Among the options: You can print booklets; print two, four, or eight pages on a single sheet of paper; resize Web pages before printing so they fit better on a page; eliminate ads from printed Web pages; and create specialized stationery. ($39.95 shareware; *www.fineprint.com.*)

The Font Creator Program. If you fancy yourself a type designer, give this program a try. It lets you create your own TrueType fonts from scratch, or take existing TrueType fonts as a starting point and edit them to your tastes. (TrueType fonts are the most common kinds of fonts and come with Windows XP.) You can also convert bitmap graphics (page 192) to TrueType outlines, so you can create fonts based on your signature, handwriting, or logo—cool stuff. ($50 shareware; *www.high-logic.com.*)

CrossFont. This unique program lets you convert TrueType and PostScript Type 1 fonts between Macs and PCs. That's all it does, but it does it exceedingly well. ($45 shareware: *www.asy.com.*)

Create a print queue

Finally, there's a way to line up the documents you want to print so that when you return home and plug in your laptop, they automatically start printing. This is called setting up a *print queue*. To make it happen, choose Control Panel → Printers and Other Hardware → Printers and Faxes, and right-click the printer you want to use. Then choose Use Printer Offline. After changing this setting, any documents you print sit in the print queue, waiting to be printed. When you return home, choose Control Panel → Printers and Other Hardware → Printers and Faxes, right-click the printer you've chosen, and select Use Printer Online. Without further ado, all of your queued documents start making their way to the printer.

Of Mice and Keyboards

Most likely, you don't give much thought to the two pieces of hardware you use most every day—your mouse and your keyboard. This section offers tips and tricks for getting the most out of these overlooked but essential pieces of hardware.

10-10 Customizing Your Mouse Settings

Moving the cursor with your mouse or touchpad can sometimes feel like you're playing—and losing—an annoying video game. Not only can cursors be hard to find, but dragging items when you use a laptop's touchpad or nub pointer sometimes requires the dexterity of a surgeon. Fortunately, XP lets you change what your cursor looks like and how it reacts to your mouse and touchpad movements.

To begin, go to Control Panel → Printers and Other Hardware → Mouse. The Mouse Properties dialog box, pictured in Figure 10-6, appears (it may look slightly different, depending on your specific mouse).

Here're some pointers for best settings:

- **Pointers** Don't like the shape of your mouse pointer, or the hourglass that Windows displays when it wants you to wait? No problem—you can change them. Click the Pointers tab, then click the Scheme pop-up menu, and choose from any of several dozen pointer designs. Choose the Dinosaur theme, and instead of an hourglass, you'll see an overweight dinosaur, for example. When you've chosen the theme you want, click OK.

  You can also customize your pointer by making it larger, or by making it solid black instead of a white arrow with a black outline. Just select the Pointers tab, and from the drop-down list under Scheme, choose "Windows Black (extra large) (system scheme)."

- **Pointer Options** When you move your mouse, do you ever wish the cursor moved more quickly—or more slowly? Changing the cursor speed is easy. Click the Pointer Options tab and in the Motion section, drag the slider to the left to slow it down; drag it to the right to speed it up. Click OK when you're done.

If you frequently lose track of your cursor you can turn on the "Show location of pointer when I press the CTRL key" box. After you select this feature, whenever you press the CTRL key, a target symbol surrounds the pointer and then vanishes. You'll never lose sight of your pointer again.

• **Buttons** Does Windows sometimes seem not to respond to your double-clicks? Or does it sometimes seem as if Windows thinks you've double-clicked, when *you* think you haven't? Then you need to adjust Windows sensitivity to double-clicking. Here's how: Click the Buttons tab, and in the Double-click speed section, drag the slider to the left to make it more sensitive; dragging it to the right to makes it less sensitive. Click OK when you're done.

Figure 10-6:
To increase your pointer's visibility, select "Display pointer trails." When you do that, your mouse leaves visible "trails" behind as it travels across your desktop, making it easier to find.

TweakUI PowerToy

If you're already a mouse power user, or you're ready to move beyond what the Mouse Properties dialog box has to offer, you can teach your mouse all kinds of new tricks using the free TweakUI PowerToy from Microsoft. Download it from *www.microsoft.com/windowsxp/pro/downloads/powertoys.asp*. After you run it, click the + sign next to the Mouse section. Three subsections appear. One of them,

Wheel, merely duplicates what you can already do in the Mouse Properties dialog box, so you can skip that one.

Note: The box on page 273 has more tips on downloads that can help you customize your mouse settings.

Here are the other two subsections and what they have to offer:

- **Hover.** When you hover your mouse over a menu or icon in order to activate a balloon of text, it can take several precious seconds for that balloon to pop open. Happily, the hover setting in TweakUI lets you change the amount of time, in milliseconds, you must hold your cursor over an area to qualify as a hover. (The default setting is 400 milliseconds.) The hover *sensitivity* box lets you decide, in pixels, how close the mouse must be to an area for it to trigger a hover response. You can test the effects of various settings by hovering your mouse over the test icon.

- **X-Mouse.** This setting lets you use "X-mouse style window activation"—a mouthful of jargon that translates to "you don't need to click a window to make it active." (Just moving the mouse over a window does the trick.) This is one of those personal things: Some people love being able to activate windows in this way because it saves a whole lot of clicking. Other people find this behavior annoying. So try it out yourself and see if you like it. The X-Mouse dialog box is shown in Figure 10-7.

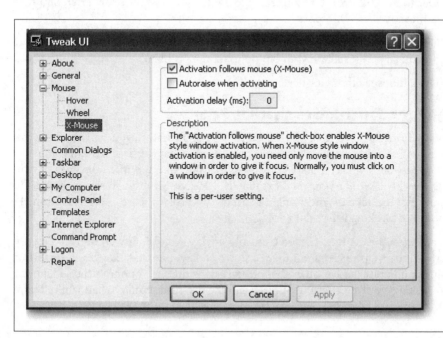

Figure 10-7:
If you choose X-mouse style window activation, this dialog box also lets you determine how many milliseconds, if any, it takes to activate the window.

Tip: If you use a mechanical mouse (one with a rubber ball on the bottom), clean it periodically to avoid—or eliminate—jerky or random-seeming cursor movements. Unplug the mouse, then remove the small access panel on the bottom, and pull out the rubber ball. Wash the ball in soapy water or a mild solvent like contact lens cleaner. Clean dirt and dust from the empty socket with a cotton swab, pop the (dried) ball back in, and close the panel. You should also clean the bottom surface of the mouse, and make sure the mouse pad or surface it's sliding across is clean.

10-11 Stopping Erratic Mouse Behavior

Mice with scroll wheels can behave erratically when used with a laptop. For instance, if you use a serial-port wheel mouse like the Microsoft IntelliMouse, your mouse may appear to jump on its own across your screen. The problem is that the touchpad or pointing device on the laptop uses *3-byte packets*, but the wheel mouse uses a *4-byte packet*. (A packet is the way that data is packaged when it's sent between the mouse and the laptop.) Your laptop may not know what to do with the packet's fourth byte (which controls the wheel), so your mouse gets the heebie-jeebies.

You've got four options if you've got a skittish scroll wheel mouse:

- Use a USB wheel mouse—a mouse that connects via the USB port—instead of a serial wheel mouse.

- Connect the serial wheel mouse to a serial-to-PS2 port converter, and connect that to the PS2 port. Or, connect it to a serial-to-USB port converter, and then connect it to the USB port.

- Check with your laptop manufacturer to see if there are any patches you can download and install on your laptop to fix the problem.

- Use a mouse without a wheel.

10-12 An Easier-to-See Insertion Point

After you've spent a long day in front of the monitor, you might think that Microsoft should've named the *insertion point*—that vertical blinking line that indicates where you can start typing—something like the *insertion sliver,* or the *barely visible insertion filament.* Fortunately, XP gives you the power to change this skinny line's thickness and blinking speed—both of which can cut down on the amount of blinking *you* end up doing.

To change either setting, choose Control Panel → Accessibility Options → Display. In the Cursor Options section there are two sliders, one that changes the insertion point's blink rate, and another that changes its width. As you move the sliders, you can see how your new settings affect a sample insertion point. When you're happy with the results, click OK; the new settings take effect immediately.

10-13 The Onscreen Keyboard

Some people are touch typists, some hunt and peck, and still others use one of Windows XP's little-known features: the onscreen keyboard. This virtual keyboard, shown in Figure 10-8, lets you "type" using your mouse, touchpad, or a joystick. It's useful for people with mobility impairments, those using a tablet PC, or in a pinch, anyone suddenly dealing with a broken keyboard.

Figure 10-8:
The onscreen keyboard can be a lifesaver if your regular keyboard—or your left wrist—breaks.

To use the onscreen keyboard, at a command prompt or in the Run box (choose Start → Run), type *osk* and press Enter. You can use the keyboard in one of three typing modes:

- **Click to select.** Click the key you want to type.

- **Hover to select.** Hover your pointer over the desired key.

ADD-IN ALERT

Teaching Your Mouse New Tricks

Try these downloads to make your mouse even more helpful around the desktop—or just more fun.

CoolMouse. This useful utility lets you assign a variety of functions to your mouse's middle button or wheel, like opening a Start menu under the mouse cursor, minimizing windows to the system tray, or rolling up windows to their title bars. You can also use your right mouse button to select favorite folders in Open/Save dialog boxes. ($24.95 shareware; *www.shelltoys.com.*)

Mouse-O-Meter. This program is a thoroughly frivolous and amazingly entertaining piece of software—an odometer for your mouse. It measures the distance, in meters, your mouse

travels, and also tracks the number of times you click your left mouse button, your right mouse button, and your keystrokes. Mouse-O-Meter reports on the totals for each, as well as the average per day, and works with any mouse. ($12 shareware; *http://surfsoftware.com.au.*)

Mouse Machine. If you repeat certain mouse movements—drawing your sword in an online game, for example—try automating them with Mouse Machine. This clever tool lets you program sequences of up to 99 moves and clicks, and then have Mouse Machine perform them automatically when you click the program's start button. (Freeware; *www.pcsupport.dk/index.htm?software/ MouseMachine.html.*)

• **Joystick or key to select.** Windows XP continually scans and highlights each of the keys on the keyboard. Press a joystick or a single key to select the key that's highlighted. (You can assign the keyboard key to hit by picking Settings → Typing Mode → "Joystick or key to select" → Advanced.)

To select one of these modes, on the keyboard, select Settings → Typing mode, then pick the one you want to use

---

ADD-IN ALERT

Keyboardery

Appendix A tells you how to make every keystroke count. To get still more out of your keyboard, try these downloads.

Keyboard Express. If you find yourself using the same keystrokes over and over, you can save yourself time and effort with Keyboard Express. This program lets you automate keystrokes so you don't have to type them time and time again, or create and schedule *macros,* which are a series of key sequences that run automatically. ($24.95 shareware; *www.keyboardexpress.com.*)

ShortKeys Lite. This text-replacement utility lets you substitute text using keystroke combinations that you define.

For example, if you frequently use the same phrase, sentence, or even paragraph, you can define a keystroke combination that pastes that text into a document when you press those keys. (Freeware, or 19.95 for full shareware version; *www.shortkeys.com.*)

IntelliType Pro. This free program from Microsoft lets you reassign your keys to do things like launch software, open a Web page, or perform menu commands. It's designed to work with Microsoft keyboards but works with some other keyboards as well. Download it from *www.microsoft.com/hardware/keyboard/download.asp.*

System Speedups

Okay, maybe Tom Cruise wasn't talking about his computer in *Top Gun* when he uttered his famous line—"I feel the need, the need for speed"—but he might as well have been. The truth is, no matter how fast your system is, it never seems fast enough. Between the time you spend waiting for programs to launch and the processor-slowing effects of that spam and virus-fighting arsenal you're running in the background, you can feel more like a computing pioneer than a 21st-century trailblazer. The good news is that Windows XP can help speed things up.

This chapter explains various ways to customize Windows XP to help prevent your PC from slowing you down. By managing your PC's memory better, using the Task Manager to find bottlenecks, and mastering a few keyboard shortcuts—to name just a few of the hints you'll find below—you can really boost your computer's performance.

Tip: Speeding up your computer is one way to happiness; speeding up *yourself* is another. The Appendix offers charts with three different kinds of useful keyboard shortcuts that can help you improve your own performance.

Managing Your Memory

This section gives you some tips to optimize your system's memory and a little-known trick that can help you decide when it's time to fork over some money to add more juice.

Note: To find out how much memory, also known as Random Access Memory (or RAM), your computer has, right-click My Computer and choose Properties → General. A Windows XP system needs at least 256 MB of RAM to work properly. Better yet, get 512 MB, or more, if you can afford it.

11-1   DOS Swap

You can speed up your system simply by replacing old DOS programs with more recent versions, if they're available. DOS applications, like old versions of WordPerfect, don't allow XP to manage memory properly, and they hoard memory by not sharing it with other programs.

11-2   Eliminating Needless Visual Effects

Microsoft gives you lots of ways to gussy up Windows XP: fading and sliding menu actions, folders that let you slap pictures on them, and icons that come with drop shadows. But all these effects can take their toll on system performance, especially if you have an older computer.

Fortunately, XP gives you lots of leeway when it comes to deciding how many bells, whistles, and assorted visual knickknackery to add to your system. Logically enough, the fewer effects you use, the faster your computer runs. Here's how to choose:

1. **Right-click My Computer and choose Properties → Advanced.**

   The Advanced tab on the System Properties dialog box appears. You can also summon System Properties from the Run box or the command line; enter *sysdm.cpl* and then press Enter. (To get to the Run box, choose Start → Run. To get to the command prompt, choose Start → Run, type *command*, and press Enter.)

2. **Under the Performance section, click Settings, and then select the Visual Effects tab.**

   The Performance Options dialog box appears, as shown in Figure 11-1.

3. **Choose the visual effects you want.**

   "Adjust for best performance" turns off all the visual effects listed. "Adjust for best appearance" has the opposite effect: it turns everything on. Selecting "Let Windows choose what's best for my computer" triggers, as you might guess, different choices on different computers. And to pick and choose individual effects yourself, choose "Custom," then decide which ones you want.

Tip: Using 32-bit color eats up a lot more memory than 16-bit color, and also puts a greater strain on your processor. If you primarily use business programs like word processors and spreadsheets, you probably won't notice a difference between the two settings. To change to 16-bit color, right-click the desktop, then choose Properties → Settings. In the Color Quality box, choose 16-bit.

11-3   Services You Don't Need

Behind the scenes, XP runs a handful of *services,* each of which perform different functions, like providing you with a Help system, allowing you to print, and offering a variety of networking features. Unfortunately, every service uses up memory and processor time; eliminating those that are unnecessary helps speed up your PC.

When it comes to deciding *which* services to turn off, some candidates are obvious. For example, if you don't have a WiFi card, there's no reason to run the Wireless Zero Configuration Service, which makes it easy to connect to wireless networks. Table 11-1 lists a bunch of services that you may want to disable.

Note: Sometimes, turning off a service only affects your current computing session; other times the service stays off the next time you turn on your PC. If you want to ensure these changes are permanent, see hint 11-4.

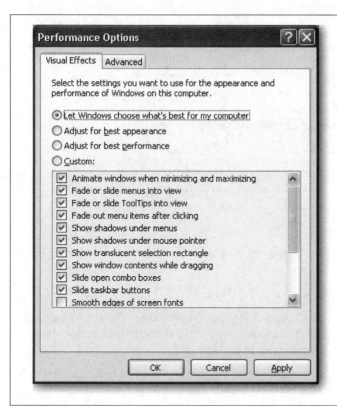

Figure 11-1:
Use the Performance Options dialog box to determine how many snazzy visual effects XP uses; fewer effects may be dull, but the trade-off is quicker system performance.

Here's how to turn off currently running services:

1. **At a command prompt or in the Run box (page 276), type in *services.msc* and press Enter.**

   The Services window appears, as shown in Figure 11-2. This program lists all Windows XP services, tells you whether they're currently running, and lets you start or stop each one.

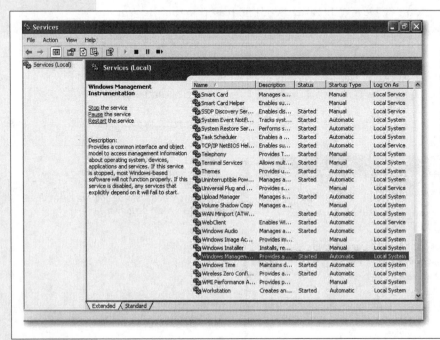

Figure 11-2:
To see how your computer responds when you turn off a service, click "Pause the service" and continue working with your PC. If your system operates with no problem, return to this screen to stop the service; if you notice any hiccups, return to this screen and restart the service.

2. **Click the Extended tab.**

   The Extended tab gives you a detailed description of each service by simply clicking on its name.

3. **Highlight any running service to decide whether to keep it or kill it.**

   Running services display "Started" in the status column. Once you highlight a service, a description of its function appears in the left-hand pane. Many services explain what happens if you turn them off.

4. **Turn off any services you don't want by clicking "Stop the service" in the left pane, or by right-clicking the service and choosing Stop.**

   Read the description of the service carefully before turning it off.

5. After you exit the Services module, if you find your computer has problems, run the module again and restart the services you've stopped.

To restart a service, highlight it and click "Start the service" in the left pane, or right-click the service and choose Start.

Table 11-1. *Windows XP Services You Might Want to Disable*

Service	What It Does
Portable Media Serial Number	Retrieves the serial number of a portable music player attached to your PC. If you don't use a portable music player, you don't need to run this service.
Task Scheduler	Schedules the running of unattended tasks. These are tasks Windows XP performs automatically, such as defragmenting your hard disk (page 6). If you don't schedule any unattended tasks, you can turn this off.
Uninterruptible Power Supply	Manages an Uninterruptible Power Supply (UPS) connected to your PC. If you don't have a UPS connected to your PC, you don't need this service.
Automatic Updates	Automatically checks for Windows updates. If you turn this service off, you can still check manually for updates by going to *http://windowsupdate.microsoft.com*.
Telnet (available only on Windows XP Professional)	Allows a remote user to log into your computer and run programs. Unless you have a specific reason to let people remotely log into your PC, turn this off—not only to speed up your PC, but because hackers often use Telnet to worm their way into your system.
Wireless Zero Configuration Service	Automatically configures a WiFi card. If you don't use, or plan to use, a WiFi card it makes sense to turn this off.

11-4   Putting Services on Permanent Leave

Turning off services each time you turn on your computer can be a hassle. If you know for sure you're not going to need a service, there's a pretty easy way to turn it off (you can always reactivate it if you change your mind). Here's how.

First, run the Services program, as described in the previous hint. Look in the Startup column for any services that are listed as Automatic (these are the ones that run automatically on startup).

Tip: For a quick way to identify all of the Automatic services, click the Startup Type column title to sort the services by Startup Type. Automatic services appear at the top of the list.

Decide which services you want to turn off. When you find a service you want to disable, right-click it and choose Properties. In the Properties dialog box that appears, chose Manual from the "Startup type" pull-down menu, as shown in Figure 11-3. From now on, the service won't start automatically—but you can still start it manually via the Services console. If you want the service disabled so it can't run *at all*, choose Disabled.

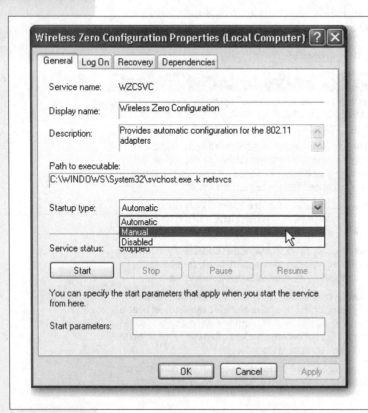

Figure 11-3:
Disabling unnecessary services so they don't launch conserves memory and limits the strain on your processor. On most PCs, for example, the Wireless Zero Configuration Service runs on startup, even if the computer doesn't use a wireless network. Therefore, it's a strong candidate to turn off if your PC doesn't have a WiFi card.

11-5   Removing Programs that Run at Startup

Services aren't the only things running in the background, slowing down your PC. Many programs do the same thing, often without you even knowing it. In some cases this behavior makes sense—antivirus software, for example. But a lot of other unnecessary freeloaders are jumping on the startup bandwagon. This hint shows you how to knock 'em off the cart.

Note: When you prevent a program from launching at startup you're not *deleting* the program—you're simply stopping it from automatically launching each time you turn on your computer.

The System Configuration Utility (Figure 11-4) is the best place to find out which programs are launching when your computer starts up. To open it, at a command prompt or in the Run box (page 276), type *msconfig* and press Enter.

Figuring out what these programs do can be tough since their names are often cryptic. Fs20.exe, for example, is the name for the EMS Free Surfer program file. (What do these engineers do when it's time to name their kids—use numbers?)

To help decipher a mysterious file name, expand the Command column near the top of the Startup tab by dragging its right handle all the way to the right. Now you can see the full listing in the Command column, including its location, such as My Computer → C: → Program Files → Free Surfer → fs20.exe. The directory location usually can help you figure out the program's name.

To stop a program from running at startup, go to the Startup tab, and uncheck the box next to it. When turning off startup programs it's best to make changes one program at a time, rather than in groups, so you don't inadvertently cause any system problems. Therefore, each time you stop a program from launching at startup, you should follow up by restarting your PC. If your computer runs without glitches, then you can move onto other programs.

Warning: Software known as *spyware* may be running on your PC without your knowledge. Hackers can program Spyware to do a lot of evil-minded things—from commandeering your browser so that it visits pornographic Web sites to monitoring your surfing habits and delivering spam-like ads. To eliminate spyware, run a program such as AdAware from *www.lavasoftusa.com.* For details on how to use it, turn to page 152.

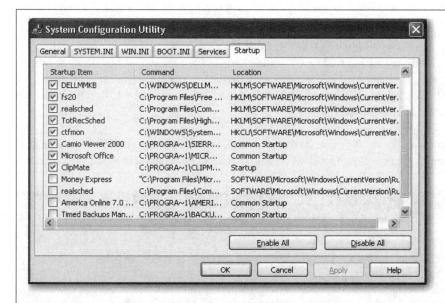

Figure 11-4:
At least once a week, you should go to this tab and see whether any unnecessary programs have been added. Sometimes, if you run a program only once, it automatically launches every time you start your PC, but doesn't bother asking if that's what you want.

11-6 Fancy Memory Trick I

Running the *kernel* in RAM may sound like some kind of shady maneuver involving the beloved *Kentucky Fried Chicken* mascot, but it's actually a pretty easy way to speed up your system's performance. The kernel is the core part of your operating system and, ordinarily, gets stored on your hard drive, which means there's a slight lag each time your PC needs to consult it. By using the faster RAM, or system memory, to store the kernel, you save a few milliseconds every time your computer needs to do something like opening and closing windows or switching between programs.

> **Note:** If you run memory-intensive applications, like graphics programs or games, or many applications at once, don't bother with this tip, as it can slow down your PC in those cases. Also, while this tip will work with 256 MB of memory, it really shines if you've got at least 512 MB.

To run the XP kernel in RAM, first you need to increase your system cache. This way, all of the XP kernel will fit in your computer's RAM. To boost the system cache, run the Registry Editor (see page 328) and go to My Computer → HKEY_ LOCAL_MACHINE → SYSTEM → CurrentControlSet → Control → SessionManager → Memory Manager. Edit the DWORD Value LargeSystemCache, and change the value to 1. Exit the Registry, reboot, and you're done.

11-7 Fancy Memory Trick II

When programs run in Windows XP, they frequently use what are called *DLLs* (Dynamic-Link Libraries), which contain shared programming instructions that different applications use in order to run. DLLs are stored in RAM whenever the system summons them; when you quit a program, XP is supposed to release the DLL from memory. But some DLLs can get stuck.

You can force Windows XP to release DLLs by adding a Registry key. Run the Registry Editor and go to My Computer → HKEY_LOCAL_MACHINE → SOFTWARE → Microsoft → Windows → CurrentVersion → Explorer. Create a new subkey called AlwaysUnloadDLL and set the default value to 1. Restart Windows to activate the change.

> **Note:** When you add this subkey, some programs—especially older Windows programs—might generate an error message or cause system problems. If this happens, delete the AlwaysUnloadDLL subkey and restart XP.

POWER USERS' CLINIC

Using the Registry to Disable Programs that Run at Startup

There's a small chance that the System Configuration Utility won't find all the programs that run at startup. Therefore, you may need to use the Registry to hunt these fugitives down and stop them from loading. Here's how: run the Registry Editor (page 328) and go to My Computer → HKEY_CURRENT_USER → Software → Microsoft → Windows → CurrentVersion → Run. The right pane lists some of the programs that automatically run at startup.

The Data field tells you the path and name of the program's executable file, which can help you determine what each program does. Right-click any program you don't want to run at startup and choose Delete. This method stops programs from running at startup for the account currently logged into Windows XP. To stop programs from running at startup for every account, go to My Computer → HKEY_ LOCAL_MACHINE → SOFTWARE → Microsoft → Windows → CurrentVersion → Run, and follow the same process to delete any programs you don't want to run at startup. When you're done, exit the Registry.

11-8   Deciding You Need More Memory

Adding more memory is the best way to speed up any computer. But, aside from your general sense that 256 MB might not be enough, or that your next door neighbor sounds awfully cool every time she talks about the 1 GB of memory her system's packing, is there any way to help gauge when it's time for more? Thankfully, the *Task Manager*—a built-in utility that monitors all the activity on your machine—has a great set of tools on its Performance tab that lays things out really clearly.

To run the Task Manager, press Ctrl-Alt-Delete. In the window that opens, click the Performance tab, shown in Figure 11-5. The Page File Usage History graph and the Available Physical Memory listing are both very helpful when trying to decide whether to add more memory. (A Page File is a file on your hard drive Windows XP uses when it needs more memory than what's available in RAM. Physical memory is the amount of RAM installed on your PC.)

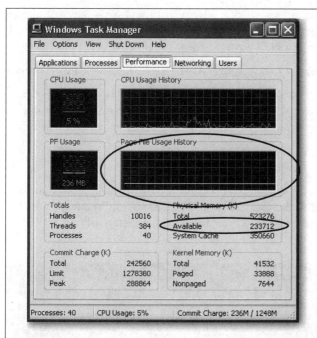

Figure 11-5:
The Task Manager's Performance tab is the best way to monitor memory use and determine if you've got enough. This system has plenty of memory available, so there's no need to buy more RAM.

Make sure the Task Manager runs in front of other open programs by choosing Options → Always on Top. That's helpful because what you want to do next is launch the group of programs you ordinarily run and then watch what happens to the Page File Usage History graph and the Available Physical Memory reading. If the graph is frequently spiking up to the top of the box or if the Available memory dips below 10,000 then it's time to buy more memory.

Processor Tricks

While today's microprocessors (also called CPUs) handle most tasks easily, certain activities like running computer-aided design software, CD-burning, and game-playing can make even a speedy system crawl.

The Task Manager (Figure 11-6) is a good way to determine how your CPU is holding up under the work you're asking it to do. Then you can make some decisions about when to launch certain programs—or whether it's time to upgrade your PC.

11-9   CPU-Draining Programs You Don't Need

Oftentimes a single program causes your system to slow down—kind of like an unruly child in a classroom sapping a teacher's attention. Want to identify which programs drain most of your CPU's power? Follow these steps:

1. **Run the Task Manager by pressing Ctrl-Alt-Delete. Then click the Processes tab.**

   The Processes tab shows all the programs and services currently running on your computer and gives details about each one, including how much of the CPU each is using.

2. **Double-click the CPU heading.**

   The Task Manager reorders the list of programs and services so those that most use the CPU are listed at the top, as shown in Figure 11-6. Frequently, the top listing is System Idle Process, which indicates what percentage of your CPU *isn't* in use.

ADD-IN ALERT

Getting More Out of Your Memory

It's a true fact: you can never have enough memory. And at a certain point, you can't buy more without investing in a new computer (page 276). If you're not ready for that kind of upgrade, here are two downloads that can help you get the most out of the memory you have:

Memory Boost Pro. This software automatically frees up unused memory when you need it, helps fine-tune how Windows uses RAM, and includes a "detective" that displays running programs and processes and how much memory they're using. It also warns you of system crashes before they happen. ($19.95 shareware; *www.rosecitysoftware. com.*)

FreeRAM XP Pro. Like Memory Boost Pro, this software frees up unused memory to give your computer more usable RAM. It doesn't include as many bells and whistles as Memory Boost Pro, but hey—it's free. Get it from *www. yourwaresolutions.com.*

---

3. **Look for any programs or processes that use a considerable amount of your CPU.**

Don't touch anything labeled System or Network Service (look in the User Name column)—killing those can lead to trouble. But otherwise, if you find any processor hogs, close them before starting any other CPU-intensive applications, such as burning a CD.

Tip: If you minimize the Task Manager, you can hold your mouse over its icon in the notification area for a quick way to see what percentage of your CPU is currently in use.

Figure 11-6:
The Task Manager's Processes tab lists the programs your PC is currently running, and reveals how much of your CPU each program uses. If System Idle Process is generating a high reading—say, above 90 percent—then your computer is really taking it easy.

11-10 Focusing Your CPU's Attention

Windows XP assigns every currently running program a priority level in order to determine how much CPU power each program receives. Should you ever want to give a particular program *more* processing power—for example, CD-burning software—you can change Windows XP's priorities so they match your needs.

In ascending order, here are the priorities Windows XP assigns:

- Low
- BelowNormal

- Normal

- AboveNormal

- High

- Realtime

The priority levels determine how quickly the processor responds to requests from the program. For example, if a Low priority program and a High priority program simultaneously ask your processor to perform a calculation, the High priority task always gets carried out first.

Windows XP automatically assigns most programs a Normal priority, but you can use the Task Manager to change these priorities at any time. Keep in mind that if you assign the Realtime priority to a program, Windows XP devotes an exceedingly high amount of CPU cycles to it, meaning there's little CPU power left over for other programs.

To alter a program's priority, run the Task Manager by pressing Ctrl-Alt-Delete, and then choose the Processes tab. Right-click the program whose priority you want to change, highlight Set Priority, and choose the priority you want as a replacement (see Figure 11-7).

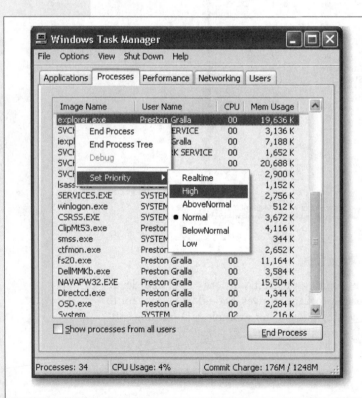

Figure 11-7:
When you set program priority levels, don't set them all at High or AboveNormal. Doing so defeats the purpose of delegating more of your CPU's power to certain programs.

Your customized priorities will last only as long as the program is running. Once you close the program, its priority level returns to whatever Windows XP ordinarily uses.

Note: Too much meddling with priorities can lead to system instability. Change one or two at a time, not 40.

11-11 A Souped-Up Alternative to Task Manager

Windows XP's Task Manager works pretty well. But if you want something with more bells and whistles, download a copy of WinTasks Professional. Among other cool features, it shows you processor and memory usage graphs for the past day, as well as the same graphs customized per process for the past 24 hours. (A process is any service or program running on your computer—anything from a word processor to XP's background program that lets you easily connect to a wireless network.) WinTasks Professional also displays all Dynamic-Link Libraries (page 282) used by each process.

WORKAROUND WORKSHOP

Reducing the Size of the Task Manager

If you're only using the Task Manager to monitor your system and don't need its title bar, menu bar, status bar and tabs, you can view it in stripped-down mode, as shown below.

Just double-click the Task Manager anywhere except inside the box that displays the running programs. Now you can reduce the size of the Task Manager window for easy, unobtrusive reference on your desktop. To toggle back to the full view, double-click the Task Manager again.

Image Name	User Name	CPU	Mem Usage
taskmgr.exe	Preston Gralla	00	3,068 K
WINWORD.EXE	Preston Gralla	00	34,676 K
SnagIt32.exe	Preston Gralla	00	700 K
DLLHOST.EXE	Preston Gralla	00	3,252 K
CIDAEMON.EXE	SYSTEM	00	208 K
wanmpsvc.exe	SYSTEM	00	1,896 K
ups.exe	SYSTEM	00	1,092 K
nvsvc32.exe	SYSTEM	00	920 K
NAVAPSVC.EXE	SYSTEM	00	952 K
mdm.exe	SYSTEM	00	2,456 K
CISVC.EXE	SYSTEM	00	140 K
Nhksrv.exe	SYSTEM	00	912 K
SPOOLSV.EXE	SYSTEM	00	3,832 K
explorer.exe	Preston Gralla	00	19,060 K
SVCHOST.EXE	LOCAL SERVICE	00	3,128 K
iexplore.exe	Preston Gralla	00	4,656 K
SVCHOST.EXE	NETWORK SERVICE	00	1,680 K
SVCHOST.EXE	SYSTEM	02	16,832 K
SVCHOST.EXE	SYSTEM	00	2,936 K
lsass.exe	SYSTEM	00	2,160 K
CERVICES EVE	CVSTEM	00	2,764 K

☐ Show processes from all users

[End Process]

WinTasks Professional even lets you create different system configuration sets that include different priorities for programs, so you can customize how your PC runs based on the tasks you want to accomplish. For example, if you sometimes use your computer mainly for games, and other times mainly for browsing the Web, you can create a game set that gives games and related programs the highest priority, and a browsing set that gives your browser the highest priority.

WinTasks Professional is available at *www.liutilities.com*. The standard version costs $29.95 and Professional version will run you $54.95.

ADD-IN ALERT

Automating Windows Tasks

While Windows' Task Manager *keeps track* of things for you, you may want to *initiate* a bunch of automatic processes yourself. Here're a few downloads that can help you.

If you perform a variety of repetitive tasks in Windows XP every day, like downloading files from an FTP site or cleaning up your hard disk, WinTask Lite can handle those chores for you. Think of it as having your own personal robot. ($99 shareware; *www.wintask.com*.)

But if you *really* want to automate Windows XP—and you're willing to get your hands dirty with some programming—using *batch files* is the best way to turn Windows XP into your private personal assistant. A holdover from DOS days, a batch file is simply a text file containing a set of commands. You then use a batch-processing program to execute one after the other, in the order they appear in the file. (You can spot batch files by their .bat extension.)

Windows XP has a set of built-in tools that let you create batch files to automate common tasks, like defragmenting

or cleaning your hard disk. But if you're dying to experiment, here are some other programs that offer much more batch-power and batch-flexibility.

WinBatch has been around since the earliest days of Windows, and has gained a sizable cult following—with good reason. It includes more than 500 separate functions for automating your system that you can combine and recombine in any way you want. So you could, for example, use it to log into a database, do a search, and then automatically save the results. ($99.99 shareware; *www.winbatch.com*.)

Batch File Compiler is a batch file program with a twist—it takes a batch file and turns it into an .exe file, so instead of running a bunch of commands in a batch file, you can run a single, compact *program*. What's the difference? Primarily, evildoers can tamper with a batch file but can't alter an .exe file, so it's a good option if you're worried about security. ($29.99 shareware; *http://bdargo.dns2go.com*.)

Security

Modern dangers don't lurk just in dark alleys, earthquake zones, or the moldy containers in your refrigerator. As computers have become linked in a global network, every connected PC has become exposed to a whole host of threats—viruses, worms, scammers and hackers, to name just a few.

While Microsoft hasn't exactly earned a reputation for prioritizing security, Windows XP offers a number of ways you can safeguard your PC from prying eyes and other potential dangers. This chapter explains how to implement a thorough security check; how to safely share files and folders with others; and how to make sure your data doesn't fall into the wrong hands.

Securing Your System

You may *want* to be generous and share files on your PC with others, but doing so can expose your computer to various security risks. This section offers hints on striking a balance so you can share in the benefits of a networked world while keeping your PC safe.

12-1   Microsoft's Baseline Security Adviser

Here's a trick few people know: Microsoft's Baseline Security Adviser, a free software download, can scan your computer for possible security holes and suggest how to fix them. Among other things, the software checks whether you have the most current security updates from Microsoft, whether you have security updates installed for the Windows Media Player, whether you have any Internet vulnerabilities, and other similar information. (For more on Windows security updates, see the box on page 292.)

Note: When installing the Baseline Security Adviser, consider turning off your antivirus software, then turning it back on after the adviser is installed. If your antivirus software runs during the installation process, it may issue security warnings. If so, simply tell the software to let the installation proceed, despite the warning.

You can download the Baseline Security Adviser from *www.microsoft.com/technet/ treeview/default.asp?url=/technet/security/tools/Tools/mbsahome.asp*. After you've downloaded the program, install it and follow the instructions to run it. After a few minutes, the program presents you with a detailed security report, like the one shown in Figure 12-1. A green check next to an item means your PC is secure, a yellow X means there may be a security issue, and a red X means you have a security problem. To get information about a problem, click the "Result details" link; to find out how to fix a problem, click "How to correct this."

Although the terminology the program uses can be difficult to understand at times, it's still worthwhile to run the check-up so you at least know about any trouble you should tackle.

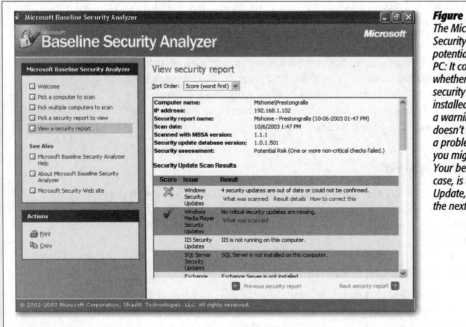

Figure 12-1:
The Microsoft Baseline Security Analyzer found potential risks on this PC: It couldn't confirm whether the most recent security updates were installed. If you receive a warning like this, it doesn't mean you have a problem—only that you might have one. Your best bet, in this case, is to use Windows Update, as outlined in the next hint.

Tip: A host of shareware offers more advanced security options. See the box on page 166.

12-2 Windows Update

Windows XP can automatically run *Windows Update* whenever your computer is on and connected to the Internet. This service checks the Microsoft Web site for downloadable improvements to the operating system and *security patches*, which are files that help your PC fight off the latest potential hacker attacks.

Windows Update is an important service, so you should make sure it's running on your PC. Here's how:

1. **Choose Start → Control Panel → System → Automatic Updates (Figure 12-2).**

   Turn on "Keep my computer up to date," if it's not already selected. This setting tells Windows XP to continually check Microsoft's Web site for updates.

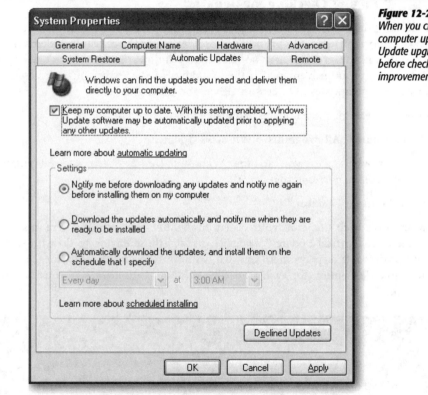

Figure 12-2:
When you choose "Keep my computer up to date," Windows Update upgrades itself if necessary before checking for other system improvements.

2. **Pick a download and installation schedule.**

   In the Settings section, select the option that says "Download the updates automatically and notify me when they are ready to be installed." This option does the download work for you, but it doesn't jump ahead and install the updates immediately—a good safeguard, as updates are occasionally problematic. If you wait a day or two before installing an update, you can check Microsoft's Web site (see the next hint) to make sure there aren't any serious bugs reported about the latest patch.

Note: XP notifies you that it has downloaded new updates by opening a little text balloon in your system tray.

---

3. Click OK.

You're done.

When you want to install the new updates, click the notification balloon, which opens a wizard that walks you through the installation.

12-3 **Manually Checking for Updates**

Windows Update only alerts you to the availability of what Microsoft considers to be very important updates—primarily those dealing with security problems. But Microsoft constantly offers new updates that Windows Update *doesn't* tell you about, including improvements to the Windows Media Player, new drivers for your video card, updates to Microsoft Office, and other goodies.

It's easy to check for these updates and install them. Here's how:

1. Choose Start → All Programs → Windows Update.

Your browser takes you to the Windows Update Web site, at *http:// windowsupdate.microsoft.com*.

2. Click "Scan for Updates."

Microsoft's Web site scans your system to identify any updates you're missing. If there are "critical updates" available (usually those having to do with security), Microsoft displays them in a list, with an Add button next to each one. Read the description for each, and click the Add button for any you want to install.

WORKAROUND WORKSHOP

Downloading Updates You've Declined

At some point you may decide *not* to install an update Windows XP tells you is available. But what happens if, for some reason, you later change your mind? It's easy to install updates you've previously declined.

Choose Control Panel → Performance and Maintenance → System → Automatic Updates and click the Declined Updates button. (If you haven't declined any updates, the button will be gray, and you won't be able to click it.) In the dialog boxes that appear, click Yes and then OK.

Windows XP doesn't immediately retrieve the updates you've skipped. Instead, the next time it scans for updates, it notifies you that the ones you've declined are available, so you can decide which ones you want to download and install.

---

3. **On the left side of the page, click Windows XP.**

This displays all the available "non-critical" updates, such as those that fix small bugs, or upgrade Microsoft programs like the Windows Media Player. Read the description for each, and click the Add button for any you want to install.

4. **When you've chosen all the updates you want to install, click "Review and install updates."**

The screen shown in Figure 12-3 appears. It lets you review all the updates you've chosen before installing them. To remove an item you've selected, click the Remove button next to its name.

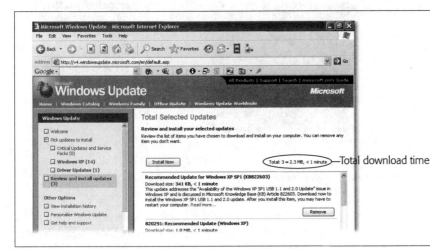

Figure 12-3:
As you select the updates you want to download, Microsoft estimates the download time for all the items on your list, based on the speed of your Internet connection.

5. **Click Install Now.**

Your PC starts downloading the files, then installs them. You may need to restart your computer to complete the installation.

Note: On occasion, Windows XP may tell you that you have to install certain updates *separately*, rather than as part of a group.

12-4 Checking for Viruses

If you've been living on the edge and don't have antivirus software installed, you can still check to see whether your PC is infected by going to the free online virus checkers run by Symantec and McAfee.

To use Symantec's virus detector, go to *http://security.symantec.com/sscv6/default. asp?langid=ie&venid=sym*, click Go, and then click Start (under the Virus Detection button). The site asks several times whether you want to install software from Symantec. Click Yes every time, and then scan your system for viruses, as shown in Figure 12-4. If the site finds any viruses, it tells you which files are infected, and what viruses they have. (To get rid of the viruses, though, you still need to buy antivirus software.)

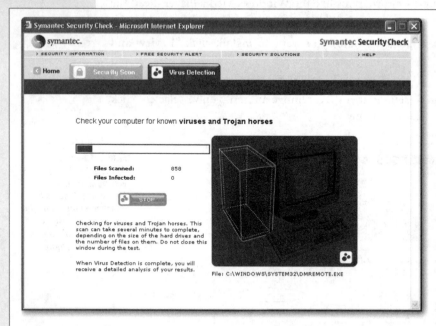

Figure 12-4:
If you don't yet have antivirus software on your PC, you can use an online virus checker, like the one from Symantec pictured here, to see if your computer is infected. For the best protection, you should run antivirus software on your PC, since it eliminates viruses in incoming email and documents before they can do any damage. (The box on page 294 tells you more about antivirus software.)

McAfee has a similar free online virus checker. Go to *www.mcafee.com*, click McAfee FreeScan, and follow the instructions. (You must register with the site before you can use the free virus-checker.) As with Symantec's checkup, McAfee's service tells you if you have any viruses, but doesn't get rid of them.

FREQUENTLY ASKED QUESTION

Antivirus Software

Do I really need antivirus software?

Yes!

New viruses infect computers across the Internet every day. Unfortunately, Windows machines are most susceptible, and the damage can be severe, causing permanently lost files and impaired—or even dead—PCs. You can minimize the threat by using third-party antivirus software, which isn't free but is *much* cheaper than recovering from a virus.

Symantec *(www.symantec.com)* and McAfee *(www.mcafee.com)* are among the leaders in the field. Their software programs not only block viruses from wreaking havoc on your PC, they can also help you eliminate a virus if you've had the misfortune of catching one.

Once you installed an antivirus program, make sure you keep it up to date. Symantec and McAfee offer Web-based updates, and you should look for new updates at least every other day.

12-5 Stripping Personal Information from Your Documents

When you save files in Microsoft Word, Excel, and PowerPoint, some personal information about you may wind up in the DNA of the document. How does this happen? When you create a new document, Microsoft Office automatically includes information you provided when you installed Office, such as your name or company name, in the background of the file. (If you're working on a document someone else created, the file contains that person's details.)

To view this information in any file, choose File → Properties. Figure 12-5 shows you the window that opens.

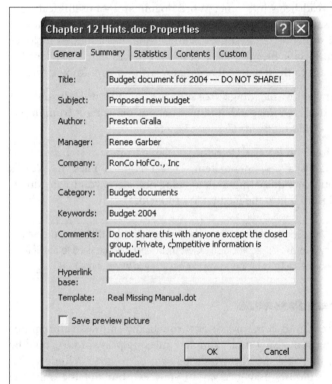

Figure 12-5:
You may not realize it, but many of your Microsoft Office documents contain personally identifying information, like the details shown here. You can delete it, but first make sure none of the information is required—by your employer, for instance.

If attaching your name to a file is more ownership than you care to claim—say the file is a spreadsheet detailing your plans to embezzle money from your company—you can tell Office to strip this information out of a document when you save it.

Using Word, Excel or PowerPoint, choose Tools → Options → Security, and select "Remove personal information from this file on save." When you next save the file, the program won't include any personal information.

Note: Unfortunately, you have to do this individually for each file you save; you can't tell Office to do it for every document you work on.

12-6   Preventing Word from Stealing Your Files

Word has a useful feature that can, unfortunately, let other people gain access to files on your PC. The feature is called *Word Fields,* and it inserts self-updating information into Word documents, such as page numbers. If, for example, you add a page to the middle of a document, Word automatically renumbers all the pages.

Some of these Word Fields are hidden, and because you can't see them, you can't tell what they're doing. For instance, the hidden field IncludeText can insert Word documents or Excel spreadsheets into other Word documents—a useful feature if you want to combine several documents. But the IncludeText command can also be used maliciously. If someone sends you a document that has a hidden Include-Text field that points to specific files and their locations on your hard disk, your PC could send those files back to the document originator without your knowledge.

You can fix the problem by downloading a free software patch from Microsoft that closes this loophole. Download the patch and instructions on using it from *http:// support.microsoft.com/default.aspx?scid=kb;en-us;329748.*

Another option is the free Hidden File Detector, available from *www.wordsite.com/ downloads/hfd.htm.* It adds a new menu item, Detect Hidden Files, to Word's Tools menu. When you select this command, a dialog box alerts you to any documents that have been inserted into the file by a Word Field.

Note: You can also fix the Word Fields problem with any downloads. In a Word document, choose Edit → Links to see if there are any links to files present. If so, delete them—that's all you need to do. (If there are no links to files, Word grays out the Links option, so you have nothing to worry about.)

12-7   Hard-to-Crack Passwords

Frequently, hackers break into computers not through any impressive programming feats, but by doing something much simpler: guessing passwords. (You'd be surprised at how many people use the word "password" as their Windows XP logon password—a ridiculously easy gateway to your PC, but not the only one that's a cinch to crack).

One of the best ways to keep your computer safe from prying eyes is to create tricky passwords. Here are several strategies to make your passwords difficult to guess:

- **Use at least eight characters in your password.** It's a simple matter of math: the longer your password, the more difficult it is to guess.

- **Mix letters and numbers.** When you mix the two, your password is more obscure than one that includes only numbers or only letters.

- **Use both lower-case and upper-case letters, if possible.** Some passwords are case-sensitive, which means the only way to type them correctly is to use the proper case. So using different cases in your password makes it much more difficult to crack.

- **Never use the name of your spouse, child, pet, hometown, or anything else associated with you.** If someone knows any details about your life, these are the first passwords they're likely to try.

- **Use a random password generator.** These tools create passwords containing a very difficult-to-guess collection of random characters. There's a free password generator on the Web at *http://world.std.com/~reinhold/passgen.html.* You can also download the free Quicky Password Generator at *www.quicky.com.*

Figure 12-6:
To prevent snooping when you're on the road with your laptop, turn off file and printer sharing, as shown here.

12-8   Safe Travels with a Laptop

If you use file sharing on a laptop while connected to a home or corporate network, you should rethink your sharing policy when you travel—particularly if you connect to wireless hot spots, where other people using that wireless juice can view and use your shared files and folders. (For more about WiFi and wireless computing, see page 237.)

But it can be cumbersome going through your PC and manually turning off sharing on all your shared folders—not to mention turning it on again for each folder when you come home. Luckily, you can turn off file sharing temporarily for all your folders at once.

Here's how. Right-click Network Neighborhood and choose Properties, then right-click the network connection you use when you travel (for example, Wireless Network Connection) and choose Properties again. Uncheck "File and Printer Sharing for Microsoft Networks" and click OK, as shown in Figure 12-6. When you return from your travels, just recheck the box.

ADD-IN ALERT

Top Security Downloads for Files and Folders

The built-in tools Windows XP uses to keep your files and folders secure work reasonably well, but there are far more powerful tools available. If you're in the market for added protection, try these downloads.

HideFolders XP. One of the best ways to keep files and folders secure is to completely hide them from other people. HideFolders XP does just that. It can make up to 64 folders invisible at once, and works with both Windows XP Home Edition and Windows XP Professional; only those with the right password can view the folders and files. It's available from various Internet download sites or directly from *www.fspro.net*. HideFolders XP is shareware, so you can try it for free, but you're expected to pay $24.95 to keep using it.

FolderLock. FolderLock lets you put a virtual lock on any file or folder by password-protecting the file. All you have to do is drag a file or folder to the "locker," and it stays locked until you unlock it. FolderLock works with either version of Windows XP and can be used with drives that utilize either FAT or NTFS compression (page 74). FolderLock, available from *www.newsoftwares.net*, is shareware and free to try, but you need to cough up $25 if you plan to keep it.

Sure Delete. When you delete files and folders from your hard disk, doesn't really delete them. The file data remains on your computer, so someone with the right tools can find it and read it. If you want to make sure your deleted files can't be recovered, Sure Delete takes out the trash—permanently. It works with FAT or NTFS compression, and with both versions of Windows XP. You can download Sure Delete for free from *www.wizard-industries.com*.

Encryption for Windows XP Pro

One of the best ways to keep your personal information and files secure is to use *encryption*. When you encrypt a file, XP scrambles the contents so that only a *person using the account that encrypted the file* can read it. Thus, when you encrypt files and then log off your account, only somebody with your account password can read the scrambled documents, making it a good choice for sensitive stuff like financial information, that note to your spouse with the code to your personal safe, and the list of names of everyone you've ever kissed.

This section explains how to encrypt files and folders using Windows XP Pro's built-in tools; the Home edition, unfortunately, doesn't include these features.

12-9   Protecting Your Data by Encrypting Files and Folders

Although encryption was once the domain of spies and computer geeks, Windows XP Professional has brought these tools to the masses, making it easy to encrypt files and folders with just a few mouse clicks.

Note: You can only use Windows XP's built-in encryption tools if you have the Professional version and your hard disk uses the NTFS file system (page 74). To check your hard disk, right-click the icon for your drive, choose Properties → General, and look at the File System entry, which indicates whether you have an NTFS file system.

Here's how to use Windows XP Professional's encryption tools:

1. **Right-click the folder or file you want to encrypt and choose Properties → General → Advanced.**

   If no Advanced button appears on the Properties dialog box, it means you aren't using NTFS, and therefore you can't use encryption.

2. **In the Advanced Attributes dialog box that appears (Figure 12-7), turn on "Encrypt contents to secure data."**

   Then click OK, then OK again to open the Confirm Attributes Changes dialog box.

Figure 12-7:
You can't compress a file or folder and also encrypt it; it's an either/or situation. Therefore if a file or folder is compressed, you can't encrypt it. You need to uncompress it first by deselecting "Compress contents to save disk space." (For more information about compressing files, turn to page 75.)

3. **Choose whether to encrypt only the selected folder, or the folder plus all the subfolders and files it contains.**

   If you only encrypt the folder, Windows XP doesn't encrypt any of the files currently in the folder, but it does encrypt any new files you create, move, or copy into the folder. If you choose all the subfolders and files, you've got everything covered.

Note: You cannot encrypt files located in My Computer → C: → Windows. Windows XP doesn't let you encrypt those files since it can slow down or damage your system.

If you're encrypting a *file* that's in an unencrypted *folder*, the Encryption Warning box appears, as shown in Figure 12-8. You can choose to encrypt the file only, or the file and the parent folder.

As a general rule, you should encrypt the folder as well as the file, because if you encrypt only the file, you may accidentally decrypt it without realizing it. Some programs save copies of your files and delete the original; in those instances, the files become decrypted as soon as you edit them. If you encrypt the folder as well, all files added to the folder are encrypted, so the saved file would automatically be encrypted.

4. **After you make your choice, click OK.**

Windows XP encrypts the file or folder.

Decrypting files and folders involves a similar process, which is just as easy—though you have to be logged into your account for it to work; otherwise the system blocks you from reading the files (which is the whole idea). So log in, then right-click the file or folder you want to decrypt, choose Properties → Advanced, and deselect "Encrypt contents to secure data." Click OK, then OK again.

Note: A file remains encrypted only when it's in an encrypted folder. So if you copy an encrypted file or send it via email, the original file in its folder stays encrypted, but the copy or sent file becomes unencrypted.

Figure 12-8:
When organizing your files and folders, consider designating several folders to contain all your sensitive information, and then encrypt those. That way, it's easy to keep track of what you need to encrypt, and what you don't.

12-10 Changing the Color of Encrypted Files and Folders

When you encrypt files and folders, they turn green when you view them in Windows Explorer. But if you want Windows XP to display them using the same color as your other files and folders—so that other people glancing at your monitor won't know what you've encrypted—you can turn off the feature. Just run Windows Explorer and choose Tools → Folder Options. Now clear the option "Show Encrypted or Compressed NTFS Files in Color." You can apply this change just to the current folder, or to all folders.

12-11 A Final Security Measure

Even if you encrypt every file on your hard disk, someone could still snoop in on your data. How? Your *paging file* or *swap file,* which XP uses to give your PC more memory when it needs it, may contain information that a program temporarily stored in memory. Consequently, even if you encrypted that information, someone might be able to be read it using the paging file. Moreover, the paging file doesn't get emptied when you turn off your computer, so when somebody turns your PC on, the file may still contain that data.

To solve the problem, you can edit the Registry to tell Windows XP to clear data out of your paging file when you turn off your computer. To activate this option, run the Registry Editor (see page 328) and go to My Computer → HKEY_LOCAL_ MACHINE → SYSTEM → CurrentControlSet → Control → Session Manager → Memory Management. Change the value of ClearPageFileAtShutdown to 1. Close the Registry and restart your computer. Now, whenever you turn off Windows XP, it clears the paging file of any data.

POWER USERS' CLINIC

Encrypting Files with One Click

Rather than editing a file's Advanced properties, as described in hint 12-9, you can encrypt files even more quickly by adding this option to the right-click context menu.

Run the Registry Editor (page xx) and go to My Computer → HKEY LOCAL MACHINE → SOFTWARE → Microsoft → Windows → CurrentVersion → Explorer → Advanced. Create a new DWORD value called EncryptionContextMenu. In

the Value Data text box, enter 00000001 and verify that the Hexidecimal option button is selected.

Once you exit the Registry Editor, Encrypt appears as an option on the context menu when you right-click a file. Now all you have to do to encrypt a file is right-click it and choose Encrypt.

Crash Recovery

In an ideal computing world, Windows XP would run problem-free, your PC would never crash, and Nigerian exiles really would want to give you a million bucks for helping them with their money-transferring problems. But it's not a perfect world, so this chapter steps in to help you recover from a serious glitch.

One critical tool for getting yourself out of trouble is *System Restore,* which may be the most useful utility ever built into Windows. This handy feature runs in the background whenever your computer is turned on, taking snapshots at regular intervals. It copies system files, information about your user accounts, and your hardware and software settings. Then, if your computer crashes or exhibits other signs of digital gremlin invasion, System Restore (Control Panel → Performance and Maintenance → System Restore) returns your PC to a *restore point,* a happy digital replica of your PC when it was working properly.

Note: Because System Restore doesn't restore *data*—just system files and settings—it isn't a replacement for conducting backups. For information about backing up your PC, turn to page 87.

13-1   Creating a Restore Point

System Restore automatically creates restore points for you (see the box on page 307 for more on when System Restore kicks in), but sometimes *you* want to decide when to take these snapshots. For example, to protect yourself when installing a new program, you may want to create a restore point *before* slapping a fresh application on our hard drive.

To manually create a restore point, choose Control Panel → Performance and Maintenance → System Restore. Then, choose Create a Restore Point (Figure 13-1), and in the next screen, name the restore point (for example, "Before installing camera"). Windows XP automatically records and displays the restore point's time and date so you don't need to include that information in your title. Finally, click Create and your system goes to work; after several seconds, a message appears telling you that XP has created the restore point. Click Close to exit the utility.

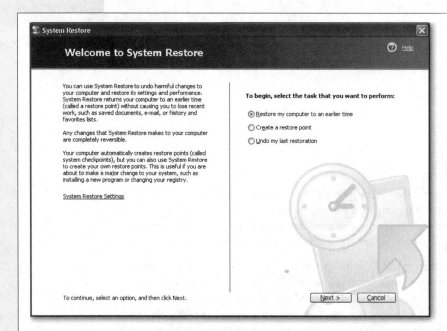

Figure 13-1:
Consider manually creating a restore point before installing new software or making any other system changes. The System Restore Settings link lets you customize how much space your hard drive uses to save restore points, as explained in hint 13-3.

13-2 Restoring Your System

Before using a restore point to return your computer to a stable state, make sure you've saved any work and closed any programs you're running. Then choose Control Panel → Performance and Maintenance → System Restore. The Restore Wizard screen appears (shown in Figure 13-2). Choose "Restore my computer to an earlier time," and from the calendar that appears, choose a date and a specific restore point, as shown in Figure 13-2, then click Next. A warning screen appears, reminding you to save your work; click Next again. After a short while, your PC shuts down and restarts in its old state.

13-3 Limiting the Size of System Restore's Files

System restore has one downside: It eats up a significant amount of disk space. Why? Because it devotes disk space to each restore point you create, which can quickly add up to several gigabytes of data. If you're trying to save hard disk space, you can shrink the amount System Restore uses.

Note: Of course, there's a trade-off: The less disk space you devote to System Restore, the fewer restore points you can create.

To change how much space System Restore uses, right-click My Computer and choose Properties → System Restore. As shown in Figure 13-2, you can change the allocated space by dragging the slider to the left (to reduce the size), or to the right (to increase it).

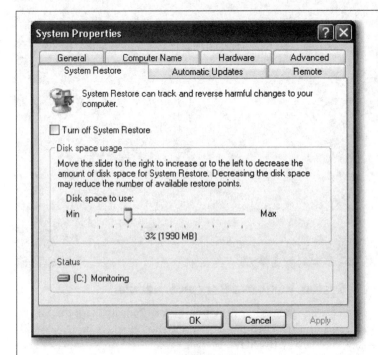

Figure 13-2:
Windows XP normally allocates 12 percent of your hard drive for System Restore. You can change this setting, or turn it off altogether, by selecting "Turn Off System Restore." If you turn it off, though, you'll be computing without a safety net.

13-4   Deleting Old Restore Points

System Restore automatically deletes its old files after 90 days or your size limit (described in the previous hint)—whichever comes first. If you're really desperate to free up disk space, you can manually delete your existing restore points. You may also want to delete old restore points if your computer falls prey to a virus. The reason? If you restore your computer to a time when it was infected, your PC might return to the sick ward.

Note: Deleting restore points is pretty much an all-or-nothing affair because XP only lets you erase all but the most recent one.

To clear out the old restore points, choose Start → All Programs → Accessories → System Tools → Disk Cleanup. After launching, the Disk Cleanup utility may take several minutes to check your system, as it calculates how much space you can save using various cleanup options. When the utility finishes checking your system, click the More Options tab, then click the "Clean up" button in the System Restore section. The Disk Cleanup utility deletes all your old restore points except the most recent one.

ADD-IN ALERT

Disk Cleanups

Windows XP's built-in Disk Cleanup program (page 306) works just fine—but why settle for just fine? You can download other tools that do an even better job of cleaning up your system, such as finding and deleting duplicate files or deleting *orphaned* shortcuts (links to programs that no longer exist). Clean-up tools designed for Windows XP abound, but here're two of the best:

• **CleanUp!** This software expands on Windows XP's Disk Cleanup tool with a few extra features that do the electronic equivalent of scrubbing your bathroom walls and cleaning behind your furniture. CleanUp! goes the extra mile by finding and deleting shortcuts to programs you've long since trashed and browser Favorites that link to dead Web sites. It also shows you a list of Registry entries that point to

files that aren't on your hard disk and lets you examine Internet Explorer AutoComplete entries, so you can delete entries for sites you don't plan to revisit. ($18 shareware; *www.emesoft.se.*)

• **System Mechanic.** This program is far more than a disk cleanup tool. In addition to normal cleanup tasks, it finds and deletes obsolete and "junk" files left behind by uninstalled programs, finds and deletes duplicate files, and fixes broken shortcuts. It also cleans out the Registry, lets you fine-tune various Windows settings, such as how to display your desktop, and has privacy tools that protect you against spyware. In all, System Mechanic offers a suite of 15 utilities. ($59.95 shareware; *www.iolo.com.*)

13-5   Changing System Restore's Backup Schedule

System Restore automatically creates a restore point every 24 hours (see the box on page 307 for more details on this schedule). However, should you want to set a different schedule—say, once every two days, or twice a day—you can make it happen by editing the Registry. You can also change how often System Restore automatically deletes old restore points.

To trigger these changes, run the Registry Editor (page 328) and go to My Computer → HKEY_LOCAL_MACHINE → SOFTWARE → Microsoft → Windows NT → CurrentVersion → SystemRestore. Then, follow any or all of these instructions, depending on which changes you want to make:

• **To change how frequently System Restore creates restore points, edit the RPGlobalInterval value.** When you edit the value, click Decimal; the Registry displays how often the utility creates a restore point, in seconds. The default number is 86400, or the number of seconds in 24 hours. For less frequent restore points, increase the number, say, to 172800 if you want a restore point created every two days. For more frequent restore points, decrease the number, say, to 43200 if you want your system to create a restore point twice a day.

- **To change how often System Restore deletes restore points, edit the RPLifeInterval value.** When you edit the value, click Decimal; the Registry displays how many seconds elapse before each Restore Points is deleted. The default is 7776000, or the number of seconds in 90 days. To delete restore points more frequently, decrease the number, say, to 3888000 to delete old restore points after 45 days. But if the amount of disk space you've devoted to System Restore points fills up sooner, Windows XP deletes old versions at more frequent intervals, no matter which interval you choose (Figure 13-2 tells you how to allot more space to System Restore).

- **To save restore points each time you start your computer, edit the RPSessionInterval value.** When you edit the value, click Decimal. By default, the setting is 0, which means it's turned off. Type a value, in seconds, indicating how often you want System Restore to save restore points each session. For example, 3600 would save a restore point every hour; 144000 creates one every four hours. Be careful with this setting, though: If you create restore points too frequently, they'll take up a substantial amount of hard disk space, which means Windows XP will delete them at relatively short intervals.

UP TO SPEED

Some Good Things to Know About System Restore

Here are some things to keep in mind about System Restore.

If you upgrade from Windows XP Home Edition to Windows XP Professional—or from Windows Me to either version of Windows XP—you lose your existing restore points.

You can't *create* restore points when you're in Safe Mode, but you can *revert* to previous restore points from Safe Mode. (For more on Safe Mode, see page 308.) If you do end up working in Safe Mode, when you're finished you might want to consider creating a restore point once you're back in Windows XP.

If you create a new user account and then use System Restore to roll back to a point before you created that account, that new user won't be able to log on (since you'll have eliminated the new account). However, the data files created by the new user won't be deleted, so you can still access them.

When you tell System Restore to stop monitoring a drive, it deletes all existing restore points for that drive. Even if you turn System Restore back on, the utility can't recreate those restore points—they're gone for good.

13-6 Getting System Restore to Ignore Certain Folders

System Restore can be a lifesaver, but it can also cause unforeseen problems by deleting files in the Windows folder or in the Program Files folder. Most of the time, this condition isn't a problem because your data files live in your Documents folder, and the whole point of restore is to jump back in time in your system foldres. But if you've set anything to save in those folders, you may find that after you restore your system, a group of files is gone.

Thankfully, you can instruct System Restore to ignore any folder you declare out of bounds. To make the change, run the Registry Editor (page 328) and go to My Computer → HKEY_LOCAL_MACHINE → System → CurrentControlSet → Control → BackupRestore → FilesNotToBackup. Create a new Multi-String Value, and give it a name that describes the folder you want to protect, such as Downloads. Double-click the value to edit it. Type the full path of the folder you want to protect and click OK, then exit the Registry. From now on, when you create a restore point, the utility completely ignores files in that folder.

13-7 Safe Mode

System Restore can get you working again, but what if you first want to diagnose a problem? *Safe Mode* is a good place to turn because it runs your computer in a stripped-down state that makes it easier to identify problems. In Safe Mode, none of your normal startup programs run (page 7), most of the hardware attached to your PC is ignored (for example, devices connected to a USB or Firewire port), and Windows XP uses only the simplest video driver possible, because video problems frequently cause XP's woes.

If your system frequently crashes, or won't boot up at all, try starting in Safe Mode. Here's how:

1. **Start your computer and it comes on, hold down the F8 key.**

   Don't wait too long before you press the F8 key; if you do, Windows XP will bypass Safe Mode and try to start normally.

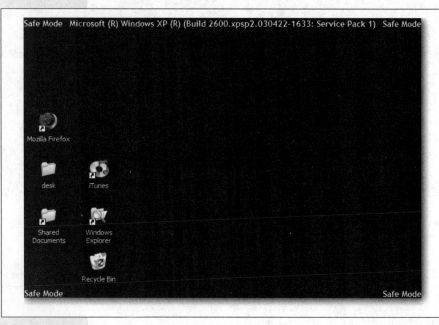

Figure 13-3:
Safe Mode actually looks a little ominous.

Note: If your computer is already running, reboot it by choosing Start → Turn Off Computer → Restart.

2. **A menu with several options appears, including "Safe Mode" and "Safe Mode with Networking." Choose Safe Mode and press Enter.**

   If you're certain your PC isn't having networking problems, then choose "Safe Mode with Networking" and press Enter. If you select this option, you can use the Internet or even a local network while you're in Safe Mode.

3. **Log into Windows XP.**

   Once you're logged in, XP looks a lot like what you can see in Figure 13-3.

4. **Troubleshoot your problem.**

   Choose Start → Help and Support. In the search box, type *troubleshooter* and press Enter. In the left-hand pane, click Full Text Search Matches, and then click the link that says "List of Troubleshooters." Choose the troubleshooter that most closely matches your problem and follow its links and advice. To exit Safe Mode, restart your computer.

ADD-IN ALERT

Troubleshooting Programs

Windows XP offers plenty of built-in troubleshooting tools, but sometimes it's worth supplementing your XP arsenal with a few additions. Here're a few of the best:

WinRescue XP. This helpful tool offers a variety of trouble-shooting and system restore modules. It has a utility that works like System Restore, offers Registry cleanup tools, includes over a dozen hardware troubleshooters, and has a backup program as well. It's shareware and free to try, but you're expected to pay $24.95 if you continue to use it. Get it from *www.superwin.com.*

RestoreIT. This program works much like System Restore, but features superior customization features that let you set and use restore points. It also lets you retrieve deleted files and can kill viruses. It's shareware and free to try, but costs $39.95 to use permanently. You can download it from *www.farstone.com.*

Bugtoaster. This free program captures the details of your system crashes and uploads the information to a Web site. Once there, the information is correlated with data from other system crashes and then analyzed. Software companies and IT departments monitor the site for bug information, then report back to the site about fixes. It's a bit of a convoluted process, but it may help you solve some system crashes. And best of all, it's free. Get it from *www. bugtoaster.com.*

Windows Media Player

Most of the programs Microsoft includes with your operating system—WordPad, Outlook Express, and Backup—tend to be pretty limited in what they can do: write a simple document, send some email, make you think you ought to pay for a better backup program. But to the company's great credit, Windows Media Player, which comes with XP, is better than decent. It's a powerful multimedia jukebox that lets you play and burn music CDs, listen to Internet radio stations, and even watch Web videos and DVDs.

The downside to Windows Media Player is that many of its multiple talents come buried inside a maze of dialog boxes and menu choices. And you might not be aware of other programs that can make Media Player even more useful.

That's what this chapter is all about: helping you get the most out of Media Player. Below you'll learn about ways to make Media Player look more stylish, help produce better sound, and what to do when your music files start skipping more than an old LP. You'll also learn some helpful tricks for playing DVDs and for speeding up the way you control the program.

Note: The hints in this chapter describe features and menus in version 9 of Windows Media Player. While most hints also work with version 8, some of the menus and buttons may be different.

You can tell which version you have by opening the player—Start → All Programs → Accessories → Entertainment → Windows Media Player—and then choosing Help → About Windows Media Player. The box that opens tells you your version (it may look something like 8.00.00.4487–which means 8). If you have version 8, you can upgrade to 9 for free by going to *www.microsoft.com/windows/windowsmedia/ download.*

14-1   Finding the Menu Bar

When you run Windows Media Player for the first time—by choosing All Programs → Accessories → Entertainment → Windows Media Player—you might not see the program's menu bar. More confusing still, the bar may suddenly appear, and just as abruptly disappear, for no apparent reason. What gives?

You can actually set the menu bar in one of two modes: permanently fixed in place or ready to appear only when your mouse is at the top of the program. If you want Windows Media Player to display the menu bar all the time, click the small double-headed arrow in the upper-left portion of the player, shown in Figure 14-1 (top). As if by magic, the menu bar appears (Figure 14-1, bottom). To make the menu bar appear only when your mouse *is at the top* of the program, click again—the menu disappears and will come out only when your mouse is up top.

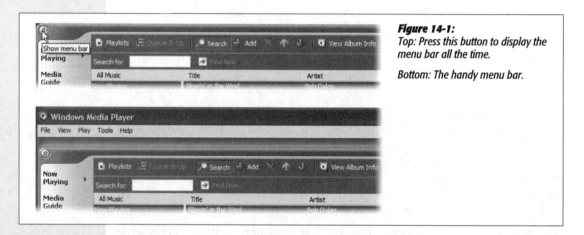

Figure 14-1:
Top: Press this button to display the menu bar all the time.

Bottom: The handy menu bar.

Tip: Windows Media Player phones home each time you launch the program by going straight to the Windows Media Guide page at *www.windowsmedia.com* (which features Microsoft-recommended content and ads). If you'd like to make this stop go to Tools → Options → Player and turn off Start Player in Media Guide.

Listening to Music

This section offers hints designed to increase your listening pleasure.

14-2   The MP3 Factor

As most power hounds and 8-year-olds know, digital comes in many formats, including MP3, .wma, .wav, and more. MP3 is the *only* format that can you play on any software player (like Windows Media Player) or physical device (like an iPod). Thus, if you want to use your PC or portable player to listen to a symphony you downloaded from a Website or rock opera from your favorite CD, you may well have to convert the files into MP3s.

Unfortunately, while Windows Media Player can *play* MP3 files, the program can't *create* MP3 files—at least not without the help of a tool, called an *encoder,* which converts files into the MP3 format.

Here're two options for creating MP3 files:

- **MP3 Power Encoder,** available for $9.95 from Cyberlink at *www.gocyberlink.com/ english/products/powerdvd/winxp_plugin.asp.*

- **MP3 XPack,** available for $9.95 from Intervideo at *www.intervideo.com/ products/custom/ms/windowsxp/media_pack.jsp.*

Tip: To find other MP3 encoders, open Windows Media Player, choose Tools → Options → Copy Music, and click "Learn more about MP3 formats."

14-3   The Graphic Equalizer

Want to try your hand at the mixing board? Windows Media Player's Graphic Equalizer lets you tweak your tunes in a bunch of ways, including raising or lowering treble and bass, changing the balance of your left and right speakers, and choosing from almost two dozen *presets*—canned groups of settings designed to make specific types of music sound better, like Rock, Rap, Techno, Country, Classical, and so on.

FREQUENTLY ASKED QUESTION

Alternatives to Windows Media Player

What options do I have besides Windows Media Player?

Windows Media Player is great for playing music, but it does have a few drawbacks, chief among them its lack of built-in support for creating MP3 files. Furthermore, some Web sites offer audio and video clips that you *can't* play using Windows Media Player; these sites require another media player like RealNetwork's RealPlayer or Apple's QuickTime program. You can solve this problem by having *several* media players on your PC. Here's an overview of the most popular, each of which has a free version.

RealPlayer (*www.real.com*) is the media-playing program from RealNetworks, a pioneer in the world of *streaming audio* (that is, audio that's broadcast, rather than offered as a file you download and save). The free version of Real-Player has comparable tools to Windows Media Player (you can rip CDs, organize your music, and burn CDs). Real-Player also lets you buy downloadable songs from its Real Music Store for around a dollar a song or subscribe to its streaming music service (called Rhapsody) which lets you listen to more than 600,000 songs for about $10 per month.

MusicMatch Jukebox (*www.musicmatch.com*), another option, creates MP3 files and plays other popular formats, too (including .wma, the Windows Media type). It also burns CDs, plays Internet radio stations, and lets you buy individual songs or subscribe to a monthly all-you-can-listen service.

Despite the big cultural differences between Windows and Macintosh, Apple offers two XP-ready programs. iTunes (*www.apple.com/itunes*) has the least cluttered interface of any major music-playing program—yet it still lets you rip and burn CDs and listen to music in many formats. It also gives you access to the iTunes music store, which has more than a million songs for sale at around a dollar a piece. But iTunes isn't really meant for playing videos (though you can watch some music videos and movie trailers by clicking on the Music Videos or Movie Trailers link in iTunes). Instead, try QuickTime, Apple's video player (*www.quicktime.com*), which is designed to play QuickTime movies, a popular format among some Web video developers.

To display the Graphic Equalizer, choose View → Enhancements → Graphic Equalizer. The Equalizer, shown in Figure 14-2, appears at the bottom of the player. If the controls are grayed out, click the "Turn on" link. To choose a preset for the genre of music you're listening to, click Custom and choose from the pop-up list that appears.

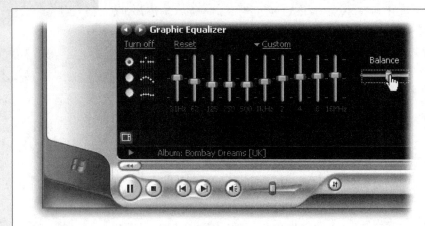

Figure 14-2:
Customize the way your music sounds by moving the sliders on the Graphic Equalizer up (toward treble) or down (toward bass). You can also change the balance between your speakers by moving the Balance slider left or right. If your PC's speakers don't have separate volume controls, this slider is the only way to change the balance between them.

To the left of the sliders, three small buttons control how they work. Select the top button if you want the sliders to move independently, the middle one if you want them to move together loosely, and the bottom one if you want them to move together in a tight group (the difference between these last two is pretty minimal).

14-4   3D WOW Sound

Want to surround yourself with Microsoft's rendition of realistic, three-dimensional sound? Windows Media Player lets you simulate a 3D surround sound effect with your speakers—even if you only have two of them—by using the SRS WOW control. The effect might not convince discerning audiophiles to ditch their stereos, but average music fans will probably notice a slightly fuller and richer sound.

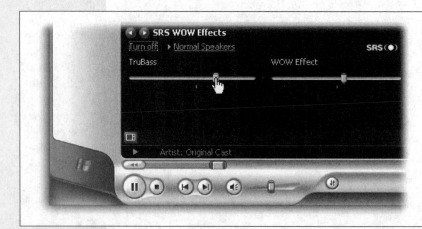

Figure 14-3:
The SRS WOW controls give your speakers a 3D sound effect, even if you have only two speakers.

Note: Not all speakers can take advantage of SRS WOW, so you may not notice any change when you use the controls. Older speakers, less expensive speakers, and laptop speakers won't deliver the audio whomp this feature is designed to produce.

To activate SRS WOW, choose View → Enhancements → SRS WOW Effects. The controls shown in Figure 14-3 appear. If the controls are grayed out, click the "Turn on" link. From the link to the right of the on/off link, choose the type of speakers you have (your choices are: large speakers, small speakers, or headphones). Adjust TruBass (a souped-up bass control) and WOW Effect with the sliders in the middle of the control panel.

14-5 Improving CD Playback Sound

When you listen to music CDs using Windows Media Player (or any music player on your computer), your tunes may sound muddy—that is, not quite as clear as when you listen to music on a normal stereo. You probably can't match the quality of a fancy stand-alone system, but you can tweak your PC's CD player to play back music in digital rather than analog form—which can help brighten up dull discs.

Launch Windows Explorer (Windows logo key+E), right-click your CD drive, and choose Properties → Hardware. Highlight your CD drive and choose Properties → Properties to open the screen pictured in Figure 14-4. At the bottom of the window, look for "Enable digital CD audio for this CD-ROM device" and make sure it's turned on, then click OK until you've closed all the dialog boxes.

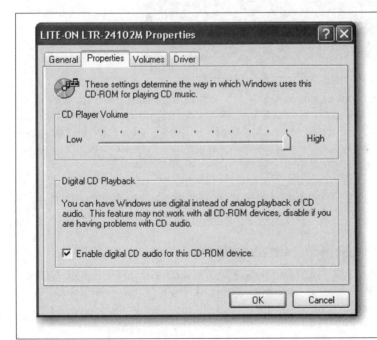

Figure 14-4:
Turning on digital audio playback can make the CDs you play on your PC sound sharper.

14-6   Groovy Visual Displays

One of Windows Media Player's cooler features is its ability to show *visualizations*—colored patterns and designs that change to reflect the current mood of the music (Figure 14-5). Windows Media Player comes with a number of visualization collections grouped by name and genre, such as Ambience, Bars and Waves, and Musical Colors (each genre includes several different visualizations).

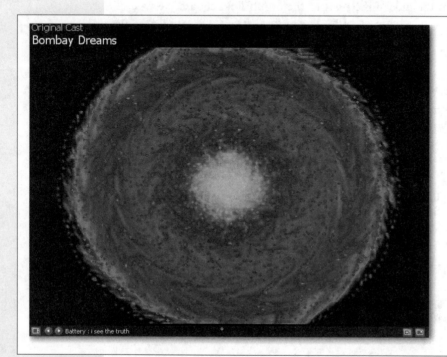

Original Cast
Bombay Dreams

Battery : i see the truth

Figure 14-5:
The visualization takes up the whole player screen. If you want it to cover your whole monitor, maximize the window by clicking the middle button in the upper right corner of the player.

To try out a visualization, choose View → Visualizations and then from the cascading series of menus, as shown in Figure 14-6, select a particular style. Once you choose the visualization you want, click the Now Playing tab in the taskbar on the left—that's where you can see the actual visualization. You can turn off visualizations by choosing View → Visualizations → No Visualizations.

Note: If you notice your PC slowing down when you're using visualizations, you may have to skip the fun, particularly if you have an older computer or one with a small memory.

14-7   Skinning Windows Media Player

You're not stuck with Windows Media Player's staid, corporate design. You can apply a *skin* of your own choosing to change the way the program looks—often drastically. (Skins are different design elements—things like fonts, button styles, and background colors—you can to a program to alter its appearance.)

More than twenty skins come with Windows Media Player (you can get many more online, too, as described in the box on page 318). Here's how to try a skin. In the task-bar on the left side of the player window, click Skin Chooser, or choose View → Go To → Skin Chooser. A list of skins pops up (Figure 14-7), and when you highlight one, a preview appears on the right—in this case, a Microsoft skin called Headspace. Choose the one you want, and then click Apply Skin to give your player an instant makeover.

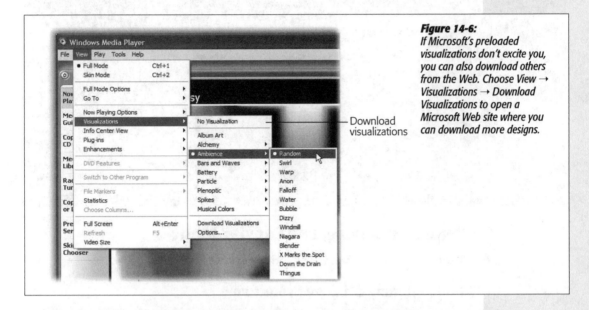

Download visualizations

Figure 14-6:
If Microsoft's preloaded visualizations don't excite you, you can also download others from the Web. Choose View → Visualizations → Download Visualizations to open a Microsoft Web site where you can download more designs.

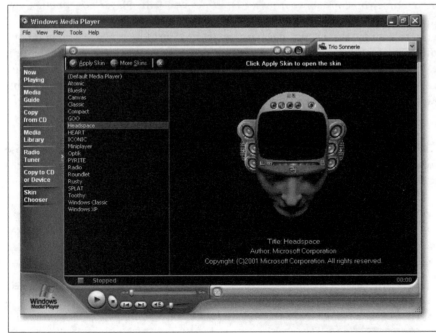

Figure 14-7:
When you apply a skin to Windows Media Player, not only does the program's entire look change, it also shrinks significantly, taking up less real estate on your screen.

Note: Skinning Windows Media Player can make certain features less recognizable, including the player's controls. If you're feeling lost, right-click anywhere on the skin to get a list of program features; choose any option you want from the list. If you want the skin to vanish press Ctrl+1 to return to Media Player's normal look.

ADD-IN ALERT

More Skins, Visualizations, and Plug-Ins

You're not limited to the skins and visualizations that come with the Windows Media Player. Microsoft offers a wide variety of free skins, visualizations, and *plug-ins*, all of which you can get from *www.wmplugins.com*. (A plug-in is a small chunk of programming that adds an additional feature to a program.)

For example, download the dancing Elvis plug-in and the King will gyrate across your Media Player (regardless of whose music is playing). The Windows Media Bonus Pack—

which includes visualizations, skins, and sound effects—is another nifty package. And if you have Windows Media Player 9, try out TweakMP PowerToy for Windows XP, which the next hint explains in more detail.

Plenty of other sites, including *www.customize.org* and Turner Classic Movies (*www.turnerclassicmovies.com/ FunStuff/VideoSkins/0,,,00.html*), offer their own collection of add-ins. Search Google for "Windows Media Player skins" to find even more sites.

Recording, Mixing, and Copying Music

The hints in this section can help bring out your inner DJ.

14-8 Turning Off Copy Protection

The first time you copy songs from a CD, Windows Media Player asks whether you want to turn on *copy protection*, which is a system Microsoft uses to assign a digital license to a song so you can't illegally copy and redistribute it. Once a song is copy protected, transferring it to a device such as a portable MP3 player may not work if the device doesn't recognize the license Microsoft has assigned it. Because there are many *legal* ways you can copy songs, this setting does you no good. So when Windows Media Player asks if you want copy protection on, just say no.

If you've already activated copy protection, can you turn if off? Yes.

Turning off copy protection is easy. Open Windows Media Player and choose Tools → Options → Privacy, then uncheck "Acquire licenses automatically for protected content," as shown in Figure 14-8.

Note: There're two terms you need to know for working with audio CDs. *Ripping*, which sounds aggressive and possibly illegal, is simply the process of copying songs *from* a CD to somewhere else (say, your hard drive). *Burning*, also a little scary sounding, refers to the process of copying songs *to* a CD (also known as making a CD). Neither process is illegal.

For a quick and helpful tutorial on how to *rip* songs from a music CD into Windows Media Player, check out *www.microsoft.com/windowsxp/using/windowsmediaplayer/videos/jukebox.mspx*. To learn how to *burn* a CD, go to *www.microsoft.com/windowsxp/using/windowsmediaplayer/getstarted/burncds2.mspx*.

14-9   Mixing Smoother CDs

If you burn mixed CDs using Windows Media Player 9, you might want to download the TweakMP PowerToy for Windows XP (*www.wmplugins.com*). The PowerToy comes with a variety of semi-helpful tools (like a mouse shortcut for moving between skin and full-screen mode), but where it really shines is in its ability to *level* the volume on music files you burn to a CD.

That service is vital when you're burning a mixed CD, because the original recordings of the songs you want to add to your CD can have widely different volume levels—leading to a mix that's seriously uneven. PowerToy automatically evens out all the songs' volumes.

After you install PowerToy, open Windows Media Player and choose Tools → Plugins → TweakMP. To turn on volume leveling, click the CD tab and select "Automatically level the volume of files when copying to an audio CD."

14-10   Preventing Skips When You Burn CDs

Sometimes when you burn a CD with digital music files stored on your computer, you may notice that the CD skips when you play it. Skipping happens for many reasons, but you can prevent it with these tricks.

Note: In addition to the hints described here, you should also close other open programs when burning a CD so your computer can devote all its resources to this task.

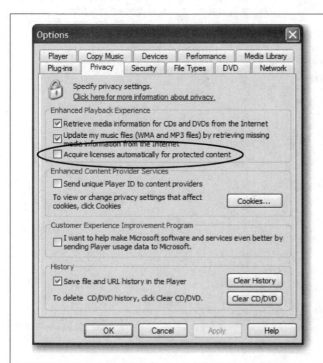

Figure 14-8:
"Acquire licenses automatically for protected content" sounds like a good idea. But, in fact, if you keep that option on, Windows Media Player can block you from listening to music you rip.

Look to the source

As the saying goes: garbage in, garbage out. If there are skips on the CD you originally used to *create* the music files, then the CDs you create *from* those files will skip too. So before burning, listen to each of the tracks you're going to burn and delete or repair any that skip. Because scratches or dirt on a CD often cause skipping, you can often fix the problem by cleaning the disc with a soft cloth, or by using a CD restoration kit (available from any music store).

Note: Always clean the *bottom* of the CD (the side without any printing); that's the side CD players read.

Change your burning method

If your original music files aren't skipping but the CDs you're creating are, you may be able to eliminate the blips by altering how your CD drive burns. First try slowing down your burning speed, which often solves the problem. In Windows Media Player, choose Tools → Options → Devices and highlight the CD drive you're using. Then choose Properties → Recording. The Recording tab appears, as shown in Figure 14-9. From the "Select a write speed" pop-up menu, choose a speed that's slower than the fastest available option and then click OK.

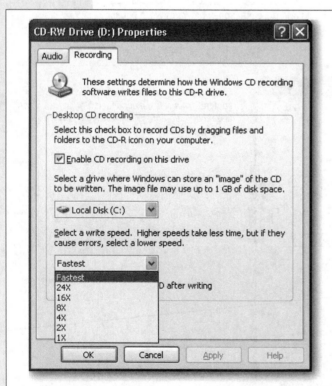

Figure 14-9:
A slow burn rate is good for burning CDs since it may help eliminate skips in music CDs. You can solve another problem using this dialog box as well: If you find you can't rip songs from a CD, make sure you turn on "Enable CD recording on this drive."

If changing the burn speed doesn't eliminate the skipping, try using analog rather than digital CD writing. In Windows Media Player, choose Tools → Options → Devices, and highlight the CD drive you're using. Then choose Properties → Audio. From the Copy section, choose Analog and click OK, then OK again. If that still doesn't work, go back to the same tab and select "Use error correction." This option slows down the CD burning process even further, which may solve the problem.

Taking Control of Your CD Player

Windows XP responds differently to different types of CDs. If you've inserted a music CD, XP launches a CD player like the Windows Media Player. If the CD contains a software program, XP usually runs the setup routine on the CD. But what if you'd prefer to make these decisions yourself? For example, you may want to *browse* through the files of a software CD and not automatically run the setup program. Or, when you insert a music CD, instead of listening to it, you might want to copy it to your PC. If so, you need to modify XP's Autorun tool, which automatically triggers a specific action each time you insert a CD.

Killing the Autorun feature on a case-by-case basis is easy: When you insert the CD into the drive, just hold down the Shift key. To prevent Autorun from doing its thing every time you insert a CD, you have to edit the Registry. Run the Registry Editor (page 328) and then go to My Computer → HKEY_LOCAL_MACHINE → SYSTEM → CurrentControlSet → Services → Cdrom. Find the AutoRun key and change its value to 0. If the key doesn't exist, create it as a DWORD value with a data value of 0. Finally, exit the Registry and reboot.

If you have XP Professional, you can turn off Autorun without using the Registry. Run the Group Policy Editor by typing gpedit.msc at a command prompt or in the Run box, and pressing Enter. Go to Local Computer Policy → Computer Configuration → Administrative Templates → System and look for the "Turn Off Autoplay" entry. Double-click it and choose Enabled, then exit the Group Policy Editor.

14-11 Saving Internet Radio Streams

These days, you don't need to visit your hometown to catch radio broadcasts of your high school's basketball games or your favorite local traffic report. Many Web sites *stream* digital audio to Internet listeners worldwide. (Streaming technology—one of the great features of the Web—broadcasts data continuously; downloadable files, on the other hand, transfer to your hard drive in one fell swoop.)

Windows Media Player lets you tune in to streaming audio (for a list of stations, click the Radio Tuner link in the taskbar), but it does let you *save* a broadcast so you can listen to it later. For this trick, you need to download and use a separate program (the box below also gives you a way to save *some* broadcasts without using an extra program). To reliably save streams, try one of these applications:

• **Super MP3 Recorder** lets you record streaming audio and then save the files to your hard drive. (The program also lets you record audio from a microphone or videotape.) When you're listening to a stream you want to record, simply start the program and tell it to begin recording; then tell it when to stop. Super MP3 (*www.supermp3recorder.com*), which works with any streaming audio format, is shareware and free to try, but costs $19.95 if you want to keep it.

• **Ripcast Streaming Audio Ripper** is a similar program, but works only with a special streaming format called Shoutcast, which many smaller and independent broadcasters use. Audio Ripper (*www.xoteck.com/ripcast*) is shareware and free to try, but costs $9.98 if you want to keep it.

WORKAROUND WORKSHOP

Saving Streams Without Extra Software

Depending on how an Internet radio station streams its audio, you can sometimes *manually* save the streams as music files without using extra software. After you've finished listening to a streaming audio file, go to My Computer → C: → Documents and Settings → [Your Account Name] → Local Settings → Temporary Internet Files. Look for files with .mp3 or .wma extensions. (Click the column labeled Type to sort your file list by file type.) The file you want may have an unintelligible name, so you may have to listen to a few possibilities before finding the one you want to archive.

When you find the file, you can save it permanently by copying it to another folder (choose Edit → Copy To Folder) and then renaming it. You can now listen to the file whenever you wish by opening it with Windows Media Player or another music player.

Video

Windows Media Player lets you watch flicks right on your PC. This section offers a few hints on getting maximum movie-watching satisfaction.

ADD-IN ALERT

Other DVD Software

Windows Media Player is a perfectly adequate program for watching DVDs. But if you want a player that can do things like take snapshots from a DVD movie or capture the audio, then you need a DVD-playing program with a little more juice. Here are three possibilities:

DirectDVD. This program gives you a full complement of DVD controls, including the ability to play Dolby Surround sound or capture images from a DVD in a variety of graphic and video formats. Perhaps DirectDVD's most powerful feature is its ability to *rip,* or copy, a DVD to the MP3 digital music format so you can play a DVD's audio on your PC or a portable MP3 player. DirectDVD (*www.orionstudios.com*) is shareware so you can try it for free, but it costs $39.95 if you want to keep using it.

Super DVD Ripper. This program can rip a DVD and save it in several PC-friendly video formats, including MPEG (Moving Picture Experts Group) and DivX (Digital video

express), which are two common formats for sharing and playing video. You can then watch the movie on a PC without a DVD drive or the DVD itself (great when you want to watch a movie while you're traveling). Super DVD Ripper can also burn movies onto a CD using the VCD (Video Compact Disc) or SVCD (Super VideoCD) formats, both of which let you watch movies using a computer's normal CD player. Super DVD Ripper (*www.dvdtodivx.net*) is shareware so you can try it for free, but if you keep it, you're expected to pay $35.95.

DVD Region-Free. This program lets you play any DVD regardless of which world region it's programmed to play in (see Hint 14-xx). DVD Region-Free is not a DVD player, but rather an add-in that works with existing DVD software. The program (*www.dvdidle.com*) is shareware so you can try it for free, but if you continue to use it, you're expected to pay $39.95.

14-12 Watching International DVDs

Windows Media Player does something that normal DVD players can't do: play DVDs from any region of the world.

Normally, DVDs are encoded so you can only play them in the region where you bought them. Thus, if you buy a DVD in Europe, Asia, or any other part of the world, you probably won't be able to play it on a DVD player purchased in the United States. (Table 14-1 lists all the regions.) But Windows Media Player lets you play DVDs from *any* region, no matter where you're located.

Warning: This trick has one significant catch: you can only change your region setting a limited number of times. The exact number of times varies according to the make and model of your DVD drive. The DVD Region dialog box, described below, tells you how many times you have remaining to change the region. If you exceed the limit, try DVD Region-Free, a plug-in described in the box on page 322.

To do watch a video from a land far, far away, you have to change the region setting on your player. Here's how:

1. **Open the Device Manager (at the command prompt or in the Run box—choose Start → Run—type** *devmgmt.msc* **and press Enter).**

   The Device Manager (see page 257) lets you change a wide variety of hardware settings, including options for your DVD drive.

2. **Find the listing for your DVD drive and right-click it. Choose Properties → DVD Region.**

   The DVD Region dialog box opens.

3. **Select the region your DVD came from (see Table 14-1), and then click OK.**

   When you choose a country, Windows XP sets the corresponding DVD region, which lets you watch the DVD in Windows Media Player.

Table 14-1. DVD Regions

Region Number	What It Encompasses
Region 1	United States and its territories, Canada
Region 2	Europe, Japan, South Africa, the Middle East
Region 3	Southeast Asia, East Asia, Hong Kong
Region 4	Australia, New Zealand, the Pacific Islands, South America, Central America, Mexico, the Caribbean
Region 5	Eastern Europe, Mongolia, North Korea, the Indian subcontinent, Africa
Region 6	China
Region 7	Reserved for future use
Region 8	Cruise ships, airplanes, and any other international vessels

Keyboard Shortcuts

In Windows Media Player, accomplishing simple tasks can sometimes take several steps. To save yourself the grief of navigating confusing menus, try using the keyboard shortcuts in Table 14-2.

Note: To see a list of more keyboard shortcuts in Windows Media Player, choose Help → Index tab and then type in "keyboard shortcuts."

Table 14-2. Windows Media Player Keyboard Shortcuts

Action	Key Combination
Display the File menu	Alt+F
Open a file	Ctrl+O
Specify a URL or path to a file	Ctrl+U
Close or stop playing a file	Ctrl+W
Exit or close the Player	Alt+F4
Display the View menu	Alt+V
Switch to full mode	Ctrl+1
Switch to skin mode	Ctrl+2
Display the menu bar in full mode	Ctrl+M
Display video in full screen	Alt+Enter
Zoom to 50 percent	Alt+1
Zoom to 100 percent	Alt+2
Zoom to 200 percent	Alt+3
Display the Play menu	Alt+P
Shuffle the order of items in a playlist	Ctrl+H
Repeat the playlist	Ctrl+T
Eject the CD or DVD (doesn't work if the PC has multiple CD-ROM or DVD drives.)	Ctrl+E
Display the Tools menu	Alt+T
Display the Help menu	Alt+H
Search for digital media files	F3
Increase the volume	F10
Decrease the volume	F9
Mute the volume	F8
Play or pause a file	Ctrl+P
Stop playback	Ctrl+S
Play the previous file	Ctrl+B
Play the next file	Ctrl+F
Play an item	Enter or Spacebar

The Registry

As you've seen throughout this book, the *Registry* lets you change, customize, or manipulate nearly every aspect of Windows XP. So what the heck is it? Actually, it's just a database that contains comprehensive settings for pretty much the whole operating system, as well as settings for the programs you run.

There's just one problem: the Registry is not particularly easy to use. But in many instances, editing the Registry is the only way to customize certain settings. In other cases, you get more options by editing the Registry rather than using menus, buttons, and dialog boxes. (XP contains so many different settings that Microsoft's engineers couldn't reasonably build a graphical interface for you to change all of them.)

Note: You actually change the Registry all the time without knowing it. For example, whenever you adjust a setting using the Control Panel, behind the scenes XP changes the Registry to put that setting into effect.

You edit the Registry using a tool built into XP called the Registry Editor. But before you learn how to use it, you need to grasp how the Registry is organized.

The five registry hives

Depending on your XP configuration and the programs you've installed, your Registry may have thousands of settings or *tens* of thousands of them. The settings are organized into five main Registry sections, called *Registry hives*. Figure 15-1 shows the structure of the Registry (the hives simply appear as folders), displayed in the Registry Editor.

Here what each Registry hive does:

- **HKEY_CLASSES_ROOT.** Contains information about file types, filename extensions, and other details related to files. It tells XP how to handle different file types, and controls basic interface options like double-clicking and context menus.

- **HKEY_CURRENT_USER.** Contains configuration information about the setup of the person currently logged into XP. It controls the desktop, as well as XP's specific appearance and behavior for that individual, including screen colors and the arrangement of the desktop. It also manages the connections to the network and to devices like digital cameras or printers.

- **HKEY_LOCAL_MACHINE.** Contains information about the computer itself, as well as the operating system. It includes specific details about all hardware, including the keyboard, printer ports, and storage devices. It also has information about security settings, installed software, system startup, drivers, and other services, like the ability to automatically connect to wireless networks.

- **HKEY_USERS.** Contains information about every user profile on the system.

- **HKEY_CURRENT_CONFIG.** Contains information about the system's current hardware setup, in the same way that HKEY_CURRENT_USER contains information about whoever's logged into the system at the moment. It has details like the type of hard disk installed in your PC, for example.

Note: When you delve into the Registry, you may notice that many of the settings seem to be exact duplicates of one another; in other words, a setting in one hive is the same as a setting in another hive. In fact, frequently one group of settings is merely an *alias* (also called a *symbolic link*)—or shortcut—for a group of settings in a different hive, so when you change those settings in one place, they take effect in both locations.

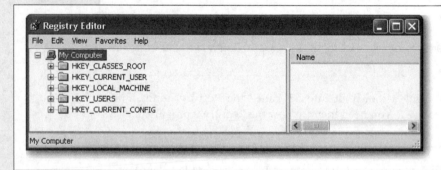

Figure 15-1:
Here's a look at the Registry's five hives through the eyes of the Registry Editor. You navigate with the Registry Editor much like Windows Explorer: expand branches by clicking +, and collapse them by clicking –.

Keys and values

Each Registry hive contains *keys*, which are your settings (like MenuShowDelay). And each key has a *value*, which contains the setting option XP or you have chosen (like 400 milliseconds).

For instance, the value for the DoubleClickSpeed key controls the amount of time between mouse clicks that must elapse before XP considers the action to be two single clicks, rather than a double-click. DoubleClickSpeed's value is 500, measured in milliseconds, although you can edit the Registry to change that number, as shown in Figure 15-2. That means that if you click your mouse twice within 500 milliseconds, XP interprets it as a double-click. If you wait longer than 500 milliseconds before your second click, XP doesn't consider it a double-click. Changing the key's value changes how XP treats those two mouse clicks—either as a double-click or as two separate clicks. So if you're a slow clicker, you might want to change that value to a larger number.

Note: DoubleClickSpeed is an example of a Registry setting that you can also change using a dialog box–in this case, the Mouse Properties dialog box (choose Start → Control Panel → Printers and Other Hardware → Mouse). When you make changes using a dialog box, XP actually makes the changes are in the Registry, which ultimately controls the setting. The dialog box is merely a convenient way to make changes to the Registry.

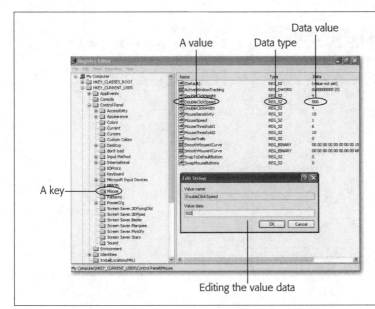

Figure 15-2:
When editing the Registry, you highlight a key in the left pane–in this case, "mouse"–and edit the values in the right pane–in this case, DoubleClickSpeed. Each value has data associated with it, which you can edit by double-clicking the value.

A key can contain one or more values. There are several types of values for Registry keys, called *data types*. Below are the Registry's primary data types:

- **REG_SZ (String value).** Made up of plain text and numbers, this data type is easy to understand and edit. It's one of the most common data types in the Registry; for instance, the value for DoubleClickSpeed is a string value (the number 500).

- **REG_MULTI_SZ (String array value).** This data type contains several strings of plain text and numbers, for example, Version 3.11.01.30.97 is the value for the version of your video BIOS. (A video BIOS is a built-in piece of software necessary for your graphics card and monitor to work.)

Note: The Registry Editor lets you edit string array values, but it doesn't let you create them.

- **REG_EXPAND_SZ (Expanded string value).** This data type contains *variables* that Windows uses to point to the location of files. (A variable is information that can change, according to the circumstances.) For example, to point to the location of the file for the Luna desktop theme, the expanded string value in the Registry would be %SystemRoot%\resources\Themes\Luna.theme. It's a variable data type because the location and exact filename of the theme can change.

- **REG_BINARY (Binary values).** Here's a data type only a PC could love. It's made up of binary data—0s and 1s that your computer can understand. The Registry represents that date by long strings of letters and numbers. Figure 15-3 shows a typical example of a binary value. As a general rule, you won't edit any binary values.

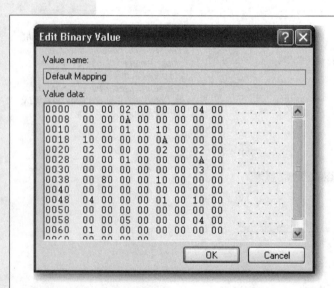

Figure 15-3:
Binary values, like the one shown here, are difficult to edit. Fortunately, you probably wouldn't ever have to. (No hints in this book involve editing binary values.)

- **REG_DWORD (DWORD values).** This data type is represented as a number. Sometimes, the Registry uses a 0 to turn on a key (and a 1 to turn it off), although it can use other numbers as well.

That's the background info. Now you're ready to get editing.

15-1 The Registry Editor

You use the Registry Editor to edit existing keys and values, create new keys and values, or delete keys and values you no longer want. Sometimes the changes take effect as soon as you make them and exit the Registry Editor; other times you have to reboot for them to work. There's no rhyme or reason as to when settings take effect—it varies from key to key.

To run the Registry Editor, open the Run box or a command prompt (choose Start → Run and then type *cmd* and press Enter), then type *Regedit* and press Enter. The first time you run the Registry Editor, it opens with the My Computer → HKEY_CURRENT_USER hive highlighted, as you can see in Figure 15-4. If you've used the Registry Editor before, it opens with the last key you edited highlighted, or the last place you were in the Registry.

Warning: Some Registry settings control vital functions on your PC, and if you adjust them, you can permanently damage your system. Don't change any settings you don't recognize or know to be safe. (All the Registry edits in this book are, of course, OK to make.)

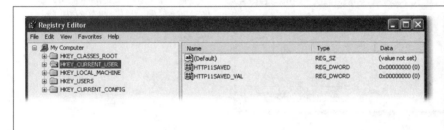

Figure 15-4:
When you use the Registry Editor for the first time, it opens to the HKEY_CURRENT_USER hive. You generally edit keys in that hive the most, because they contain your personal XP settings.

The Registry is organized hierarchically, like a hard disk, and you browse through it with the Registry Editor the same way you browse through your files using Windows Explorer. Clicking a + sign opens the next level down; clicking a – sign closes the current level or folder.

WORKAROUND WORKSHOP

Navigating the Registry

Each Registry key can contain subkeys, and those subkeys can contain subkeys, and so on, which are all organized in folders, much like a hard drive. This arrangement is useful visually, but navigating it using a mouse can give your clicking finger a workout. For a less taxing option, use these shortcuts:

- With the cursor in a key, press the right arrow on your keyboard to reveal subkeys.

- Pressing the left arrow closes a key and moves up one level in the key hierarchy.

- To jump to the next subkey that begins with a specific letter, press that letter on your keyboard.

Even with keyboard shortcuts, sometimes finding the key you want to edit in the Registry is like navigating a maze—with lots of dead ends before you reach your goal. A faster way to find the key you need is to use the Find command by pressing Ctrl+F (same as Edit → Find).

Editing keys and values

Frequently, you use the Registry Editor to edit a value that already exists. To edit a key's value, first navigate to the key you want to change. When you do that, the values show up in the right-hand pane of the Registry Editor (shown back in Figure 15-2). Double-click the value you want to edit and a box appears that lets you edit the value, as shown in Figure 15-5. Click OK when you're done.

Tip: Because the Registry Editor doesn't highlight the key you're editing, it's often hard to see where you are. (An open folder icon appears next to the key, but it's easy to miss.) To see which key you're editing, look at the status bar at the bottom of the Registry Editor—it should display the current key (as in Figure 15-4). If it doesn't, from the Registry Editor menu, choose View → Status Bar.

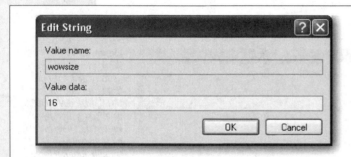

Figure 15-5:
Double-click a value, and the Registry Editor lets you edit it using this dialog box. You can't edit the value name from here, only the data.

To rename a key, select it, and from the Registry Editor menu choose Edit → Rename. You can also right-click the key and choose Edit → Rename.

Adding keys and values

Sometimes in order to customize XP or give it a new feature, you have to *add* a key or a value to the Registry, as opposed to editing one that already exists. In this case, you create that key or value right in the Registry Editor. For example, if you want to add a new option to the menu that pops up when you right-click a file in Windows Explorer (which lets you quickly copy files to a folder), you have to create a new key called Copy To.

To add a new key, you first have to select the appropriate *parent key* in the left-hand pane of the Registry Editor. A parent key is the key one level up in the Registry from the key you want to create. For example, the parent key of the Mouse key is the Control Panel. The full path is:

My Computer → HKEY_CURRENT_USER → Control Panel → Mouse

Once you've highlighted the appropriate parent key, choose Edit → New → Key. Then type the new key's name. For a quicker way, right-click the parent key, and choose Edit → New → Key.

A key by itself does nothing; in order for the key to control XP, you need to give it a value. It's a two-step process. First you name the value and define what type of value it is. Then you enter the actual data for the value.

To add a value to a key:

1. **In the left-hand pane of the Registry Editor, select the key you want.**

   If you haven't created the key yet, do so as outlined above.

2. **From the menu, choose Edit → New and from the submenu, select the type of value you want to create.**

   There are five types of values you can create, as detailed on pages 327–328. When creating a new value, be sure you choose the proper type, as shown in Figure 15-6.

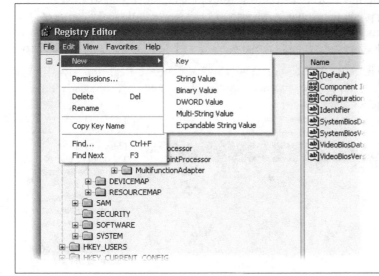

Figure 15-6:
The first step in adding a new value to any key in the Registry is choosing a value type from the Edit → New menu. For example, a key that controls an on/off setting would probably use a DWORD value (page 328). The hints in this book specify which type of value to use.

3. **Type the name of the new value and press Enter.**

   Type it exactly as written in the hints throughout this book, including capitalizations.

4. **Press Enter again. The same dialog box shown in Figure 15-5 appears.**

   Enter the data for the value—again, exactly as the instructions indicate—and press Enter. Exit the Registry. Your settings may take effect immediately, or you might have to reboot. (Each hint indicates whether rebooting is necessary.)

Deleting keys and values

Sometimes you need to delete a key or a value in the Registry. For example, if there's a feature in XP that causes a conflict, or perhaps you've created a key and later decide you don't want that feature any more, deleting is the way to go.

Open the Registry Editor and go to the key or value you need to delete (try the search and navigation tips in the box on page 329). Once you find a key or value, deleting it is simple: Select it and press Delete.

15-2   An Important Registry Precaution

The Registry can be rather unforgiving. Once you change it, there's no Undo command—and unlike most other Windows programs, the Registry Editor doesn't ask whether you want to save your changes, giving you a chance to back out. That means that if you make a change to the Registry and later want to go back to your original settings, you have to remember the often arcane and complicated changes you made and re-edit the Registry back to the way it was.

Actually, there's an easier way to restore your previous settings when you change the Registry: Back up the Registry before you edit or change anything, so you can easily go back to your previous settings if you want. In fact, you should make copies of your Registry not only to protect against an editing escapade that goes awry, but also to ensure that you can restore your system if it crashes while you're editing the Registry.

As luck would have it, there's a great way to back up the Registry—right in the Registry Editor. You can use it to back up the entire Registry, a Registry hive, or individual branches and keys.

Figure 15-7:
The quickest way to back up the Registry is to use the Export Registry File screen. If you want to back up only a portion of the Registry, choose "Selected branch" at the bottom of the screen.

To back up the Registry:

1. **Open the Registry Editor by typing *Regedit* in the Run box or a command prompt and pressing Enter. Then highlight the part of the Registry you want to back up.**

   If you want to back up the entire Registry, highlight My Computer. To back up a single hive, highlight just that hive. To back up a key or portion of the Registry and all keys underneath it, highlight that key or portion of the Registry. If you're only editing a single key or value, you can just back up a portion of the Registry. But for general safety's sake, you should back up the entire Registry every month or so.

2. **Choose File → Export.**

   The Export Registry File dialog box appears, as shown in Figure 15-7.

3. **Give the file a name, choose a location and save it.**

   The saved file ends in a .reg extension. Give the file a descriptive name, so you recognize it if you later need to restore the Registry. You may want to include the date as well; for example, fullbackup1009.reg.

If you want to restore the Registry to its pre-edited state, run the Registry Editor, choose File → Import, and then import the backup file. (You only need to use the backup if, after you edit the Registry, your computer doesn't work properly.)

Note: A .Reg file is the easiest way to back up the Registry, but it doesn't back up two sets of Registry keys: the SAM and Security keys that control password policies, user rights, and related information. However, unless you have a complex system with many accounts, these keys aren't absolutely vital. And if you're not editing these keys, backing them up isn't important, since you aren't changing them.

15-3   Editing the Registry with .Reg Files

If you're the cautious type and the idea of touching the Registry makes your skin itch with anxiety, there's another way you can edit the Registry that may give you more peace of mind: using .Reg files. These are regular text files you can create or edit with Notepad or another text editor and then merge into the Registry to make your changes. You can create a .Reg file from scratch, or export one from a portion of the Registry. When you use a .Reg file, you don't have to edit the Registry itself, so you're less likely to get yourself in a jam if you make a mistake.

Warning: Never use a word processor like Microsoft Word to edit .Reg files. Word processors add extra characters to the file that the Registry doesn't understand, causing big problems when the file is merged into the Registry.

The best way to create a .Reg file is to export an existing portion of the Registry, then edit that file with a text editor like Notepad. To do it, first open the Registry Editor and highlight the key or portion of the Registry you want to export, then choose File → Export. Choose a name and location for the file, and make sure it ends in .reg. You can export an individual key, a branch of the Registry, a hive, or the entire Registry. (For more details on exporting from the Registry, see the backup instructions in the previous hint.)

After you export the key, you can edit it by running Notepad (or another text editor) and opening the file. Here, for example, is the exported "My Computer → HKEY_CURRENT_USER → Control Panel → don't load" key as it looks in Notepad:

```
Windows Registry Editor Version 5.00
[HKEY_CURRENT_USER\Control Panel\don't load]
"ncpa.cpl"="Yes"
"odbccp32.cpl"="No"
```

You edit a .Reg file as you would any other text file. As you can see, the first line of the .Reg file starts with Windows Registry Editor Version 5.00. Don't change this line; Windows XP uses it to confirm that the file does in fact contain Registry information. (Previous versions of Windows have a different first line. For Windows 95/98/Me and Windows NT 4, the first line reads either REGEDIT4 or Registry Editor 4.)

The names of Registry keys are surrounded by brackets, and they include the full path name to the subkey, like [HKEY_CURRENT_USER\Control Panel\don't load] in this example. There may be multiple keys and subkeys, although this example just has one key. After each key are the key values and data. Values and data are both surrounded by quotation marks, as you can see in the above example. DWORD values, however, are preceded by *dword:* and don't have quotation marks surrounding them. Similarly, binary values are preceded by *hex:* and don't have quotation surrounding them. (For more about data types, like DWORD values and binary values, see pages 327–328.)

Edit the value and data according to the instructions in the hint you're using and save the file, using the same name. This example adds to the Registry a new value that stops the Phone and Modem Options applet from appearing in the Control Panel. So the new .Reg file looks like this (the new information appears on the last line):

```
Windows Registry Editor Version 5.00
[HKEY_CURRENT_USER\Control Panel\don't load]
"ncpa.cpl"="Yes"
"odbccp32.cpl"="No"
"telephon.cpl"="No"
```

When you've made your changes, import the .Reg file back into the Registry by opening the Registry Editor and choosing File → Import, then browsing to the edited file and opening it. An even easier way to import it is to find the file using Windows Explorer and double-click it. When you do so, XP asks whether you want to import the file. Answer yes, and XP imports it and makes the change to the Registry. This point can be very confusing: You may at first think that double-clicking a .Reg file opens it for editing, but it doesn't—it *merges* it into the Registry.

15-4   Protecting the Registry

As mentioned in the previous tip, when you double-click a .Reg file, XP merges it directly into the Registry instead of simply opening it up for editing as you might expect. Accidentally double-clicking a .Reg file can cause serious problems: Instead of opening a file, you inadvertently make changes to the Registry.

To avoid this fiasco, you can change the action XP takes when you double-click a .Reg file, so XP opens the file for editing in Notepad rather than merging it into the Registry. Here's how:

1. **In Windows Explorer, choose Tools → Folder Options → File Types.**

   This opens the File Types dialog box.

2. **Highlight the REG entry and click Advanced.**

   The Edit File Type dialog box opens, where you can change the action XP takes when you double-click a .Reg file.

3. **Highlight the Edit entry and click the Edit button.**

   A dialog box appears. The Action box should have the word "edit" in it, as in Figure 15-8.

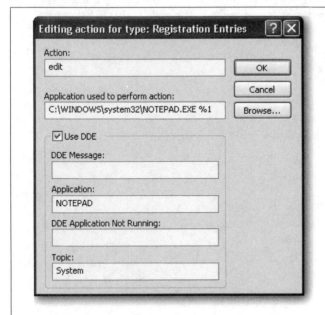

Figure 15-8:
Using this screen, you can change the action XP performs when you double-click a .Reg file—in this case, opening the file in Notepad for editing rather than immediately making a Registry change.

4. In the box that says "Application used to perform action," enter *C:\WINDOWS\ system32\NOTEPAD.EXE %1* and click OK, and OK again in every dialog box that appears.

This path tells XP to use Notepad to open .Reg files when you double-click them. If you want to use another text editor, use its full path and name instead of the path to Notepad. Make sure you add *%1* after the application's name, because that tells the text editor to open the file you double-click.

15-5 Creating a Registry Favorites List

Navigating through the many levels of the Registry can be time-consuming and frustrating, especially when you're trying to find a key you know you edited before. You can't leave a trail of electronic breadcrumbs to find your way back, but you can add keys you use frequently to the Registry Editor's Favorites list. That way, you can quickly return to keys you've used before.

Adding a key to the list is simple: just highlight it and choose Favorites → Add to Favorites. You can do this at any level of the Registry, not just with individual keys. So, for example, if you often edit keys found within My Computer → HKEY_CURRENT_USER → HARDWARE, you can put that location on your Favorites list. To use the Favorites list, click the Favorites menu; a menu opens with your Favorites listed at the bottom (Figure 15-9).

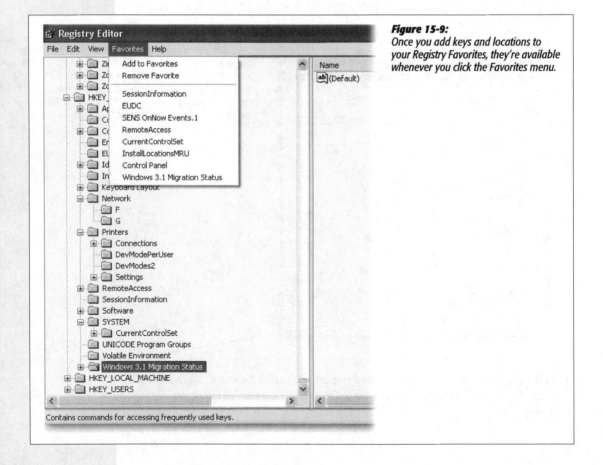

Figure 15-9:
Once you add keys and locations to your Registry Favorites, they're available whenever you click the Favorites menu.

Tip: There's one problem with Favorites: it uses the name of the current key, but not its full path. So, for example, if you add the key "My Computer → HKEY_LOCAL_MACHINE → SOFTWARE → Netscape → Netscape 6 → 6.2.1 (en)" to your Favorites, it shows up as "6.2.1 (en)" on the Favorites menu, which isn't particularly descriptive when you're scanning the menu six months later.

As you're adding a favorite, edit the name of the key or branch to something you're more likely to remember. It's easy: when you click Add To Favorites, an Add To Favorites dialog box appears. To rename a Favorite, in the Favorite name box that appears, type a more descriptive name you're likely to recognize.

15-6 Printing the Registry

Looking through the Registry with the Registry Editor can be maddeningly confusing. There are literally thousands of entries, all nested within one another, and many are very similar. It's like being stuck in the most complicated maze you can imagine. In some cases, you may find it easier to look through the Registry on paper. With the Registry Editor, you can print out a single key, a branch of the Registry, a whole hive, or the entire Registry.

Printing the whole Registry, or even an entire hive, takes a substantial amount of time and paper, so start by printing small sections, then go back and print more if you need other information.

To print any portion of the Registry, navigate to the key, subkey, or section you want to print, and then choose File → Print, or press Ctrl+P. That prints the current key, plus every subkey and value beneath it.

ADD-IN ALERT

Other Registry Tools

The Registry Editor is a perfectly serviceable tool, as far as it goes. But if you're planning to do a lot of tinkering with the Registry, it doesn't go far enough. For instance, it doesn't offer a way to clean out old, unused Registry entries, or include easy-to-use editing tools. So if you want more bells and whistles, try the following software downloads:

Registry First Aid. When you install and uninstall software, and as your system ages, the Registry begins to fill up with old or unnecessary Registry entries that clog up your system. Registry First Aid finds these obsolete entries and lets you delete them. ($21 shareware; *www.rosecitysoftware.com*.)

Registry Commander. This free utility gives you a host of features the Windows Registry Editor left out, such as a history list that lets you jump to recently edited keys, the ability to bookmark keys, a way to copy and paste entire keys, and advanced searches. Get it at *www.aezay.dk*.

Resplendent Registrar. This exceedingly powerful Registry editor includes even more tools, such as a search-and-replace feature, a Registry defragmenter to reclaim wasted disk space, an activity monitor that tracks all Registry activity, and a tool for comparing the contents of two Registry keys—plus lots of other helpful features. ($21 shareware: *www.resplendance.com*.)

Registry Mechanic. This program analyzes your Registry and fixes any problems it finds. It also backs up the Registry before making any changes. That way, if a particular fix just creates more problems, you can easily restore your Registry to the state it was in before Registry Mechanic got involved. ($19.95 shareware; *www.winguides.com*.)

Windows XP Keyboard Shortcuts

Mice are great—if you're a cat. But real power hounds prefer the time-saving keyboard shortcuts.

Since it's not easy to find—let alone remember—Windows XP keyboard shortcuts, the tables in this appendix offer handy reminders, divided into three categories: surprisingly handy shortcuts that use the Windows logo key (Table A-1); common keyboard shortcuts that work in most Windows programs (Table A-2); and dialog box shortcuts (Table A-3).

Tip: Remember that for all the key combinations listed here, you need to start by holding down the first key listed, and then, while keeping the first key pressed, press the other keys.

Table A-1. *Windows Logo Key Shortcuts*

Shortcut Key Combination	What It Does
Windows Key	Displays or hides the Start menu.
Windows Key+Break (the key with the word "Break" printed on it)	Displays the System Properties dialog box.
Windows Key+D	Shows the desktop.
Windows Key+M	Minimizes all windows.
Windows Key+Shift+M	Restores minimized windows.
Windows Key+E	Opens Windows Explorer.
Windows Key+F	Searches for a file or folder.
Windows Key+F1	Displays Windows Help.
Windows Key+R	Opens the Run dialog box.

Table A-2. *Common Windows XP Keyboard Shortcuts*

Shortcut Key Combination	What It Does
Shift+F10	Displays the shortcut menu for the selected item (equivalent to right-clicking with the mouse).
Shift+Delete	Deletes the selected item permanently without placing it in the Recycle Bin.
Shift with any of the arrow keys	Selects more than one contiguous item in a window or on the desktop, or selects text within a document.
Right Arrow	Opens the next menu to the right, or opens a submenu.
Left Arrow	Opens the next menu to the left, or closes a submenu.
Home	Goes to the top of the active window.
F6	Cycles through screen elements in a window or on the desktop.
F5	Refreshes the active window.
F3	Searches for a file or folder.
F2	Renames the selected item.
F10	Activates the menu bar in the active program.
Esc	Cancels the current task.
Ctrl+A	Selects all.
Ctrl+Z	Undoes the previous action.
Ctrl+X	Cuts.
Ctrl+C	Copies.
Ctrl+V	Pastes.
Ctrl+Up Arrow	Moves the insertion point to the beginning of the previous paragraph.
Ctrl+Shift with any of the arrow keys	Highlights a block of text.
Ctrl+Right Arrow	Moves the insertion point to the beginning of the next word.
Ctrl+Left Arrow	Moves the insertion point to the beginning of the previous word.
Ctrl+F4	Closes the active document in programs that allow you to have multiple documents open simultaneously.
Ctrl+Esc	Displays the Start menu.
Ctrl+Down Arrow	Moves the insertion point to the beginning of the next paragraph.
Ctrl while dragging an item	Makes a copy of the item you're dragging.
Backspace	In My Computer or Windows Explorer, opens the folder one level up.
Alt+Tab	Switches between open items.
Alt+F4	Closes the active item, or quits the active program.
Alt+Esc	Cycles through items in the order they were opened.
Alt+Enter	Displays the properties of the selected object.

Table A-3. *Windows XP Dialog Box Shortcuts*

Shortcut Key Combination	What It Does
Ctrl+Tab	Moves forward through tabs in a dialog box.
Ctrl+Shift+Tab	Moves backward through tabs in a dialog box.
Tab	Moves forward through options in a dialog box.
Shift+Tab	Moves backward through options in a dialog box.
Space Bar	Selects or clears the checkbox if the active option is a checkable.
Arrow keys	Selects a button if the active option is a group of option buttons.
F1	Displays Help in the current program.
F4	Displays the items in the active list.
Backspace	Opens a folder one level up if a folder is selected in the Save As or Open dialog box.
Alt+underlined letter	Carries out the underlined letter's corresponding command or selects the corresponding option in a dialog box.

Index

protecting with WEP, 242–243
security, 153
unplugged icon, 243
WMA files, 75
Word, 110–116
compressing files, 75
creating your own keyboard shortcuts, 112–113
digital signatures, 115
frequently used symbols, 113
hyperlinks, 170
invisible ink, 111
preventing access to files, 296
special characters, 111
Translate feature, 113
watermarks, 118
Word Count, 115
WordPad, 106

X

X1, 86

Y

Yahoo! Instant Messenger, 163
Yahoo! mail, 204
Yahoo! Messenger
free add-ons, 165
sending text messages, 164
YahooPOPs!, 204

Z

Zero Configuration WiFi Services, 238
zipped files and folders, 76–78
ZoneAlarm, 147
ZoneAlarm IM Secure, 165
ZoneAlarm IM Secure Pro, 166

Index